ACCA

PAPER P1

PROFESSIONAL ACCOUNTANT

In this new syllabus first edition approved by ACCA

- We **discuss** the **best strategies** for studying for ACCA exams
- We **highlight** the **most important elements** in the syllabus and the **key skills** you will need
- We **signpost** how each chapter links to the syllabus and the study guide
- We **provide** lots of **exam focus points** demonstrating what the examiner will want you to do
- We **emphasise key points** in regular **fast forward summaries**
- We **test your knowledge** of what you've studied in **quick quizzes**
- We **examine your understanding** in our **exam question bank**
- We **reference all the important topics** in our **full index**

BPP's **i-Learn** and **i-Pass** products also support this paper.

FOR EXAMS IN DECEMBER 2007 AND JUNE 2008

First edition April 2007

ISBN 9780 7517 3300 6

British Library Cataloguing-in-Publication Data
A catalogue record for this book
is available from the British Library

Published by

BPP Learning Media Ltd
BPP House, Aldine Place
London W12 8AA

www.bpp.com/learningmedia

Printed in Great Britain by
W M Print
45-47 Frederick Street
Walsall, West Midlands
WS2 9NE

Your learning materials, published by BPP Learning
Media Ltd, are printed on paper sourced from
sustainable, managed forests.

We are grateful to the Association of Chartered Certified
Accountants for permission to reproduce past
examination questions. The suggested solutions in the
exam answer bank have been prepared by BPP Learning
Media Ltd, unless where otherwise stated.

Contents

The BPP Learning Media Effective Study Package

Distance Learning from BPP Professional Education

You can access our exam-focussed interactive e-learning materials over the **Internet**, via BPP Learn Online, hosted by BPP Professional Education.

BPP Learn Online offers **comprehensive tutor support**, **revision guidance** and **exam tips**.

Visit www.bpp.com/acca/learnonline for further details.

Learning to Learn Accountancy

BPP's ground-breaking **Learning to Learn Accountancy** book is designed to be used both at the outset of your ACCA studies and throughout the process of learning accountancy. It challenges you to consider how you study and gives you helpful hints about how to approach the various types of paper which you will encounter. It can help you **focus your studies on the subject and exam**, enabling you to **acquire knowledge**, **practise and revise efficiently and effectively**.

How the BPP ACCA-approved Study Text can help you pass

How the BPP ACCA-approved Study Text can help you pass

Tackling studying

We know that studying for a number of exams can seem daunting, particularly when you have other commitments as well.

- We therefore provide guidance on **what you need to study efficiently and effectively** – to use the limited time you have in the best way possible.

- We explain the **purposes** of the **different features** in the BPP Study Text, demonstrating how they help you and improve your chances of passing.

Developing exam awareness

We never forget that you're aiming to pass your exams, and our Texts are completely focused on helping you do this.

- In the section **Approaching and passing P1** we introduce the key themes of the syllabus, describe the skills you need and summarise how to succeed.

- The **Introduction** to each chapter of this Study Text sets the chapter in the context of the syllabus and exam.

- We provide specific tips, **Exam focus points**, on what you can expect in the exam and what to do (and not to do!) when answering questions.

And our Study Text is **comprehensive**. It covers the syllabus content. No more, no less.

Using the Syllabus and Study Guide

We set out the Syllabus and Study Guide in full.

- Reading the **introduction to the Syllabus** will show you what **capabilities** (skills) you'll have to demonstrate, and how this exam links with other papers.

- The topics listed in the **Syllabus** are the **key topics** in this exam. By quickly looking through the Syllabus, you can see the breadth of the paper. Reading the Syllabus will also highlight topics to look out for when you're reading newspapers or *student accountant* magazine.

- The **Study Guide** provides the **detail**, showing you precisely what you'll be studying. Don't worry if it seems a lot when you look through it; BPP's Study Text will carefully guide you through it all.

- Remember the Text shows at the start of every chapter which areas of the Syllabus and Study Guide are covered in each chapter.

Testing what you can do

Testing yourself helps you develop the skills you need to pass the exam and also confirms that you can recall what you have learnt.

- We include **Questions** within chapters, and the **Exam question bank** provides lots more practice.

- Our **Quick Quizzes** test whether you have enough knowledge of the contents of each chapter.

- Question practice is particularly important if English is not your first written language. ACCA offers an **International Certificate in Financial English** promoting language skills within the international business community.

BPP
LEARNING MEDIA

Example chapter

Topic list

The Topic list gives an overview of the chapter.

Introduction

The Introduction sets the chapter in the context of the whole syllabus.

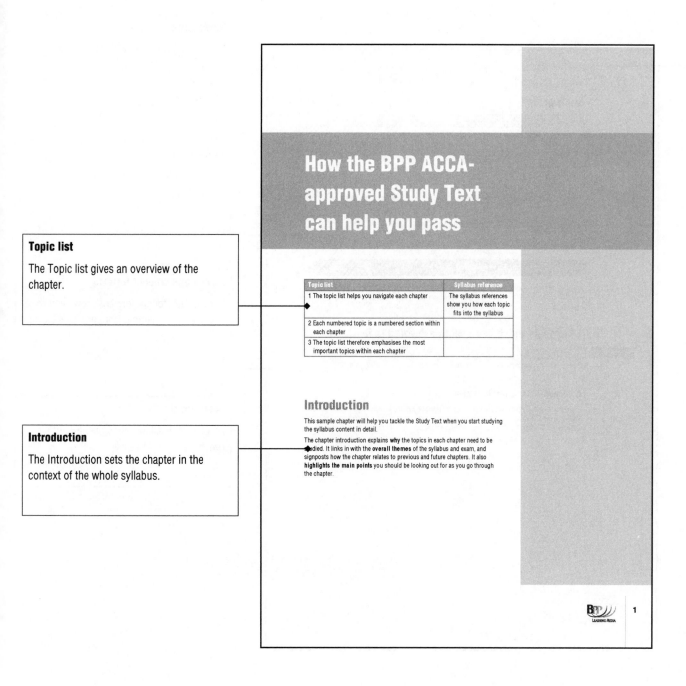

How the BPP ACCA-approved Study Text can help you pass

Topic list	Syllabus reference
1 The topic list helps you navigate each chapter	The syllabus references show you how each topic fits into the syllabus
2 Each numbered topic is a numbered section within each chapter	
3 The topic list therefore emphasises the most important topics within each chapter	

Introduction

This sample chapter will help you tackle the Study Text when you start studying the syllabus content in detail.

The chapter introduction explains **why** the topics in each chapter need to be studied. It links in with the **overall themes** of the syllabus and exam, and signposts how the chapter relates to previous and future chapters. It also **highlights the main points** you should be looking out for as you go through the chapter.

BPP LEARNING MEDIA   1

Study guide

		Intellectual level
	We list the topics in ACCA's Study guide that are covered in each chapter	The intellectual level indicates the depth in which the topics will be covered

Exam guide

The Exam guide highlights ways in which the main topics covered in each chapter may be examined.

Knowledge brought forward from earlier studies

Knowledge brought forward boxes summarise information and techniques that you are **assumed to know** from your earlier studies. As the exam may test your knowledge of these areas, you should **revise** your previous study material if you are unsure about them.

1 Key topic which has a section devoted to it

FAST FORWARD

Fast forwards give you a **summary** of the content of each of the main chapter sections. They are listed together in the roundup at the end of each chapter to allow you to review each chapter quickly.

1.1 Important topic within section

The headings within chapters give you a good idea of the **importance** of the topics covered. The larger the header, the more important the topic is. The headers will help you navigate through the chapter and locate the areas that have been highlighted as important in the front pages or in the chapter introduction.

Study guide

The Study guide links with ACCA's own guidance.

Exam guide

The Exam guide describes the examinability of the chapter.

Knowledge brought forward

Knowledge brought forward shows you what you need to remember from previous exams.

Fast forward

Fast forwards allow you to preview and review each section easily.

---

2 BPP
LEARNING MEDIA

BPP
LEARNING MEDIA

Example

Examples show you how theory is put into practice.

Key term

Key terms are the core vocabulary.

Exam focus point

Exam focus points provide specific links to the exam.

Formula to learn

You must remember these formulae in the exam.

Question

Questions provide vital practice of what you've learnt.

Case Study

Case Studies link what you've learnt with the business environment.

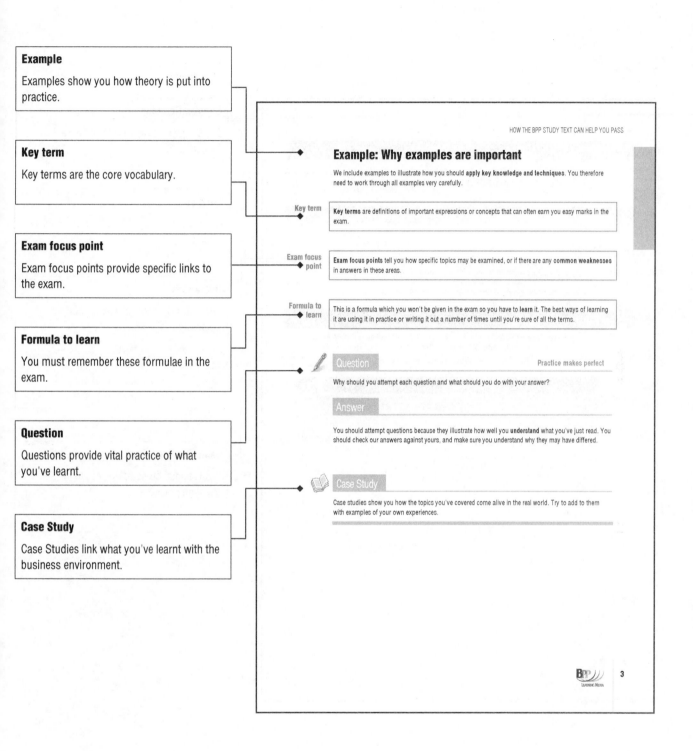

Chapter Roundup

- Fast forwards give you a **summary** of the content of each of the main chapter sections. They are listed together in the roundup at the end of each chapter to allow you to review each chapter quickly.

Quick Quiz

1 What are the main purposes of the Quick Quiz?

2 What should you do if you get Quick Quiz questions wrong?

    A   Nothing as you now know where you went wrong
    B   Note the correct answer and go on to the next chapter
    C   Practise full questions on this topic when you revise
    D   Go back and look through the topic again to ensure you know it

Answers to Quick Quiz

1 The main purposes of the Quick Quiz are to check how much you've remembered of the topics covered and to practise questions in a variety of formats.

2   D   Go back and look through the topic again to ensure that you know it.

Now try the questions below from the Exam Question Bank

Number	Level	Marks	Time
Questions that give you practice of what you've learnt in each chapter	Examination	25	45 mins

Chapter Roundup

The Chapter Roundup lists all the Fast forwards.

Quick Quiz

The Quick Quiz speedily tests your knowledge.

Exam Question Bank

Each chapter cross-references to further question practice.

Learning styles

BPP's guide to studying, *Learning to Learn Accountancy*, provides guidance on identifying how you learn and the variety of intelligences that you have. We shall summarise some of the material in *Learning to Learn Accountancy*, as it will help you understand how to you are likely to approach the Study Text:

If you like	Then you might focus on	How the Study Text helps you
Word games, crosswords, poetry	Going through the detail in the Text	Chapter introductions, Fast forwards and Key terms help you determine the detail that's most significant
Number puzzles, Sudoku, Cluedo	Understanding the Text as a logical sequence of knowledge and ideas	Chapter introductions and headers help you follow the flow of material
Drawing, cartoons, films	Seeing how the ways material is presented show what it means and how important it is	The different features and the emphasis given by headers and emboldening help you see quickly what you have to know
Attending concerts, playing a musical instrument, dancing	Identifying patterns in the Text	The sequence of features within each chapter helps you understand what material is really crucial
Sport, craftwork, hands on experience	Learning practical skills such as preparing a set of accounts	Examples and question practice help you develop the practical skills you need

If you want to learn more about developing some or all of your intelligences, *Learning to Learn Accountancy* shows you plenty of ways in which you can do so.

Studying efficiently
and effectively

BPP
LEARNING MEDIA

What you need to study efficiently and effectively

Positive attitude

Yes there is a lot to learn. But look at the most recent ACCA pass list. See how many people have passed. They've made it; you can too. Focus on all the **benefits** that passing the exam will bring you.

Exam focus

Keep the exam firmly in your sights throughout your studies.

- Remember there's lots of **helpful guidance** about P1 in this first part of the Study Text.
- Look out for the **exam references** in the Study Text, particularly the types of question you'll be asked.

Organisation

Before you start studying you must organise yourself properly.

- We show you how to **timetable** your study so that you can ensure you have enough time to cover all of the syllabus – and revise it.
- Think carefully about the way you take **notes**. You needn't copy out too much, but if you can summarise key areas, that shows you understand them.
- Choose the notes **format** that's most helpful to you; lists, diagrams, mindmaps.
- Consider the **order** in which you tackle each chapter. If you prefer to get to grips with a theory before seeing how it's applied, you should read the explanations first. If you prefer to see how things work in practice, read the examples and questions first.

Active brain

There are various ways in which you can keep your brain active when studying and hence improve your **understanding** and **recall** of material.

- Keep asking yourself how the topic you're studying fits into the **whole picture** of this exam. If you're not sure, look back at the chapter introductions and Study Text front pages.
- Go carefully through every **example** and try every **question** in the Study Text and in the Exam question bank. You will be thinking deeply about the syllabus and increasing your understanding.

Review, review, review

Regularly reviewing the topics you've studied will help fix them in your memory. Your BPP Texts help you review in many ways.

- Important points are emphasised **in bold**.
- **Chapter Roundups** summarise the **Fast forward** key points in each chapter.
- **Quick Quizzes** test your grasp of the essentials.

BPP Passcards present summaries of topics in different visual formats to enhance your chances of remembering them.

Timetabling your studies

As your time is limited, it's vital that you calculate how much time you can allocate to each chapter. Following the approach below will help you do this.

Step 1   Calculate how much time you have

Work out the time you have available per week, given the following.

- The standard you have set yourself

- The time you need to set aside for work on the Practice & Revision Kit, Passcards, i-Learn and i-Pass

- The other exam(s) you are sitting

- Practical matters such as work, travel, exercise, sleep and social life

Hours

Note your time available in box A.   A [ ]

Step 2   Allocate your time

- Take the time you have available per week for this Study Text shown in box A, multiply it by the number of weeks available and insert the result in box B.   B [ ]

- Divide the figure in box B by the number of chapters in this Study Text and insert the result in box C.   C [ ]

Remember that this is only a rough guide. Some of the chapters in this Study Text are longer and more complicated than others, and you will find some subjects easier to understand than others.

Step 3   Implement your plan

Set about studying each chapter in the time shown in box C. You'll find that once you've established a timetable, you're much more likely to study systematically.

Short of time: Skim study technique

You may find you simply do not have the time available to follow all the key study steps for each chapter, however you adapt them for your particular learning style. If this is the case, follow the **Skim study** technique below.

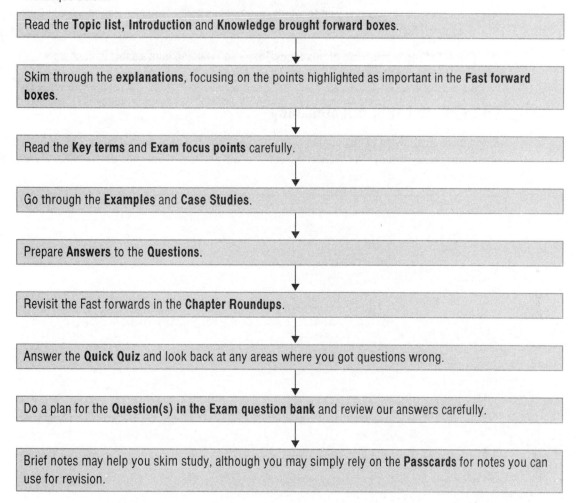

Read the **Topic list, Introduction** and **Knowledge brought forward boxes**.

Skim through the **explanations**, focusing on the points highlighted as important in the **Fast forward boxes**.

Read the **Key terms** and **Exam focus points** carefully.

Go through the **Examples** and **Case Studies**.

Prepare **Answers** to the **Questions**.

Revisit the Fast forwards in the **Chapter Roundups**.

Answer the **Quick Quiz** and look back at any areas where you got questions wrong.

Do a plan for the **Question(s) in the Exam question bank** and review our answers carefully.

Brief notes may help you skim study, although you may simply rely on the **Passcards** for notes you can use for revision.

Revision

When you are ready to start revising, you should still refer back to this Study Text.

- As a source of **reference** (you should find the index particularly helpful for this)
- As a way to **review** (the Fast forwards, Exam focus points, Chapter Roundups and Quick Quizzes help you here)

Remember to keep careful hold of this Study Text – you will find it invaluable in your work.

Learning to Learn Accountancy

BPP's guide to studying for accountancy exams, **Learning to Learn Accountancy**, challenges you to think about how you can study effectively and gives you lots and lots of vital tips on studying, revising and taking the exams.

BPP LEARNING MEDIA

Studying P1

Approaching P1

1 What's it all about

1.1 Underlying themes

The **P1 Professional Accountant** syllabus has been written with a different focus to the exams that you have sat so far. The exam is not about learning law, accounting standards or calculation techniques; instead it seeks to promote the underlying themes of **professionalism, responsibility, accountability and ethics**. The syllabus shows how accounting is **underpinned by governance and ethics**, and the need for accountants to **repay the trust** that society puts in them. Governance is itself supported by **sound internal control systems, internal audit** and **rigorous risk management**. The examiner has stressed that the paper's main themes should be seen as interconnected.

1.2 Governance and responsibility

Chapter 1 demonstrates the importance of the underlying themes of the syllabus. Corporate governance is a central part of the syllabus. Instead of going straight into the detailed requirements of the corporate governance reports, it discusses in detail the **concepts** that underpin good corporate governance, the **constituencies** (shareholders and other stakeholders) that corporate governance is designed to serve and the **extent of corporate responsibilities** towards different stakeholders.

Chapter 2 deals with the basis of corporate governance legislation and codes, whether they are based on **principles or a detailed rulebook** and how governance codes incorporate wider ideas of social responsibility. **Chapter 3** covers governance best practice, drawing on examples from different codes from all over the world.

1.3 Internal control and review

Chapters 4 and 5 demonstrate the **importance of internal control and audit**. These are emphasised because management failing to ensure that adequate internal control systems are in place has led to some of the major corporate scandals over the years; Barings is an example of what results when control systems are inadequate.

In **Chapter 4** we look at the main features of internal control systems. Some of this material you will have covered in your auditing studies, but in this paper we are not primarily concerned with the detailed accounting controls, but more with the **overall control framework and environment** – and how **internal control links to corporate governance and risk management**.

In **Chapter 5** we deal with the role of internal audit in internal control. In this chapter we are not focusing on the detailed work that internal audit does; you will have covered that in your auditing studies. In this paper we are concerned with the factors that determine the **effectiveness of internal audit**, and **threats to internal audit**, most importantly the key ethical threat of lack of independence.

1.4 Identifying, assessing and controlling risks

Chapters 6-9 cover risk management, another area where failings can lead to corporate collapse. **Chapter 6** identifies the **common risks** that many organisations face. It shows that you shouldn't just think in terms of the audit risks that you've previously studied; organisations may be affected by other significant risks which however have little direct impact on its financial statements.

Chapters 7-9 cover how organisations deal with risk. You need to be aware of the **main analysis frameworks** and the main types of response (risk avoidance, reduction, transfer, acceptance). However the examiner also stresses the importance of organisational structure and culture issues; the **responsibilities of board and staff for managing risks** and the **culture of risk awareness** within the organisation.

1.5 Professional values and ethics

In this section the syllabus requires you to think carefully about the ethical assumptions that guide individual behaviour and underpin the role of accountancy. **Chapter 10** is a very important chapter in this text, dealing with the **ethical and social responsibility stances** of individuals and also the **factors** that determine the individual's position. The examiner also wishes you to **question the role of the accountant** in protecting shareholder wealth and focusing on the performance of capital investment; does this mean that accountancy is a servant of capital and makes the implicit assumptions about morality that capitalism does.

This questioning approach extends to **Chapter 11** where you are expected to **look critically** at the ethical codes accountants follow as well as the codes that businesses operate. It is true that you need to have a good knowledge of what the accountancy profession's codes say on **ethical threats and conflicts** and to be able to use that knowledge in determining solutions to ethical dilemmas. However you are also expected to question how much help the codes actually are in resolving dilemmas and whether the ethical framework presented is in the best interests of society and the accountancy profession.

Chapter 12 looks at **social and environmental issues**, concentrating on what organisations have done to address issues such as **sustainability** and the implications for accounting, disclosure, control systems and audit.

2 Skills you have to demonstrate

2.1 Knowledge and application

Even with exams you've previously taken, you'll remember that passing didn't only mean reproducing knowledge; you also had to **apply** what you knew. At Professional level, the balance is tilted much more towards application. You will need a sound basis of technical knowledge; the exams will detect whether you have the necessary knowledge. However you won't pass if you just spend your time acquiring knowledge; developing application skills is vital.

2.2 Application skills

What application skills do you need? Many P1 questions will include detail in a scenario about a specific organisation. The following skills are particularly important when you're dealing with question scenarios.

- **Identifying the most important features** of the organisation and the organisation's environment; clues to these will be scattered throughout the scenario. The technical knowledge that you have should help you do this, but you will also need business awareness and imagination

- **Using analysis techniques** that will give you more insight into the data that you're given

- **Selecting real-life examples** that are relevant to the scenario

- **Making informed judgements** that follow from your analysis about what the organisation is doing and should be doing

- **Communicating clearly and concisely** your analysis and recommendations. Perhaps you will be reporting to a specific individual; if so you should take into account the needs of this individual

3 How to pass

3.1 Study the whole syllabus

You need to be comfortable with **all areas of the syllabus**. Compulsory Question 1 will always span a number of syllabus areas and other questions may do so as well. In particular you must have a very good knowledge and awareness of the themes in the ethical section of the syllabus, since the examiner has stated that compulsory Question 1 will always include an element on ethics.

The examiner has also stressed that study and revision should cover all of the syllabus in detail. Students should not question spot or prioritise one area of the syllabus over another.

3.2 Focus on themes, not lists

There are quite a number of lists in the texts. This is inevitable because corporate governance guidance quoted as best practice is often in list form; sometimes also lists are the clearest way of presenting information. However the examiner has stressed that passing the exam is not a matter of learning and reproducing lists. Good answers will have to **focus on the details in the scenario** and **bring out the underlying themes** that relate to the scenario; the points in them will have more depth than a series of single-line bullet points.

3.3 Read around

Wider reading will help you understand the main issues businesses face. Reading the business pages of newspapers will highlight key business risks organisations face and topical corporate governance issues. General news pages may cover significant ethical and corporate responsibility issues. Have a look as well at websites of organisations promoting social responsibility such as CERES.

3.4 Lots of question practice

You can **develop application skills** by attempting questions in the Exam Question Bank and later on questions in the BPP Learning Media Practice and Revision Kit.

3.5 Analysing question requirements

For P1 it's particularly important to **consider the question requirements carefully** to make sure you understand exactly what the question is asking, and whether each question part has to be answered in the context of the scenario or is more general.

You also need to be sure that you understand all the **tasks** that the question is asking you to perform and the **significance of the question verbs**. A lower level verb such as define will require a more descriptive answer; a higher level verb such as evaluate will require a more applied, critical answer.

The examiner has stressed that **higher-level requirements and verbs** will be most significant in this paper, for example critically evaluating a statement and arguing for or against a given idea or position.

3.6 Analysing question scenarios

When reading through the scenario you need to think widely about how the scenario relates to the underlying themes of the syllabus, and also important content from whatever areas of the syllabus the question covers:

(a) In questions on **corporate governance**, you are likely to be looking out for **weaknesses** in the current arrangements and trying to **recommend improvements** that are line with governance best practice.

(b) With **control systems** questions, you are most likely to be interested in the **design and appropriateness of the control systems**, whether there are **obvious shortcomings** with them, and also **details of the control environment** and the **organisation's culture and ethos** that will influence how effective the control systems are.

(c) With **risks** you are looking for the **most significant risks**. If these are not highlighted, you should look for the risks that are **connected with the organisation's strategy** or which **relate to significant changes** that the organisation and its business environment are going through, or are about to go though. You should also try to determine the extent to which **risk awareness is embedded** in the **organisation's culture**.

(d) If you are asked how organisations should **respond to particular risks**, you'll need to use the scenario detail to determine how serious these risks are, and suggest **responses** that are **relevant** to **counter the risks** and are **appropriate for the organisation**. It's no use for example suggesting that the organisation sets up a large risk management function if it is not big enough to warrant one.

(e) With **ethical issues** you are looking to determine not only the **ethical issues at stake**, but the **ethical position of the organisation** and individuals and the **factors that determine the ethical position**, since these will have to be considered when you think about solutions to the ethical problems.

(f) Look out in any question scenarios or frameworks for hints that you may have to provide a critique of the **overall framework or model** that is being operated. If you're basing your answer on content from corporate governance or ethical codes, will you have to criticise the principles or rules on which they are founded. If you have to make recommendations that benefit shareholders, is the shareholders' viewpoint the most valid or should other stakeholders' interests be taken into account.

3.7 Consider the moral and ethical frameworks

The examiner has stressed that these will affect the judgements you make when answering questions as they do in real-life. In particular the stakeholders **affected** by **business and strategic decisions** and whether some stakeholders are being favoured over others need to be considered.

Remember the exam is designed to make you take a questioning approach to wide issues, and this may mean having to argue in favour of a viewpoint with which you don't agree.

3.8 Answering questions

Well-judged, clear recommendations grounded in the scenario will always score well as markers for this paper have a wide remit to reward good answers. You need to be **selective**; as we've said, lists of points memorised from texts and reproduced without any thought won't score well. Similarly scenario details should only be used if they support the points you're making.

4 Brought forward knowledge

You will have covered some of the corporate governance, company law and ethics contents of P1 in law and auditing papers that you have previously sat.

However because of students studying this paper will have sat different variants of the law and auditing exams, and because of the complications resulting from the transition to the new syllabus, this text includes full coverage of the knowledge you need for this exam even though some of it has been covered in other exams.

5 ACCA ethics module

Under the rules affecting the transition into the new syllabus, you are not required to sit the new ethics module if you started studying for ACCA exams under the old syllabus. However we would **strongly recommend** that you sit the module before taking P1. The module will give you insights to a range of ethical perspectives that will be valuable in your professional career, and will also assist you in tackling the ethics content of the P1 syllabus and indeed the syllabuses of other Professional level exams.

Syllabus

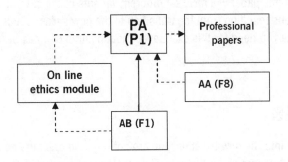

AIM

To apply relevant knowledge, skills and exercise professional judgement in carrying out the role of the accountant relating to governance, internal control, compliance and the management of risk within an organisation, in the context of an overall ethical framework.

MAIN CAPABILITIES

On successful completion of this paper, candidates should be able to:

A Define governance and explain its function in the effective management and control of organisations and of the resources for which they are accountable

B Evaluate the professional accountant's role in internal control, review and compliance

C Explain the role of the accountant in identifying and assessing risk

D Explain and evaluate the role of the accountant in controlling and mitigating risk

E Demonstrate the application of professional values and judgement through an ethical framework that is in the best interests of society and the profession, in compliance with relevant professional codes, laws and regulations.

RELATIONAL DIAGRAM OF MAIN CAPABILITIES

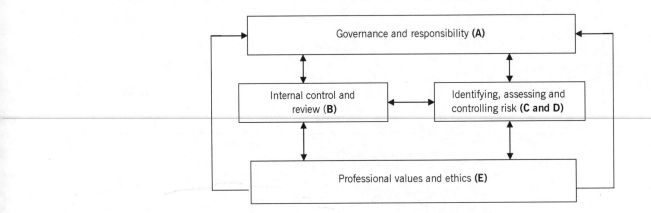

INTELLECTUAL LEVELS

The syllabus is designed to progressively broaden and deepen the knowledge, skills and professional values demonstrated by the student on their way through the qualification.

The specific capabilities within the detailed syllabuses and study guides are assessed at one of three intellectual or cognitive levels:

Level 1: Knowledge and comprehension
Level 2: Application and analysis
Level 3: Synthesis and evaluation

Very broadly, these intellectual levels relate to the three cognitive levels at which the Knowledge module, the Skills module and the Professional level are assessed.

Each subject area in the detailed study guide included in this document is given a 1, 2, or 3 superscript, denoting intellectual level, marked at the end of each relevant line. This gives an indication of the intellectual depth at which an area could be assessed within the examination. However, while level 1 broadly equates with the Knowledge module, level 2 equates to the Skills module and level 3 to the Professional level, some lower level skills can continue to be assessed as the student progresses through each module and level. This reflects that at each stage of study there will be a requirement to broaden, as well as deepen capabilities. It is also possible that occasionally some higher level capabilities may be assessed at lower levels.

RATIONALE

The syllabus for Paper P1, *Professional Accountant*, acts as the gateway syllabus into the professional level. It sets the other Essentials and Options papers into a wider professional, organisational, and societal context.

The syllabus assumes essential technical skills and knowledge acquired at the Fundamentals level where the core technical capabilities will have been acquired, and where ethics, corporate governance, internal audit, control, and risk will have been introduced in a subject-specific context.

The PA syllabus begins by examining the whole area of governance within organisations in the broad context of the agency relationship. This aspect of the syllabus focuses on the respective roles and responsibilities of directors and officers to organisational stakeholders and of accounting and auditing as support and control functions.

The syllabus then explores internal review, control, and feedback to implement and support effective governance, including compliance issues related to decision-making and decision-support functions. The syllabus also examines the whole area of identifying, assessing, and controlling risk as a key aspect of responsible management.

Finally, the syllabus covers personal and professional ethics, ethical frameworks – and professional values – as applied in the context of the accountant's duties and as a guide to appropriate professional behaviour and conduct in a variety of situations.

DETAILED SYLLABUS

A   Governance and responsibility

1.   The scope of governance

2.   Agency relationships and theories

3.   The board of directors

4.   Board committees

5.   Directors' remuneration

6.   Different approaches to corporate governance

7.   Corporate governance and corporate social responsibility

8.   Governance: reporting and disclosure

B   Internal control and review

1.   Management control systems in corporate governance

2.   Internal control, audit and compliance in corporate governance

3.   Internal control and reporting

4.   Management information in audit and internal control

C   Identifying and assessing risk

1.   Risk and the risk management process

2.   Categories of risk

3.   Identification, assessment and measurement of risk

D   Controlling risk

1.   Targeting and monitoring risk

2.   Methods of controlling and reducing risk

3.   Risk avoidance, retention and modelling

E   Professional values and ethics

1.   Ethical theories

2.   Different approaches to ethics and social responsibility

3.   Professions and the public interest

4.   Professional practice and codes of ethics

5.   Conflicts of interest and the consequences of unethical behaviour

6.   Ethical characteristics of professionalism

7.   Social and environmental issues in the conduct of business and of ethical behaviour

Study Guide

A   GOVERNANCE AND RESPONSIBILITY

1.   The scope of governance

a) Define and explain the meaning of corporate governance.[2]

b) Explain, and analyse the issues raised by the development of the joint stock company as the dominant form of business organisation and the separation of ownership and control over business activity.[3]

c) Analyse the purposes and objectives of corporate governance.[2]

d) Explain, and apply in context of corporate governance, the key underpinning concepts of:[3]
   i)   fairness
   ii) openness/transparency
   iii) independence
   iv) probity/honesty
   v)   responsibility
   vi) accountability
   vii) reputation
   viii)judgment
   ix) integrity

e) Explain and assess the major areas of organisational life affected by issues in corporate governance.[3]
   i)   duties of directors and functions of the board (including performance measurement)
   ii) the composition and balance of the board (and board committees)
   iii) reliability of financial reporting and external auditing
   iv) directors' remuneration and rewards
   v)   responsibility of the board for risk management systems and internal control
   vi) the rights and responsibilities of shareholders, including institutional investors
   vii) corporate social responsibility and business ethics.

f) Compare, and distinguish between public, private and non-governmental organisations (NGO) sectors with regard to the issues raised by, and scope of, governance.[3]

g) Explain and evaluate the roles, interests and claims of, the internal parties involved in corporate governance.[3]
   i)   Directors
   ii) Company secretaries
   iii) Sub-board management
   iv) Employee representatives (e.g. trade unions)

h) Explain and evaluate the roles, interests and claims of, the external parties involved in corporate governance.[3]
   i)   Shareholders (including shareholders' rights and responsibilities)
   ii) Auditors
   iii) Regulators
   iv) Government
   v)   Stock exchanges
   vi) Small investors (and minority rights)
   vii) Institutional investors (see also next point)

i) Analyse and discuss the role and influence of institutional investors in corporate governance systems and structures, for example the roles and influences of pension funds, insurance companies and mutual funds.[2]

2.   Agency relationships and theories

a) Define agency theory.[2]

b) Define and explain the key concepts in agency theory.[2]
   i)   Agents
   ii) Principals
   iii) Agency
   iv) Agency costs
   v)   Accountability
   vi) Fiduciary responsibilities
   vii) Stakeholders

c) Explain and explore the nature of the principal-agent relationship in the context of corporate governance.[3]

d) Analyse and critically evaluate the nature of agency accountability in agency relationships.[3]

e) Explain and analyse the following other theories used to explain aspects of the agency relationship.[2]
   i)   Transaction costs theory
   ii) Stakeholder theory

3. **The board of directors**

a) Explain and evaluate the roles and responsibilities of boards of directors.[3]

b) Describe, distinguish between and evaluate the cases for and against, unitary and two-tier board structures.[3]

c) Describe the characteristics, board composition and types of, directors (including defining executive and non-executive directors (NED).[2]

d) Describe and assess the purposes, roles and responsibilities of NEDs.[3]

e) Describe and analyse the general principles of legal and regulatory frameworks within which directors operate on corporate boards:[2]
   i)   legal rights and responsibilities,
   ii)   time-limited appointments
   iii) retirement by rotation,
   iv)   service contracts,
   v)   removal,
   vi)   disqualification
   vii) conflict and disclosure of interests
   viii) insider dealing/trading

f) Define, explore and compare the roles of the chief executive officer and company chairman.[3]

g) Describe and assess the importance and execution of, induction and continuing professional development of directors on boards of directors.[3]

h) Explain and analyse the frameworks for assessing the performance of boards and individual directors (including NEDs) on boards.[2]

4. **Board committees**

a) Explain and assess the importance, roles and accountabilities of, board committees in corporate governance.[3]

b) Explain and evaluate the role and purpose of the following committees in effective corporate governance:[3]
   i)   Remuneration committees
   ii)   Nominations committees
   iii) Risk committees.

5. **Directors' remuneration**

a) Describe and assess the general principles of remuneration. [3]
   i)   purposes
   ii)   components
   iii) links to strategy
   iv)   links to labour market conditions.

b) Explain and assess the effect of various components of remuneration packages on directors' behaviour. [3]
   i)   basic salary
   ii)   performance related
   iii) shares and share options
   iv)   loyalty bonuses
   v)   benefits in kind

c) Explain and analyse the legal, ethical, competitive and regulatory issues associated with directors' remuneration.[3]

6. **Different approaches to corporate governance**

a) Describe and compare the essentials of 'rules' and 'principles' based approaches to corporate governance. Includes discussion of 'comply or explain'.[3]

b) Describe and analyse the different models of business ownership that influence different governance regimes (e.g. family firms versus joint stock company-based models).[2]

c) Describe and critically evaluate the reasons behind the development and use of codes of practice in corporate governance (acknowledging national differences and convergence).[3]

d) Explain and briefly explore the development of corporate governance codes in principles-based jurisdictions.[2]
   i)   impetus and background
   ii)   major corporate governance codes
   iii) effects of

e) Explain and explore the Sarbanes-Oxley Act (2002) as an example of a rules-based approach to corporate governance.[2]
   i) impetus and background
   ii) main provisions/contents
   iii) effects of

f) Describe and explore the objectives, content and limitations of, corporate governance codes intended to apply to multiple national jurisdictions.[2]
   i) Organisation for economic cooperation and development (OECD) Report (2004)
   ii) International corporate governance network (ICGN) Report (2005)

7. Corporate governance and corporate social responsibility

a) Explain and explore social responsibility in the context of corporate governance.[2]

b) Discuss and critically assess the concept of stakeholders and stakeholding in organisations and how this can affect strategy and corporate governance.[3]

c) Analyse and evaluate issues of 'ownership,' 'property' and the responsibilities of ownership in the context of shareholding.[3]

d) Explain the concept of the organisation as a corporate citizen of society with rights and responsibilities.[3]

8. Governance: reporting and disclosure

a) Explain and assess the general principles of disclosure and communication with shareholders.[3]

b) Explain and analyse 'best practice' corporate governance disclosure requirements (for example under the UK Combined Code 2003 Schedule C).[2]

c) Define and distinguish between mandatory and voluntary disclosure of corporate information in the normal reporting cycle.[2]

d) Explain and explore the nature of, and reasons and motivations for, voluntary disclosure in a principles-based reporting environment

(compared to, for example, the reporting regime in the USA).[3]

e) Explain and analyse the purposes of the annual general meeting and extraordinary general meetings for information exchange between board and shareholders.[2]

f) Describe and assess the role of proxy voting in corporate governance.[3].

B INTERNAL CONTROL AND REVIEW

1. Management control systems in corporate governance

a) Define and explain internal management control.[2]

b) Explain and explore the importance of internal control and risk management in corporate governance.[3]

c) Describe the objectives of internal control systems.[2]

d) Identify, explain and evaluate the corporate governance and executive management roles in risk management (in particular the separation between responsibility for ensuring that adequate risk management systems are in place and the application of risk management systems and practices in the organisation).[3]

e) Identify and assess the importance of the elements or components of internal control systems.[3]

2. Internal control, audit and compliance in corporate governance

a) Describe the function and importance of internal audit.[1]

b) Explain, and discuss the importance of, auditor independence in all client-auditor situations (including internal audit).[3]

c) Explain, and assess the nature and sources of risks to, auditor independence. Assess the hazard of auditor capture.[3]

d) Explain and evaluate the importance of compliance and the role of the internal audit committee in internal control.[3]

e) Explore and evaluate the effectiveness of internal control systems.[3]

f) Describe and analyse the work of the internal audit committee in overseeing the internal audit function.[2]

g) Explain and explore the importance and characteristics of, the audit committee's relationship with external auditors.[2]

3. Internal control and reporting

a) Describe and assess the need to report on internal controls to shareholders.[3]

b) Describe the content of a report on internal control and audit.[2]

4. Management information in audit and internal control

a) Explain and assess the need for adequate information flows to management for the purposes of the management of internal control and risk.[3]

b) Evaluate the qualities and characteristics of information required in internal control and risk management and monitoring.[3]

C IDENTIFYING AND ASSESSING RISK

1. Risk and the risk management process

a) Define and explain risk in the context of corporate governance.[2]

b) Define and describe management responsibilities in risk management.[2]

2. Categories of risk

a) Define and compare (distinguish between) strategic and operational risks.[2]

b) Define and explain the sources and impacts of common business risks.[2]
   i) market

ii) credit
iii) liquidity
iv) technological
v) legal
vi) health, safety and environmental
vii) reputation
viii) business probity
ix) derivatives

c) Recognise and analyse the sector or industry specific nature of many business risks [2]

3. Identification, assessment and measurement of risk

a) Identify, and assess the impact upon, the stakeholders involved in business risk.[3]

b) Explain and analyse the concepts of assessing the severity and probability of risk events.[2]

c) Describe and evaluate a framework for board level consideration of risk.[3]

d) Describe the process of (externally) reporting internal control and risk.[2]

D CONTROLLING RISK

1. Targeting and monitoring of risk

a) Explain and assess the role of a risk manager in identifying and monitoring risk.[3]

b) Explain and evaluate the role of the risk committee in identifying and monitoring risk.[3]

c) Describe and assess the role of internal or external risk auditing in monitoring risk.[3]

2. Methods of controlling and reducing risk

a) Explain the importance of risk awareness at all levels in an organisation.[2]

b) Describe and analyse the concept of embedding risk in an organisation's systems and procedures [3]

c) Describe and evaluate the concept of embedding risk in an organisation's culture and values.[3]

d) Explain and analyse the concepts of spreading and diversifying risk and when this would be appropriate.[2]

3. Risk avoidance, retention and modelling

a) Define the terms 'risk avoidance' and 'risk retention'.[2]

b) Explain and evaluate the different attitudes to risk and how these can affect strategy.[3]

c) Explain and assess the necessity of incurring risk as part of competitively managing a business organisation.[3]

d) Explain and assess attitudes towards risk and the ways in which risk varies in relation to the size, structure and development of an organisation [3]

E PROFESSIONAL VALUES AND ETHICS

1. Ethical theories

a) Explain and distinguish between the ethical theories of relativism and absolutism.[2]

b) Explain, in an accounting and governance context, Kohlberg's stages of human moral development.[3]

c) Describe and distinguish between deontological and teleological/consequentialist approaches to ethics.[2]

d) Apply commonly used ethical decision-making models in accounting and professional contexts
   i) American Accounting Association model
   ii) Tucker's 5-question model

2. Different approaches to ethics and social responsibility.

a) Describe and evaluate Gray, Owen & Adams (1996) seven positions on social responsibility.[2]

b) Describe and evaluate other constructions of corporate and personal ethical stance:[2]
   i) short-term shareholder interests
   ii) long-term shareholder interests
   iii) multiple stakeholder obligations

iv) shaper of society

c) Describe and analyse the variables determining the cultural context of ethics and corporate social responsibility (CSR).[2]

3. Professions and the public interest

a) Explain and explore the nature of a 'profession' and 'professionalism'.[2]

b) Describe and assess what is meant by 'the public interest'.[2]

c) Describe the role of, and assess the widespread influence of, accounting as a profession in the organisational context.[3]

d) Analyse the role of accounting as a profession in society.[2]

e) Recognise accounting's role as a value-laden profession capable of influencing the distribution of power and wealth in society.[3]

f) Describe and critically evaluate issues surrounding accounting and acting against the public interest.[3]

4. Professional practice and codes of ethics

a) Describe and explore the areas of behaviour covered by *corporate* codes of ethics.[3]

b) Describe and assess the content of, and principles behind, *professional* codes of ethics.[3]

c) Describe and assess the codes of ethics relevant to accounting professionals such as the IFAC or professional body codes eg ACCA.[3]

5. Conflicts of interest and the consequences of unethical behaviour

a) Describe and evaluate issues associated with conflicts of interest and ethical conflict resolution.[3]

b) Explain and evaluate the nature and impacts of ethical threats and safeguards.[3]

c) Explain and explore how threats to independence can affect ethical behaviour.[3]

6. Ethical characteristics of professionalism

a) Explain and analyse the content and nature of ethical decision-making using content from Kohlberg's framework as appropriate.[2]

b) Explain and analyse issues related to the application of ethical behaviour in a professional context.[2]

c) Describe and discuss 'rules based' and 'principles based' approaches to resolving ethical dilemmas encountered in professional accounting.[2]

7. Social and environmental issues in the conduct of business and ethical behaviour

a) Describe and assess the social and environmental effects that economic activity can have (in terms of social and environmental 'footprints').[3]

b) Explain and assess the concept of sustainability and evaluate the issues concerning accounting for sustainability (including the contribution of 'full cost' accounting).[3]

c) Describe the main features of internal management systems for underpinning environmental accounting such as EMAS and ISO 14000.[1]

d) Explain the nature of social and environmental audit and evaluate the contribution it can make to the development of environmental accounting.[3]

The exam paper

The exam is a three-hour paper consisting of two sections.

		Number of marks
Section A:	1 compulsory case study	50
Section B:	Choice of 2 from 3 questions (25 marks each)	50
		100

Section A will be a compulsory case study question with typically four or five sub-requirements relating to the same scenario information. The question will usually assess and link a range of subject areas across the syllabus. It will require students to demonstrate high-level capabilities to understand the complexities of the case and evaluate, relate and apply the information in the case study to the requirements.

The case study will be between 400 and 700 words long. The examiner has stressed the importance of reading the case in detail, taking notes as appropriate and getting a feel for what the issues are. Scenarios may be drawn from any situation involving aspects of governance; this is likely to be, but need not be, in an organisational setting.

Professional marks will be available in Section A for presentation, logical flow of argument and quality of argument.

Section B questions are more likely to assess a range of discrete subject areas from the main syllabus section headings; they may require evaluation and synthesis of information contained within short scenarios and application of this information to the question requirements.

Although one subject area is likely to be emphasised in each Section B question, students should not assume that questions will be solely about content from that area. Each question will be based on a shorter case scenario to contextualise the question.

The paper will have a global focus; no numerical questions will be set.

Analysis of pilot paper

Section A

1   Corporate governance arrangements; acquisition risks; board structure; non-executive directors; environmental reporting

Section B

2   Directors' remuneration; remuneration committee; conflicts of interest
3   Professional ethics; integrity; deontological and consequentialist approaches
4   Internal control systems; reputation risks; ethical responsibilities

The pilot paper is reproduced in full from page 39.

Pilot paper

Paper P1

Professional Accountant

Time allowed

Reading and planning: 15 minutes
Writing: 3 hours

This paper is divided into two sections:

Section A – This ONE question is compulsory and MUST be attempted

Section B – TWO questions ONLY to be attempted

Do NOT open this paper until instructed by the supervisor.

During reading and planning time only the question paper may be annotated. You must NOT write in your answer booklet until instructed by the supervisor.

This question paper must not be removed from the examination hall.

Warning

The pilot paper cannot cover all of the syllabus nor can it include examples of every type of question that will be included in the actual exam. You may see questions in the exam that you think are more difficult than any you see in the pilot paper.

SECTION A: This question is compulsory and MUST be attempted

Question 1

Chemco is a well-established listed European chemical company involved in research into, and the production of, a range of chemicals used in industries such as agrochemicals, oil and gas, paint, plastics and building materials. A strategic priority recognised by the Chemco board some time ago was to increase its international presence as a means of gaining international market share and servicing its increasingly geographically dispersed customer base. The Chemco board, which operated as a unitary structure, identified JPX as a possible acquisition target because of its good product 'fit' with Chemco and the fact that its geographical coverage would significantly strengthen Chemco's internationalisation strategy. Based outside Europe in a region of growth in the chemical industry, JPX was seen by analysts as a good opportunity for Chemco, especially as JPX's recent flotation had provided potential access to a controlling shareholding through the regional stock market where JPX operated.

When the board of Chemco met to discuss the proposed acquisition of JPX, a number of issues were tabled for discussion. Bill White, Chemco's chief executive, had overseen the research process that had identified JPX as a potential acquisition target. He was driving the process and wanted the Chemco board of directors to approve the next move, which was to begin the valuation process with a view to making an offer to JPX's shareholders. Bill said that the strategic benefits of this acquisition was in increasing overseas market share and gaining economies of scale.

While Chemco was a public company, JPX had been family owned and operated for most of its thirty-five year history. Seventy-five percent of the share capital was floated on its own country's stock exchange two years ago, but Leena Sharif, Chemco's company secretary, suggested that the corporate governance requirements in JPX's country were not as rigorous as in many parts of the world. She also suggested that the family business culture was still present in JPX and pointed out that it operated a two-tier board with members of the family on the upper tier. At the last annual general meeting, observers noticed that the JPX board, mainly consisting of family members, had 'dominated discussions' and had discouraged the expression of views from the company's external shareholders. JPX had no non-executive directors and none of the board committee structure that many listed companies like Chemco had in place. Bill reported that although JPX's department heads were all directors, they were not invited to attend board meetings when strategy and management monitoring issues were being discussed. They were, he said, treated more like middle management by the upper tier of the JPX board and that important views may not be being heard when devising strategy. Leena suggested that these features made the JPX board's upper tier less externally accountable and less likely to take advice when making decisions. She said that board accountability was fundamental to public trust and that JPX's board might do well to recognise this, especially if the acquisition were to go ahead.

Chemco's finance director, Susan Brown advised caution over the whole acquisition proposal. She saw the proposal as being very risky. In addition to the uncertainties over exposure to foreign markets, she believed that Chemco would also have difficulties with integrating JPX into the Chemco culture and structure. While Chemco was fully compliant with corporate governance best practice, the country in which JPX was based had few corporate governance requirements. Manprit Randhawa, Chemco's operations director, asked Bill if he knew anything about JPX's risk exposure. Manprit suggested that the acquisition of JPX might expose Chemco to a number of risks that could not only affect the success of the proposed acquisition but also, potentially, Chemco itself. Bill replied that he would look at the risks in more detail if the Chemco board agreed to take the proposal forward to its next stage.

Finance director Susan Brown, had obtained the most recent annual report for JPX and highlighted what she considered to be an interesting, but unexplained, comment about 'negative local environmental impact' in its accounts. She asked chief executive Bill White if he could find out what the comment meant and whether JPX had any plans to make provision for any environmental impact. Bill White was able to report, based on his previous dealings with JPX, that it did not produce any voluntary environmental reporting. The Chemco board broadly supported the idea of environmental reporting although company secretary Leena Sharif recently told Bill White that she was unaware of the meaning of the terms 'environmental footprint' and 'environmental reporting' and so couldn't say whether she was supportive or not. It was agreed, however, that relevant information on JPX's environmental performance and risk would be necessary if the acquisition went ahead.

Required

(a)   Evaluate JPX's current corporate governance arrangements and explain why they are likely to be considered inadequate by the Chemco board.   **(10 marks)**

(b)   Manprit suggested that the acquisition of JPX might expose Chemco to a number of risks. Illustrating from the case as required, identify the risks that Chemco might incur in acquiring JPX and explain how risk can be assessed.   **(15 marks)**

(c)   Construct the case for JPX adopting a unitary board structure after the proposed acquisition. Your answer should include an explanation of the advantages of unitary boards and a convincing case FOR the JPX board changing to a unitary structure.   **(10 marks)**

(d)   Explain FOUR roles of non-executive directors (NEDs) and assess the specific contributions that NEDs could make to improve the governance of the JPX board.   **(7 marks)**

(e)   Write a memo to Leena Sharif defining 'environmental footprint' and briefly explaining the importance of environmental reporting for JPX.   **(8 marks)**

(Total = 50 marks)

Question 1

This question is an example of what's likely to be a common type of question on this paper, evaluate the inadequacies and suggest improvements. However parts (c) and (d) are quite specific about which areas you have to discuss, indicating you need a detailed knowledge of corporate governance issues to underpin your discussions. The question part on risk is mixed in with this discussion on corporate governance, indicating how different parts of the syllabus will be combined in the case study question.

This question covers material from a number of chapters, and you can expect Question 1 to be drawn from areas covered across the whole Text.

Section B: TWO questions ONLY to be attempted

Question 2

In a recent case, it emerged that Frank Finn, a sales director at ABC Co, had been awarded a substantial over-inflation annual basic pay award with no apparent link to performance. When a major institutional shareholder, Swanland Investments, looked into the issue, it emerged that Mr Finn had a cross directorship with Joe Ng, an executive director of DEF Co. Mr Ng was a non-executive director of ABC and chairman of its remunerations committee. Swanland Investments argued at the annual general meeting that there was "a problem with the independence" of Mr Ng and further, that Mr Finn's remuneration package as a sales director was considered to be poorly aligned to Swanland's interests because it was too much weighted by basic pay and contained inadequate levels of incentive.

Swanland Investments proposed that the composition of Mr Finn's remuneration package be reconsidered by the remunerations committee and that Mr Ng should not be present during the discussion. Another of the larger institutional shareholders, Hanoi House, objected to this, proposing instead that Mr Ng and Mr Finn both resign from their respective non-executive directorships as there was "clear evidence of malpractice". Swanland considered this too radical a step, as Mr Ng's input was, in its opinion, valuable on ABC's board.

Required

(a)   Explain FOUR roles of a remuneration committee and how the cross directorship undermines these roles at ABC Co.   **(12 marks)**

(b)   Swanland Investments believed Mr Finn's remuneration package to be 'poorly aligned' to its interests. With reference to the different components of a director's remuneration package, explain how Mr Finn's remuneration might be more aligned to shareholders' interests at ABC Co.

(8 marks)

(c)   Evaluate the proposal from Hanoi House that both Mr Ng and Mr Finn be required to resign from their respective non-executive positions.   **(5 marks)**

(Total = 25 marks)

Question 2

This question has some similiarities to Question 1, requiring knowledge of specific areas of good corporate governance practice and application of that knowledge to identify weaknesses and recommend improvements. Ethics part (c) is only worth 5 marks; you may well encounter more complex ethical situations requiring discussion worth more marks.

Chapter 3 of this Text thoroughly covers the issues involved in this question.

Question 3

At a recent conference on corporate social responsibility, one speaker (Professor Cheung) argued that professional codes of ethics for accountants were not as useful as some have claimed because:

"they assume professional accountants to be rules-driven, when in fact most professionals are more driven by principles that guide and underpin all aspects of professional behaviour, including professional ethics."

When quizzed from the audience about his views on the usefulness of professional codes of ethics, Professor Cheung suggested that the costs of writing, implementing, disseminating and monitoring ethical codes outweighed their usefulness. He said that as long as professional accountants personally observe the highest values of probity and integrity then there is no need for detailed codes of ethics.

Required

(a) Critically evaluate Professor Cheung's views on codes of professional ethics. Use examples of ethical codes, where appropriate, to illustrate your answer. **(12 marks)**

(b) With reference to Professor Cheung's comments, explain what is meant by 'integrity' and assess its importance as an underlying principle in corporate governance. **(7 marks)**

(c) Explain and contrast a deontological with a consequentialist based approach to business ethics. **(6 marks)**

(Total = 25 marks)

Question 3

More an essay than a scenario-based question, but a clear illustration that you will be expected to discuss ethical theory without necessarily having to apply it to a practical scenario.

Chapters 10 and 11 of this Text cover the areas you need to discuss in this question.

Question 4

As part of a review of its internal control systems, the board of FF co, a large textiles company, has sought your advice as a senior accountant in the company.

FF's stated objective has always been to adopt the highest standards of internal control because it believes that by doing so it will not only provide shareholders with confidence in its governance but also enhance its overall reputation with all stakeholders. In recent years, however, FF's reputation for internal control has been damaged somewhat by a qualified audit statement last year (over issues of compliance with financial standards) and an unfortunate internal incident the year prior to that. This incident concerned an employee, Miss Osula, expressing concern about the compliance of one of the company's products with an international standard on fire safety. She raised the issue with her immediate manager but he said, according to Miss Osula, that it wasn't his job to report her concerns to senior management. When she failed to obtain a response herself from senior management, she decided to report the lack of compliance to the press. This significantly embarrassed the company and led to a substantial deterioration in FF's reputation.

The specifics of the above case concerned a fabric produced by FF Co, which, in order to comply with an international fire safety standard, was required to resist fire for ten minutes when in contact with a direct flame. According to Miss Osula, who was a member of the quality control staff, FF was allowing material rated at only five minutes fire resistance to be sold labelled as ten minute rated. In her statement to the press, Miss Osula said that there was a culture of carelessness in FF and that this was only one example of the way the company approached issues such as international fire safety standards.

Required

(a) Describe how the internal control systems at FF Co differ from a 'sound' system of internal control, such as that set out in the Turnbull guidance, for example. **(10 marks)**

(b) Define 'reputation risk' and evaluate the potential effects of FF's poor reputation on its financial situation. **(8 marks)**

(c) Explain, with reference to FF as appropriate, the ethical responsibilities of a professional accountant both as an employee and as a professional. **(7 marks)**

(Total = 25 marks)

Question 4

An illustration that Section B questions may cover topics from across the syllabus, even though there isn't the emphasis that there is for Section A questions on linking those different areas. Again part (a) is an identify the problems requirement, although here you aren't expected to recommend improvements in detail. Part (b) illustrates that you might be asked questions about a specific risk rather than be expected to cover the range of key risks that an organisation faces.

Chapters 4, 6 and 11 between them deal with the issues you need to include.

Part A
Governance and responsibility

Scope of corporate governance

Topic list	Syllabus reference
1 Definitions of corporate governance	A1
2 Corporate governance and agency theory	A2
3 Stakeholders in corporate governance	A1
4 Major issues in corporate governance	A1

Introduction

We start this Text by discussing corporate governance, a fundamental topic in this paper. You have encountered corporate governance already in your law and auditing studies, but this syllabus requires a deeper understanding of what has driven the development of corporate governance codes over the last fifteen years.

We start by looking at the principles that underpin corporate governance codes. Some will be familiar from what you have learnt about ethics in Auditing. We shall examine ethics in detail in Part E of this Text, but you'll find that certain ethical themes recur throughout this book.

In Section 2 we show how corporate governance has partly developed in response to the problem of agency – the difficulty of ensuring that shareholders are able to exercise sufficient control over directors and managers, their agents. In Section 3 we consider the interests of other stakeholders in corporate governance. As we shall see in later chapters, a key issue in the development of corporate governance is how much, if at all, directors/managers should consider the interests of stakeholders other than shareholders.

In the last section we introduce other major corporate governance issues; we shall see how corporate governance guidelines address these in the next two chapters.

Study guide

		Intellectual level
A1	**The scope of governance**	
(a)	Define and explain the meaning of corporate governance	2
(b)	Explain and analyse the issues raised by the development of the joint stock company as the dominant form of business organisation and the separation of ownership and control over business activity	3
(c)	Analyse the purpose and objectives of corporate governance	2
(d)	Explain and apply in the context of corporate governance the key underpinning concepts	3
(e)	Explain and assess the major areas of organisational life affected by corporate governance	3
(f)	Compare and distinguish between public, private and non-governmental organisations with regard to the issues raised by, and the scope of, governance	3
(g)	Explain and evaluate the roles, interests and claims of the internal parties involved in corporate governance	3
(h)	Explain and evaluate the roles, interests and claims of the external parties involved in corporate governance	3
(i)	Analyse and discuss the role and influence of institutional investors in corporate governance systems and structures, for example the roles and influences of pension funds, insurance companies and mutual funds	2
A2	**Agency relationships and theories**	
(a)	Define agency theory	2
(b)	Define and explain the key concepts in agency theory	3
(c)	Explain and explore the nature of the principal-agent relationship in the context of corporate governance	3
(d)	Analyse and critically evaluate the nature of agency accountability in agency relationships	2
(e)	Explain and analyse the following other theories used to explain aspects of the agency relationship: Transactions cost theory and Stakeholder theory	2

Exam guide

You may be asked about the significance of the underlying concepts in Section 1, or to analyse a corporate governance scenario in terms of the responsibilities directors have towards various stakeholders. The issues highlighted in the last section could well be important problems in a scenario question.

1 Definitions of corporate governance

FAST FORWARD

Corporate governance, the system by which organisations are directed and controlled, is based on a number of concepts including transparency, independence, accountability and integrity.

1.1 What is corporate governance?

Key term

Corporate governance is the **system** by which organisations are directed and controlled. (Cadbury report)

Corporate governance is a **set of relationships** between a company's directors, its shareholders and other stakeholders. It also provides the structure through which the objectives of the company are set, and the means of achieving those objectives and monitoring performance, are determined. (OECD)

Although mostly discussed in relation to large quoted companies, governance is an issue for all corporate bodies, commercial and not for profit, including public sector and non-governmental organisations.

Exam focus point

An exam question on corporate governance might start by asking you to define what corporate governance is.

There are a number of elements in corporate governance:

(a) The management, awareness, evaluation and mitigation of **risk** is fundamental in all definitions of good governance. This includes the operation of an **adequate and appropriate system of control.**

(b) The notion that **overall performance is enhanced** by **good supervision** and **management** within **set best practice guidelines** underpins most definitions.

(c) Good governance provides a **framework** for an organisation to pursue its strategy in an **ethical and effective** way and **offers safeguards against misuse of resources**, human, financial, physical or intellectual.

(d) Good governance is not just about externally established codes, it also requires a willingness to **apply the spirit** as well as the letter of the law.

(e) Good corporate governance can **attract new investment** into companies, particularly in developing nations.

(f) **Accountability** is generally a major theme in all governance frameworks, including accountability not just to shareholders but also other **stakeholders.**

(g) Corporate governance **underpins capital market confidence in companies** and in the government/regulators/tax authorities that administer them.

1.2 Corporate governance concepts

One view of governance is that it is based on a series of underlying concepts.

1.2.1 Fairness

The directors' deliberations and also the systems and values that underlie the company must be **balanced** by taking into account everyone who has a legitimate interest in the company, and respecting their rights and views. In many jurisdictions, corporate governance guidelines reinforce legal protection for certain groups, for example minority shareholders.

1.2.2 Openness/transparency

In the context of corporate governance, transparency means **corporate disclosure to stakeholders**. Disclosure in this context obviously includes information in the financial statements, not just the numbers and notes to the accounts but also narrative statements such as the directors' report and the operating and financial review. It also includes all **voluntary disclosure**, that is disclosure above the minimum required by law or regulation. Voluntary corporate communications include management forecasts, analysts' presentations, press releases, information placed on websites and other reports such as stand-alone environmental or social reports.

The main reason why transparency is so important relates to the agency problem that we shall discuss in Section 2, the potential conflict between owners and managers. Without effective disclosure the position could be unfairly weighted towards managers, since they have far more knowledge of the company's activities and financial situation than owner/investors. Avoidance of this **information asymmetry** requires not only effective disclosure rules, but strong internal controls that ensure that the information that is disclosed is **reliable**.

1.2.3 Independence

Independence is an important concept in relation to directors. Corporate governance reports have increasingly stressed the importance of **independent non-executive directors**; directors who are not primarily employed by the company and who have very strictly controlled other links with it. They should will thus be free from conflicts of interest and in a better position to **promote the interests of shareholders and other stakeholders**. Freed from pressures that could influence their activities, independent non-executive directors should be able to carry out **effective monitoring** of the company in conjunction with equally independent external auditors on behalf of shareholders.

Non-executive directors' lack of links and limits on the time that they serve as non-executive directors should promote **avoidance of managerial capture** – accepting executive managers' views on trust without analysing and questioning them.

1.2.4 Probity/honesty

Hopefully this should be the most self-evident of the principles, relating not only to telling the truth, but also not **misleading** shareholders and other stakeholders by presenting information in a slanted way.

1.2.5 Responsibility

The South African King report stresses that for management to be held properly responsible, there must be a system in place that allows for **corrective action** and **penalising mismanagement**. Responsible management should do, when necessary, whatever it takes to set the company on the right path.

King states that the board of directors must act responsively to, and with responsibility towards, all stakeholders of the company. However the responsibility of directors to other stakeholders, both in terms of to **whom** they are responsible and the **extent** of their responsibility, remains a key point of contention in corporate governance debates. We shall discuss the importance of stakeholders later in this chapter.

1.2.6 Accountability

Key term

> Corporate **accountability** refers to whether an organisation (and its directors) are answerable in some way for the consequences of their actions.

The UK Cadbury report emphasises that boards of directors are accountable to shareholders. However Cadbury stresses that making the accountability work is the responsibility of **both** parties. Directors, as we have seen, do so through the quality of information that they provide whereas shareholders do so through their willingness to **exercise their responsibility as owners**, which means using the available mechanisms to query and assess the actions of the board.

As with responsibility one of the biggest debates in corporate governance is the extent of management's **accountability** towards **other stakeholders** such as the community within which the organisation operates. This has led on to a debate that we shall discuss in Chapter 10 about the contents of accounts themselves; for what should accounts actually account.

1.2.7 Reputation

We shall see later on in this Text how risks to an organisation's reputation depend on how likely other risks are to crystallise. In the same way directors' concern for an organisation's reputation will be demonstrated by the extent to which they fulfil the other principles of corporate governance. There are purely **commercial reasons** for promoting the organisation's reputation, that the price of publicly traded shares is often dependent on reputation and hence reputation is often a very valuable asset of the organisation.

1.2.8 Judgement

Judgement means that the board **making decisions that enhance the prosperity** of the organisation. This means that board members must acquire a broad enough knowledge of the **business and its environment** to be able to provide meaningful direction to it. This has implications not only for the attention directors have to give to the organisation's affairs, but also the way the directors are recruited and trained.

As you will see when you come to study Paper P3, the complexities of senior management mean that the directors have to bring **multiple conceptual skills** to management that aim to maximise long-term returns. This means that corporate governance can involve balancing many competing people and resource claims against each other; although as we shall see risk management is an integral part of corporate governance, corporate governance isn't just about risk management.

1.2.9 Integrity

The UK Cadbury report provides an excellent summary:

Key term

> '**Integrity** means straightforward dealing and completeness. What is required of financial reporting is that it should be honest and that it should present a balanced picture of the state of the company's affairs. The integrity of reports depends on the integrity of those who prepare and present them.'

Integrity can be taken as meaning someone of **high moral character**, who sticks to principles no matter the pressure to do otherwise. In working life this means adhering to principles of professionalism and probity. **Straightforward dealing in relationships** with the different people and constituencies whom you meet is particularly important; trust is vital in relationships and belief in the integrity of those with whom you are dealing underpins this.

The Cadbury report definition highlights the need for **personal honesty and integrity** of preparers of accounts. This implies qualities beyond a mechanical adherence to accounting or ethical regulations or guidelines. At times accountants will have to use judgement or face financial situations which aren't covered by regulations or guidance, and on these occasions integrity is particularly important.

Integrity is an essential principle of the **corporate governance relationship**, particularly in relationship to representing shareholder interests and exercising agency (discussed in Section 2). As with financial reporting guidance, ethical codes don't cover all situations and therefore depend for their effectiveness on the qualities of the accountant. In addition we have seen that a key aim of corporate governance is to inspire confidence in participants in the market and this significantly depends upon a **public perception** of **competence and integrity**.

Exam focus point

> The Pilot paper asks for an explanation of what integrity is, and its importance in corporate governance; other principles might be tested by similar questions.

2 Corporate governance and agency theory

Agency is extremely important in corporate governance as often the directors/managers are acting as agents for the owners. Corporate governance frameworks aim to ensure directors/ managers **fulfil their responsibilities** as agents by requiring disclosure and suggesting they be rewarded on the basis of performance.

2.1 Nature of agency

You will have encountered agency in your earlier studies, but a brief revision will be helpful.

Key term

Agency relationship is a contract under which one or more persons (the principals) engage another person (the agent) to perform some service on their behalf that involves delegating some decision-making authority to the agent. (Jensen and Meckling)

There are a number of specific types of agent. These have either evolved in particular trades or developed in response to specific commercial needs. Examples include factors, brokers, estate agents, del credere agents, bankers and auctioneers.

2.2 Accountability and fiduciary responsibilities

2.2.1 Accountability

Key term

In the context of agency, **accountability** means that the agent is **answerable under the contract** to his principal and must account for the resources of his principal and the money he has gained working on his principal's behalf.

Two problems potentially arise with this:

- How does the principal **enforce this accountability** (the agency problem see below); as we shall see the corporate governance systems developed to monitor the behaviour of directors have been designed to address this issue

- What if the agent is **accountable to parties other than his principal** – how does he reconcile possibly conflicting duties (the stakeholder view see Section 3)

2.2.2 Fiduciary duty

A legal definition of fiduciary duty is as follows.

Key term

Fiduciary duty is a duty imposed upon certain persons because of the position of trust and confidence in which they stand in relation to another. The duty is more onerous than generally arises under a contractual or tort relationship. It requires full disclosure of information held by the fiduciary, a strict duty to account for any profits received as a result of the relationship, and a duty to avoid conflicts of interest.

Under English law company directors owe a fiduciary duty to the company to exercise their powers bona fide in what they **honestly consider to be the interests** of the company. This duty is **owed to the company** and not generally to individual shareholders. In exercising the powers given to them by the constitution the directors have a fiduciary duty not only to act bona fide but also only to use their powers **for a proper purpose.** The powers are restricted to the purposes for which they were given.

Clearly the concepts of fiduciary duty and accountability are very similar though not identical. Where certain wider responsibilities are enshrined in law, do directors have a duty to go beyond the law, or can they regard the law as defining what society as a whole requires of them.

2.2.3 Fiduciary relationship with stakeholders

Evan and Freeman have argued that **management bears a fiduciary relationship to stakeholders** and to the corporation as an abstract entity. It must act in the interests of the **stakeholders as their agent**, and it must act in the interests of the **corporation to ensure the survival** of the firm, safeguarding the long-term stakes of each group. Adoption of these principles would require significant changes to the way corporations are run. Evan and Freeman propose a '**stakeholder board of directors'**, with one representative for each of the stakeholder groups and one for the company itself. Each stakeholder representative would be elected by a stakeholder assembly. Company law would have to develop to protect the interests of stakeholders.

2.2.4 Performance

The agent who agrees to act as agent for reward has a **contractual obligation** to perform his agreed task. An unpaid agent is not bound to carry out his agreed duties. Any agent may refuse to perform an illegal act.

2.2.5 Obedience

The agent must act strictly in **accordance with his principal's instructions** provided these are lawful and reasonable. Even if he believes disobedience to be in his principal's best interests, he may not disobey instructions. Only if he is asked to commit an illegal act may he do so.

2.2.6 Skill

A paid agent undertakes to maintain the standard of **skill and care** to be expected of a person in his profession.

2.2.7 Personal performance

The agent is presumably selected because of his personal qualities and owes a duty to **perform his task himself** and not to delegate it to another. But he may delegate in a few special circumstances, if delegation is necessary, such as a solicitor acting for a client would be obliged to instruct a stockbroker to buy or sell listed securities on a Stock Exchange.

2.2.8 No conflict of interest

The agent owes to his principal a duty not to put himself in a situation where his **own interests conflict** with those of the principal; for example, he must not sell his own property to the principal (even if the sale is at a fair price).

2.2.9 Confidence

The agent must keep in **confidence** what he knows of his principal's affairs even after the agency relationship has ceased.

2.2.10 Any benefit

Any benefit must be handed over to the principal unless he **agrees** that the agent may **retain it**. Although an agent is entitled to his agreed remuneration, he must account to the principal for any other **benefits**. If he accepts from the other party any **commission or reward** as an inducement to make the contract with him, it is considered to be a bribe and the contract is fraudulent.

2.3 Agency in the context of corporate governance

Agency is a significant issue in corporate governance because of the **dominance of the joint-stock company**, the company limited by shares as a form of business organisation. For larger companies this has led to the **separation of ownership of the company** from its **management.** The owners (the shareholders) can be seen as the **principal,** the management of the company as the **agents**.

Although ordinary **shareholders** (equity shareholders) are the owners of the company to whom the board of directors are accountable as agents, the actual powers of shareholders tend to be restricted. They normally have no right to inspect the books of account, and their forecasts of future prospects are gleaned from the annual report and accounts, stockbrokers, journals and daily newspapers.

The day-to-day running of a company is the responsibility of the directors and other managers to whom the directors delegate, not the shareholders. For these reasons, therefore, there is the potential for **conflicts of interest** between management and shareholders.

2.4 The agency problem

The agency problem in joint stock companies derives from the principals (owners) not being able to run the business themselves and therefore having to rely on agents (directors) to do so for them. This **separation of ownership from management** can cause issues if there is a breach of trust by directors by intentional action, omission, neglect or incompetence. This breach may arise because the directors are **pursuing their own interests** rather than the shareholders or because they have **different attitudes to risk-taking** to the shareholders.

For example, if managers hold none or very little of the equity shares of the company they work for, what is to stop them from working inefficiently, concentrating too much on achieving short-term profits and hence maximising their own bonuses, not bothering to look for profitable new investment opportunities, or giving themselves high salaries and perks?

One power that shareholders possess is the right to **remove the directors** from office. But shareholders have to take the initiative to do this, and in many companies, the shareholders lack the energy and organisation to take such a step. Ultimately they can vote in favour of a takeover or removal of individual directors or entire boards, but this may be **undesirable** for other reasons.

2.5 Agency costs

To alleviate the agency problem, shareholders have to take steps to exercise control. However agency theory assumes that it will be **expensive and difficult**:

- To verify what the agent is doing, partly because the agent has available more information about his activities than the principal does
- To introduce mechanisms to control the activities of the agent

Agency costs arise therefore from attempts by principals to monitor the activities of agents, and may be viewed in monetary terms, resources consumed or time taken in monitoring. There will also be costs involved in establishing methods of control such as contracts. These costs may not just be incurred by the shareholders. To fulfil the requirements imposed on them (and to obtain the rewards of fulfilment) managers will spend time and resources proving that they are maximising shareholder value by for example providing increased disclosure.

Exam focus point	Your syllabus stresses the significance of agency problems in joint stock companies.

2.6 Resolving the agency problem: alignment of interests

Agency theory sees employees of businesses, including managers, as individuals, each with his or her own objectives. Within a department of a business, there are departmental objectives. If achieving these various objectives leads also to the achievement of the objectives of the organisation as a whole, there is said to be **alignment of interests.**

Key term

> **Alignment of interests** is accordance between the objectives of agents acting within an organisation and the objectives of the organisation as a whole. Alignment of interests is sometimes referred to as goal congruence, although goal congruence is used in other ways, as you will see in your P3 studies.

Alignment of interests may be better achieved and the 'agency problem' better dealt with by giving managers some profit-related pay, or by providing incentives that are related to profits or share price. Examples of such remuneration incentives are:

(a) **Profit-related/economic value-added pay**

Pay or bonuses related to the size of profits or economic value-added (covered in Chapter 3).

(b) **Rewarding managers with shares**

This might be done when a private company 'goes public' and managers are invited to subscribe for shares in the company at an attractive offer price. In a **management buy-out** or **buy-in** (the latter involving purchase of the business by new managers; the former by existing managers), managers become joint owner-managers.

(c) **Executive share option plans (ESOPs)**

In a share option scheme, selected employees are given a number of share options, each of which gives the holder the right after a certain date to subscribe for shares in the company at a fixed price. The value of an option will increase if the company is successful and its share price goes up, therefore giving managers an incentive to take decisions to increase the value of the company, actions congruent with wider shareholder interests.

Such measures might merely encourage management to adopt **'creative accounting'** methods which will distort the reported performance of the company in the service of the managers' own ends.

An alternative approach is to attempt to **monitor managers' behaviour,** for example by establishing **'management audit'** procedures, to introduce **additional reporting requirements**, or to seek **assurances** from managers that shareholders' interests will be foremost in their priorities. The most significant problem with monitoring is likely to be the **agency costs** involved, as they may imply **significant shareholder engagement** with the company.

2.7 Transaction costs theory

Transactions cost theory is based on the work of Cyert and March and broadly states that the way the company is **organised** or **governed** determines its control over transactions. Companies will try to keep as many transactions as possible in-house (being able to do that because they have grown so large) in order to **reduce uncertainties** about dealing with suppliers, and about purchase prices and quality. To do this, companies will tend towards **vertical integration** (being involved at all stages of the production process or supply chain).

Further insights of transaction cost theory are that managers behave rationally up to a point and are also **opportunistic** ie organise their transactions to pursue their own interests. Thus despite differences of emphasis, transaction cost theory and agency theory are largely attempting to tackle the same problem, namely to ensure that company managers pursue shareholders' best interests rather than their own.

3 Stakeholders in corporate governance

FAST FORWARD

Directors and managers need to be aware of the **interests of stakeholders** in governance, however their responsibility towards them is judged.

Governance reports have emphasised the role of **institutional investors** (insurance companies, pension funds, investment houses) in directing companies towards good corporate governance.

3.1 Stakeholders

Key term

Stakeholders are any entity (person, group or possibly non-human entity) that can affect or be affected by the actions or policies of an organisation. It is a bi-directional relationship. Each stakeholder group has different **expectations** about what it wants and different claims upon the organisation.

3.2 Stakeholder theory

Stakeholder theory proposes **corporate accountability** to a broad range of stakeholders. It is based on companies being so large, and their impact on society being so significant that they cannot just be responsible to their shareholders.

Modern corporations have been seen as **so powerful, socially, economically and politically**, that **unrestrained use of their power** will inevitably **damage other people's rights**. For example, they may blight an entire community by closing a major factory, thus enforcing long-term unemployment on a large proportion of the local workforce. They may use their purchasing power or market share to impose unequal contracts on suppliers and customers alike. They may exercise undesirable influence over government through their investment decisions. There is also the argument that corporations exist within society and are **dependent upon it for the resources** they use. Some of these resources are obtained by direct contracts with suppliers but others are not, being provided by government expenditure.

There is considerable dispute about whose interests should be taken into account. The **legitimacy of each stakeholder's claim** will depend on your ethical and political perspective on whether certain groups should be considered as stakeholders. Should for example distant (developing world) communities, other species, the natural environment in general or future generations be considered as legitimate stakeholders.

 Case Study

Animals

To what extent do you consider animals should be considered as stakeholders? This is more than just a hypothetical question.

- Vegetarians do not eat meat because they believe that eating meat is wrong. Animals are ends in themselves, and do not exist just for our pleasure.

- Some anti-vivisection campaigners, such as Body Shop, a cosmetics retailer, state they are against 'animal testing'.

- Even if animals are to be eaten, some cultures require them to be treated well, according to humane standards, as animals are capable of suffering.

- The moral status of particular species of animals varies from **culture** to **culture**. Pigs, obviously, are 'unclean' in Judaism and Islam. Beef is forbidden to Hindus. British people do not eat 'horse', although horses are eaten in other European countries. Similarly, eating dogs is perfectly acceptable in some cultures, but is totally unacceptable elsewhere. Guinea pigs are a food staple in the Andes countries, but are school pets in Britain. In some cultures, insects are eaten; in others, not.

- How would your views differ if you believed, as is the case in some religions, that animals contain the reincarnated souls of dead people?

- How would your view change if you believed that, like humans, some animal species are able to 'learn', exhibit altruistic behaviour, and that our sense of right and wrong results from evolutionary adaptation of the social behaviour patterns of our primate ancestors? (De Waal, 2001).

Donaldson and Preston suggested that there are two motivations for organisations responding to stakeholder concerns.

3.2.1 Instrumental view of stakeholders

This reflects the view that organisations have **mainly economic responsibilities** (plus the legal responsibilities that they have to fulfil in order to keep trading). In this viewpoint fulfilment of responsibilities towards stakeholders is desirable because it contributes to companies maximising their profits. Therefore a business does not have any moral standpoint of its own; it merely reflects whatever the concerns are of the stakeholders it cannot afford to upset, such as customers looking for green companies or talented employees looking for pleasant working environments.

3.2.2 Normative view of stakeholders

This is based on the idea that organisations have moral duties towards stakeholders; thus accommodating stakeholder concerns is an end in itself. This suggests the existence of **ethical and philanthropic responsibilities** as well as economic and legal responsibilities and organisations focusing on being **altruistic**.

The normative view is based on the ideas of the German philosopher Immanuel Kant. We shall discuss these in detail in Chapter 10. For now Kant argued for the existence of **civil duties** that are important in maintaining and increasing the net good in society. Duties include the **moral duty to take account of the concerns and opinions** of others. Not to do so will result in breakdown of social cohesion leading to everyone being morally worse off.

Exam focus point

In the exam you are likely to see a number of questions like the one the examiner issued, where the reasons for the validity of a particular stakeholder's claim on an organisation had to be explored.

3.3 Classifications of stakeholders

Stakeholders can be classified by their proximity to the organisation.

Stakeholder group	Members
Internal	Employees, management
Connected	Shareholders, customers, suppliers, lenders, trade unions, competitors
External	The government, local government, the public, pressure groups, opinion leaders

There are other ways of classifying stakeholders, such as Evan-Freeman's narrow-wide, Clarkson's primary-secondary and Mahoney's active-passive classifications.

3.3.1 Narrow and wide stakeholders

Stakeholder group	Members
Narrow	Those most affected by the organisation's strategy – shareholders, managers, employees, suppliers, dependent customers
Wide	Those less affected by the organisation's strategy – government, less dependent customers, the wider community

One implication of this classification might appear to be that organisations should pay most attention to narrow stakeholders, less to wider stakeholders.

3.3.2 Primary and secondary stakeholders

Stakeholder group	Members
Primary	Those without whose participation the organisation will have difficulty continuing as a going concern, such as customers, suppliers and government (tax and legislation)
Secondary	Those whose loss of participation won't affect the company's continued existence such as broad communities (and perhaps management)

Clearly an organisation **must** keep its primary stakeholders happy. The distinction between this classification and the narrow-wide classification is that the narrow-wide classification is based on how much the **organisation affects** the stakeholder; the primary-secondary classification is based on how much the **stakeholders affect the organisation**.

3.3.3 Active and passive stakeholders

Stakeholder group	Members
Active	Those who seek to participate in the organisation's activities. Obviously includes managers and shareholders, but may also include other groups not part of the organisation's structure such as regulators or pressure groups
Passive	Those who do not seek to participate in policy-making such as most shareholders, local communities and government

Passive stakeholders may nevertheless still be interested and powerful. If corporate governance arrangements are to develop, there may be a need for powerful passive shareholders to take a more active role. Hence as we shall see below there has been emphasis on institutional shareholders who own a large part of listed companies' shares actively using their power as major shareholders to promote better corporate governance.

3.4 Assessing the relative importance of stakeholder interests

Apart from the problem of taking different stakeholder interests into account, an organisation also faces the problem of **weighing shareholder interests** when considering future strategy. How for example do you compare the interest of a major shareholder with the interest of a local resident coping with the noise and smell from the company's factory?

3.5 Stakeholder power

One way of weighing stakeholder interests is to look at the power they exert. The greater the power of a stakeholder group, the greater its influence will be on strategy.

Mendelow classifies stakeholders on a matrix whose axes are power held and likelihood of showing an interest in the organisation's activities. These factors will help define the type of relationship the organisation should seek with its stakeholders, and how it should view their concerns. Mendelow's matrix represents a continuum, a map for plotting the relative influence of stakeholders. Stakeholders in the bottom right of the continuum are more significant because they combine the highest power and influence.

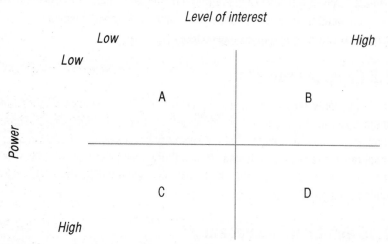

(a) **Key players** are found in segment D: the organisation's strategy must be **acceptable** to them, at least. An example would be a major customer.

(b) Stakeholders in segment C must be treated with care. While often passive, they are capable of moving to segment D. They should therefore be **kept satisfied.** Large institutional shareholders might fall into segment C.

(c) Stakeholders in segment B do not have great ability to influence strategy, but their views can be important in influencing more powerful stakeholders, perhaps by lobbying. They should therefore be **kept informed.** Community representatives and charities might fall into segment B.

(d) Minimal effort is expended on segment A.

Stakeholder mapping is used to assess the significance of stakeholders. This in turn has implications for the organisation.

(a) The framework of corporate governance and the direction and control of the business should recognise **stakeholders' levels** of **interest** and **power**.

(b) Companies may try to **reposition** certain stakeholders and discourage others from repositioning themselves, depending on their attitudes.

(c) Key **blockers** and **facilitators** of change must be identified.

(d) Stakeholder mapping can also be used to establish **future priorities**.

3.6 Reconciling viewpoints of different stakeholders

Jensen argued that **enlightened long-term value maximisation** offers the best, fairest, method of reconciling the competing interests of stakeholders. Jensen argued that the problem with traditional stakeholder theory is that it gave no indication of how to trade off competing interests; lacking therefore measurable targets, managers are left unaccountable for their actions.

3.7 Role of stakeholders

Corporate governance reports worldwide have concentrated significantly on the roles, interests and claims of the internal and external stakeholders involved.

3.8 Directors

The powers of directors to run the company are set out in the company's **constitution or articles.**

Under corporate governance best practice there is a distinction between the role of **executive directors**, who are involved **full-time in managing the company**, and the **non-executive directors**, who primarily focus on **monitoring**. However under company law in most jurisdictions the legal duties of directors apply to both executive and non-executive directors.

3.9 Company secretary

The UK Cadbury report gave a new dimension to the company secretary's function. It said that, in addition to the legal role, he or she has an important role to play in improving the corporate governance of listed companies. The report states that the secretary has a key role in ensuring that board procedures are **observe**d and **regularly reviewed**. The Cadbury report also suggests that the company secretary may be seen as a source of guidance on the responsibilities of the board and its chairman and on the implementation of corporate governance reports.

3.10 Sub-board management

Their interests are similar to the directors in many respects, and they may be concerned with corporate governance from the viewpoint of being potential main board directors. They will also be interested in how corporate governance decisions **impact on their current position** (how much decision-making will be delegated to them and in what areas? What parameters will they be obliged to follow?). As employees, managers will also have **interests in pay and working conditions** as described below.

3.11 Employees

Employees of course play a vital role in an organisation in the **implementation of strategy**; they need to **comply with the corporate governance systems** in place and **adopt appropriate culture**. Their commitment to the job may be considerable involving changes when taking the job (moving house), dependency if in the job for a long time (not just financial but in utilising skills that may not be portable elsewhere) and fulfilment as a human being (developing a career, entering relationships).

Employees will focus on how the company is **performing**, and how the company's performance will impact on their **pay** and **working conditions**. UK company law has required the directors to have regard to the interests of the company's employees in general as well as the interests of its members. Other European jurisdictions have gone further in terms of employee participation.

Employees also have information requirements. Surveys suggest that the most interesting information for employees is information **concerned with the immediate work environment** and which is **future-orientated.** There are a number of ways on which this information can be provided:

- An organisation-wide employee report

- Organisation-wide information on financial results, but breaking down information on personnel or sales to a unit level

- Including statements by managers on their individual activities

- Producing separate inserts about each division

3.12 Trade unions

A good relationship with trade unions can have many benefits for a company. Trade unions can for example distribute **information to employees** or **ascertain their views**. Trade unions are also exercising their influence through **pension funds**, pressing for change by use of voting rights. The strength of trade unions varies from country to country; in France where union rights are extended to all employees, unionisation has a greater impact on corporate decision-making than it can do in the UK where only union members benefit from collective bargaining agreements

3.13 Suppliers

Major suppliers will often be key stakeholders, particularly in businesses where **material costs and quality** are significant. Supplier co-operation is also important if organisations are trying to improve their management of assets by keeping inventory levels to a minimum; they will need to rely on suppliers for reliability of delivery. If the **relationship with suppliers deteriorates** because of a poor payment record, suppliers can limit or withdraw credit and charge higher rates of interest. They can also reduce their level of service, or even switch to supplying competitors.

3.14 Customers

Customers have increasingly high **expectations of the goods and services** they buy, both from the private and public sectors. These include not just low costs, but value for money, quality and service support.

In theory, if consumers are not happy with their purchases, they will take their business elsewhere next time. With increasingly competitive markets, consumers are able to exercise increasing levels of power over companies.

More sophisticated analysis of consumer behaviour has also enhanced the importance of consumers. Dissatisfied customers are **more likely to make their views known** than satisfied customers. Moreover businesses now believe that normally the costs of retaining existing customers are significantly less than those of obtaining new customers.

Consumers are increasingly evaluating goods and services not just on the basis of how they will satisfy their immediate material needs, but also how they will satisfy their **deeper moral needs**. For example, a shopper may prefer one brand of baked beans not for its taste but because the manufacturer supports a good cause of which the consumer approves.

3.15 External auditors

The external audit is one of the most important corporate governance procedures; it enables investors to have much greater **confidence** in the information that their agents, the directors/managers, are supplying. However the main focus of the external audit is on giving assurance that the accounts give a true and fair view.

Because of the significance of the external audit, the external auditors must be independent. As the UK Cadbury report comments: 'The central issue is to ensure that an appropriate relationship exists between the auditors and the managers whose financial statements they are auditing.'

A balance is required between working constructively with company management and at the same time serving the interests of shareholders. Cadbury suggests that the balance could be attained by companies **establishing audit committees** and the accounting profession **developing effective accounting standards**.

3.16 Regulators

Key term

> **Regulation** can be defined as any form of interference with the operation of the free market. This could involve regulating demand, supply, price, profit, quantity, quality, entry, exit, information, technology, or any other aspect of production and consumption in the market.

This category includes government bodies such as health and safety executives and regulators such as the financial services authorities amongst many others relevant to specific types of industry.

3.16.1 Methods of regulation

Legislators and regulators affect organisations' governance and risk management. They establish **rules and standards** that provide the impetus for management to ensure that risk management and control systems meet minimum requirements. They also conduct inspections and audits that provide useful information and recommendations regarding possible improvements. Regulators will be particularly interested in **maintaining shareholder-stakeholder confidence** in the information with which they are being provided.

In specific situations regulators may have other actions available.

 Case Study

Competition authorities are responsible for ensuring diversity wherever possible, but sometimes the industry is a natural monopoly.

The two main methods used to regulate monopoly industries are as follows.

(a)   **Price control**

The regulator agreeing the output prices with the industry. Typically, the price is progressively reduced in real terms each year by setting price increases at a rate below that of inflation. This has been used with success by regulators in the UK but can be confrontational.

(b)   **Profit control**

The regulator agreeing the maximum profit that the industry can make. A typical method is to fix maximum profit at x% of capital employed. However this does not provide any incentive to make more efficient use of assets: the higher the capital employed, the higher the profit.

In addition the regulator will be concerned with:

(a)   Actively **promoting competition** by encouraging new firms in the industry and preventing unreasonable barriers to entry.

(b)   Addressing **quality** and **safety** issues and considering the **social implications** of service provision and pricing.

3.16.2 Costs of regulation

The potential costs of regulation include the following.

(a)   **Enforcement costs**

Regulation can only be effective if it is properly monitored and enforced. **Direct costs** of enforcement include the setting up and running of the regulatory agencies – employing specialist staff, monitoring behaviour, prosecuting offenders (or otherwise ensuring actions are modified in line with regulations). **Indirect costs** are those incurred by the regulated (eg the firms in the industry) in conforming to the restrictions.

(b) **Regulatory capture**

This refers to the process by which the regulator becomes **dominated and controlled by the regulated firms**, such that it acts increasingly in the firm's interests, rather than those of consumers. This is a phenomenon that has been observed in the USA (where economic regulation has always been more widespread).

(c) **Unintended consequences of regulation**

An example is the so-called 'Aversch-Johnson effect'. This refers to the tendency of rate-of-return (profit) regulation to encourage firms to become too capital-intensive and hence minimise their return on capital. In other words, firms regulated in this way have an incentive to choose a method of production that is not least-cost, because it involves too high a ratio of capital to labour.

3.16.3 Regulation and stakeholders

Where privatisation has perpetuated monopolies over natural resources, industry regulatory authorities have the role of ensuring that **consumers' interests** are not subordinated to those of other stakeholders, such as employees, shareholders and tax authorities. The regulator's role may be 'advisory' rather than statutory. It may extend only to a part of a company's business, necessitating a fair allocation of costs across different activities of the company.

 Case Study

Benston (2000) provides six reasons for the regulation imposed to protect consumers of banking, securities, and insurance. Regulations are imposed to:

* Maintain consumer confidence in the financial system

* Assure that a supplier on whom consumers (eg of a major utility) rely does not fail

* Assure that consumers receive sufficient information to make 'good' decisions and are dealt with fairly

* Assure fair pricing of financial services

* Protect consumers from fraud and misrepresentation

* Prevent invidious discrimination against individuals

3.16.4 Regulators and corporate governance

Regulators will also be concerned with how corporate governance guidance affects the way organisations deal with changing circumstances.

 Case Study

A good example of a major change requiring a different approach to regulation has been the liberalisation of the activities by financial institutions in many countries. The traditional separation of financial institutions into banks, insurance companies, brokers, investment companies has been abolished and financial institutions engage in all these activities. The risks to which a multiproduct financial institution is exposed can be significantly different to the risks that each of the individual component parts eg the banking division are exposed.

In practice, the task of keeping regulation up-to-date and relevant is made more challenging by the pace of innovation in financial products and the development of financial markets and institutions and by globalisation.

The question that arises is: How much regulation should then be? And Is there perhaps an optimal level of regulation?

According to McMenamin in *Financial Management – An Introduction*, 'regulation is essentially a question of balance .... too little or ineffective regulation leaves the markets open to abuse, too much regulation makes markets rigid, costly to operate and uncompetitive'.

3.17 Government

Governments do not have a direct economic/financial interest in companies (except for those in which they hold shares). However, governments often have a strong indirect interest in companies' affairs, hence the way they are run and the information that is provided about them:

(a)   Governments raise **taxes** on sales and profits and on shareholders' dividends. They also expect companies to act as tax collectors for income tax and sales tax. The tax structure might influence investors' preferences for either dividends or capital growth.

(b)   Governments establish and determine the **overall regulatory and control climate** in a country. This involves exertion of fiscal pressure, and other methods of state intervention. Governments also determine whether the regulatory framework is **principles or rules based** (discussed later in the text).

(c)   Governments may **provide funds** towards the cost of some investment projects. They may also encourage private investment by offering tax incentives.

(d)   In the UK, the government has made some attempts to encourage more private individuals to become company shareholders, by means of:

   (i)   Attractive **privatisation** issues (such as in the electricity, gas and telecommunications industries)

   (ii)   **Tax incentives**, such as ISAs (Individual Savings Accounts), to encourage individuals to invest in shares.

(e)   Governments also influence companies, and the relationships between companies, their directors, shareholders and other stakeholders.

3.18 Stock exchanges

Stock exchanges provide a means for companies to **raise money** and investors to **transfer their shares** easily. Stock exchanges list companies whose shares can be held by the general public (called public companies in many jurisdictions); many such companies have a clear separation between ownership and management.

Stock exchanges are important because they provide **regulatory frameworks** in principle-based jurisdictions. In most countries listing rules apply to companies whose shares are listed on the stock exchange. Stock exchange regulation can therefore have a significant impact on the way corporate governance is implemented. The UK is a good example of this, with the comply or explain approach being consistent with the approach of self-regulation of London institutions. In America by contrast a more legalistic and rules-based approach has been adopted, in line with the regulatory approach that is already in place.

3.19 Institutional investors

Key term

> **Institutional investors** manage funds invested by individuals.

Institutional investors are now the biggest investors in many stock markets but they might also invest venture capital, or lend directly to companies. UK trends show that institutional investors can wield great powers over the companies in which they invest.

Question	Institutional investors

Before looking at the following paragraph, see if you can list the major types of institutional investor in the UK.

The major institutional investors in the UK are:

- **Pension funds**

- **Insurance companies**

- **Investment and unit trusts** (set up to invest in portfolios of shares)

- **Venture capital organisations** (investors particularly interested in companies that are seeking to expand)

3.19.1 Advantages and disadvantages of institutional investment

In some respects the **institutional investor** fulfils a desirable role. People should ideally be in pensionable employment or have personal pension plans, and the funds from which their pensions will be payable should be held separately from the companies by whom they are employed. Similarly, investors should have the opportunity to invest through the medium of insurance companies, unit trusts and investment trusts.

However, the dominance of the equity markets by institutional investors has possibly undesirable consequences as well.

(a) For capital markets to be truly competitive there should be no **investors** who are of **such size** that they **can influence prices**. In the UK, transactions by the largest institutions are now on such a massive scale that considerable price movements can result.

(b) Many institutions tend to **avoid shares** which are seen as **speculative** as they feel that they have a duty to their 'customers' to invest only in 'blue chip' shares (ie those of leading commercially sound companies). As a result, the shares of such companies tend to be relatively expensive.

(c) Fund managers are sometimes accused of **'short-termism'** in that they will tend to seek short-term speculative gains or simply sell their shares and invest elsewhere if they feel that there are management shortcomings. However arguably institutional investors have become so influential that they are less able to divest from companies without suffering a substantial loss in order to liquidate their holdings. They have therefore been forced to adopt a more long-term outlook.

3.19.2 Role of institutional investors

UK guidance has placed significant emphasis on the role of institutional investors in promoting good corporate governance. The UK Combined Code states that institutional shareholders should enter into a dialogue with companies based on the **mutual understanding of objectives**, taking into account the size and complexity of the companies and the risks they face. Their representatives should attend company annual general meetings and make considered use of their votes.

UK guidance stresses that institutional investors should consider in particular companies' governance arrangements that relate to **board structure and composition.** They should enter a dialogue about departures from the Code if they do not accept the companies' position.

 Case Study

The UK Combined Code refers to guidance in the Institutional Shareholders' Committee's ' The Responsibilities of Institutional Shareholders and Agents – Statement of Principles'. The Code suggests best practice in four areas.

(a)   Setting out how institutional investors will **discharge their responsibilities** – what they will require of investee companies, meetings, monitoring, intervention and voting strategies.

(b)   **Monitoring performance** – review of documentation, attending annual general meetings, entering a dialogue; the aim should to identify problems at an early stage. They may need to share information with other shareholders although they should avoid becoming insiders.

(c)   **Intervention** if the financial interests of the institutional shareholders' clients are threatened (see below).

(d)   **Evaluating and reporting** to their clients the impact and effectiveness of what they have done, including the votes they have cast.

3.19.3 Means of exercising institutional investors' influence

A number of different methods may be effective.

(a)   **One-to-one meetings** – to discuss strategy, whether objectives are being achieved, how the company is achieving its objectives, the quality of management. However new information cannot be divulged to any single analyst or investor in these meetings as it would give that investor an information advantage over others.

(b)   **Voting** – generally institutional investors would prefer to work behind the scenes and to avoid voting against the board if possible; if they were intending to oppose a resolution, they should normally state their intention in advance. Most corporate governance reports emphasise the importance of institutional investors exercising their votes regularly and responsibly.

(c)   **Focus list** – putting companies' names on a list of underperforming companies; such companies' boards may face challenges.

(d)   **Contributing to corporate governance rating systems** that measure key corporate governance performance indicators such as number of non-executive directors, role of the board and the transparency of the company.

3.19.4 Intervention by institutional shareholders

In extreme circumstances the institutional shareholders may intervene more actively, by for example calling an **extraordinary general meeting** in an attempt to unseat the board. The UK Institutional Shareholders' Committee has identified a number of reasons why institutional investors might intervene:

- Fundamental concerns about the **strategy** being pursued in terms of products, markets and investments

- **Poor operational performance**, particularly if one or more key segments has persistently underperformed

- Management being dominated by a small group of executive directors, with the **non-executive directors failing to hold management to account**

BPP LEARNING MEDIA

- **Major failures in internal controls**, particularly in sensitive areas such as health and safety, pollution or quality
- **Failure** to **comply with laws and regulations or governance codes**
- **Excessive levels of directors' remuneration**
- **Poor attitudes towards corporate social responsibility**

3.20 Small investors

The Organisation for Economic Co-operation and Development suggested that a key principle of corporate governance is that all shareholders should be treated **equally**. However if institutional investors become more influential, they may be treated better by company managers.

Small investors may not have the same ease of access to information that institutional investors possess, nor the level of understanding of experts employed by institutional investors. These problems can handicap their position.

3.21 Stakeholder and agency theory

Quinn and Jones argued that agency theory does not allow managers to **avoid their normal moral obligations,** particularly avoiding harm to others, respecting the autonomy of others, telling the truth and honouring agreements. Only after fulfilling these can they maximise shareholder wealth. The agency-principal relationship can only be meaningful if managers attend to the moral principles.

The opposite view was forcefully argued by Milton Friedman. Friedman claimed that managers are responsible to owners who generally are aiming to make as much money as possible. If managers are argued to have social responsibilities, then they have to act in some ways that are not in the interest of the owners, **their principals**, and they will be spending money for purposes other than which they are authorised. They therefore are not acting properly as agents; instead they are in effect raising taxes and deciding how these taxes should be spent, which is the proper function of government, not agents.

3.22 Stakeholder theory and company law

Although company law reforms in various countries have attempted to place some emphasis on ethical and social responsibility, a key foundation of company law in most jurisdictions remains the **fiduciary and legal obligations** that managers have to **maximise shareholder wealth**. Therefore under law, if managers are to fulfil responsibilities to a wider stakeholder base, there must, according to capitalist thinking, be a business profit case for doing so (Freidman's argument above).

Some commentators have tried to reconcile stakeholder and agency theory by arguing that managers are stakeholders, responsible as **agents to all other stakeholders**. Although stakeholders have divergent interests that may be difficult to reconcile, that does not absolve management from at least trying to reconcile their interests; managers are, after all, certainly responsible to all shareholders and different shareholders also have divergent interests.

4 Major issues in corporate governance

FAST FORWARD

Key issues in corporate governance reports have included the **role of the board**, the **quality of financial reporting and auditing**, **directors' remuneration**, **risk management** and **corporate social responsibility**.

We shall expand on these issues in the next two chapters, but for now let's examine the major areas that have been affected by corporate governance.

4.1 Duties of directors

The corporate governance reports have aimed to build on the directors' duties as defined in statutory and case law duties of directors. These include the **fiduciary duties** to act in the **best interests of the company**, use their powers for a **proper purpose**, **avoid conflicts of interest** and exercise a **duty of care**.

4.2 Composition and balance of the board

A feature of many corporate governance scandals has been boards dominated by a **single senior executive** or 'small kitchen cabinet' with other board members merely acting as a rubber stamp. Sometimes the single individual may bypass the board to action his own interests. The report on the UK Guinness case suggested that the Chief Executive, Ernest Saunders, paid himself a £3million reward without consulting the other directors.

Even if an organisation is not dominated by a single individual, there may be other weaknesses. The organisation may be run by a small group centred round the chief executive and chief financial officer, and appointments may be made by personal recommendation rather than a formal, objective process.

As we shall see, the board must also be **balanced** in terms of skills and talents from several **specialisms** relevant to the organisation's situation and also in terms of **age** (to ensure senior directors are bringing on newer ones to help succession planning).

4.3 Reliability of financial reporting and external auditors

Issues concerning **financial reporting and auditing** are seen by many investors as crucial because of their central importance in ensuring management accountability. They have thus been the focus of much debate and litigation. Whilst focusing the corporate governance debate solely on accounting and reporting issues is inadequate, the greater regulation of practices such as off-balance sheet financing has led to **greater transparency** and a **reduction in risks** faced by investors.

External auditors may not carry out the necessary questioning of senior management because of fears of **losing the audit**, and internal auditors do not ask awkward questions because the chief financial officer **determines their employment prospects**. Often corporate collapses are followed by criticisms of external auditors, such as the Barlow Clowes affair where poorly planned and focused audit work failed to identify illegal use of client monies.

4.4 Directors' remuneration and rewards

Directors being paid excessive salaries and bonuses has been seen as one of the major corporate abuses for a large number of years. It is thus inevitable that the corporate governance codes have targeted this issue.

4.5 Responsibility of the board for risk management and internal control systems

Boards that meet irregularly or fail to consider systematically the organisation's activities and risks are clearly not fulfilling their responsibilities. Sometimes the failure to carry out proper oversight is due to a **lack of information** being provided, which in turn may be due to inadequate systems being in place for the **measurement** and **reporting of risk**.

4.6 Rights and responsibilities of shareholders

We saw in Section 3 how shareholders' rights and the role of shareholders, particularly institutional shareholders, has been the subject of much debate. Shareholders should have the right to receive all **material information** that may affect the value of their investment and to **vote** on measures affecting the organisation's **governance**.

4.7 Corporate social responsibility and business ethics

The lack of consensus about the issues for which businesses are responsible and the stakeholders to whom they are responsible has inevitably made corporate social responsibility and business ethics an important part of the corporate governance debate.

The South African King report optimistically comments that 'The relationship between a company and its stakeholders should be mutually beneficial… This inclusive approach is the way to create sustained business success and steady long-term growth in corporate value.' The UK's Hampel report however emphasises responsibility towards shareholders, and states that it is impractical for boards to be given lots of responsibilities towards the wider stakeholder community.

4.8 Public and non-governmental corporate governance

Many of the principles that apply to company corporate governance also apply to government bodies or other major entities such as charities. Boards will be required to act with **integrity**, to **supervise the body's activities properly** and to **ensure appropriate control and risk management and reporting systems** are being maintained.

However there are certain ways in which companies might differ from other types of organisation such as in their ownership (principals), their raison d'etre and the legal/regulatory environment within which they operate.

4.8.1 Composition of boards

This may be determined by regulation or may be tailored by the body's constitution. There may be more than one board; possibly an **executive board** for overseeing operations, and a **stakeholder board** containing representatives of all major stakeholder groups, which determines objectives and ensures stakeholder interests are being represented.

4.8.2 Conduct of directors

Directors may be subject to **organisation or sector-specific** controls to ensure that they act in the public interest.

 Case Study

The BBC Trust has recently been introduced as a new means of governing the British Broadcasting Corporation. The Trust aims to ensure greater transparency and give the public a say in setting the strategic direction of the BBC. To do this, the Trustees keep in close contact with licence fee payers via research, direct engagement with the public and through Audience Research Councils.

The Trust's role includes judging performance against the six public purposes established in the BBC's Charter. The Trust also approves the Statements of Programme Policy drawn up by the Executive Board of the BBC setting out, in broad terms, the BBC's plans for the UK public services for the year ahead. The Trust aims to ensure the plans contribute to the BBC fulfilling its public service remit. If the Executive Board wants to make a significant change to an existing service licence or introduce a new service, the Trust has first to give permission. The Trust won't allow proposals to go ahead without carrying out a Public Value Test. The Trust also regulates the commercial services and trading activities of the BBC, enforcing the BBC's commitment to fair trading.

4.8.3 Compulsory regulations vs voluntary best practice

Certain guidelines that are voluntary best practice in the corporate sector may be compulsory for some other sorts of organisation, for example maintenance of an internal audit department.

4.8.4 Disclosure of internal control

Central government bodies in the UK are an example of bodies who are required to make disclosures about specific controls such as risk registers, training, key performance indicators and reporting systems.

Chapter Roundup

- **Corporate governance**, the system by which organisations are directed and controlled, is based on a number of concepts including transparency, independence, accountability and integrity.

- **Agency** is extremely important in corporate governance as often the directors/managers are acting as agents for the owners. Corporate governance frameworks aim to ensure directors/ managers fulfil their **responsibilities** as agents by requiring disclosure and suggesting they be rewarded on the basis of performance.

- Directors and managers need to be aware of the **interests of stakeholders** in governance, however their responsibility towards them is judged.

- Governance reports have emphasised the role of **institutional investors** (insurance companies, pension funds, investment houses) in directing companies towards good corporate governance.

- Key issues in corporate governance reports have included the **role of the board**, the **quality of financial reporting and auditing**, **directors' remuneration**, **risk management** and **corporate social responsibility**.

Quick Quiz

1   Corporate governance focuses on companies' relationships with all stakeholders, not just shareholders.

    True   ☐

    False   ☐

2   Name five concepts that underlie corporate governance.

3   Fill in the blank

    .... means straightforward dealing and completeness

4   Why is agency a significant issue in corporate governance?

5   What does fiduciary mean?

6   Name three methods of rewarding management that can help to ensure alignment of interests.

7   Which of the following is not generally classified as an institutional shareholder?

    A   Pension funds
    B   Investment trusts
    C   Central government
    D   Venture capitalists

8   What are the main fiduciary duties of directors?

Answers to Quick Quiz

1 True

2 Any five of:

Fairness, Openness/Transparency, Independence, Probity/Honesty, Responsibility, Accountability, Reputation, Judgement and Integrity

3 Integrity

4 Because of the separation of ownership (principal) from management (agent)

5 Fiduciary means that persons owe a duty to others because of the position of trust and confidence they hold in relation to those others.

6 Profit-related/ economic value-added pay, shares, executive share option plans

7 C Central government

8 Acting in the best interests of the company, using their powers for a proper purpose, avoiding conflicts of interest, the duty of care

Now try the question below from the Exam Question Bank

Number	Level	Marks	Time
Q1	Examination	25	45 mins

Approaches to corporate governance

2

Topic list	Syllabus reference
1 Basis of corporate governance guidance	A6
2 Corporate governance codes	A6
3 Sarbanes-Oxley	A6
4 Corporate social responsibility	A7

Introduction

Having described the underlying principles and issues behind the development of corporate governance in Chapter 1, in this chapter we discuss how corporate governance codes have developed. In Section 1 we see the development of many codes in the context of a desire to develop principles-based guidance and also as a function of the share ownership patterns of the economies to which the codes relate. In Section 2 we discuss briefly the main codes that have been developed worldwide, both in individual countries and for a number of jurisdictions (the OECD and ICGN reports).

Because of the differing approach to regulation generally, and also specifically because of the fall-out from the collapse of Enron, America has developed a more prescriptive approach to corporate governance, the Sarbanes-Oxley Act. We cover this legislation in Section 3. We give more detail about it than other regulations/guidance, since the examiner has emphasised its importance as the most influential corporate governance instrument of recent times, influencing practice globally because of the international significance of American business.

In the last section we discuss the very important topic of corporate social responsibility, what concepts lie behind it and how it has influenced the development of corporate governance. Corporate social responsibility ideas are significant in Part E of the syllabus, which we shall cover in Chapters 10 to 12.

Study guide

		Intellectual level
A6	**Different approaches to corporate governance**	
(a)	Describe and compare the essentials of rules and principles based approaches to corporate governance. Includes discussion of comply or explain	3
(b)	Describe and analyse the different models of business ownership that influence different governance regimes (eg family firms vs joint stock company-based models)	2
(c)	Describe and critically evaluate the reasons behind the development and use of codes of practice in corporate governance (acknowledging national differences and convergence)	3
(d)	Explain and briefly explore the development of corporate governance codes in principles-based jurisdictions (impetus and background, major corporate governance codes, effects)	2
(e)	Explain and explore the Sarbanes-Oxley Act as an example of a rules-based approach to corporate governance (impetus and background, main provisions/contents, effects)	2
(f)	Describe and explore the objectives, content and limitations of corporate governance codes intended to apply to multiple national jurisdictions (OECD, ICGN)	2
A7	**Corporate governance and corporate social responsibility**	
(a)	Explain and explore social responsibility in the context of corporate governance	2
(b)	Discuss and critically assess the concept of stakeholders and stakeholding in organisations and how this can affect strategy and corporate governance	3
(c)	Analyse and evaluate issues of ownership, property and the responsibilities of ownership in the context of shareholding	3
(d)	Explain the concept of the organisation as a corporate citizen of society with rights and responsibilities	3

Exam guide

You may well have to discuss the implications of basing governance guidance on principles. The examiner has stated that knowledge of the main features and advantages and disadvantages of codes in general is important, but line-by-line knowledge isn't required.

As regards specific codes, the main themes of Sarbanes-Oxley may be tested. The examiner has stressed that although the UK Combined Code sets out good practice (and students from anywhere in the world would do well to have some knowledge of UK practice), answers based on the students' local codes of practice would be equally acceptable. Students in countries without detailed codes could use UK or international codes to underpin their answers.

The existence of wider social responsibilities is likely to be a theme in many questions.

1 Basis of corporate governance guidance

Many governance codes have adopted a **principles-based approach** allowing companies flexibility in interpreting the codes' requirements and to explain if they have departed from the provisions of the code.

Insider systems are where listed companies are owned by a small number of major shareholders.

Outsider systems are where shareholdings are more widely dispersed, and the management-ownership split is more of an issue.

1.1 Principles or rules?

A continuing debate on corporate governance is whether the guidance should predominantly be in the form of principles, or whether there is a need for detailed laws or regulations.

Case Study

A principles-based approach to regulating the behaviour of motorists might say that motorists should drive safely having regard to traffic and road conditions whereas a rules-based approach might specify that motorists should not drive at speeds in excess of 100 km.

This example of motoring regulation indicates a basic weakness with both types of regime. Using a principles-based approach, what criteria can be used to determine when a motorist is not driving safely? The motorist being involved in an accident perhaps, but the accident may have been due to other factors. A problem with a rules-based approach is that attention is focused on whether the rules have been broken, and not perhaps on more relevant factors. For example a motorist driving on a motorway at 100 km per hour on a day where the motorway was seriously affected by snow might be obeying the law, but would clearly be driving at an undesirably fast speed.

Case Study

An example from sport of the differences between a principles and rules-based approach was the clash between the Australian cricket umpire Darrell Hair and the Pakistani cricket team in the Fourth Test between England and Pakistan in 2006. The resulting furore led to the Pakistan cricket captain, Inzamam-ul-Haq being suspended for a number of matches and Hair losing his position as a Test match umpire.

Hair suspected that members of the Pakistan team had been tampering with the match ball and penalised Pakistan with a five-run penalty, a penalty laid down in the rules of cricket. When Pakistan protested by not resuming play after the next scheduled match interval, Hair and his umpiring colleague, Billy Doctrove, abandoned the match, a decision that was not rescinded despite Pakistan later stating that they were happy to resume play.

Hair claimed his actions were in accordance with the rules of cricket. However he was criticised on a number of grounds:

(a) That there was insufficient evidence of ball-tampering; thus it can be difficult to see even using a rules-based approach whether the rules have been broken.

(b) That Hair should have acted in accordance with the 'spirit of cricket' (meaning here perhaps the principle of trying to ensure that the game continues with all parties in as happy a frame of mind as possible) and given the Pakistanis a verbal warning before applying a penalty that they would regard as a challenge to their integrity.

(c) That once the Pakistanis indicated their willingness to play, the umpires should have resumed the game because of the principle of aiming to keep the spectators of the game happy. Failure to follow this principle had tangible results in the form of the loss of income from the following day's cricket, which should have been the final day of the match.

1.2 Characteristics of a principles-based approach

(a) The approach focuses on **objectives** (for example the objective that shareholders holding a minority of shares in a company should be treated fairly) rather than the mechanisms by which these objectives will be achieved. Possibly therefore principles are easier to integrate into strategic planning.

(b) A principles-based approach can lay stress on those elements of corporate governance to which rules **cannot easily be applied**. These include overall areas such as the requirement to maintain sound systems of internal control, and 'softer' areas such as organisational culture and maintaining good relationships with shareholders and other stakeholders.

(c) Principles-based approaches can applied across **different legal jurisdictions** rather being founded in the legal regulations of one country. The OECD guidelines, which we shall cover later in this chapter, are a good example of guidance that is applied internationally.

(d) Where principles-based approached have been established in the form of corporate governance codes, the specific recommendations that the codes make are generally enforced on a **comply or explain basis**.

(e) Principles-based approaches have often been adopted in jurisdictions where the governing bodies of **stock markets** have had the prime role in setting standards for companies to follow.

1.3 Characteristics of a rules-based approach

(a) Rules-based systems place **more emphasis** on definite **achievements** rather than underlying factors and control systems. The EMAS environmental management system (discussed further in Chapter 12) is a good example of a system based on rules, with requirements for **targets to be set** and disclosure requirements of whether or not targets have been achieved.

(b) Rules-based approaches allow no leeway; the **key issue** is whether or not you have complied with the rules.

(c) It should in theory be **easy to see** whether there has been compliance with the rules. However that depends on whether the rules are **unambiguous**, and the **clarity of evidence** of compliance or non-compliance (a problem with the cricket example above).

(d) Enforcers of a rules-based approach (regulators, auditors) may find it difficult to deal with **questionable situations** that are not covered sufficiently in the rulebook. This as we shall see was a problem with Enron; the company kept a number of its financial arrangements off its balance sheet. Although this approach can be seen as not true and fair, Enron could use it because it did not breach the accounting rules then in existence in America.

(e) Rules-based approaches to corporate governance tend to be found in legal jurisdictions and culture that lay great emphasis on **obeying the letter of the law** rather than the spirit. They often take the form of legislation themselves, notably the Sarbanes-Oxley Act which we shall discuss later in this chapter as the most relevant example of a rules-based approach.

1.4 Advantages of a principles-based approach

Possible advantages of basing corporate governance codes on a series of principles are:

(a)   It avoids the need for **inflexible legislation** that companies have to comply with even though the legislation is not appropriate.

(b)   It is less burdensome in **terms of time and expenditure.** Although governments have not been directly involved in many of the bodies that have established corporate governance practice; they clearly have a major interest and have made their views known. In many countries there are continual pressures from business for governments to 'reduce the burden of red-tape.'

(c)   A **principles-based approach** allows companies to **develop their own approach** to corporate governance that is appropriate for their circumstances within the limits laid down by stock exchanges.

(d)   Enforcement on a **comply** or **explain basis** means that businesses can explain why they have departed from the specific provisions if they feel it is appropriate.

(e)   A principles-based approach accompanied by disclosure requirements puts the **emphasis on investors** making up their own minds about what businesses are doing (and whether they agree departures from the codes are appropriate).

1.5 Principles-based approach in action: The Hampel report

Of the major corporate governance reports, the Hampel report (1998) in the UK came out the strongest in favour of a principles-based approach. The committee preferred relaxing the regulatory burden on companies and was against treating the corporate governance codes as sets of rules, judging companies by whether they have complied ('box-ticking'). The report states that there may be **guidelines** which will normally be appropriate but the differing circumstances of companies meant that sometimes there are valid reasons for exceptions.

'Good corporate governance is not just a matter of prescribing particular corporate structures and complying with a number of hard and fast rules. There is a need for broad principles. All companies should then apply these flexibly and with commonsense to the varying circumstances of individual companies. Companies' experience of the Cadbury and Greenbury codes has been rather different. Too often they believe that the codes have been treated as sets of prescriptive rules. The shareholders or their advisers would only be interested only in whether the letter of the rule has been complied with.'

1.6 Criticisms of a principles-based approach

A number of commentators criticised the Hampel report for the approach it took, and their criticism can be seen as identifying potential problems with a principles– based approach in general.

(a)   The principles set out in the Hampel report have been criticised as **so broad** that they are of very little use as a guide to best corporate governance practice. For example the suggestion that non-executive directors from a wide variety of backgrounds can make a contribution is seen as not strong enough to encourage companies away from recruiting directors by means of the 'old boy network' (relying on their current business and social contacts).

(b)   It has also been suggested that the Hampel comments about **box-ticking** are incorrect for two reasons. Firstly, shareholders do not apply that approach when assessing accounts. Secondly, it is far less likely that disasters will strike companies with a 100% compliance record since they are unlikely to be content with token compliance, but will have set up procedures that contribute significantly to their being governed well.

There are other dangers with a **principles-based approach**:

(a) There may be **confusion over what is compulsory and what isn't**. Although codes may state that they are not prescriptive, their adoption by the local stock exchange means that specific recommendations in the codes effectively become rules, which companies have to **obey in order to retain their listing**.

(b) Some companies may perceive a principles-based approach as **non-binding** and fail to comply without giving an adequate or perhaps any explanation. Not only does this demonstrate a failure to understand the **purpose of principles-based codes** but it also casts aspersions on the integrity of the companies' decision-makers.

(c) Shareholders and stock markets may be as intolerant of companies who **fail to comply with principles** as they are of companies who **break rules**.

1.7 Influence of ownership

A key distinction that has been drawn between the corporate governance systems worldwide in different regimes has been between the insider and outsider models of ownership, although in practice most regimes fall somewhere in between the two.

1.8 Insider systems

Insider or relationship-based systems are where most companies listed on the local stock exchange are owned and controlled by a **small number of major shareholders**. The shareholders may be members of the company's founding families, banks, other companies or the government.

The reason for the concentration of share ownership is the legal system; there tends to be more diverse shareholder ownership in jurisdictions such as the UK that have **strong protection** for minority shareholders.

1.8.1 Advantages of insider systems

(a) It is easier to establish ties between **owners and managers**; in particular controlling families often participate in the management of companies.

(b) The agency problem is reduced if the owners are also involved in **management**.

(c) Even if the owners are not involved in management, it should be easier to **influence company management** through **ownership and dialogue**.

(d) A smaller base of shareholders may be more flexible about **when** profits are made and hence more able to take a **long-term view**.

1.8.2 Disadvantages of insider systems

(a) There may be **discrimination against minority shareholders** as regards for example availability of information and ultimately expropriation of the wealth of minorities.

(b) Evidence suggests that controlling families tend **not to be monitored effectively** by banks or by other large shareholders.

(c) Insider systems often do not develop **more formal governance structures** until they need to, for example as a forum for resolving family disagreements or dealing with controversial issues such as succession planning.

(d) Insider firms, particularly family firms, may be reluctant to employ outsiders in influential positions and may be **unwilling to recruit independent non-executive directors**.

(e)   Evidence suggests that **insider systems are more prone to opaque financial transactions** and misuse of funds.

(f)   For capital markets to be truly competitive there should be no **investors** who are on **their own** of **such size** that they **can influence prices**. As we have already seen in many capital markets, transactions by the largest shareholders are now on such a massive scale that considerable price movements can result.

(g)   As previously discussed, many large shareholders (particularly financial institutions) tend to **avoid shares** that are seen as **speculative** and invest only in 'blue chip' shares (ie those of leading commercially sound companies). As a result, the shares of such companies tend to be relatively expensive.

Case Study

Sir Adrian Cadbury, chairman of the committee that produced the seminal Cadbury report in the UK, also was responsible for a report in 2000; *Family firms and their Governance; creating Tomorrow's Company from Today's.* In the report Cadbury discussed the stages of establishing corporate governance structures in a family firm, from a family assembly through to a board of directors including members from outside the family. Cadbury commented that establishing a formal board was the key stage of progressing from an organisation based on family relationships to an organisation based on business relationships, and that the establishment of a board provided necessary clarification of responsibilities and the process for taking decisions.

Cadbury commented that in order to manage growth successfully, family firms had to:

- Be able to recruit and retain the very best people for the business
- Develop a culture of trust and transparency
- Define logical and efficient organisational structures

1.9 Outsider systems

Outsider systems are ones where shareholding is more widely dispersed, and there is the **manager-ownership separation**. These are sometimes referred to as Anglo-American or Anglo-Saxon regimes.

1.9.1 Advantages of outsider systems

(a)   The separation of ownership and management has provided an impetus for the development of **more robust legal and governance regimes** to **protect shareholders**.

(b)   Shareholders have voting rights that they can use to **exercise control**.

(c)   Hostile takeovers are far more frequent, and the threat of these acts as a **disciplining mechanism** on company management.

1.9.2 Disadvantages of outsider systems

(a)   Companies are more likely to have an **agency problem** and **significant costs of agency**.

(b)   The larger shareholders in these regimes have often had **short-term priorities** and have preferred to sell their shares rather than leave the company.

Exam focus point

Although the British and American systems can both be classified as outsider systems, don't necessarily assume that exam scenarios will always be about such systems. Some questions may well be set on insider systems, and focus on the implications for corporate governance of operating within insider systems.

2 Corporate governance codes

Globalisation, the **treatment of investors** and **major corporate scandals** have been major driving forces behind corporate governance developments.

Major governance guidance includes the **UK Combined Code** the **South African King report** and the **Singapore Code of Corporate Governance**. International guidance includes the **OECD principles** and the **ICGN report**.

2.1 The driving forces of governance code development

Corporate governance issues came to prominence in the USA during the 1970s and in the UK and Europe from late 1980s. The main, but not the only, drivers associated with the increasing demand for the development of governance were:

(a)   **Increasing internationalisation and globalisation** meant that investors, and institutional investors in particular, began to invest outside their home countries. The King report in South Africa highlights the role of the free movement of capital, commenting that investors are promoting governance in their own self-interest.

(b)   The **differential treatment of domestic and foreign investors**, both in terms of reporting and associated rights/dividends, also the excessive influence of majority shareholders in insider jurisdictions, caused many investors to call for parity of treatment.

(c)   Issues concerning **financial reporting** were raised by many investors and were the focus of much debate and litigation. Shareholder confidence in what was being reported in many instances was eroded. Whilst corporate governance development isn't just about better financial reporting requirements, the regulation of practices such as off-balance sheet financing has led to greater transparency and a reduction in risks faced by investors.

(d)   The characteristics of individual countries may have a **significant influence** in the way corporate governance has developed. The King report emphasises the importance of qualities that are fundamental to the South African culture such as collectiveness, consensus, helpfulness, fairness, consultation and religious faith in the development of best practice.

(e)   An increasing number of **high profile corporate scandals** and collapses including Polly Peck International, BCCI, and Maxwell Communications Corporation prompted the development of governance codes in the early 1990s. However the scandals since then have raised questions about further measures that may be necessary.

2.2 Development of corporate governance codes

To combat these problems codes of best practice were developed in many jurisdictions. The UK Cadbury report suggests that a voluntary code coupled with disclosure would prove more effective than a statutory code in promoting the key principles of **openness, integrity and accountability**.

Nevertheless the Cadbury report acknowledges the need for codes to go beyond broad principles and provide some specific guidelines. These would promote an **understanding of directors' responsibilities** and **openness about the ways they have been discharged**. Specific guidelines would also help in **raising standards of financial reporting** and **business conduct;** if this did not occur, then statutory regulation would probably be inevitable.

2.3 Major governance codes – UK

2.3.1 The Cadbury report

The Cadbury committee in the UK was set up because of the lack of confidence perceived in financial reporting and in the ability of auditors to provide the assurances required by the users of financial statements. The main difficulties were considered to be in the relationship between **auditors and boards of directors**. In particular, the commercial pressures on both directors and auditors caused pressure to be brought to bear on auditors by the board and the auditors often capitulated. Problems were also perceived in the ability of the board of directors to control their organisations.

(a) **Corporate governance responsibilities**

The roles of those concerned with the financial statements are described in the Cadbury report, published in 1992.

(i) The **directors** are responsible for the corporate governance of the company.

(ii) The **shareholders** are linked to the directors via the financial reporting system.

(iii) The **auditors** provide the shareholders with an external objective check on the directors' financial statements.

(iv) Other concerned **users**, particularly employees (to whom the directors owe some responsibility) are indirectly addressed by the financial statements.

(b) **Code of Best Practice**

The **Code of Best Practice** included in the Cadbury report and subsequently amended by later reports was aimed at the directors of all UK public companies, but the directors of all companies were encouraged to use the Code.

Provisions in the Cadbury report included:

(a) The board of directors should meet on a **regular basis**, retain full control over the company and monitor executive management. Certain matters such as major acquisitions or disposals of assets, should be **referred** automatically to the **board**. There should be a **clear division of responsibilities** at the head of a company, with no one person having complete power. Generally this would mean the posts of chairman and chief executive being held by different people.

(b) The report sees non-executive directors as important figures because of the **independent judgement** they bring to bear on important issues. There should be at **least three non-executive** directors on the board, a **majority** of whom should be **independent** of management.

(c) The report contains provisions about the length of **directors' service contracts** and **disclosure of remuneration** that are developed further in the Greenbury and Hampel reports (see below).

(d) The (internal) **audit committee** was seen by the Cadbury committee as a key board committee. The audit committee should **liase** with **internal** and **external auditors**, and provide a forum for both to express their concerns. The committee should also **review** half yearly and annual **statements**.

(e) The annual report should present a **balanced** and **understandable assessment** of the company's position. The directors should **explain** their **responsibilities** for preparing accounts. Statements should also be made about the company's ability to continue as a **going concern**, and the effectiveness of its **internal controls**.

2.3.2 The Greenbury code

In 1995, the **Greenbury committee** published a code which established principles for the determination of **directors' pay** and detailing disclosures to be given in the annual reports and accounts.

The Greenbury code went beyond the Cadbury code. The Greenbury code recommends that the **remuneration committee** should determine executive directors' remuneration and that this committee should be comprised solely of non-executive directors. Directors' **service contracts** should be **limited to one year**.

2.3.3 The Hampel report

The **Hampel committee** followed up in 1998 matters raised in the Cadbury and Greenbury reports, as we have seen aiming to restrict the regulatory burden on companies and substituting principles for detail whenever possible. Under Hampel:

(a)   The accounts should contain a **statement** of how the company applies the corporate governance principles.

(b)   The accounts should **explain their policies**, including any circumstances justifying departure from best practice.

2.3.4 Combined Code

The London Stock Exchange subsequently issued a combined corporate governance code, which was derived from the recommendations of the Cadbury, Greenbury and Hampel reports. The Combined Code is summarised in an Appendix to this Text.

Since the publication of the Combined Code a number of reports in the UK have been published about specific aspects of corporate governance.

- The **Turnbull report** (1999, revised 2005) focused on risk management and internal control.
- The **Smith report** (2003) discussed the role of audit committees.
- The **Higgs report** (2003) focused on the role of the non-executive director.

We shall discuss some of the detailed provisions of these codes later in this Text.

2.4 Major governance codes – South Africa

South Africa's major contribution to the corporate governance debate has been the **King report**, first published in 1994 and updated in 2002 to take account of developments in South Africa and elsewhere in the world.

The King report differs in emphasis from other guidance by advocating an integrated approach to corporate governance in the interest of a wide range of stakeholders – embracing the social, environmental and economic aspects of a company's activities. The report encourages active engagement by companies, shareholders, business and the financial press and relies heavily on disclosure as a regulatory measure.

2.5 Singapore Code of Corporate Governance

The Singapore Code (published 2001, revised 2005) of Corporate Governance takes a similar approach to the UK's Combined Code with the emphasis being on companies giving a detailed description of their governance practices and explaining any deviation from the Code. Some guidelines, particularly on directors' remuneration, go beyond what is in UK guidance. Revisions to the Code in 2005 reflected recent concerns; they included expanding the role of the audit committee, requiring companies to have procedures in place for whistle-blowing and the separation of substantive motions in general meetings.

2.6 Effects of corporate governance reports

The OECD report (see below) emphasises that codes may leave shareholders and other stakeholders with uncertainty concerning their **status**. Market credibility therefore requires that their status in terms of **coverage**, **implementation**, **compliance** and **sanctions** should be clearly specified.

As far as the UK Codes are concerned, a survey of institutional investors carried out in 2000, two years after the Combined Code was first issued, suggested that provisions of the Codes had had varying impacts. There had been effective implementation of proposals relating to **board structure**, **non-executive directors** and **board committees**. However the reports had had only a limited effect on **director remuneration levels**, though there had been greater compliance with guidance relating to **length of directors' service contracts** and **severance arrangements**.

2.7 Convergence of international guidance

Because of increasing international trade and cross-border links, there is significant pressure for the development of internationally comparable practices and standards. Accounting and financial reporting is one area in which this has occurred. Increasing international investment and integration of international capital markets has also led to pressure for standardization of governance guidelines, as international investors seek **reassurance about the way their investments are being managed** and the **risks** involved.

Unsurprisingly the convergence models that have been developed lie between the **insider/outsider** models and between **profit-orientated and ethical stakeholder approaches**.

2.8 OECD guidance

The Organisation for Economic Co-operation and Development (OECD) has carried out an extensive consultation with member countries, and developed a **set of principles of corporate governance** that countries and companies should work towards achieving. The OECD has stated that its interest in corporate governance arises from its concern for **global investment**. Corporate governance arrangements should be credible and should be understood across national borders. Having a common set of accepted principles is a step towards achieving this aim.

The OECD developed its Principles of Corporate Governance in 1998 and issued a revised version in April 2004. They are non-binding principles, intended to assist governments in their efforts to evaluate and improve the legal, institutional and regulatory framework for corporate governance in their countries.

They are also intended to provide guidance to stock exchanges, investors and companies. The focus is on stock exchange listed companies, but many of the principles can also apply to private companies and state-owned organisations.

The OECD principles deal mainly with governance problems that result from the **separation of ownership and management** of a company. Issues of ethical concern and environmental issues are also relevant, although not central to the problems of governance.

2.8.1 The OECD principles

The OECD principles are grouped into five broad areas:

(a) **The rights of shareholders**

Shareholders should have the right to **participate and vote in general meetings** of the company, **elect** and **remove members of the board** and **obtain relevant and material information** on a timely basis. Capital markets for corporate control should function in an **efficient and timely manner**.

(b) **The equitable treatment of shareholders**

All shareholders of the same class of shares should be treated equally, including **minority shareholders** and **overseas shareholders**. **Impediments** to **cross-border shareholdings** should be **eliminated**.

(c)   **The role of stakeholders**

Rights of stakeholders should be **protected**. All stakeholders should have **access to relevant information** on a regular and timely basis. **Performance-enhancing mechanisms** for employee participation should be **permitted to develop**. Stakeholders, including employees, should be able to **freely communicate their concerns** about illegal or unethical relationships to the board.

(d)   **Disclosure and transparency**

Timely and accurate disclosure must be made of all material matters regarding the company, including the financial situation, foreseeable risk factors, issues regarding employees and other stakeholders and governance structures and policies. The company's approach to disclosure should promote the provision of analysis or advice that is relevant to decisions by investors.

(e)   **The responsibilities of the board**

The board is responsible for the **strategic guidance** of the company and for the **effective monitoring** of management. Board members should act on a fully informed basis, in good faith, with due diligence and care and in the **best interests of the company and its shareholders**. They should treat **all shareholders fairly**. The board should be able to exercise **independent judgement**; this includes assigning independent non-executive directors to appropriate tasks.

Exam focus point

This summary is worth remembering for the exam because it incorporates many key ideas from corporate governance codes around the world.

2.9 ICGN report

The International Corporate Governance Network (ICGN) published a report in 2005 aiming to enhance the guidance produced by the OECD. The purpose is to provide **practical guidance** for boards to meet expectations so that they can **operate efficiently** and **compete for scarce capital effectively**. The ICGN believes that if investors and companies establish **productive communication** on governance issues, the prospects for economic prosperity will be enhanced.

The ICGN guidance emphasises the following points in particular:

2.9.1 Board

(a)   The **structure of boards** will depend on **national models.** Boards should be responsible for guiding corporate strategy, monitoring performance and the effectiveness of corporate governance arrangements, dealing with succession issues, aligning remuneration with the company's interests, ensuring the integrity of systems and overseeing disclosure.

(b)   Directors should have appropriate **skills, knowledge and experience**, demonstrate **independent judgement** and **fulfil their fiduciary duties to** shareholders and the company.

(c)   Directors should be **re-elected at least once every three years.**

(d)   The board's chair should not be the current or former Chief Executive Officer. Corporations should establish **audit, compensation and nomination/governance committees.**

(e)   There should be a formal process for **evaluating the work of the board** and **individual directors**.

2.9.2 Shareholders

(a) Companies should **act to protect shareholders' rights** to vote; divergence from shareholders having one vote for each share they own should be justified. Shareholders should be able to vote on removing individual directors and auditors. Shareholders should have the right to put resolutions that are **advisory or binding** on a board of directors.

(b) Major changes affecting the **equity, economic interests** or **share ownership rights** of existing shareholders should not be made without prior shareholder approval.

(c) Institutional shareholders should be able to **discharge their fiduciary duties** to vote. They should be able to consult with management.

(d) Shareholders should be able to take **action against inequitable treatment**.

2.9.3 Audit and accounts

(a) The company should aim to **excel in the financial returns it achieves** compared with a benchmark based on the performance of its sector peer group.

(b) There should be full **disclosure** of ownership, voting rights, shareholder agreements and significant relationships.

(c) The audit committee should **oversee the company's relationship with the external auditor**.

2.9.4 Ethics and stakeholders

(a) Corporations should implement a **code of ethics** and conduct their activities in an **economically, socially and environmentally responsible manner.** The board is responsible for determining, implementing and maintaining a culture of **integrity**.

(b) Companies should have procedures for **monitoring related party transactions** and **conflicts of interest**.

(c) The board should be responsible for **managing successful and productive relationships** with the corporation's stakeholders. There should be disclosure of policies involving stakeholders. In particular there should be measures **aligning employee interests** with **stakeholder and other interests**, such **as employee share ownership** or other **profit-sharing programs**.

2.10 Significance of international codes

Codes such as the OECD code have been developed from best practice in a number of jurisdictions. As such, they can be seen as **representing an international consensus**. They stress global issues that are important to companies operating in a number of jurisdictions. The OECD code for example emphasises the importance of **eliminating impediments to cross-border shareholdings** and **treating overseas shareholders fairly**.

Although the OECD code is **non-binding**, its principles have been incorporated into national guidance by a number of companies including Greece and China. The OECD principles have also been used by organisations such as the World Bank as a basis for assessing the corporate governance frameworks and practices in individual countries. These assessments are used to determine the level of policy dialogue with, and technical assistance given to, these countries.

2.11 Limitations of international codes

A number of problems have been identified with international codes.

(a) International principles represent a **lowest common denominator** of general, fairly bland, principles.

(b) Any attempt to strengthen the principles will be extremely difficult because of **global differences** in legal structures, financial systems, structures of corporate ownership, culture and economic factors.

(c) As international guidance has to be based on **best practice** in a number of regimes, development will always lag behind changes in the most advanced regimes.

(d) The codes have **no legislative power**.

2.12 Contribution of corporate governance codes

However the individual provisions of the codes are viewed, they have undoubtedly made a number of contributions to the corporate environment:

(a) The reports have **highlighted the contributions good corporate governance** can make to companies.

(b) The codes have **emphasised certain dangers** that have contributed to corporate governance failure, for example individuals having too great an influence.

(c) The provisions have **provided benchmarks** that can be used to judge the effectiveness of internal controls and risk management systems.

(d) The guidelines have **promoted specific good practice** in a number of areas, for example non-executive directors, performance-related pay and disclosure.

(e) The recommendations have highlighted the importance of basic concepts and highlighted how these can be put into practice, for example **accountability** through recommendations about organisation-stakeholder relationships and **transparency** by specifying disclosure requirements.

2.13 Impact of corporate governance codes

A survey by McKinsey in 2002 suggested that investors were **prepared to pay a premium** to invest in a company with good corporate governance. Important signs of good corporate governance for investors included boards with a majority of independent non-executive directors, significant director share ownership and share-based compensation, formal director evaluation and good responsiveness to shareholder requests for information.

As far as company performance is concerned, surveys suggest that firms with strong shareholder rights had higher firm value, higher profits, higher sales growth and also lower capital expenditure and fewer acquisitions. The reason may be active shareholders ensure accountability and transparency, and give managers less scope to take risks or be negligent about internal control systems. On the other hand there appears to be little evidence that **leadership structure and board composition** have much impact on corporate performance.

3 Sarbanes-Oxley

The **Sarbanes-Oxley legislation** requires directors to **report on the effectiveness of the controls over financial reporting, limits the services auditors can provide** and requires listed companies to establish an **audit committee**. It adopts a **rules-based** approach to governance.

3.1 The Enron scandal

The most significant scandal in America in recent years has been the Enron scandal, when one of the country's biggest companies filed for bankruptcy. The scandal also resulted in the disappearance of Arthur Andersen, one of the Big Five accountancy firms who had audited Enron's accounts. The main reasons why Enron collapsed were over-expansion in energy markets, eventually too much reliance on derivatives' trading which eventually went wrong, breaches of federal law, and misleading and dishonest behaviour. However enquiries into the scandal exposed a number of weaknesses in the company's governance.

3.1.1 A lack of the transparency in the accounts

This particularly related to certain investment vehicles that were kept off balance sheet. Various other methods of inflating revenues, offloading debt, massaging quarterly figures and avoiding taxes were employed.

3.1.2 Ineffective corporate governance arrangements

The company's management team was criticised for being arrogant and over ambitious. The Economist suggested that Enron's Chief Executive Officer, Kenneth Lay, was like a cult leader with his staff and employees fawning over his every word and following him slavishly. The non-executive directors were weak, and there were conflicts of interest. The chair of the audit committee was Wendy Gramm; her husband, Senator Phil Gramm, received substantial political donations from Enron.

3.1.3 Inadequate scrutiny by the external auditors

Arthur Andersen failed to spot or failed to question dubious accounting treatments. Since Andersen's consultancy arm did a lot of work for Enron, there were allegations of conflicts of interest.

3.1.4 Information asymmetry

That is the agency problem of the directors/managers knowing more than the investors. The investors included Enron's employees. Many had their personal wealth tied up in Enron shares, which ended up being worthless. They were actively discouraged from selling them. Many of Enron's directors, however, sold the shares when they began to fall, potentially profiting from them. It is alleged that the Chief Financial Officer, Andrew Fastow, concealed the gains he made from his involvement with affiliated companies.

3.1.5 Executive compensation methods

These were meant to align the interests of shareholders and directors, but seemed to encourage the overstatement of short-term profits. Particularly in the USA, where the tenure of Chief Executive Officers is fairly short, the temptation is strong to inflate profits in the hope that share options will have been cashed in by the time the problems are discovered.

3.2 The Sarbanes-Oxley Act 2002

In the US the response to the breakdown of stock market trust caused by perceived inadequacies in corporate government arrangements and the Enron scandal was the **Sarbanes-Oxley Act 2002.** The Act applies to all companies that are required to file periodic reports with the Securities and Exchange Commission (SEC). The Act was the most far-reaching US legislation dealing with securities in many years and has major implications for public companies. Rule-making authority was delegated to the SEC on many provisions.

Sarbanes-Oxley shifts responsibility for financial probity and accuracy to the board's **audit committee**, which typically comprises three independent directors, one of whom has to meet certain financial literacy requirements (equivalent to non-executive directors in other jurisdictions).

Along with rules from the Securities and Exchange Commission, Sarbanes-Oxley requires companies to increase their financial statement **disclosures**, to have an internal **code of ethics** and to impose **restrictions on share trading** by, and **loans to**, corporate officers.

3.3 Detailed provisions of the Sarbanes-Oxley Act

3.3.1 Public Oversight Board

The Act set up a new regulator, **The Public Company Accounting Oversight Board (PCAOB),** to oversee the audit of public companies that are subject to the securities laws.

The Board has powers to set **auditing, quality control, independence and ethical standards** for registered public accounting firms to use in the preparation and issue of audit reports on the financial statements of listed companies. In particular the board is required to set standards for registered public accounting firms' reports on listed company statements on their internal control over financial reporting. The board also has **inspection and disciplinary powers** over firms.

3.3.2 Auditing standards

Audit firms should **retain working papers** for at least seven years, have **quality control standards** in place such as second partner review. As part of the audit they should review internal control systems to ensure that they **reflect the transactions** of the client and provide **reasonable assurance** that the transactions are recorded in a manner that will **permit preparation** of the **financial statements** in accordance with **generally accepted accounting principles**. They should also review records to check whether **receipts and payments** are being made **only in accordance with management's authorisation**.

3.3.3 Non-audit services

Auditors are expressly prohibited from carrying out a number of services including internal audit, bookkeeping, systems design and implementation, appraisal or valuation services, actuarial services, management functions and human resources, investment management, legal and expert services. **Provision of other non-audit services** is only allowed with the **prior approval** of the **audit committee**.

3.3.4 Quality control procedures

There should be **rotation** of lead or reviewing audit partners every five years and other procedures such as independence requirements, consultation, supervision, professional development, internal quality review and engagement acceptance and continuation.

3.3.5 Auditors and audit committee

Auditors should discuss **critical accounting policies**, **possible alternative treatments**, the management letter and unadjusted differences with the audit committee.

3.3.6 Audit committees

Audit committees should be established by all listed companies.

All members of audit committees should be **independent** and should therefore not accept any **consulting** or **advisory fee** from the company or be affiliated to it. At least one member should be a financial expert. Audit committees should be responsible for the **appointment, compensation** and **oversight** of auditors. Audit committees should establish mechanisms for dealing with complaints about accounting, internal controls and audit.

3.3.7 Corporate responsibility

The **chief executive officer** and **chief finance officer** should certify the **appropriateness** of the **financial statements** and that those **financial statements fairly present** the **operations and financial condition** of the issuer. If the company has to prepare a restatement of accounts due to material non-compliance with standards, the **chief finance officer** and **chief executive officer** should **forfeit their bonuses.**

3.3.8 Off balance sheet transactions

There should be **appropriate disclosure** of **material off-balance sheet transactions** and other relationships (transactions that are not included in the accounts but that impact upon financial conditions, results, liquidity or capital resources).

3.3.9 Internal control reporting

Annual reports should contain **internal control reports** that state the responsibility of management for establishing and maintaining an **adequate internal control structure** and **procedures for financial reporting.** Annual reports should also contain an **assessment** of the **effectiveness** of the **internal control structure** and **procedures** for **financial reporting**. Auditors should report on this assessment.

Companies should also report whether they have adopted a **code of conduct** for senior financial officers and the content of that code.

3.3.10 Whistleblowing provisions

Employees of **listed companies** and **auditors** will be granted whistleblower protection against their employers if they **disclose private employer information** to parties involved in a fraud claim.

3.4 Impact of Sarbanes-Oxley in America

The biggest expense involving compliance that companies are incurring is fulfilling the requirement to ensure their **internal controls** are properly documented and tested. US companies had to have efficient controls in the past, but they are now having to document them more comprehensively than before, and then have the external auditors report on what they have done.

The Act also formally stripped accountancy firms of almost all non-audit revenue streams that they used to derive from their audit clients, for fear of conflicts of interest.

For lawyers, the Act strengthens requirements on them to whistleblow internally on any wrongdoing they uncover at client companies, right up to board level.

3.5 International impact of Sarbanes-Oxley

The Act also has a significant **international dimension**. About 1,500 non-US companies, including many of the world's largest, list their shares in the US and are covered by Sarbanes-Oxley. There were complaints that the new legislation conflicted with local corporate governance customs, and following an intense round of lobbying from outside the US, changes to the rules were secured. For example, German employee representatives, who are non-management, can sit on audit committees, and audit committees do not have to have board directors if the local law says otherwise, as it does in Japan and Italy.

As also America is such a significant influence worldwide, arguably Sarbanes-Oxley may influence certain jurisdictions to adopt a more rules-based approach.

3.6 Criticisms of Sarbanes-Oxley

Monks and Minnow have criticised Sarbanes-Oxley for **not being strong enough** on some issues, for example the selection of external auditors by the audit committee, and at the same time being over-rigid on others. Directors may be less likely to consult lawyers in the first place if they believe that legislation could override lawyer-client privilege.

In addition Monks and Minnow allege a Sarbanes-Oxley compliance industry has sprung up focusing companies' attention on complying with all aspects of the legislation, significant or much less important. This has distracted companies from **improving information flows** to the market and then allowing the market to make well-informed decisions. The Act has also done little to address the temptation provided by generous stock options to inflate profits, other than requiring possible forfeiture if accounts are subsequently restated.

Most significantly perhaps there is recent evidence of companies turning away from the US Stock markets and towards other markets such as London. An article in the *Financial Times* suggested that this was partly due to companies tiring of the **increased compliance costs** associated with Sarbanes-Oxley implementation. In addition the nature of the **regulatory regime** may be an increasingly significant factor in listing decisions. A rules-based approach means compliance must be absolute; the comply or explain choice is not available.

4 Corporate social responsibility

FAST FORWARD

> Debates on organisations' **social responsibilities** focus on what these responsibilities are, how organisations should deal with stakeholders and what aspects of an organisation's environment, policies and governance are affected.

4.1 Significance of corporate social responsibility

Businesses, particularly large ones, are subject to increasing expectations that they will exercise corporate social responsibility. Carroll's model of social responsibility suggests there are four levels of social responsibility.

4.1.1 Economic responsibilities

Companies have economic responsibilities to **shareholders** demanding a good return, to **employees** wanting fair employment conditions and **customers** who are seeking good-quality products at a fair price. Businesses are set up to be properly functioning economic units and so this responsibility forms the basis of all others.

4.1.2 Legal responsibilities

Since laws **codify society's moral views**, obeying those laws must be the foundation of compliance with social responsibilities. Although in all societies corporations will have a minimum of legal responsibilities, there is perhaps more emphasis on them in continental Europe than in the Anglo-American economies where the focus of discussion has been whether many legal responsibilities constitute excessive red tape.

4.1.3 Ethical responsibilities

These are responsibilities that require corporations to act in a **fair and just way** even if the law does not compel them to do so.

4.1.4 Philanthropic responsibilities

According to Carroll, these are **desired** rather than being required of companies. They include charitable donations, contributions to local communities and providing employees with the chances to improve their own lives.

4.2 Corporate social responsibility and stakeholders

Inevitably discussion on corporate social responsibilities has been tied in with the stakeholder view of corporate activity, the view that as businesses benefit from the goodwill and other tangible aspects of society, that they owe it **certain duties** in return, particularly towards those affected by its activities.

4.2.1 Problems of dealing with stakeholders

Whatever the organisation's view of its stakeholders, certain problems in dealing with them on corporate social responsibility may have to be addressed.

(a) Collaborating with stakeholders may be **time-consuming** and **expensive**.

(b) There may be **culture clashes** between the company and certain groups of stakeholders, or between the values of different groups of stakeholders with companies caught in the middle.

(c) There may be **conflict between company and stakeholders** on certain issues when they are trying to collaborate on other issues.

(d) **Consensus** between different groups of stakeholders may be difficult or impossible to achieve, and the solution may not be economically or strategically desirable.

(e) Influential stakeholders' **independence** (and hence ability to provide necessary criticism) may be compromised if they become too closely involved with companies.

(f) Dealing with certain stakeholders (eg public sector organisations) may be complicated by their being **accountable in turn to the wider public**.

4.3 Impact of corporate social responsibility on strategy and corporate governance

Social responsibilities can impact on what companies do in a number of ways.

4.3.1 Objectives and mission statements

If the organisation publishes a mission statement to inform stakeholders of strategic objectives, **mention of social objectives** is a sign that the board believes that they have a significant impact on strategy.

4.3.2 Ethical codes of conduct

As part of their guidance to promote **good corporate behaviour** among their employees, some organisations publish a **business code of ethics**. We shall look at these in Chapter 11.

4.3.3 Corporate social reporting and social accounts

We shall see in Chapter 12 how organisations, as part of their reporting on operational and financial matters, report on **ethical or social conduct**. Some go further, **producing social accounts** showing quantified impacts on each of the organisation's stakeholder constituencies.

4.3.4 Corporate governance

Impacts on corporate governance could include representatives from key stakeholder groups on the board, or perhaps even a **stakeholder board of directors**. It also implies the need for a binding corporate governance code that regulates the rights of stakeholder groups.

4.4 Corporate citizenship

Key term

> **Corporate citizenship** is the business strategy that shapes the values underpinning a company's mission and the choices made each day by its executives, managers and employees as they engage with society. Three core principles define the essence of corporate citizenship, and every company should apply them in a manner appropriate to its distinct needs: minimizing harm, maximizing benefit, and being accountable and responsive to stakeholders. (Boston Center for Corporate Citizenship)

Much of the debate in recent years about **corporate social responsibility** has been framed in terms of corporate citizenship, partly because of unease about using words like ethics and responsibility in the context of business decisions. Matten et al have suggested that there are three perspectives or corporate citizenship.

4.4.1 Limited view

This is based on **voluntary philanthropy** undertaken in the business's interests. The main stakeholder groups that the corporate citizen engages with are local communities and employees. Citizenship in action takes the form of limited focus projects.

4.4.2 Equivalent view

This is based on a wider general definition of **corporate social responsibility** that is partly voluntary and partly imposed. The organisation focuses on a broad range of stakeholders and responds to the demands of society. Self-interest is not the primary motivation, instead the organisation is focused on legal requirements and ethical fulfilment.

4.4.3 Extended view

This view is based round a partly voluntary, partly imposed view of **active social and political** citizenship. Corporations must respect citizens' rights, particularly as governments have failed to provide some of the safeguards necessary for their society's citizens. Again the focus is on a wide range of stakeholders, with a combination of self interest promoting corporate power and wider responsibility towards society.

Under the extended view, organisations will promote:

- **Social rights** of citizens by provision (for example provision of decent working conditions)
- **Civil rights**, by intervening to promote citizens' individual rights themselves or to pressurize governments to promote citizens' rights
- **Political rights** by channelling (allowing individuals to promote their causes by using corporate power)

Case Study

Companies have devised a number of different definitions of corporate citizenship.

Abbott Laboratories

Global citizenship reflects how a company advances its business objectives, engages its stakeholders, implements its policies, applies its social investment and philanthropy, and exercises its influence to make productive contributions to society.

At Abbott, global citizenship also means thoughtfully balancing financial, environmental and social responsibilities with providing quality health care worldwide. Our programs include public education; environment, health and safety; and access to health care. These efforts reflect an engagement and partnership with stakeholders in the pursuit of sustainable solutions to challenges facing the global community.

AT&T

For AT&T, corporate citizenship means caring about the communities it is involved with, keeping the environment healthy, making AT&T a safe and rewarding place to work and behaving ethically in all its business dealings.

Coca-Cola

Responsible corporate citizenship is at the heart of The Coca-Cola Promise, which is based on four core values – in the marketplace, the workplace, the environment and the community:

- **Marketplace**. We will adhere to the highest ethical standards, knowing that the quality of our products, the integrity of our brands and the dedication of our people build trust and strengthen relationships. We will serve the people who enjoy our brands through innovation, superb customer service, and respect for the unique customs and cultures in the communities where we do business.

- **Workplace**. We will treat each other with dignity, fairness and respect. We will foster an inclusive environment that encourages all employees to develop and perform to their fullest potential, consistent with a commitment to human rights in our workplace. The Coca-Cola workplace will be a place where everyone's ideas and contributions are valued, and where responsibility and accountability are encouraged and rewarded.

- **Environment**. We will conduct our business in ways that protect and preserve the environment. We will integrate principles of environmental stewardship and sustainable development into our business decisions and processes.

- **Community**. We will contribute our time, expertise and resources to help develop sustainable communities in partnership with local leaders. We will seek to improve the quality of life through locally-relevant initiatives wherever we do business.

DHL

DHL takes its definition of Corporate Citizenship from the World Economic Forum: Corporate citizenship is about the contribution a company makes to society through its core business activities, its social investment and philanthropy programs, and its engagement in public policy.

Texas Instruments

Beyond the bottom line, the worth of a corporation is reflected in its impact in the community. At TI, our philosophy is simple and dates back to our founding fathers. Giving back to the communities where we operate makes them better places to live and work, in turn making them better places to do business. TI takes its commitment seriously and actively participates in community involvement through three ways – philanthropy, civic leadership and public policy and grass roots efforts.

4.5 Impact of the concept of corporate citizenship

Looking at the definitions, it seems that the only one that adds a **fresh perspective** to the concept of the company in society is the extended view, since it emphasises the **political role of the corporation** and therefore the importance of its **accountability**. It also provides perspectives on the organisation as a **global participant**, having to cope with different concepts of citizenship worldwide.

4.6 Ownership and corporate social responsibility

Having talked about the social responsibilities of companies, we also need to consider the responsibilities of shareholders in companies. One view is that shareholders, by buying shares in a company in the hope of greater returns than a safe investment say in government stock, buy a responsibility; they should be insisting that those managing the company carry out a policy that is consistent with the **public welfare**.

One of the main problems with this view in relation to large corporations is the **wide dispersion of shareholders**. This means that shareholders with small percentage holdings have negligible influence on managers. In addition the ease with which shareholders can **dispose of shares** on the stock markets arguably loosens their feeling of obligation in relation to their property. This then raises the question of why the speculative (and possibly short-term) interests of shareholders should prevail over the longer-term interests of other stakeholders.

In corporate governance discussions, the idea of ownership responsibilities have had a significant influence because of the importance of **institutional shareholders**. Not only do they have the level of shareholdings that can be used as a lever to pressure managers, but they themselves have **fiduciary responsibilities** as trustees on behalf of their investors.

Exam focus point	In the exam you may have to bring these ideas in when discussing the role of institutional shareholders.

4.7 Critiques of corporate social responsibility

Corporate social responsibility has been attacked for introducing concepts that are counter to good order in the free market. The underlying idea is that economic self-interest and allocative efficiency ensure **maximum economic growth** and hence **maximum social welfare**.

On the other hand other critics of corporate social responsibility argue that corporate social responsibility often tends to be restricted to what should be disclosed in the accounts that organisations themselves prepare, and that the range of concerns and stakeholders to which organisations are accountable is limited. More fundamentally critics claim that corporate social responsibility's supporters operate and hence acquiesce in the free market and take attention away from the need for **fundamental structural change** in economies.

Nevertheless supporters argue that corporate social responsibility and reporting can be extended to illuminate **inequalities in distribution** in society and **limitations of traditional accounting methods**. Reporting has a major role in making organisations more visible and transparent.

Case Study

Scottish Power's corporate social responsibility programme has been developed from multi-stakeholder consultation. The stakeholders emphasised the need for the company to prioritise its most significant social and environmental impacts. This consultation identified 12 impacts, and Scottish Power's 2005/06 report detailed what had been done to address these:

(a) **Provision of energy**

Scottish Power was the largest developer of onshore wind in the UK, and second largest in the US, and planned to invest £170 million in Flue Gas Desulphurisation to reduce SO2 emissions.

(b) **Health and safety**

The Lost-Time Accident rate fell and the company improved its occupational health risk registers that assess potential health impacts and help to assess health monitoring requirements. More widely, over 50,000 children attended its Child Electrical Safety Education programmes.

(c) **Customer experience**

Internal and external surveys showed high and improving levels of customer satisfaction, and a flat volume of complaints; two other key performance measures, customer minutes lost and customer interruptions, improved during the year.

(d) **Climate change and emission to air**

Scottish Power reduced emissions of carbon dioxide per unit of electricity and burned 100,000 tonnes of waste derived fuel and Biomass to reduce the amount of coal used.

(e) **Waste and resource usage**

An increased volume of ash was resold to avoid landfill and internal energy usage was reduced, although the power stations did use an increased amount of water.

(f) **Biodiversity**

The company set aside further windfarm habitat management areas and supported research into golden eagle and hen harrier interaction with wind turbines and blanket bog restoration.

(g) **Sites, siting and infrastructure**

Scottish Power continued to develop windfarms.

(h) **Employee experience**

The company attempted to minimise the number of employees leaving the business through restructuring and planned to measure employee satisfaction through the 100 best companies model.

(i) **Customers with special circumstances**

Scottish Power contributed £2 million to the Scottish Power Energy People Trust.

(j) **Community**

The company's overall community investment increased, and it won awards for its community activity. Scottish Power acknowledged that its presence can affect local communities by providing jobs or sharing resources, or on the other hand, works traffic or noise. 'It is important that our communities trust us, as we often need their cooperation to do our job effectively. Our relationship with local communities is something we can never take for granted, and as a result we must work hard to maintain that trust.'

(k) **Procurement**

Procurement activities were accredited to the environmental standard ISO 14001. An action plan was ready for implementation across UK procurement activities, aiming to ensure a consistent and proactive approach to the environment and working with suppliers. Scottish Power also stressed that many suppliers are seen as an extension of its business, and must be expected to adhere to acceptable, social, environmental and business performance standards.

(l) **Economic**

The decision to invest in FGD technology at its Longannet plant would extend the life of the plant, secure existing jobs, improve environmental performance and provide additional construction jobs.

Question
Combined Code

The Combined Code is a London Stock Exchange requirement for listed companies. It is recommended for other companies. Some argue that the code should be mandatory for all companies.

Required

(a) Discuss the benefits of the Combined Code to shareholders and other interested users of financial statements.

(b) Discuss the merits and drawbacks of having such provisions in the form of a voluntary code.

Answer

(a) **Benefits of the Combined Code**

Shareholders

Of key importance to the shareholders are the suggestions that the Combined Code makes in respect of the **annual general meeting**. In the past, particularly for large listed companies, AGMs have sometimes been forbidding and unhelpful to shareholders. The result has been poor attendance and low voting on resolutions.

The Combined Code requires that separate **resolutions** are made for identifiably different items which should assist shareholders in understanding the proposals laid before the meeting.

It also requires that **director** members of various important board committees (such as the remuneration committee) be **available** at AGMs to answer shareholders' questions.

Internal controls

Another important area for shareholders is the emphasis placed on directors monitoring and assessing **internal controls** in the business on a regular basis. While it is a statutory requirement that directors safeguard the investment of the shareholders by instituting internal controls, this additional emphasis on quality should increase shareholders' confidence in the business.

Directors re-election

The requirements of the code also make the **directors more accessible** to the shareholders. They are asked to submit to re-election every three years. They are also asked to make disclosure in the financial statements about their responsibilities in relation to preparing financial statements and going concern.

Audit committee

Lastly, some people would argue that the existence of an **audit committee** will lead to shareholders having greater confidence in the reporting process of an entity.

Other users

The key advantage to other users is likely to lie in the increased emphasis on internal controls as this will assist the company in operating smoothly and increasing viability of operations, which will be of benefit to customers, suppliers and employees.

(b) **Voluntary code**

Adherence to the combined code is not a statutory necessity, although it is possible that in the future, such a code might become part of company law.

Advantages

The key merit of the code being voluntary for most companies is that it is **flexible**. Companies can review the code and make use of any aspects which would benefit their business.

If they adopt aspects of the code, they can disclose to shareholders what is being done to ensure **good corporate governance**, and what aspects of the code are not being followed, with reasons.

This flexibility is important, for there will be a **cost of implementing** such a code, and this cost might outweigh the benefit for small or owner-managed businesses.

Disadvantages

Critics would argue that a voluntary code allows companies that should comply with the code to **get away with non-compliance** unchallenged.

They would also argue that the **type of disclosure** made to shareholders about degrees of compliance could be **confusing and misleading** to shareholders and exacerbate the problems that the code is trying to guard against.

Chapter Roundup

- Many governance codes have adopted a **principles-based approach** allowing companies flexibility in interpreting the codes' requirements and to explain if they have departed from the provisions of the code.

- **Insider systems** are where listed companies are owned by a small number of major shareholders.

- **Outsider systems** are where shareholdings are more widely dispersed, and the management-ownership split is more of an issue.

- **Globalisation**, the **treatment of investors** and **major corporate scandals** have been major driving forces behind corporate governance developments.

- Major governance guidance includes the **UK Combined Code**, the **South African King report** and the **Singapore Code of Corporate Governance**. International guidance includes the **OECD principles** and the **ICGN report**.

- The **Sarbanes-Oxley legislation** requires directors to **report on the effectiveness of the controls over financial reporting, limits the services auditors can provide** and requires listed companies to establish an **audit committee**. It adopts a **rules-based** approach to governance.

- Debates on organisations' **social responsibilities** focus on what these responsibilities are, how organisations should deal with stakeholders and what aspects of an organisation's environment, policies and governance are affected.

Quick Quiz

1   Box-ticking is a major criticism of a principles-based approach to corporate governance.

   True   ☐

   False   ☐

2   Fill in the blank

   Countries where most listed companies are owned and controlled by a small number of major shareholders are known as .... systems.

3   Which UK report concentrated on establishing principles for the determination of directors' pay and disclosures about directors' remuneration in the accounts?

   A   The Cadbury report
   B   The Greenbury report
   C   The Hampel report
   D   The Turnbull report

4   What are the five major areas covered by the OECD principles?

5   Which major corporate scandal primarily prompted the development of the Sarbanes-Oxley rules?

6   Which of the following types of work are external auditors not expressly prohibited from carrying out for audit clients under the Sarbanes-Oxley rules?

   A   Internal audit
   B   Systems design and implementation
   C   Taxation advice
   D   Investment management

7   Sarbanes-Oxley requires accounts to include an assessment of the effectiveness of the internal control structure and the procedures for financial reporting.

   True   ☐

   False   ☐

8   ....is the business strategy that shapes the values underpinning a company's mission and the choices made each day by its executives, managers and employees as they engage with society.

Answers to Quick Quiz

1   False. Box-ticking is a major criticism of a rules-based approach.

2   Insider systems

3   B   The Greenbury report

4   Rights of shareholders, equitable treatment of shareholders, role of stakeholders, disclosure and transparency, responsibilities of the board

5   Enron

6   C   Taxation advice (although the approval of the client's audit committee is required)

7   True

8   Corporate citizenship

Now try the question below from the Exam Question Bank

Number	Level	Marks	Time
Q2	Introductory	n/a	45 mins

BPP
LEARNING MEDIA

Corporate governance practice and reporting

Topic list	Syllabus reference
1 Role of the board	A3, A4
2 Board membership and roles	A3
3 Directors' remuneration	A5
4 Relationships with shareholders and stakeholders	A8
5 Reporting on corporate governance	A8

Introduction

In this chapter we see in more detail how corporate governance reports have tried to address the issues we've discussed in the first two chapters, particularly the last section of Chapter 1. A quick glance at the contents of this chapter reveals that a properly-functioning board is central to good corporate governance and hence we spend a lot of time discussing who should be on the board and what they should be doing. Section 3 deals with the perennially controversial area of directors' remuneration.

In the last two sections we deal with the areas of relationships with shareholders and stakeholders. Section 4 focuses on methods of communication, particularly general meetings. Section 5 deals with what is reported to shareholders. Remember that one aspect of the principal-agent problem is information asymmetry, agents (directors/managers) being in possession of more information than principals (shareholders). The disclosure provisions in legislation and corporate governance reports aim to address this issue.

In this chapter we have tried to mix and match codes with issues, mentioning specific codes such as the UK Greenbury Code on directors' remuneration that contain particularly important governance provisions. However the examiner has stressed that worldwide convergence has meant that similar codes operate in many jurisdictions, and that it will be acceptable to refer to **relevant** provisions of your local code or international codes when answering questions.

Study guide

		Intellectual level
A3	**The board of directors**	
(a)	Explain and evaluate the roles and responsibilities of boards of directors	3
(b)	Describe, distinguish between and evaluate the cases for and against unitary and two-tier structures	3
(c)	Describe the characteristics, board composition and types of directors (including defining executive and non-executive directors)	2
(d)	Describe and assess the purposes, roles and responsibilities of non-executive directors	3
(e)	Describe and analyse the general principles of the legal and regulatory frameworks within which directors operate on corporate boards	2
(f)	Define, explore and compare the roles of the chief executive and company chairman	3
(g)	Describe and assess the importance, and execution, of induction and continuing professional development of directors on boards of directors	3
(h)	Explain and analyse the frameworks for assessing the performance of boards and individual directors (including NEDs) on boards	2
A4	**Board committees**	
(a)	Explain and assess the importance, roles and accountabilities of board committees in corporate governance	3
(b)	Explain and evaluate the role and purpose of the following committees in effective corporate governance: remuneration committee, nominations committee, risk committee	3
A5	**Directors' remuneration**	
(a)	Describe and assess the general principles of remuneration	3
(b)	Explain and assess the effect of various components of remuneration packages on directors' behaviour	3
(c)	Explain and analyse the legal, ethical, competitive and regulatory issues associated with directors' remuneration	3
A8	**Governance: reporting and disclosure**	
(a)	Explain and assess the general principles of disclosure and communication with shareholders	3
(b)	Explain and analyse best practice corporate governance disclosure requirements for example under the UK Combined Code	2
(c)	Define and distinguish between mandatory and voluntary disclosure of corporate information in the normal reporting cycle	2
(d)	Explain and explore the nature of, and reasons and motivations for, voluntary disclosure in a principles-based reporting environment (compared with for example the reporting regime in the USA)	3
(e)	Explain and analyse the purposes of the annual general meeting and extraordinary general meetings for information exchange between the board and shareholders	2
(f)	Describe and assess the role of proxy voting in corporate governance	3

Exam guide

The exam is likely to include many questions like Question 1 in the pilot paper, requiring assessment of the strength of corporate governance arrangements in a particular organisation. This chapter provides the benchmarks against which arrangements can be assessed. You may also see quite specific part questions on aspects of corporate governance such as the role of non-executive directors.

1 Role of the board

FAST FORWARD

The board should be responsible for taking major **policy** and **strategic** decisions.

Directors should have a **mix of skills** and their **performance** should be assessed regularly.

Appointments should be conducted by formal procedures administered by a **nomination committee**.

1.1 Definition of board's role

If the board is to act effectively, its role must be defined carefully.

Case Study

The South African King report provides a good summary of the role of the board.

> 'To define the purpose of the company and the values by which the company will perform its daily existence and to identify the stakeholders relevant to the business of the company. The board must then develop a strategy combining all three factors and ensure management implements that strategy.'

The UK Higgs report provides an alternative definition.

> 'The board is collectively responsible for promoting the success of the company by directing and supervising the company's affairs.
>
> The board's role is to provide entrepreneurial leadership of the company, within a framework of prudent and effective controls which enable risk to be assessed and managed.
>
> The board should set the company's strategic aims, ensure that the necessary financial and human resources are in place for the company to meet its objectives and review management performance.
>
> The board should set the company's values and standards and ensure that its obligations to its stakeholders and others are understood and met.'

1.2 Scope of role

To be effective, boards must **meet frequently**. The Singapore Code of Corporate Governance emphasises the need for boards to meet regularly and as warranted by circumstances. Companies should amend their constitutions to provide for telephonic and videoconference meetings. The ICGN guidelines emphasise the importance of the non-executive directors meeting in the absence of the executive directors as often as required and on a regular basis.

1.2.1 Matters for board decision

The UK Cadbury report suggests that the board should have a **formal schedule of matters** specifically reserved to it for decision at board meetings. Some would be decisions such as **mergers and takeovers** that are **fundamental** to the business and hence should not be taken solely by executive managers. Other decisions would include **acquisitions and disposals of assets of the company** or its subsidiaries that are material to the company and **investments, capital projects, bank borrowing** facilities, **loans** and their repayment, foreign currency transactions, all **above a certain size** (to be determined by the board).

1.2.2 Other tasks

- Monitoring the Chief Executive Officer
- Overseeing strategy
- Monitoring risks, control systems and governance
- Monitoring the human capital aspects of the company eg succession, morale, training, remuneration etc
- Managing potential conflicts of interest
- Ensuring that there is effective communication of its strategic plans, both internally and externally

 Case Study

For the voluntary sector, the UK's *Good Governance, A Code for the Voluntary and Community Sector* stresses the board of trustees' role in ensuring compliance with the objects, purposes and values of the organisation and with its governing document. The Code stresses that the Board must ensure that the organisation's vision, mission, values and activities remain true to its objects.

The Code also lays more stress than the governance codes targeted at listed companies on trustees focusing on the strategic direction of their organisation and not becoming involved in day-to-day activities. The Chief Executive Officer should provide the link between the board and the staff team, and the means by which board members hold staff to account. Where in smaller organisations trustees need to become involved in operational matters, they should separate their strategic and operational roles.

1.3 Attributes of directors

In order to carry out effective scrutiny, directors need to have **relevant expertise** in industry, company, functional area and governance. The board as a whole needs to contain a **mix of expertise** and show a **balance** between **executive management** and **independent non-executive directors**. The South African King report, reporting within a racially-mixed region, stresses the importance also of having a good **demographic balance**.

1.3.1 Possession of necessary information

As we have seen above, in many corporate scandals, the board were not given full information. The UK's Higgs report stresses that it is the responsibility both of the chairman to decide what information should be made available, and directors to satisfy themselves that they have **appropriate information** of **sufficient quality** to make sound judgements. The South African King report highlights the importance of the board receiving **relevant non-financial information**, going beyond assessing the financial and qualitative performance of the company, looking at **qualitative measures** that involve **broader stakeholder interests**.

1.4 Role and function of nomination committee

In order to ensure that balance of the board is maintained, corporate governance codes recommend the board should set up a **nomination committee,** to oversee the process for board appointments and make recommendations to the board. The nomination committee needs to consider:

- The **balance** between executives and independent non-executives
- The **skills**, **knowledge** and **experience** possessed by current board
- The **need for continuity** and succession planning
- The desirable **size** of the board
- The need to attract board members from a **diversity** of backgrounds

Codes stress that as well as considering these issues when appointments are made, the nomination committee should regularly review the **structure, size** and **composition** of the board, and keep under review the **leadership needs** of the company.

It should also consider whether non-executive directors are spending **enough time** on their duties and other issues relating to re-election and reappointment of directors, also membership of board committees.

Case Study

One area of concern is whether individual directors are exercising disproportionate influence on the company. For example Boots prohibited the chairman of the remuneration committee from serving on the audit committee and vice versa.

The UK Combined Code emphasises that the procedures for recruiting directors must be formal, rigorous and transparent. To help ensure this a majority of committee members should be **independent non-executive directors** (discussed below). The Combined Code recommends that an **external search consultancy** and **open advertising** should be used, particularly when appointing a non-executive director or chairman.

Case Study

The UK Higgs report made a number of suggestions about possible sources of non-executive directors:

- Companies operating in international markets could benefit from having at least one non-executive director with international experience

- Lawyers, accountants and consultants can bring skills that are useful to the board

- Listed companies should consider appointing directors of private companies as non-executive directors

- Including individuals with charitable or public sector experience but strong commercial awareness can increase the breadth of diversity and experience on the board

1.5 Induction of new directors

The UK Higgs report provides detailed guidance on the development of an induction programme tailored to the needs of the company and individual directors.

Build an understanding of the nature of the company, its business and its markets	• The company's products or services • Group structure/subsidiaries/joint ventures • The company's constitution, board procedures and matters reserved for the board • The company's principal assets, liabilities, significant contracts and major competitors • Major risks and risk management strategy • Key performance indicators • Regulatory constraints
Build a link with the company's people	• Meetings with senior management • Visits to company sites other than headquarters, to learn about production and services, meet employees and build profile • Participating in boards' strategy development
Build an understanding of the company's main relationships including meetings with auditors	• Major customers • Major suppliers • Major shareholders and customer relations policy

1.6 Continuing professional development of board

The Higgs report points out that to remain effective, directors should **extend their knowledge and skills** continuously. The report suggests that professional development of potential directors ought to concentrate on the **role of the board**, **obligations** and **entitlements** of existing directors and the **behaviours** needed for effective board performance.

For existing directors, significant issues that professional development should cover on a regular basis include:

- Strategy

- Management of human and financial resources

- Audit and remuneration issues

- Legal and regulatory issues

- Risk management

- The effective behaviours of a board director such as influencing skills, conflict resolution, chairing skills and board dynamics

- The technical background of the company's activities so that directors can properly appreciate the strategic considerations (for example in fast evolving fields such as financial services or technology)

The Higgs report suggests that a variety of approaches to training may be appropriate including lectures, case studies and networking groups.

1.7 Performance of board

Appraisal of the board's performance is an important control over it, aimed at **improving board effectiveness, maximising strengths and tackling weaknesses**. It should be seen as an essential part of the **feedback** process within the company and may prompt the board to change its **methods** and/or **objectives**. The UK Higgs report recommends that **performance of the board** should be **assessed** once a year, and provides a list of the criteria that could be used:

- Performance against objectives
- Contribution to testing and development of strategy and setting of priorities
- Contribution to robust and effective risk management
- Contribution to development of corporate philosophy (values, ethics, social responsibilities)
- Appropriate composition of board and committees
- Responses to problems or crises
- Are matters reserved for the board the right ones
- Are decisions delegated to managers the right ones
- Internal and external communication
- Board fully informed of latest developments
- Effectiveness of board committees
- Quality of information
- Quality of feedback provided to management
- Adequacy of board meetings and decision-making
- Fulfilling legal requirements

Parker suggests that a key aspect of board appraisal is whether the board focuses on long-term issues and vision, or spends too much time on day-to-day management matters.

 Case Study

Corporate governance a practical guide published by the London Stock Exchange and the accountants RSM Robson Rhodes suggests that board evaluation needs to be in terms of clear objectives. Boards ought to be learning lessons from specific decisions they have taken (Did they receive adequate information? Did they address the main issues well?)

Considering how the board is working as a team is also important; this includes issues such as encouragement of criticism, existence of factions, whether dominant players are restricting the contribution of others. The guidance suggests involving an external facilitator to help discover key issues.

The guide also compares the working of an effective board with other types of board and suggests that boards should consider which unsuccessful elements they demonstrate.

Type of board	Strengths	Weaknesses
Effective board	• Clear strategy aligned to capabilities • Vigorous implementation of strategy • Key performance drivers monitored • Effective risk management • Focus on views of City and other stakeholders • Regular evaluation of board performance	

Type of board	Strengths	Weaknesses
The rubber stamp	<ul><li>Makes clear decisions</li><li>Listens to in-house expertise</li><li>Ensures decisions are implemented</li></ul>	<ul><li>Fails to consider alternatives</li><li>Dominated by executives</li><li>Relies on fed information</li><li>Focuses on supporting evidence</li><li>Does not listen to criticism</li><li>Role of non-executives limited</li></ul>
The talking shop	<ul><li>All opinions given equal weight</li><li>All options considered</li></ul>	<ul><li>No effective decision-making process</li><li>Lack of direction from chairman</li><li>Failure to focus on critical issues</li><li>No evaluation of previous decisions</li></ul>
The number crunchers	<ul><li>Short-term needs of investors considered</li><li>Prudent decision-making</li></ul>	<ul><li>Excessive focus on financial impact</li><li>Lack of long-term, wider awareness</li><li>Lack of diversity of board members</li><li>Impact of social and environmental issues ignored</li><li>Risk averse</li></ul>
The dreamers	<ul><li>Strong long-term focus</li><li>Long-term strategies</li><li>Consider social and environmental implications</li></ul>	<ul><li>Insufficient current focus</li><li>Fail to identify or manage key risks</li><li>Excessively optimistic</li></ul>
The adrenalin junkies	<ul><li>Clear decisions</li><li>Decisions implemented</li></ul>	<ul><li>Lurch from crisis to crisis</li><li>Excessive focus on short-term</li><li>Lack of strategic direction</li><li>Internal focus</li><li>Tendency to micro-manage</li></ul>
The semi-detached	<ul><li>Strong focus on external environment</li><li>Intellectually challenging</li></ul>	<ul><li>Out of touch with the company</li><li>Little attempt to implement decisions</li><li>Poor monitoring of decision-making</li></ul>

1.8 Performance of individual directors

Separate appraisal of the performance of the Chairman and the CEO should be carried out by the non-executive directors, but **all** directors should have some form of individual appraisal. Criteria that could be applied include the following.

- **Independence** – free thinking, avoids conflicts of interest

- **Preparedness** – knows key staff, organisation and industry, aware of statutory and fiduciary duties

- **Practice** – participates actively, questioning, insists on obtaining information, undertakes professional education

- **Committee work** – understands process of committee work, exhibits ideas and enthusiasm

- **Development of the organisation** – makes suggestions on innovation, strategic direction and planning, helps win the support of outside stakeholders

We shall discuss the appraisal of non-executive directors specifically in the next section.

1.9 Legal and regulatory frameworks

When defining the scope of their role, boards must comply with the **legal and regulatory framework** of the jurisdiction(s) within which they operate. These affect not just the scope of the board's role, but also the appointment and removal of directors. You will have covered key aspects of the framework in your company law studies, but we include a brief reminder of the main elements of the law in most jurisdictions.

1.9.1 Legal rights

Directors are entitled to **fees and expenses** as directors according to the company's constitution, and emoluments and compensation for loss of office in line with their service contracts (discussed below).

1.9.2 Legal responsibilities

Directors have a **duty of care** to show **reasonable competence** and may have to **indemnify the company** against loss caused by their negligence. In the UK case of *Re City Equitable Fire and Insurance Co Ltd 1925* below, this duty was analysed into three propositions.

(a) A director is expected to show the **degree of skill** that may **reasonably be expected** from a person of his knowledge and experience. The standard set is personal to the person in each case. An accountant who is a director of a mining company is not required to have the expertise of a mining engineer, but he should show that of an accountant.

(b) A director is **required to attend board meetings** when he is able but he has no duty to concern himself with the affairs of the company at other times.

(c) In the absence of grounds for suspicion and subject to normal business practice, he is **entitled to leave** the **routine conduct** of the business **in the hands of its management** and may trust them, accepting the information and explanations which they provide, if they appear to be honest and competent.

Directors are also said to be in a **fiduciary position** in relation to the company. They must act honestly in what they consider to be the best interest of the company.

1.9.3 Conflict and disclosure of interests

As **agents**, directors have a **general duty to avoid a conflict of interest**. In particular:

(a)   The directors must **retain their freedom of action** and **not fetter their discretion** by agreeing to vote as some other person may direct.

(b)   The directors owe a fiduciary duty to **avoid a conflict of duty and personal interest.**

(c)   The directors **must not obtain any personal advantage** from their position as directors **without the consent of the company** for whatever gain or profit they have obtained.

Any **action** against a director in connection with a conflict of interest will normally be **taken by the company**. The type of remedy will vary with the breach of duty.

(a)   The director may have to **account for a personal gain**.

(b)   If he contracts with the company in a conflict of interest the **contract may be rescinded by the company**. However the company cannot both affirm the contract and recover the director's profit.

(c)   The court may declare that a transaction is **ultra vires** or **unlawful**.

A company may, either by its **constitution** or by **passing a resolution** in general meeting, **authorise or ratify** the conduct of directors in breach of duty. There must be **full disclosure** to members of the relevant facts.

1.9.4 Time-limited appointments

Under the company's constitution or the director's service contract, some roles, particularly chief executive or chairman may be for a fixed period. Ordinary directors may have to retire from the board on reaching a **retirement age** (65 or 70) and may or may not be able to seek re-election.

In addition some corporate governance guidelines suggest non-executive directors should hold their post for a limited length of time. The UK Higgs report suggests that a non-executive director should normally serve two three year terms; value may be added in exceptional circumstances by a non-executive director serving for longer, but the reasons need to be explained to shareholders. Higgs suggests that after nine years on the board, non-executive directors should face annual re-election.

1.9.5 Service contracts

Service contracts set out terms and conditions of directors' appointment, including the duration of the appointment (fixed term contract) or the required minimum period of notice (a rolling contract). Legal provisions in many regimes have tended to focus on requirements for companies to keep **contracts** and make them **available for shareholder inspection**. In many countries, it has been corporate governance codes that have dealt with the most controversial issues, including remuneration, the term of the contract and payments on termination of contract.

1.9.6 Retirement by rotation

Directors are often required to retire from the board and seek re-election, generally once every three years, although managing directors may be exempt from these provisions. The provisions may be enshrined in law, but in most jurisdictions, the company's **constitution or articles** prescribe the roles on rotation. Directors will generally be entitled to seek re-election if they have retired by rotation. However, retirement by rotation provisions allow shareholders a regular opportunity to vote directors out of office.

1.9.7 Departure from office

A director may leave office in the following ways.

- **Resignation** (written notice may be required)
- Not **offering himself for re-election** when his term of office ends
- **Death**
- **Dissolution of the company**
- Being **removed** from office
- Being **disqualified** (by virtue of the constitution or by the court)

1.9.8 Disqualification

Directors may be disqualified from serving on the board under the **company's constitution**, for example, for becoming bankrupt, suffering mental disorder or being absent from the court without permission.

Directors may also be legally disqualified by the **court or government action**. Depending on the regime, possible grounds for disqualification may include failing to keep proper accounting records and trading when their company is insolvent.

Case Study

Under UK law a company's articles (constitution) may provide for the removal of a director from office. For example some company articles provide that a director may be removed from office by extraordinary resolution (75% vote in favour) passed in general meeting or even by a resolution of the board of directors. These provisions permit a company to dismiss a director without observing the formalities of the statutory procedures. However if the director also has a service agreement he may still be entitled to compensation for its breach by his dismissal.

In addition to any provisions of the articles for removal of directors, a director may be removed from office under statute by ordinary resolution (50+% vote in favour) of which special notice (28 days) to the company has been given by the person proposing it:

This statutory power of removal overrides the articles and any service agreement (but the director may claim damages for breach of the agreement). The power is, however, limited in its effect in two ways.

(i) A member who gives special notice to remove a director cannot insist on the inclusion of his resolution in the notice of a meeting unless he qualifies by representing sufficient members (that is members who either have one twentieth of the voting rights or are at least 100 members on whose shares an average of at least £100 has been paid up).

(ii) A director may be irremovable if he has 'weighted' voting rights and can prevent the resolution from being passed.

1.9.9 Insider dealing/trading

In most regimes it is a criminal offence to use inside information to buy or sell shares in a stock market. **Inside information** has been defined as information that is specific and precise, has not yet been made public, and if made public would have a significant effect on the share price. As well as being a criminal offence, it is also an abuse of **directors' roles as agents**, a clear instance of directors using the superior information they have for their benefit.

2 Board membership and roles

FAST FORWARD

Division of responsibilities at the head of an organisation is most simply achieved by separating the roles of chairman and chief executive.

Independent non-executive directors have a key role in governance. Their number and status should mean that their views carry significant weight.

2.1 Board membership

Key issues for consideration are:

- **Size** – with greater size can come greater opportunities for representation of varied views. However this can be at the expense of ease of operation and coherence of decision-making

- **Inside/outside mix** – what proportion should be executive decision-makers whose main employment is by the company and what proportion should be outsiders?

- **Diversity** – the issues here include male/female mix, representation from ethnic minorities, representatives from professions other than business (for example academia)

2.2 Chairman and CEO

Ultimate leadership of the organisation consists of a number of strands, most importantly

- Heading the board of directors – the **chairman**

- Leading the management team at and below board level – the **Chief Executive Officer or CEO**

2.2.1 Role of chairman

The UK Higgs report provides a thorough analysis of the role of the chairman. Higgs comments that the chairman is 'pivotal in creating the conditions for overall board and individual director effectiveness, both inside and outside the boardroom'. The chairman is responsible for:

(a) **Running the board and setting its agenda**

   The chairman should ensure the board focuses on **strategic matters** and takes account of the key issues and the concerns of all board members.

(b) **Ensuring the board receives accurate and timely information**

   We shall discuss this further later in the Text, but good information will enable the board to **take sound decisions** and **monitor the company effectively.**

(c) **Ensuring effective communication with shareholders**

   The chairman should take the lead in ensuring that the board **develops an understanding** of the **views of major investors**.

(d) **Ensuring that sufficient time is allowed for discussion of controversial issues**

   All members should have enough time to **consider critical issues** and not be faced with unrealistic deadlines or decision-making.

(e) **Taking the lead in providing an induction programme for new directors**

   The programme should be **comprehensive, formal and tailored**.

(f)   **Taking the lead in board development**

The chairman is responsible for **addressing the development needs** of the board as a whole and enhancing the effectiveness of the whole team, also meeting the development needs of individual directors.

(g)   **Facilitating board appraisal**

The chairman should ensure the performance of the whole board, board committees and individuals is evaluated at least once a year.

(h)   **Encouraging active engagement by all the members of the board**

(i)   **Reporting in and signing off accounts**

Financial statements in many jurisdictions include a **chairman's statement** that must be compatible with other information in the financial statements. The chairman may also be responsible for signing off the financial statements.

Case Study

Higgs goes on to provide a description of an effective chairman, who:

- Upholds the highest standards of integrity and probity

- Leads board discussions to promote effective decision-making and constructive debate

- Promotes effective relationships and open communication between executive and non-executive directors

- Builds an effective and complementary board initiating change and planning succession

- Promotes the highest standards of corporate governance

- Ensures a clear structure for, and the effective running of, board committees

- Establishes a close relationship of trust with the CEO, providing support and advice whilst respecting executive responsibility

- Provides coherent leadership of the company

2.2.2 Role of CEO

The CEO is responsible for **running the organisation's business** and for **proposing and developing the group's strategy** and overall commercial objectives in consultation with the directors and the board. The CEO is also responsible for **implementing the decisions of the board** and its committees, **developing the main policy statements** and **reviewing** the business's **organisational structure and operational performance.**

The CEO is the senior executive in charge of the management team and is answerable to the board for its performance. He will have to formalise the roles and responsibilities of the management team, including determining the degree of delegation.

A guidance note supplementing the UK Combined Code suggests that the major responsibilities of the CEO will be as follows:

(a) **Business strategy and management**

The CEO will take the lead in **developing objectives and strategy** having regard to the organisation's stakeholders, and will be primarily responsible for ensuring that the organisation achieves its objectives, optimising the use of resources.

(b) **Investment and financing**

The CEO will **examine major investments**, capital expenditure, acquisitions and disposals and be responsible for identifying new initiatives.

(c) **Risk management**

The CEO will be responsible for **managing the risk profile** in line with the risk appetite accepted by the board. He will also be responsible for ensuring that appropriate internal controls are in place.

(d) **Board committees**

The CEO will make **recommendations** to be discussed by the board committees on **remuneration policy**, **executive remuneration** and **terms of employment**, also on the role and capabilities relating to future director employments.

2.3 Division of responsibilities

All governance reports acknowledge the importance of having a division of responsibilities at the head of an organisation to avoid the situation where one individual has **unfettered control** of the decision-making process.

The simplest way to do this is to require the roles of **chairman** and **CEO** to be held by two different people, for the following reasons.

(a) It reflects the reality that both jobs are **demanding roles** and ultimately the idea that no one person would be able to do both jobs well. The CEO can then run the company; the chairman can run the board.

(b) The separation of roles avoids the risk of **conflicts of interest**.

(c) The board cannot make the CEO **truly accountable** for management if it is led by the CEO.

(d) Separation of the roles means that the board is more able to **express its concerns effectively** by providing a point of reporting (the chairman) for the non-executive directors.

The UK Combined Code also suggests that the CEO should not go on to become Chairman of the same company. If a CEO did become chairman, the main risk is that he will interfere in matters that are the responsibility of the new CEO and thus exercise undue influence over him or her.

2.3.1 Alternative arrangements

The UK Cadbury report recommends that if the posts were held by the same individual, there should be a **strong independent element** on the board with a recognised senior member. The UK Higgs report suggests that a **senior independent non-executive director** should be appointed who would be available to shareholders who have concerns that have not been resolved through the normal channels.

2.4 Board committees

Many companies operate a series of board sub-committees responsible for supervising specific aspects of governance. Operation of a committee system does not absolve the main board of its responsibilities for the areas covered by the board committees.

However good use of committees seems to have had a positive effect on the governance of many companies. Higgs found evidence that committees had given assurance that important board duties were being discharged rigorously.

The main board committees are:

- **Internal audit committee** – arguably the most important committee, responsible for liasing with external audit, supervising internal audit and reviewing the annual accounts and internal controls. The audit committee's work is discussed further in Chapter 5.

- **Nomination committee** – responsible for recommending the appointments of new directors to the board; we have discussed their work above.

- **Remuneration committee** – responsible for advising on executive director remuneration policy and the specific package for each director (discussed in Section 3).

- **Risk committee** – responsible for overseeing the organisation's risk response and management strategies (discussed in Chapter 8).

Corporate governance guidance has concentrated on the work of the audit, remuneration and nomination committees. The Higgs report recommends that no one individual should serve on all committees; most reports recommend that the committees should be staffed by non-executive directors and preferably **independent non-executive directors**. We shall now consider the role of non-executive directors to see why their role is deemed to be so significant.

2.5 Non-executive directors

Key term

> **Non-executive directors** have no executive (managerial) responsibilities.

Non-executive directors should provide a **balancing influence**, and play a key role in **reducing conflicts of interest** between management (including executive directors) and shareholders. They should provide **reassurance** to shareholders, particularly institutional shareholders, that management is acting in the interests of the organisation.

2.6 Role of non-executive directors

The UK's Higgs report provides a useful summary of the role of non-executive directors.

(a) **Strategy**. Non-executive directors should contribute to, and challenge the direction of, strategy.

(b) **Scrutiny**. Non-executive directors should scrutinise the performance of executive management in meeting goals and objectives and monitor the reporting of performance. They should represent the shareholders' interests to ensure agency issues don't arise to reduce shareholder value.

(c) **Risk**. Non-executive directors should satisfy themselves that financial information is accurate and that financial controls and systems of risk management are robust. (These may include industry-specific systems such as in the chemical industry.)

(d)   **People**. Non-executive directors are responsible for determining appropriate levels of remuneration for executives, and are key figures in the appointment and removal of senior managers and in succession planning.

The UK Higgs report suggests that non-executive directors have 'an important and inescapable relationship with shareholders'. Higgs recommends that one or more non-executive directors should take direct responsibility for shareholder concerns, and should attend regular meetings with shareholders.

2.6.1 Advantages of non-executive directors

Non-executive directors can bring a number of advantages to a board of directors.

(a)   They may have **external experience and knowledge which executive directors do not possess.** The experience they bring can be in many different fields. They may be executive directors of other companies, and thus have experience of different ways of approaching corporate governance, internal controls or performance assessment. They can also bring knowledge of markets within which the company operates.

(b)   Non-executive directors can provide a **wider perspective** than executive directors who may be more involved in detailed operations.

(c)   Good non-executive directors are often a **comfort factor** for third parties such as investors or creditors.

(d)   The English businessman Sir John Harvey-Jones has pointed out that there are **certain roles** non-executive directors are well-suited to play. These include 'father-confessor' (being a confidant for the chairman and other directors), 'oil-can' (intervening to make the board run more effectively) and acting as 'high sheriff' (if necessary taking steps to remove the chairman or chief executive).

(e)   The most important advantage perhaps lies in the dual nature of the non-executive director's role. Non-executive directors are **full board members** who are expected to have the level of knowledge that full board membership implies.

At the same time they are meant to provide the so-called **strong, independent element** on the board. This should imply that they have the knowledge and detachment to be able to **monitor the company's affairs effectively**. In particular they should be able to assess fairly the remuneration of executive directors when serving on the remuneration committee, and to be able to discuss knowledgeably with auditors the affairs of the company on the audit committee.

In addition, of course, appointing non-executive directors ensures compliance with corporate governance regulations or codes.

2.6.2 Problems with non-executive directors

Nevertheless there are a number of difficulties connected with the role of non-executive director.

(a)   In many organisations, non-executive directors may **lack independence**. There are in practice a number of ways in which non-executive directors can be linked to a company, as suppliers or customers for example. Even if there is no direct connection, potential non-executive directors are more likely to agree to serve if they admire the company's chairman or its way of operating.

(b)   There may be a **prejudice in certain companies** against widening the recruitment of non-executive directors to include people proposed other than by the board or to include stakeholder representatives.

(c)   High-calibre non-executive directors may gravitate towards the **best-run companies**, rather than companies which are more in need of input from good non-executives.

(d)   Non-executive directors may have **difficulty imposing** their views upon the board. It may be easy to dismiss the views of non-executive directors as irrelevant to the company's needs. This may imply that non-executive directors need good persuasive skills to influence other directors. Moreover, if executive directors are determined to push through a controversial policy, it may prove difficult for the more disparate group of non-executive directors to oppose them effectively.

(e)   Sir John Harvey-Jones has suggested that not enough emphasis is given to the role of non-executive directors in **preventing trouble**, in warning early on of potential problems. Contrawise, when trouble does arise, non-executive directors may be expected to play a major role in rescuing the situation, which they may not be able to do.

(f)   Perhaps the biggest problem which non-executive directors face is the **limited time** they can devote to the role. If they are to contribute valuable experience, they are likely to have time-consuming other commitments. In the time they have available to act as non-executive directors, they must contribute as knowledgeable members of the full board and fulfil their legal responsibilities as directors. They must also serve on board committees. Their responsibilities mean that their time must be managed effectively, and they must be able to focus on areas where the value they add is greatest.

(g)   Some commentators have suggested that non-executive directors can **damage company performance** by **weakening board unity** and **stifling entrepreneurship**. Agrawal and Knoeber suggested that boards are often expanded for political reasons, to include stakeholder representatives with concerns other than maximisation of financial performance.

2.7 Number of non–executive directors

Most corporate governance reports acknowledge the importance of having a significant presence of non-executive directors on the board. The question has been whether organisations should follow the broad principles expressed in the Cadbury report:

'The board should include non-executive directors of sufficient character and number for their views to carry significant weight.'

or whether they should follow prescriptive guidelines. New York Stock Exchange rules now require listed companies to have a majority of non-executive directors (ie more than half the board); other codes, such as the Singapore code, suggest at least a third of the board should be independent (non-executive) directors.

2.8 Independence of non-executive directors

Various safeguards can be put in place to ensure that non-executive directors remain independent. Those suggested by the corporate governance reports include:

(a)   Non-executive directors should have **no business**, **financial** or other **connection** with the company, apart from fees and shareholdings. Recent reports such as the UK Higgs report have widened the scope of business connections to include anyone who has been an employee or had a material business relationship over the last few years, or served on the board for more than ten years.

(b)   **Cross-directorships**, where an executive director of Company A is a non-executive director of Company B, and an executive director of Company B is a non-executive director of Company A, are a particular threat to independence. This is often increased by cross-shareholdings. The problem is that non-executive directors will sit in judgement on executive directors when for example they consider their remuneration. Having one director sit in judgement on another who in turn is sitting in judgement on him is an obvious conflict of interest, with directors being concerned with their own interests rather than shareholders'.

(c)   They should **not take part in share option schemes** and their service should not be pensionable, to maintain their independent status.

(d)   **Appointments** should be for a **specified term** and reappointment should not be automatic. The board as a whole should decide on their nomination and selection.

(e)   Procedures should exist whereby non-executive directors may take **independent advice**, at the company's expense if necessary.

However the requirements do vary jurisdiction by jurisdiction, reflecting different approaches to the drafting of codes of governance. In some jurisdictions factors that impair independence are stressed, others emphasise positive qualities that promote independence. Ultimately, as the ICGN guidelines point out, all definitions come down to non-executive directors being **independent-minded**, which means exercising objective judgement in the best interests of the corporation whatever the consequences for the director personally.

Exam focus point	Whenever a question scenario features non-executive directors, watch out for threats to, or questions over, their independence. The pilot paper included a question on threats to independence.

 Case Study

The UK Higgs report summed up the attributes of the effective non– executive director:

- Upholds the highest ethical standards of integrity and probity

- Supports executives in their leadership of the business while monitoring their conduct

- Questions intelligently, debates constructively, challenges rigorously and decides dispassionately

- Listens sensitively to the views of others inside and outside the board

- Gains the trust and respect of other board members

- Promotes the highest standards of corporate governance and seeks compliance with the provisions of the Code wherever possible

Higgs suggests that the following issues should be considered when appraising the performance of non-executive directors:

- Preparation for meetings
- Attendance level
- Willingness to devote time and effort to understand the company and its business
- Quality and value of contributions to board meetings
- Contribution to development of strategy and risk management
- Demonstration of independence by probing, maintaining own views and resisting pressure from others
- Relationships with fellow board members and senior management
- Up-to-date awareness of technical and industry matters
- Communication with other directors and shareholders

2.9 Multi-tier boards

Some jurisdictions take the split between executive and other directors to its furthest extent.

2.9.1 Corporate governance arrangements in Germany

Institutional arrangements in German companies are based on a **dual board**.

(a) **Supervisory board**

A **supervisory board** has workers' representatives and shareholders' representatives including banks' representatives. The board has no executive function, although it does review the company's direction and strategy and is responsible for **safeguarding stakeholders' interests**. It must receive formal reports the state of the company's affairs and finance; it approves the accounts and may appoint committees and undertake investigations. The board should be composed of members who, as a whole, have the required **knowledge, abilities and expert experience** to complete their tasks properly and are sufficiently independent.

(b) **Management board**

A **management or executive board**, composed entirely of managers, will be responsible for the **running** of the business. The supervisory board appoints the management board. Membership of the two boards is entirely separate.

2.9.2 Corporate governance arrangements in Japan

In Japan there are three different types of board of director.

- **Policy boards** – concerned with long-term strategic issues
- **Functional boards** – made up of the main senior executives with a functional role
- **Monocratic boards** – with few responsibilities and having a more symbolic role

Perhaps unsurprisingly one of the main features of this structure is that decision-making is **generally thorough** but slow. This has been considered as acceptable in a culture where the stress is on long-term decisions. Directors are supposed to continue to promote the interests of employees once they join the board, in line with corporate culture. Entry of executives onto the board is **controlled** by the chairman, who may seek the advice of others (frequently bankers).

2.10 Unitary boards vs multi-tier boards

2.10.1 Advantages of unitary boards

(a) All participants in the single board have equal legal responsibility for management of the company and strategic performance. This implies a **more involved approach** by those directors who are not executive directors and therefore act in an independent and 'supervisory' capacity.

(b) If all the directors attend the same meetings, the **independent directors** are **less likely** to be **excluded from decision-making and given restricted access to information**. Boards that take all views into account in decision-making may end up making better decisions.

(c) The **presence of non-executive directors** with different perspectives and viewpoints to question the actions and decisions of executive directors as they are taking place **should lead to better decisions being made**.

(d) The **relationship** between **different types of directors** may be **better** as a single board promotes easier co-operation.

2.10.2 Disadvantages of unitary boards

(a) Asking a non-executive or independent director to be **both manager and monitor** is **too awkward and demanding a task**.

(b) The time requirements on non-executive directors may be **onerous,** both in terms of the time spent in board meetings and the commitment required to **obtain sufficient knowledge** about the company to properly fulfil their monitoring role.

(c) As operated in the UK, the unitary board system makes **no specific provision for employees** to be **represented on the management board**, other than by the people who employ them.

(d) The unitary board **emphasises the divide between the shareholders and the directors** as there is no crossover between them, and it **means that the general meeting** is the only place where shareholder grievance or concern can be heard.

2.10.3 Advantages of multi-tier boards

(a) The main argument in favour of multi-tier boards is the **clear and formal separation** between the monitors and those being monitored.

(b) The supervisory/policy board has the **capacity** to be an **effective guard** against management inefficiency or worse. Indeed its very existence may be a **deterrent** to fraud or irregularity in a similar way to the independent audit.

(c) The supervisory board system should **take account of the needs of stakeholders** other than shareholders, specifically **employees**, who are clearly important stakeholders in practice. The system actively **encourages transparency within the company**, between the boards and, through the supervisory board, to the employees and the shareholders. It also **involves the shareholders and employees** in the supervision and appointment of directors.

2.10.4 Disadvantages of multi-tier boards

(a) **Confusion over authority** and therefore a **lack of accountability** can arise with multi-tier boards. This criticism has been particularly levelled at Japanese companies where the consequence is allegedly often over-secretive procedures.

(b) In practice, the board may not be as effective as it seems in theory. The **management board may restrict the information passed on** to the supervisory board and the boards may only liase infrequently.

(c) The supervisory board may not be as **independent** as would be wished, depending on how rigorous the appointment procedures are. In addition, members of the supervisory board can be, indeed are likely to be, shareholder representatives; this could detract from legal requirements that shareholders don't instruct directors how to manage if the supervisory board was particularly strong.

| **Exam focus point** | The Pilot paper asked about the arguments for adopting a unitary board structure. |

2.10.5 The future global position

Proposals to introduce two (or more) tier boards have been particularly criticised in the UK and USA. This has affected the debate on enhancing the role of non-executive directors. Critics claim that moves to increase the involvement of non-executive directors (influenced ironically by Sarbanes-Oxley) are a step on the slippery slope towards two-tier boards.

The German and Japanese models also appear to be coming under pressure to change as a result of globalisation of capital markets and cross-border mergers and acquisitions.

3 Directors' remuneration

Directors' remuneration should be set by a **remuneration committee** consisting of independent non-executive directors.

Remuneration should be dependent upon **organisation** and **individual performance**.

Accounts should disclose **remuneration policy** and (in detail) the **packages of individual directors**.

3.1 Purposes of directors' remuneration

Clearly adequate remuneration has to be paid to directors in order to attract individuals of **sufficient calibre**. Remuneration packages should be structured to ensure that individuals are **motivated to achieve performance levels** that are in the company and shareholders' best interests as well as their own personal interests.

3.1.1 Need for guidance

However, directors being paid excessive salaries and bonuses has been seen as one of the major corporate abuses for a large number of years. It is thus inevitable that the corporate governance provisions have targeted it. However this is not necessarily to the disadvantage of the high-performing director, since guidance issued has been underpinned by a distinction between reasonable rewards that are justified by performance, and high rewards that are not justified and are seen as unethical.

3.2 Role and function of remuneration committee

The remuneration committee plays the key role in establishing remuneration arrangements. In order to be effective, the committee needs both to **determine** the organisation's **general policy** on the **remuneration of executive directors** and **specific remuneration packages** for each director.

The UK Combined Code suggests measures to ensure that the committee is **independent**, including requiring the committee to be staffed by **independent non-executive directors,** thus ensuring that executive directors do not set their own remuneration levels. Measures to ensure independence include stating that the committee should have **no personal interests** other than as shareholders, no conflicts of interest and no day-to-day involvement in running the business.

3.3 Remuneration policy

Issues connected with remuneration policy may include the following:

- The **pay scales** applied to each director's package
- The **proportion** of the **different types of reward** within each package
- The **period** within which performance related elements become payable
- What proportion of rewards should be related to **measurable performance** or enhanced shareholder value, and the balance between **short and long-term performance elements**
- **Transparency of directors' remuneration**, including pension rights, in the annual accounts

When establishing remuneration policy, boards have to take account the position of their **company relative to other companies**. However the UK Combined Code points out the need for directors to treat such comparisons with caution, in view of the risk of an upward ratchet in remuneration levels with no corresponding improvement in performance.

3.3.1 Performance measures

A key issue in determining remuneration policy is what performance measures to use to determine the remuneration of directors. There are a number of potential problems with this decision:

- Simply, the **choice of the wrong measure**, achieving performance that does not benefit the company significantly

- Excessive focus on short-term results, particularly **annual financial performance** (which can also be manipulated)

- Remuneration operating with a **time delay**, being based on what happened some time ago rather than current performance

Other issues the remuneration committee have to consider include:

- The potentially complex relationships with a variety of **strategic goals and targets** (including cost of capital, return on equity, economic value added, market share, revenue and profit growth, cost containment, cash management, compliance goals, revenue and environment goals)

- The **differentials at management/director level** (difficult with many layers of management)

- The **ability of managers to leave**, taking clients and knowledge to a competitor or their own new business

- **Individual performance** and additional work/effort

3.4 Remuneration packages

Packages will need to **attract, retain and motivate directors** of sufficient quality, whilst at the same time taking into account shareholders' interests as well. However assessing executive remuneration in an imperfect market for executive skills may prove problematic. The committee needs to be mindful of the **implications** of **all aspects** of the package, also the individual contributions made by each director.

3.4.1 Basic salary

Basic salary will be in accordance with the terms of the directors' **contract of employment**, and is not related to the performance of the company or the director. Instead it is determined by the **experience** of the director and what other companies might be prepared to pay (the **market rate**).

3.4.2 Performance related bonuses

Directors may be paid a cash bonus for good (generally accounting) performance. To guard against excessive payouts, some companies impose limits on bonus plans as a fixed percentage of salary or pay.

Transaction bonuses tend to be much more controversial. Some chief executives get bonuses for acquisitions, regardless of subsequent performance, possibly indeed further bonuses for spinning off acquisitions that have not worked out.

3.4.3 Shares

Directors may be awarded shares in the company with limits (a few years) on when they can be sold in return for good performance.

3.4.4 Share options

Share options give directors the right to purchase shares at a specified exercise price over a specified time period in the future. If the price of the shares rises so that it exceeds the exercise price by the time the options can be exercised, the directors will be able to purchase shares at lower than their market value.

We discussed in Chapter 1 how share options can be used to **align management and shareholder interests**, particularly options held for a long time when value is dependent on long-term performance. The UK Combined Code states that shares granted or other forms of remuneration should not vest or be exercisable in **less than three years.** Directors should be encouraged to hold their shares for a further period after vesting or exercise. Grants should be phased rather than being in one block.

The performance criteria used for share options are a matter of particular debate. Possible criteria include the company's performance relative to a group of **comparable companies**.

There are various tricks that can be used to reduce or eliminate the risk to directors of not getting a reward through stock options. Possibilities include grants that **fail to discount for overall market gains,** or are cushioned against loss of value through **compensatory bonuses** or **repricing.**

The UK Combined Code states that non-executive directors should not normally be offered share options, as options may impact upon their independence.

3.4.5 Benefits in kind

Benefits in kind could include transport (eg a car), health provisions, life assurance, holidays, expenses and loans. The remuneration committee should consider the benefit to the director and the cost to the company of the complete package. Also the committee should consider how the directors' package relates to the package for employees; ideally perhaps the package offered to the directors should be an extension of the package applied to the employees.

Loans may be **particularly problematic.** Recent corporate scandals have included a number of instances of abuses of loans, including a $408 million loan to WorldCom Chief Executive Officer Bernie Ebors. Using corporate assets to make loans when directors can obtain loans from commercial organisations seems very doubtful, and a number of jurisdictions prohibit loans to directors of listed companies.

3.4.6 Pensions

Many companies may pay pension contributions for directors and staff. In some cases however, there may be separate schemes available for directors at higher rates than for employees. The UK Combined Code states that as a general rule only basic salary should be **pensionable.** The Code emphasises that the remuneration committee should consider the pension consequences and associated costs to the company of basic salary increases and any other changes in pensionable remuneration, especially for directors close to retirement.

Exam focus point

> The Pilot paper asked for a description of the different elements of the remuneration package.

3.5 Service contracts and termination payments

Length of service contracts can be a particular problem. If service contracts are too long, and then have to be terminated prematurely, the perception often arises that the amounts paying off directors for the remainder of the contract are essentially rewards for failure. Most corporate governance guidance suggests that service contracts greater than 12 months need to be carefully considered and should ideally be avoided. A few are stricter; Singapore's code suggests that notice periods should be six months or less.

Some companies have cut the notice period for dismissing directors who fail to meet performance targets from one year to six months. Other solutions include continuing to pay a director to the end of his contract, but ceasing payment if the director finds **fresh employment**, or paying the director for **loss of office** in the form of **shares.**

3.6 Remuneration of non-executive directors

To avoid the situation where the remuneration committee are solely responsible for determining their own remuneration, the Combined Code states that the board or the shareholders should determine the remuneration of non-executive directors within the limits prescribed by the company's constitution.

3.7 Remuneration disclosures

In order for readers of the accounts to achieve a fair picture of remuneration arrangements, the annual report would need to disclose:

- Remuneration policy
- Arrangements for individual directors

The UK Directors' Remuneration Report Regulations emphasise the importance of detailed disclosure of **performance conditions** attached to remuneration packages, such as the reasons for choosing those conditions and the methods used to determine whether the conditions have been met. A key comparison required by regulations is a line graph showing the total shareholder return on the company's shares over a five year period and the total shareholder return on a holding of a portfolio of shares over the same period representing a named broad equity market index.

Other disclosures that may be required by law or considered as good practice include the **duration of contracts with directors**, and **notice periods and termination payments** under such contracts. Details of **external remuneration consultants** employed by the remuneration committee to advise on determining remuneration should be provided.

Case Study

A good example of where specific country disclosure requirements have gone further are the provisions in the Singapore Code of Corporate Governance which also prescribes disclosure of:

- The remuneration packages of the top five **key executives** who are not directors
- Details of the remuneration of employees who are **immediate family members** of the directors

3.8 Voting on remuneration

Along with disclosure, the directors also need to consider whether members need to signify their approval of remuneration policy by voting on the **remuneration statement** and elements of the remuneration packages, for example long-term incentive schemes. Any vote could be binding on the company or advisory. The legal impediment to voting on the overall remuneration of individual directors is the employment **contract** between the company and its directors; the shareholders cannot force the company to commit a breach of contract.

4 Relationships with shareholders and stakeholders

The board should maintain a **regular dialogue with shareholders**, particularly **institutional shareholders**. **The annual general meeting** is the most significant forum for communication.

How much organisations consider the interests of other stakeholders will depend on their **legal responsibilities** and the extent to which they view **stakeholders as partners**.

4.1 Rights of shareholders

The OECD guidelines stress the importance of the **basic rights of shareholders**. These include the right to secure methods of ownership registration, convey or transfer shares, obtain relevant and material information, participate and vote in general meetings and share in the profits of the company. Under the OECD guidelines shareholders should also have the right to participate in, and be sufficiently informed on, decisions concerning fundamental changes such as amendments to the company's constitution.

The guidelines also stress the importance of treating all shareholders of the same class equally, particularly protecting minority shareholders against poor treatment by controlling shareholders.

4.2 Relationships with shareholders

A key aspect of the relationship is the accountability of directors to shareholders. This can ultimately be ensured by requiring all directors to submit themselves for **regular re-election** (the corporate governance reports suggest once every three years is reasonable).

The need for regular communication with shareholders is emphasised in most reports. Particularly important is communication with **institutional shareholders** such as pension funds who may hold a significant proportion of shares. The UK Combined Code states that non-executive directors, in particular the senior independent director, should maintain regular contact with shareholders. The board as a whole should use a variety of means for ascertaining major shareholders' opinions, for example face-to-face contact, analysts or brokers' briefings and surveys of shareholders' opinions.

4.3 General meetings

The annual general meeting is the most important formal means of communication, and the governance guidance suggests that boards should **actively encourage** shareholders to attend annual general meetings. The UK Hampel report contains some useful recommendations on how the annual general meeting could be used to **enhance communications** with shareholders, by giving shareholders an opportunity to ask questions and use their votes.

(a) Notice of the AGM and related papers should be **sent** to shareholders **at least 20 working days** before the meeting.

(b) · Companies should consider providing a **business presentation** at the **AGM**, with a question and answer session.

(c) The chair of the key sub-committees (audit, remuneration) should be available to answer questions.

(d) Shareholders should be able to **vote separately** on each substantially separate issue; the practice of 'bundling' unrelated proposals in a single resolution should cease.

(e) Companies should propose a resolution at the AGM relating to the **report and accounts**.

(f)   The Combined Code **emphasises the importance of institutional shareholders** attending annual general meetings and **using their votes,** to translate their intentions into practice. Institutional shareholders should provide their clients with details of how they've voted.

(g)   Codes with international jurisdiction, such as the OECD principles, emphasise the importance of **eliminating impediments to cross-border voting**.

The most important document for communication with shareholders is the annual report and accounts, covered in Section 5 below.

4.4 Proxy votes

Key term

> A **proxy** is a person appointed by a shareholder to vote on behalf of that shareholder at company meetings.

Under most regimes a member of a company, who is entitled to attend and vote at a meeting of the company, has a statutory right to appoint an agent, called a 'proxy', to attend and vote for him. There may be rules governing how many proxies a member can appoint, whether the proxy has to be a member, whether the proxy has a right to speak and when the proxy can vote.

4.4.1 The Myners report

The Myners report in the UK *Review of the Impediments to Voting UK shares* (2004) aimed to address concerns about problems in administering proxy votes and the beneficial owners not taking sufficient interest in the votes. The report makes a number of recommendations.

(a)   **Beneficial owners**

Beneficial share owners should ensure that their agreements with investment managers and custodians who are accountable to them should include **voting standards**, **establish a chain of responsibility** and an **information flow** on voting and **require reports** by investment managers on how they have **discharged their responsibilities**. Investment managers should decide a voting policy and stick to it.

(b)   **Electronic voting**

The report recommends the adoption of **electronic voting** to enhance the efficiency of the voting process and to reduce the loss of proxy votes.

(c)   **Stock lending**

The report comes down against **stock lending** on the grounds that voting rights are effectively transferred, and lending sometimes takes place specifically to transfer voting rights. Myners recommends that stock should be recalled if there are votes on contentious issues.

(d)   **Investment managers**

Investment managers should **report to their clients** how they have exercised their voting responsibilities.

(e)   **Procedures at meetings**

Myners addresses the situation where votes at company meetings are decided on a show of hands, with one vote per member present, unless a poll is called. Only if a poll is called can proxies be included under UK law. Myners suggests that a **poll** should be called on **all resolutions**. The report also recommends that proxy forms should include a **vote withheld box**, to identify the extent to which shareholders are consciously abstaining. The report also recommends giving the right to speak and the right to vote on a show of hands to anyone who has been appointed to act as a proxy by a member (an alternative to filling in a proxy form).

4.5 Relationships with stakeholders

How much the board is responsible for the interests of stakeholders other than shareholders is a matter of debate. The Hampel committee claimed that although relationships with other stakeholders were important, making the directors responsible to other stakeholders would mean there was no clear yardstick for judging directors' performance.

However the OECD guidelines see a rather wider importance for stakeholders in corporate governance, concentrating on employees, creditors and the government. Companies should behave ethically and have regard for the environment and society as a whole.

The OECD guidelines stress that the corporate governance framework should therefore ensure that respect is given to the **rights of stakeholders** that are protected by law. These rights include rights under labour law, business law, contract law and insolvency law.

The OECD guidelines also state that corporate governance frameworks should permit **'performance-enhancing mechanisms** for stakeholder participation'. Examples of this are employee representation on the board of directors, employee share ownership, profit-sharing arrangements and the right of creditors to be involved in any insolvency proceedings.

The UK Hermes Principles emphasise that companies should support **voluntary and statutory** measures that **minimise the externalisation of costs** to the detriment of society at large.

5 Reporting on corporate governance

Annual reports must **convey** a **fair and balanced view** of the organisation. They should state whether the organisation has complied with governance regulations and codes. It is considered best practice to give specific disclosures about the board, internal control reviews, going concern status and relations with stakeholders.

5.1 Importance of reporting

The Singapore code of corporate governance summed up the importance of reporting and communication rules:

'Companies should engage in regular, effective and fair communication with shareholders... In disclosing information, companies should be as descriptive, detailed and forthcoming as possible, and avoid boilerplate disclosures.'

Good disclosure helps reduce the gap between the information available to directors and the information available to shareholders, and thus addresses one of the key difficulties of the agency relationship between directors and shareholders.

5.2 Principles vs compulsory

The emphasis in principles-based corporate governance regimes is on **complying or explaining**; companies either act in accordance with the principles and guidelines laid down in the code or explain why and specifically how or in what regard they have not done so.

The London Stock Exchange requires the following general disclosures:

(a)   A **narrative statement** of how companies have **applied the principles** set out in the Combined Code, providing explanations which enable their shareholders to assess how the principles have been applied.

(b)   A **statement** as to whether or not they **complied** throughout the accounting period with the **provisions** set out in the Combined Code. Listed companies that did not comply throughout the accounting period with all the provisions must specify the provisions with which they did not comply, and give reasons for non-compliance.

Beyond these basic requirements disclosure guidelines in principles-based regimes tend to be based on the ideas of **providing balanced and detailed information** that enables shareholders to assess the company's potential. They acknowledge that **judgement** is important in deciding what to disclose.

 Case Study

An example quoted in UK guidance is the resignation of directors from a subsidiary company. If one director resigns, it would probably not be mentioned; however if a number of directors resign within a short space of time, it might well merit disclosure. The key test in deciding whether to include an item is the **potential future significance** of the issue.

5.3 Reporting requirements

The corporate governance reports suggest that the directors should **explain** their **responsibility for preparing accounts**. They should **report that the business is a going concern**, with supporting assumptions and qualifications as necessary.

In addition further statements may be required depending on the jurisdiction such as:

(a) Information about the **board of directors**: the composition of the board in the year, information about the independence of the non-executives, frequency of, and attendance at, board meetings, how the board's performance has been evaluated. The South African King report suggests a charter of responsibilities should be disclosed

(b) Brief reports on the **remuneration, audit and nomination committees** covering terms of reference, composition and frequency of meetings

(c) Information about **relations with auditors** including reasons for change and steps taken to ensure auditor objectivity and independence when non-audit services have been provided

(d) A statement that the directors have reviewed the **effectiveness** of **internal controls**, including risk management

(e) A statement on relations and **dialogue with shareholders**

(f) A statement that the company is a **going concern**

(g) **Sustainability reporting,** defined by the King report as including the nature and extent of social, transformation, ethical, safety, health and environmental management policies and practices

(h) An **operating and financial review (OFR)**. The UK's Accounting Standards Board summarised the purpose of such a review:

'The Operating and Financial Review (OFR) should set out the directors' analysis of the business, in order to provide to investors a historical and prospective analysis of the reporting entity 'through the eyes of management'. It should include discussion and interpretation of the performance of the business and the structure of its financing, in the context of known or reasonably expected changes in the environment in which it operates.'

Furthermore the information organisations provide cannot just be backward-looking. The King report points out investors want a forward-looking approach and to be able to assess companies against a **balanced scorecard.** Companies will need to weigh the need to keep commercially sensitive information private with the expectations that investors will receive full and frank disclosures. They should also consider the need of other stakeholders.

However in the UK the government executed an about–turn on its proposals to make the OFR compulsory under statute. The result is that the contents of the OFR is now subject to a statement of **best practice** rather than a reporting standard.

5.4 Voluntary disclosure

Voluntary disclosure can be defined as any disclosure above the **mandated minimum**. Examples include a Chief Executive Officer's report, a social/environmental report, additional risk or segmental data. The UK's Department of Trade and Industry set out the process that companies should consider following when deciding what to include in the OFR, and these principles are useful for voluntary disclosure in general:

(a) The process should be **planned** and **transparent,** and communicated to everyone responsible for preparing the information.

(b) The process should involve **consultation** within the business, and with shareholders and other key groups.

(c) The process should ensure that **all relevant information** should be taken into account.

(d) The process should be **comprehensive**, **consistent** and **subject to review**.

Question   Codes and corporate governance

Briefly explain what is meant by corporate governance and discuss how the main measures recommended by the corporate governance codes should contribute towards better corporate governance.

Answer

Definition of corporate governance

Corporate governance can be defined broadly as the **system** by which an **organisation** is **directed and controlled.** It is concerned with systems, processes, controls, accountability and decision making at the heart of and at the highest level of an organisation. It is therefore concerned with the way in which top managers **execute their responsibilities** and authority and how they **account** for that authority to those who have entrusted them with assets and resources. In particular it is concerned with the potential abuse of power and the need for openness, integrity and accountability in corporate decision making.

Recommendations of corporate governance codes

Clearly, a company must have senior executives. The problem is how to ensure as far as possible that the actions and decisions of the executives will be for the benefit of shareholders. Measures that have been recommended by various corporate governance codes include the following.

Directors

(a) A listed company is required by the Combined Code to appoint **non-executive directors**, most of whom should be **independent.** The non-executives are intended to provide a check or balance against the power of the chairman and chief executive.

(b) The posts of **chairman and CEO** should not be held by the same person, to prevent excessive executive power being held by one individual.

(c) Non-executive directors should **make up** the **membership** of the remuneration committee of the board, and should determine the remuneration of executive directors. This is partly to prevent the executives deciding their own pay, and rewarding themselves excessively. Another purpose is to try to devise incentive schemes for executives that will motivate them to **achieve results** for the company that will also be in the best interests of the shareholders.

Risk assessment

The requirement in many codes for a risk audit should ensure that the board of directors is **aware** of the **risks** facing the company, and have **systems** in place for managing them. In theory, this should provide some protection against risk for the company's shareholders.

Dialogue with shareholders

The Combined Code encourages **greater dialogue** between a **company** and its **shareholders**. Institutional investor organisations are also encouraging greater participation by shareholders, for example in voting.

Audits

The **audit committee** of the board is seen as having a **major role** to play, in promoting dialogue between the external auditors and the board. Corporate governance should be improved if the views of the **external auditors** are given greater consideration.

Chapter Roundup

- The board should be responsible for taking major **policy** and **strategic** decisions.

- Directors should have a **mix of skills** and their **performance** should be assessed regularly.

- Appointments should be conducted by formal procedures administered by a **nomination committee**.

- **Division of responsibilities** at the head of an organisation is most simply achieved by separating the roles of chairman and chief executive.

- **Independent non-executive directors** have a key role in governance. Their number and status should mean that their views carry significant weight.

- Directors' remuneration should be set by a **remuneration committee** consisting of independent non-executive directors.

- Remuneration should be dependent upon **organisation** and **individual performance**.

- Accounts should disclose **remuneration policy** and (in detail) the **packages of individual directors**.

- The board should maintain a **regular dialogue with shareholders**, particularly **institutional shareholders**. **The annual general meeting** is the most significant forum for communication.

- How much organisations consider the interests of other stakeholders will depend on their **legal responsibilities** and the extent to which they view **stakeholders as partners**.

- Annual reports must **convey** a **fair and balanced view** of the organisation. They should state whether the organisation has complied with governance regulations and codes. It is considered best practice to give specific disclosures about the board, internal control reviews, going concern status and relations with stakeholders.

Quick Quiz

1   What according to the City Equitable Fire and Insurance Company case were the three main duties of directors?

2   What are the main features of the induction programme recommended by the Higgs report?

3   How did the Cadbury report suggest that the board's responsibilities should be defined?

4   How can an organisation ensure that there is a division of responsibilities at its highest level?

5   What according to the Greenbury report were the key principles in establishing a remuneration policy?

6   The UK Combined Code recommends that a remuneration committee should be staffed by executive directors.

   True   ☐

   False   ☐

7   Which of the following is not a recommendation of the UK Hampel report in relation to annual general meetings?

   A   Notice of the AGM should be sent to shareholders at least 20 working days before the meeting.

   B   To simplify voting, the key proposals made at the AGM should be combined in one resolution.

   C   Companies should propose a resolution at the AGM relating to their report and accounts.

   D   Institutional shareholders should provide their clients with details of how they've voted at Annual General Meetings.

8   Fill in the blank

   An .... sets out the directors' analysis of the business, in order to provide to investors a historical and prospective analysis of the reporting entity 'through the eyes of management'.

Answers to Quick Quiz

1. • A director is expected to show the degree of skill that may reasonably be expected from a person of his knowledge and experience

   • A director is required to attend board meetings when he is able but has no duty to concern himself with the affairs of the company at other times

   • In the absence of grounds for suspicion, and subject to normal business practice, a director is entitled to leave the routine conduct of the business in the hands of its management

2. Building an understanding of the nature of the company, its business and markets; building a link with the company's people; building an understanding of the company's main relationships

3. Boards should have a formal schedule of matters reserved for their decisions including decisions such as approval of mergers and acquisitions, major acquisitions and disposals of assets and investments, capital projects, bank borrowing facilities, major loans and their repayment, foreign currency transactions above a certain limit.

4. • Splitting the roles of chairman and chief executive
   • Appointing a senior independent non-executive director
   • Having a strong independent element on the board with a recognised leader

5. • Directors' remuneration should be set by independent members of the board

   • Any form of bonus should be related to measurable performance or enhanced shareholder value

   • There should be full transparency of directors' remuneration including pension rights in the annual accounts

6. False. The remuneration committee should be staffed by independent non-executive directors.

7. B   The Hampel report recommends that shareholders should be able to vote separately on each substantially separate issue.

8. An operating and financial review sets out the directors' analysis of the business, in order to provide to investors a historical and prospective analysis of the reporting entity 'through the eyes of management'.

Now try the question below from the Exam Question Bank

Number	Level	Marks	Time
Q3	Introductory	n/a	45 mins

Part B
Internal control and review

BPP
LEARNING MEDIA

Internal control systems

4

Topic list	Syllabus reference
1 Purposes of internal control systems	B1
2 Internal control frameworks	B1
3 Control environment	B1
4 Control procedures	B1
5 Internal controls and risk management	B1
6 Costs and benefits of internal controls	B1

Introduction

In this chapter we cover the main elements of internal control. You will have encountered internal controls in your auditing studies; in this chapter we take an overview of the main elements rather than looking at controls in detail.

This is a very important chapter; the examiner has stressed how important a sound system of internal control is and how internal controls need to be judged in the context of overall strategic considerations. Hence at the end of this chapter we briefly consider internal controls in the context of risk management. We also look at wider cost-benefit considerations; is it worth implementing internal controls for the benefits they will bring. Again we shall consider these themes when in Chapter 8 we examine different methods of risk management.

Study guide

		Intellectual level
B1	**Management control systems in corporate governance**	
(a)	Define and explain internal management control	2
(b)	Explain and explore the importance of internal control and risk management in corporate governance	3
(c)	Describe the objectives of internal control systems	2
(e)	Identify and assess the importance of elements or components of internal control systems	3
B2	**Internal control, audit and compliance in corporate governance**	
(e)	Explore and evaluate the effectiveness of internal control systems	3

Exam guide

You may be asked to provide an appropriate control framework for an organisation or assess a framework that is described in a scenario. Look out in particular for whether the underlying control environment appears to be sound.

1 Purposes of internal control systems

Internal controls should help organisations counter risks, maintain the quality of financial reporting and comply with laws and regulations. They provide **reasonable assurance** that organisations will fulfil their strategic objectives.

Key term

An **internal control** is any action taken by management to enhance the likelihood that established objectives and goals will be achieved. Management plans, organises and directs the performance of sufficient actions to provide reasonable assurance that objectives and goals will be achieved. Thus, control is the result of proper planning, organising and directing by management.   (*Institute of Internal Auditors*)

1.1 Elements of control systems

Basic concepts in talking about control include the following.

Plan, target, standard, objective	What the system is designed to achieve, eg budgeted revenues
	Objectives for the process being controlled must exist, for without an aim or purpose control has no meaning. Objectives and targets are set in response to environmental pressures such as customer demand
Sensor	Detects the actual control system behaviour, and gathers information about it – eg sales force and output from sales order processing system
Inputs, processes and outputs	The main stages of operations

Comparator	Compares actual system behaviour with the plan, eg management accounts with variances.
Effector	Enacts control action to change the actual system behaviour eg instructions from a manager.
	It must be possible to **take action** so that failures to meet objectives can be reduced. Action could involve changing objectives, inputs, process or the whole system.

This concept of control involves more than just measuring results and taking corrective action. Control in the broad sense also embraces the **formulation of objectives** – deciding what are the 'right things' that need to be done – as well as monitoring their attainment by way of feedback.

1.1.1 The cybernetic control system

A **cybernetic control system describes the process of control within a system**. A general cybernetic control model has **six key stages**.

- Identification of system objectives
- Setting targets for system objectives
- Measuring achievements/outputs of the system
- Comparing achievements with targets
- Identifying what corrective action might be necessary
- Implementing corrective action

1.1.2 Important characteristics of control systems

Fisher has suggested that management control systems can be viewed in terms of the following criteria.

- Flexibility and ease of achievement of targets
- Relative importance of numerical and subjective performance measures
- Relative importance of short and long-term measures
- Consistency of measures used across organisation
- Whether management actively intervenes or intervenes by exception
- How automatic control mechanisms are
- Extent of participation below top management
- Extent of reliance on social relationships

1.2 Effectiveness of control systems

In order for internal controls to function properly, they have to be well-directed. Managers and staff will be more able (and willing) to implement controls successfully if it can be demonstrated to them what the objectives of the control systems are. Objectives also provide a yardstick for the board when they come to monitor and assess how controls have been operating.

1.3 Turnbull guidelines

The UK Turnbull report (revised in 2005) provides a helpful summary of the main purposes of an internal control system.

Turnbull comments that internal control consists of 'the **policies**, **processes**, **tasks, behaviours** and other aspects of a company that taken together:

(a) Facilitate its **effective** and **efficient operation** by enabling it to respond appropriately to significant **business, operational, financial, compliance** and other risks to achieving the company's objectives. This includes the **safeguarding of assets** from inappropriate use or from loss and fraud and ensuring that **liabilities** are **identified** and **managed**.

(b) Help ensure the **quality** of **internal** and **external reporting**. This requires the **maintenance of proper records and processes** that generate a flow of **timely, relevant and reliable information** from within and without the organisation.

(c) Help ensure **compliance with applicable laws and regulations,** and also with internal policies with respect to the conduct of business'

1.3.1 Characteristics of internal control systems

The Turnbull report summarises the key characteristics of the internal control systems. They should:

- Be **embedded** in the operations of the company and **form part of its culture**

- Be capable of **responding quickly** to evolving risks within the business

- Include procedures for **reporting immediately to management** significant control failings and weaknesses together with control action being taken

The Turnbull report goes on to say that a sound system of internal control reduces but does not eliminate the possibilities of losses arising from **poorly-judged decisions**, **human error, deliberate circumvention of controls**, **management override of controls** and **unforeseeable circumstances.** Systems will provide reasonable (not absolute) assurance that the company will not be hindered in achieving its business objectives and in the orderly and legitimate conduct of its business, but won't provide certain protection against all possible problems.

Exam focus point

Particularly important areas include safeguarding of shareholders' investment and company assets, facilitation of operational effectiveness and efficiency, and contribution to the reliability of reporting. These areas need to be borne in mind in any question on internal control systems, although questions will doubtless cover other aims as well.

2 Internal control frameworks

FAST FORWARD

Internal control frameworks include the **control environment** within which **internal controls** operate. Other important elements are the **risk assessment and response processes,** the **sharing of information** and **monitoring** the environment and operation of the control system.

2.1 Need for control framework

Organisations need to consider the overall framework of controls since controls are unlikely to be very effective if they are developed sporadically around the organisation, and their effectiveness will be very difficult to measure by internal audit and ultimately by senior management.

2.2 Control environment and control procedures

Key term

> The **internal control framework** comprises the **control environment** and **control procedures**. It includes all the policies and procedures (internal controls) adopted by the directors and management of an entity to assist in achieving their objective of ensuring, as far as practicable, the orderly and efficient conduct of its business, including adherence to internal policies, the safeguarding of assets, the prevention and detection of fraud and error, the accuracy and completeness of the accounting records, and the timely preparation of reliable financial information. Internal controls may be incorporated within computerised accounting systems. However, the internal control system extends beyond those matters which relate directly to the accounting system.

Perhaps the simplest framework for internal control draws a distinction between

- **Control environment** – the overall context of control, in particular the **culture**, **infrastructure** and **architecture** of control and **attitude** of directors and managers towards control
- **Control procedures** – the detailed controls in place

We shall examine both these elements in detail in the next two sections.

The Turnbull report also highlights the importance of

- Information and communication processes
- Processes for monitoring the continuing effectiveness of the system of internal control

Exam focus point

> There may be some marks available for a general description of key features of a business's control systems.

2.3 The COSO framework

The control framework that the Committee of Sponsoring Organisations (COSO) of the Treadway Commission has developed links objectives with risk management. All elements of this framework affect what COSO call the objectives categories:

- Strategic development
- Operations
- Reporting
- Compliance

A significant advantage of the COSO framework is that it focuses on a wide concept of internal control and is not just limited to financial control. We shall examine this framework further in the context of risk management in Chapter 8.

2.4 The COCO framework

A slightly different framework is the **criteria of control** or COCO framework developed by the Canadian Institute of Chartered Accountants (CICA).

2.4.1 Purpose

The COCO framework stresses the need for all aspects of activities to be **clearly directed with a sense of purpose**. This includes overall objectives, mission and strategy; management of risk and opportunities; policies; plans and performance measures. The corporate purpose should drive control activities and ensure controls achieve objectives.

2.4.2 Commitment

The framework stresses the importance of managers and staff making an **active commitment** to identify themselves with the organisation and its values, including ethical values, authority, responsibility and trust.

2.4.3 Capability

Managers and staff must be equipped with the **resources and competence necessary** to operate the control systems effectively. This includes not just knowledge and resources but also communication processes and co-ordination.

2.4.4 Action

If employees are sure of the purpose, are committed to do their best for the organisation and have the ability to deal with problems and opportunities then the actions they take are more likely to be successful.

2.4.5 Monitoring and learning

An essential part of commitment to the organisation is a commitment to its evolution. This includes:

- Monitoring external environments
- Monitoring performance
- Reappraising information systems
- Challenging assumptions
- Reassessing the effectiveness of internal controls

Above all each activity should be seen as part of a **learning process** that lifts the organisation to a higher dimension.

<table>
<tr>
<td>Exam focus
point</td>
<td>This emphasises the importance of feedback and continuous improvement in control systems and is something worth looking for in exam scenarios – does the organisation appear capable of making essential improvements.</td>
</tr>
</table>

2.5 Limitations of internal controls

However, any internal control system can only provide the directors with **reasonable assurance** that their objectives are reached, because of **inherent limitations**. This is why auditors cannot obtain all their evidence from tests of the systems of internal control. The limitations include:

- The **costs of control** not **outweighing** their **benefits**

- The **potential for human error or fraud**

- **Collusion between employees**

- The **possibility of controls being by-passed** or overridden by management

- Controls being designed to cope with **routine and not non-routine transactions**

- Controls depending on the **method of data processing** – they should be **independent** of the method of data processing

3 Control environment

The **control environment** is influenced by **management's attitude** towards control, the **organisational structure** and the **values** and **abilities** of employees.

3.1 Nature of control environment

Key term

The **control environment** is the overall attitude, awareness and actions of directors and management regarding internal controls and their importance in the entity. The control environment encompasses the management style, and corporate culture and values shared by all employees. It provides the background against which the various other controls are operated.

The following factors are reflected in the control environment.

- The **philosophy** and **operating style** of the directors and management

    The entity's **culture**, whether control is seen as an integral part of the organisational framework, or something that is imposed on the rest of the system

- The entity's **organisational structure** and methods of assigning authority and responsibility (including segregation of duties and supervisory controls)

- The directors' **methods of imposing control**, including the internal audit function, the functions of the board of directors and personnel policies and procedures

- The **integrity, ethical values** and **competence** of directors and staff

The UK Turnbull report highlighted a number of elements of a strong control environment.

- **Clear strategies** for dealing with the significant risks that have been identified

- The company's **culture, code of conduct, human resource policies** and **performance reward systems** supporting the business objectives and risk management and internal control systems

- Senior management demonstrating through its actions and policies commitment to **competence, integrity** and **fostering a climate of trust** within the company

- **Clear definition** of **authority, responsibility** and **accountability** so that decisions are made and actions are taken by the appropriate people

- **Communication** to employees what is expected of them and scope of their freedom to act

- People in the company having the **knowledge, skills** and **tools** to support the achievements of the organisation's objectives and to manage its risks effectively.

However, a strong control environment does not, by itself, ensure the effectiveness of the overall internal control system although it will have a major influence upon it.

The control environment will have a major impact on the establishment of business objectives, the structuring of business activities, and dealing with risks.

Exam focus point

An organisation with a poor control environment featured in one of the pilot paper questions.

4 Control procedures

FAST FORWARD

Controls can be classified in various ways including **corporate**, **management**, **business process** and **transaction**; **administrative** and **accounting**; **prevent**, **detect** and **correct**; **discretionary** and **non-discretionary**; **voluntary** and **mandated**; **manual** and **automated**.

The mnemonic **SPAMSOAP** can be used to remember the main types of control.

Key term

> **Control procedures** are those policies and procedures in addition to the control environment which are established to achieve the entity's specific objectives.   (UK Auditing Practices Board)

4.1 Classification of control procedures

You may find internal controls classified in different ways, and these are considered below.

4.1.1 Corporate, management, business process and transaction controls

This classification is based on the idea of a pyramid of controls from corporate controls at the top of the organisation, to transaction controls over the day-to-day operations.

- **Corporate controls** include general policy statements, the established core culture and values and overall monitoring procedures such as the internal audit committee

- **Management controls** encompass planning and performance monitoring, the system of accountabilities to superiors and risk evaluation

- **Business process controls** include authorisation limits, validation of input, and reconciliation of different sources of information

- **Transaction controls** include complying with prescribed procedures and accuracy and completeness checks

4.1.2 Administrative controls and accounting controls

Administrative controls are concerned with achieving the objectives of the organisation and with implementing policies. The controls relate to the following aspects of control systems.

- Establishing a suitable organisation structure
- The division of managerial authority
- Reporting responsibilities
- Channels of communication

Accounting controls aim to provide accurate accounting records and to achieve accountability. They apply to the following.

- The recording of transactions
- Establishing responsibilities for records, transactions and assets

4.1.3 Prevent, detect and correct controls

Prevent controls are controls that are designed to prevent errors from happening in the first place. Examples of **prevent controls** are as follows.

- Checking invoices from suppliers against goods received notes before paying the invoices

- Regular checking of delivery notes against invoices, to ensure that all deliveries have been invoiced

- Signing of goods received notes, credit notes, overtime records and so forth, to confirm that goods have actually been received, credit notes properly issued, overtime actually authorised and worked and so on

Question   Prevent controls

How can prevent controls be used to measure performance and efficiency?

Answer

In the above examples the system outputs could include information, say, about the time lag between delivery of goods and invoicing:

(a)   As a measure of the **efficiency of the invoicing section**

(b)   As an **indicator of the speed and effectiveness** of **communications** between the despatch department and the invoicing department

(c)   As **relevant background information** in assessing the effectiveness of cash management

You should be able to think of plenty of other examples. Credit notes reflect customer dissatisfaction, for example: how quickly are they issued?

Detect controls are controls that are designed to detect errors once they have happened. Examples of **detect controls** in an accounting system are bank reconciliations and regular checks of physical inventory against book records of inventory.

Correct controls are controls that are designed to minimise or negate the effect of errors. An example of a **correct control** would be back-up of computer input at the end of each day, or the storing of additional copies of software at a remote location.

4.1.4 Discretionary and non-discretionary controls

Discretionary controls are controls that, as their name suggests, are subject to human discretion. For example a control that goods are not dispatched to a customer with an overdue account may be discretionary (the customer may have a good previous payment record or be too important to risk antagonising).

Non-discretionary controls are provided automatically by the system and cannot be bypassed, ignored or overridden. For example, checking the signature on a purchase order is discretionary, whereas inputting a PIN number when using a cash dispensing machine is a non-discretionary control.

4.1.5 Voluntary and mandated controls

Voluntary controls are chosen by the organisation to support the management of the business. Authorisation controls, that certain key transactions require approval by a senior manager, are voluntary controls.

Mandated controls are required by law and imposed by external authorities. A financial services organisation may be subject to the control that only people authorised by the financial services regulatory body may give investment advice.

4.1.6 Manual and automated controls

Manual controls demonstrate a one-to-one relationship between the processing functions and controls, and the human functions.

Automated controls are programmed procedures designed to prevent, detect and correct errors all the way through processing.

Manual controls are often used in conjunction with automated controls, for example when an exception report is reviewed.

4.1.7 General and application controls

These controls are used to reduce the risks associated with the computer environment. **General controls** are controls that relate to the environment in which the application system is operated. **Application controls** are controls that prevent, detect and correct errors and irregularities as transactions flow through the business system.

4.1.8 Financial and non-financial controls

Financial controls focus on the key transaction areas, with the emphasis being on the **safeguarding of assets** and the **maintenance of proper accounting records** and **reliable financial information**.

Non-financial controls tend to concentrate on wider performance issues. **Quantitative non-financial controls** include numeric techniques such as **performance indicators**, the **balanced scorecard** and **activity-based management**. **Qualitative non-financial controls** include many topics we have already discussed, such as organisational structures, rules and guidelines, strategic plans and human resource policies.

Exam focus point

> Remember the importance of the control system looking well beyond financial controls and including quantitative performance indicators and a variety of non-financial controls.

4.2 Types of procedure

The UK Auditing Practices Board's SAS 300 *Accounting and internal control systems and risk assessments* lists some specific control procedures.

- **Approval** and **control** of **documents**
- Controls over **computerised applications** and the information technology environment
- **Checking** the **arithmetical accuracy** of the records
- Maintaining and reviewing **control accounts** and trial balances
- **Reconciliations**
- **Comparing** the results of cash, security and stock **counts** with **accounting records**
- **Comparing internal data** with **external sources** of information
- **Limiting** direct physical **access** to assets and records

The old UK Auditing Practices Committee's guideline *Internal controls* gave a useful summary that is often remembered as a mnemonic, SPAMSOAP.

Segregation of duties
Physical
Authorisation and approval
Management
Supervision
Organisation
Arithmetical and accounting
Personnel

At Professional level, you should be thinking in particular about higher level 'management' controls. Using the above mnemonic, we can give examples of higher level internal controls.

(a) **Segregation of duties**. For example, the chairman/Chief Executive roles should be split.

(b) **Physical**. These are measures to secure the custody of assets, eg only authorised personnel are allowed to move funds on to the money market.

(c) **Authorisation and approval**. All transactions should require authorisation or approval by an appropriate responsible person; limits for the authorisations should be specified, eg a remuneration committee is staffed by non-executive directors to decide directors' pay.

(d) **Management** should provide control through analysis and review of accounts, eg variance analysis, provision of internal audit services.

(e) **Supervision** of the recording and operations of day-to-day transactions. This ensures that all individuals are aware that their work will be checked, reducing the risk of falsification or errors, eg budgets, managers' review, exception or variance reports.

(f) **Organisation**: identify reporting lines, levels of authority and responsibility. This ensures everyone is aware of their control (and other) responsibilities, especially in ensuring adherence to management policies, eg avoid staff reporting to more than one manager. Procedures manuals will be helpful here.

(g) **Arithmetical and accounting**: to check the correct and accurate recording and processing of transactions, eg reconciliations, trial balances.

(h) **Personnel**. Attention should be given to selection, training and qualifications of personnel, as well as personal qualities; the quality of any system is dependent upon the competence and integrity of those who carry out control operations, eg use only qualified staff as internal auditors.

Exam focus point

In the exam you will be expected not to regurgitate the SPAMSOAP mnemonic but to apply it to assess the overall adequacy of the control framework.

5 Internal controls and risk management

FAST FORWARD

An organisation's internal controls should be designed to counter the **risks** that are a consequence of the objectives it pursues.

5.1 Turnbull guidance

The UK Turnbull report stresses the links between internal controls and risk very strongly. Turnbull states that in order to determine its policies in relation to internal control and decide what constitutes a sound system of internal control, the board should consider:

- The **nature and extent of risks** facing the company

- The **extent and categories of risk** which it regards as acceptable for the company to bear

- The **likelihood of the risks** concerned materialising

- The company's ability to **reduce the incidence and impact on the business** of risks that do materialise

- The **costs of operating particular controls** relative to the benefit obtained in managing the related risks

COSO points out that an organisation needs to establish **clear and coherent objectives** in order to be able to tackle risks effectively. The risks that are important are those that are **linked with achievement** of the organisation's objectives. In addition there should be control mechanisms that identify and adjust for the risks that arise out of changes in economic, industry, regulatory and operating conditions.

Question   Responses to risk

A new employee in the marketing department has asked you about the business objective of meeting or exceeding sales targets.

Required

(a)   What are the main risks associated with the business objective to meet or exceed sales targets?

(b)   How can management reduce the likelihood of occurrence and impact of the risk?

(c)   What controls should be associated with reducing the likelihood of occurrence and impact of the risk?

Answer

This question is based on an example in the COSO guidance.

(a)   One very important risk would be having insufficient knowledge of customers' needs.

(b)   Managers can compile buying histories of existing customers and undertake market research into new customers.

(c)   Controls might include checking progress of the development of customer histories against the timetable for those histories and taking steps to ensure that the data is accurate.

COSO also suggests that the links between risks and controls may be complex. Some controls, for example calculation of staff turnover, may indicate how successful management has been in responding to several risks, for example competitor recruiting and lack of effectiveness of staff training and development programmes. On the other hand some risks may require a significant number of internal controls to deal with them.

5.2 Changing risks

Turnbull stresses that the internal control system has a key role in the management of key business risks.

Turnbull goes to stress that an organisation's risks are **continually changing**, as its objectives, internal organisation and business environment are continually evolving. New markets and new products bring further risks and also change overall organisation risks. Diversification may reduce risk (the business is not over-dependent on a few products) or may increase it (the business is competing in markets in which it is ill-equipped to succeed). Therefore the organisation needs to constantly re-evaluate the nature and extent of risks to which it is exposed.

6 Costs and benefits of internal controls

Sometimes the benefits of controls will be outweighed by their costs, and organisations should compare them. However it is difficult to put a monetary value on many **benefits** and **costs** of controls, and also the potential losses if controls are not in place.

6.1 Benefits of internal controls

The benefits of internal control, even well-directed ones, are not limitless. Controls can provide reasonable, not absolute, assurance that the organisation is progressing towards its objectives, safeguarding its assets and complying with laws and regulations. Internal controls cannot guarantee success as there are plenty of **environmental factors** (economic indicators, competitor actions) beyond the organisation's control.

In addition we have seen that there are various inherent limitations in control systems including faulty decision-making and breakdowns occurring because of human error. The control system may also be vulnerable to **employee collusion** and **management override** of controls **undermining** the **control systems.**

However the benefits of internal control are not always measurable in financial terms; they may include improvements in **efficiency and effectiveness**. There may also be indirect benefits; improved control systems resulting in external audit being able to place more reliance on the organisation's systems, hence needing to do less work and (hopefully) charging a lower audit fee.

6.2 Costs of internal controls

As well as realising the limitations of the benefits of controls, it is also important to realise their costs. Some costs are obvious, for example the salary of a night security officer to keep watch over the premises. There are also **opportunity costs** through for example increased manager time being spent on review rather than dealing with customers for example.

More general costs include reduced **flexibility**, **responsiveness** and **creativity** within the organisation.

One common complaint is the controls stifle initiative, although this is not always well-founded, particularly if the initiative involves too casual an approach to risk management.

6.3 Benefits vs Costs

The principle that the costs of controls need to be compared with benefits is reasonable. The internal controls may not be felt to be worth the reduction in risk that they achieve.

However the comparison of benefits and costs may be difficult in practice:

- It can be difficult to **estimate the potential monetary loss or gain** that could occur as a result of exposure to risk if no measures are taken to combat the risk.

- It can be difficult to assess by how much the **possible loss or gain** is affected by a control measure, particularly if the benefit of control is to reduce, but not eliminate the risk (something which will be true for many controls).

- As we have seen, many benefits of controls are **non-monetary,** for example improvements in employee attitudes or the reputation of the organisation.

Exam focus point

Remembering costs vs. benefits arguments should help you keep your answer in perspective. A common complaint of examiners of papers where internal controls are tested is that the controls many students suggest are too elaborate and hence not appropriate for the organisations described in the questions.

Chapter Roundup

- **Internal controls** should help organisations counter risks, maintain the quality of financial reporting and comply with laws and regulations. They provide **reasonable assurance** that organisations will fulfil their strategic objectives.

- Internal control frameworks include the **control environment** within which **internal controls** operate. Other important elements are the **risk assessment and response processes,** the **sharing of information** and **monitoring** the environment and operation of the control system.

- The **control environment** is influenced by **management's attitude** towards control, the **organisational structure** and the **values** and **abilities** of employees.

- Controls can be classified in various ways including **corporate**, **management**, **business process** and **transaction; administrative** and **accounting; prevent, detect** and **correct; discretionary** and **non-discretionary; voluntary** and **mandated; manual** and **automated.**

- The mnemonic **SPAMSOAP** can be used to remember the main types of control.

- An organisation's internal controls should be designed to counter the **risks** that are a consequence of the objectives it pursues.

- Sometimes the benefits of controls will be outweighed by their costs, and organisations should compare them. However it is difficult to put a monetary value on many **benefits** and **costs** of controls, and also the potential losses if controls are not in place.

Quick Quiz

1   What according to Turnbull should a good system of internal control achieve?

2   What are the main components of the criteria of control framework?

3   What are the main factors that will be reflected in the organisation's control environment?

4   Match the control and control type

(a)   Checking of delivery notes against invoices
(b)   Back-up of computer input
(c)   Bank reconciliation

(i)   Prevent
(ii)   Detect
(iii) Correct

5   A .... control is required by law and imposed by external authorities.

6   List the eight types of control given in SAS 300.

7   Which of the following is an example of a business process control?

A   Audit committee
B   Reporting process to superiors
C   Authorisation limits
D   Completeness of input check

8   When deciding whether the benefits of controls justify the costs, organisations should focus on the financial benefits and costs.

True   ☐
False ☐

Answers to Quick Quiz

1   • Facilitate effective and efficient operation by enabling it to respond to significant risks
    • Help ensure the quality of internal and external reporting
    • Help ensure compliance with applicable laws and regulations

2   • Purpose
    • Commitment
    • Capability
    • Action
    • Monitoring and learning

3   • The philosophy and operating style of the directors and management

    • The entity's organisational structure and methods of assigning authority and responsibility (including segregation of duties and supervisory controls)

    • The directors' methods of imposing control, including the internal audit function, the functions of the board of directors and personnel policies and procedures

    • The integrity, ethical values and competence of directors and staff

4   (a)   (i)
    (b)   (iii)
    (c)   (ii)

5   Mandated

6   • Approval and control of documents
    • Controls over computerised applications and the information technology environment
    • Checking the arithmetical accuracy of the records
    • Maintaining and reviewing control accounts and trial balances
    • Reconciliations
    • Comparing the results of cash, security and inventory counts with accounting records
    • Comparing internal data with external sources of information
    • Limiting direct physical access to assets and records

7   C   A   Audit committee is a corporate control
        B   Reporting process to superiors is a management control
        C   Authorisation limit is a business process control
        D   Completeness of input check is a transaction control

8   False. Organisations might also consider the improvements in efficiency and effectiveness that internal controls can bring, and these can't necessarily be measured in financial terms. Likewise there may be opportunity losses in terms of management time being spent on operating controls which can't be measured financially.

Now try the question below from the Exam Question Bank

Number	Level	Marks	Time
Q4	Examination	25	45 mins

Internal audit

Topic list	Syllabus reference
1 The role of internal audit	B2
2 Internal and external audit	B2
3 Standards for internal audit	B2
4 Reporting the results of internal audit	B2
5 Assessing the performance of internal audit	B2
6 The internal audit committee	B2

Introduction

In this chapter we concentrate on the internal audit function. In your auditing studies you have studied what internal audit does, and we briefly recap its role here and also revisit the important differences between internal and external audit.

The main focus of this chapter is on internal audit's significance as an internal control. We stress the importance of independence if internal audit is to act effectively and we also review the other standards that internal audit should follow and the criteria by which internal audit will be assessed.

In Chapter 3 we mentioned the internal audit committee briefly as a key board committee, and we look in detail at its work of supervising internal audit and its other functions in the last section.

Study guide

		Intellectual level
B2	**Internal control, audit and compliance in corporate governance**	
(a)	Describe the function and importance of internal audit	1
(b)	Explain, and discuss the importance of, auditor independence in all client audit situations (including internal audit)	3
(c)	Explain, and assess the nature and sources of risks, to auditor independence. Assess the hazard of auditor capture	3
(d)	Explain and evaluate the importance of compliance and the role of the internal audit committee in internal control	3
(f)	Describe and analyse the work of the internal audit committee in overseeing the internal audit function	2
(g)	Explain, and explore the importance and characteristics of, the audit committee's relationship with external auditors	2
D1	**Targeting and monitoring of risk**	
(c)	Describe and assess the role of internal or external risk auditing in monitoring risk	3

Exam guide

Scenarios where internal audit independence is threatened are likely to be set in the exam, and you may also have to judge, based on the detail you're given, how effective a particular internal audit function is. Any or all aspects of an internal audit committee's work may be set in the exam.

1 The role of internal audit

FAST FORWARD ▶▶

> The role of internal audit will **vary** according to the **organisation's objectives** but is likely to include review **of internal control systems**, **risk management**, **legal compliance** and **value for money**.

Key term

> **Internal audit** is an independent appraisal function established within an organisation to examine and evaluate its activities as a service to the organisation. The objective of internal audit is to assist members of the organisation in the effective discharge of their responsibilities. To this end, internal audit furnishes them with analyses, appraisals, recommendations, counsel and information concerning the activities reviewed. (UK Institute of Internal Auditors)
>
> **Internal audit** is an appraisal or monitoring activity established by management and directors for the review of the accounting and internal control systems as a service to the entity. It functions by, amongst other things, examining, evaluating and reporting to management and the directors on the adequacy and effectiveness of components of the accounting and internal control systems.
> (UK Auditing Practices Board)

1.1 The need for internal audit

The Turnbull report in the UK stated that listed companies without an internal audit function should **annually review** the need to have one, and listed companies with an internal audit function should review annually its **scope, authority** and **resources**.

Turnbull states that the need for internal audit will depend on:

- The **scale, diversity** and **complexity** of the company's activities
- The **number of employees**
- **Cost-benefit considerations**
- **Changes** in the organisational structures, reporting processes or underlying information systems
- **Changes** in **key risks**
- **Problems** with **internal control systems**
- An **increased number** of **unexplained** or **unacceptable** events

Although there may be alternative means of carrying out the routine work of internal audit, those carrying out the work may be involved in operations and hence lack **objectivity**.

1.2 Objectives of internal audit

The role of the internal auditor has expanded in recent years as internal auditors seek to monitor all aspects (not just accounting) of organisations, and add value to their employers. The work of the internal auditor is still prescribed by management, but it may cover the following broad areas.

(a) **Review of the accounting and internal control systems**. The establishment of adequate accounting and internal control systems is a responsibility of management and the directors. Internal audit is often assigned specific responsibility for the following tasks.

    (i) Reviewing the design of the systems
    (ii) Monitoring the operation of the systems by risk assessment and detailed testing
    (iii) Recommending cost effective improvements

Review will cover both financial and non-financial controls.

(b) **Examination of financial and operating information**. This may include review of the means used to identify, measure, classify and report such information and specific enquiry into individual items including detailed testing of transactions, balances and procedures.

(c) **Review of the economy, efficiency and effectiveness** of operations.

(d) **Review of compliance** with laws, regulations and other external requirements and with internal policies and directives and other requirements including appropriate authorisation of transactions.

(e) **Review of the safeguarding of assets**. Are valuable, portable items such as computers or cash secured, is authorisation needed for dealing in investments?

(f) **Review of the implementation of corporate objectives**. This includes review of the effectiveness of planning, the relevance of standards and policies, the organisation's corporate governance procedures and the operation of specific procedures such as communication of information.

(g)   **Identification of significant business** and financial **risks, monitoring** the **organisation's overall risk management policy** to ensure it operates effectively, and **monitoring** the **risk management strategies** to ensure they continue to operate effectively.

(h)   **Special investigations** into particular areas, for example suspected fraud.

1.3 Internal audit and risk management

Internal audit will play a significant part in the organisation's risk management processes, being required to assess and advise on how risks are countered. Internal audit's work will be influenced by **business objectives**, the risks that may **prevent** the organisation **achieving its objectives** and the organisation's attitude towards risk (that is its degree of risk acceptance or risk aversion). Internal audit will assess:

- The **adequacy of the risk management and response processes** for identifying, assessing, managing and reporting on risk

- The risk management and control **culture**

- The **internal controls** in operation to **limit risks**

- The **operation and effectiveness** of the **risk management processes**

The areas auditors will concentrate on will depend on the **scope** and **priority** of the audit assignment, the **risks identified**, the probability of those **risks crystallizing** and their **likely impact**. Where the risk management framework is insufficient, auditors will have to rely on their own **risk assessment** and **recommend an appropriate framework** be introduced. Where a adequate framework for risk management and control is embedded in operations, auditors will aim to use **management assessment of risks** and concentrate on **auditing the risk management processes**.

1.4 Independence of internal audit

Auditors should be independent of the activities audited.

Although an internal audit department is part of an organisation, it should be **independent** of the **line management** whose sphere of authority it may audit.

 Case Study

Spencer Pickett in the *Internal Auditing Handbook* suggests that the concept of independence involves a number of key qualities:

Objectivity	Judgements are made in a state of detachment from the situation or decision
Impartiality	Not taking sides, in particular not being influenced by office politics in determining the work carried out and the reports given
Unbiased views	Avoiding the perception that internal audit is out to 'hit' certain individuals or departments
Valid opinion	The audit opinion should be based on all relevant factors, rather than being one that pleases everyone
No spying for management	Again internal audit should serve the whole organisation; also managers who want their staff targeted might be trying to cover up their own inadequacies

No no-go areas	Being kept away from certain areas will fatally undermine the usefulness of internal audit and mean that aggressive (incompetent?) managers are not checked
Sensitive areas audited	Internal audit must have the abilities and skills to audit complex areas effectively
Senior management audited	Internal audit must cover the management process and not just audit the detailed operational areas
No backing-off	Audit objectives must be pursued fully in a professional manner and auditors must not allow aggressive managers to deflect them from doing necessary work and issuing valid opinions

1.5 Threats to independence

1.5.1 Involvement in systems design

If internal audit has been involved in the design of systems, it is very doubtful that they can audit what they have recommended.

1.5.2 Overfamiliarity

As a result of working for the same organisation, and being involved with the same issues, internal auditors may develop close professional or personal relationships with the managers and staff they are auditing. This may well make it very difficult to achieve independence.

As we shall see in Chapter 10, an organisation's culture and informal networks of staff can have a big influence on individuals' attitudes to ethics.

1.5.3 Reporting relationships

The principle that internal audit should be **independent** of the **line management** whose sphere of authority it audits ideally should extend to internal audit being **independent of the finance director**. The department should report to the **board** or to a special **internal audit committee** and not to the finance director.

The reason for this is best seen by thinking about what could happen if the internal audit department reported some kind of irregularity to a finance director without realising that the finance director was actually involved. The director would take the report and decide that it was all very interesting, but not worth pursuing. A very different line might be taken by another, independent director!

Exam focus point

> You may encounter other threats in the exam, possibly linked to the factors described in the case example above.

1.6 Dealing with threats to independence

Independence of internal auditors can be achieved by the following.

- Management should ensure staff recruited to internal audit internally **do not conduct audits** on departments in which they have worked.

- Where internal audit staff have also been involved in **designing** or **implementing new systems**, they should not **conduct post-implementation audits**.

- Internal auditors should have **appropriate scope** in carrying out their responsibilities, and unrestricted access to records, assets and personnel.

- **Rotation of staff** over specific departmental audits should be implemented.

1.6.1 Review and consultancy

Consultancy projects (one-off projects designed to address ad-hoc issues) are playing an **increasing role** in the work of **internal audit**. Taking on these projects enables internal auditors to extend their skills, and the organisation to draw on the knowledge of internal auditors. However there are dangers in becoming too involved in consultancy projects.

(a)   Internal audit staff may be diverted to consultancy projects, and the regular audit reviews may be **inadequately resourced**.

(b)   By taking on consultancy projects, and suggesting **solutions** internal audit could be getting too involved in **operational concerns**. There is a serious potential lack of independence if internal audit has to review solutions that **internal audit** staff have provided.

(c)   Management is relying on internal audit to **solve problems** instead of having operational staff and managers solve or preferably prevent them.

Certain steps therefore need to be taken in order to avoid these problems:

(a)   The **terms of reference** of the internal audit department should draw a clear distinction between **regular audit services** and **consultancy work**.

(b)   **Enough resources** for **regular work** should be **guaranteed**; consultancy work should be separately resourced and additional resources obtained if necessary.

(c)   If managers are concerned about **improving controls**, reviewing these improvements can legitimately be included in the work of internal audit.

(d)   **Regular audit reviews** and **consultancy projects** can be undertaken by different staff.

(e)   If consultancy work **identifies serious control weaknesses**, these must be incorporated into **internal audit reviews** as **high risk areas**.

1.7 Recruiting internal auditors

The decision about where to recruit internal auditors from will partly depend on the skills available internally and externally. Clearly an internal recruit has **familiarity** with the organisation that an external recruit would lack. However there are a number of arguments in favour of recruiting externally.

1.7.1 Other experience

An external recruit can bring in **fresh perspectives** gained from working elsewhere. He can use his experience of other organisations' problems to **identify likely risk areas** and **recommend practical solutions and best practice from elsewhere**.

1.7.2 Independence of operational departments

An internal recruit is likely to have built up **relationships and loyalties** with people whom he has already worked, perhaps owing people favours. Equally he could have **grievances or have come into conflict with** other staff. These could **compromise his independence** when he comes to audit their departments.

1.7.3 Prejudices and biases

An internal recruit is likely to have **absorbed the perspectives and biases** of the organisation, and thus be more inclined to treat certain individuals or departments strictly, whilst giving others the benefit of the doubt when maybe that is not warranted.

2 Internal and external audit

FAST FORWARD

> **Internal auditors** are **employees** of the organisation whose work is designed to **add value** and who report to the **audit committee. External auditors** are from **accountancy firms** and their role is to **report on the financial statements to shareholders**.
>
> Both **internal and external auditors** review controls, and **external auditors** may **place reliance** on **internal auditors' work** providing they assess its worth.

Key term

> **External audit** is a periodic examination of the books of account and records of an entity carried out by an independent third party (the auditor), to ensure that they have been properly maintained, are accurate and comply with established concepts, principles, accounting standards, legal requirements and give a true and fair view of the financial state of the entity.

2.1 Differences between internal and external audit

The following table highlights the differences between internal and external audit.

	Internal audit	External audit
Purpose	Internal audit is an activity designed to **add value** and improve an **organisation's operations**. Its work can cover any aspect of an organisation's business or operations, and is not just concerned with issues affecting the **truth and fairness of the financial statements**.	External audit is an exercise to enable auditors to **express an opinion on the financial statements**.
Reporting to	Internal audit reports to the **board of directors**, or others charged with governance, such as the audit committee.	The external auditors report to the **shareholders**, or members, of a company on the stewardship of the directors.
Relating to	Internal audit's work relates to the **operations of the organisation**.	External audit's work relates to the **financial statements**. They are concerned with the financial records that underlie these.
Relationship with the company	Internal auditors are very often **employees of the organisation**, although sometimes the internal audit function is outsourced.	External auditors are **independent of the company and its management**. They are appointed by the shareholders.

The table shows that although some of the procedures that internal audit undertake are very similar to those undertaken by the external auditors, the whole **basis** and **reasoning** of their work is fundamentally **different**.

The **difference** in **objectives** is particularly important. Every definition of internal audit suggests that it has a **much wider scope** than external audit, which has the objective of considering whether the accounts give a true and fair view of the organisation's financial position.

The growing recognition by management of the benefits of good internal control, and the complexities of an adequate system of internal control have led to the development of internal auditing as a form of control over all other internal controls. The emergence of internal auditors as specialists in internal control is the result of an evolutionary process similar in many ways to the evolution of external auditing.

Required

Explain why the internal and external auditors' review of internal control procedures differ in purpose.

Answer

The internal auditors **review and test the system of internal control** and report to management in order to **improve the information** received by managers and to help in their task of running the company. The internal auditors will recommend changes to the system to make sure that management receive objective information that is efficiently produced. The internal auditors will also have a duty to search for and discover fraud.

In most jurisdictions excluding America, the external auditors **review the system of internal control** in order to **determine the extent of the substantive work** required on the year-end accounts. The external **auditors report** to the **shareholders** rather than the managers or directors. It is usual, however, for the external auditors to issue a letter of weakness to the managers, laying out any areas of weakness and recommendations for improvement in the system of internal control. The external auditors report on the **truth and fairness** of the financial statements, not directly on the system of internal control. The external auditors do not have a specific duty to detect fraud, although they should plan the audit procedures so as to have reasonable assurance that they will detect any material misstatement in the accounts on which they give an opinion.

3 Standards for internal audit

Internal audit standards cover **professional proficiency, scope of work, performance, management**, and most importantly **independence**.

3.1 IIA Standards

Whatever the scope of internal audit all staff should be aware of the standards to which they are working.

The Institute of Internal Auditors has produced a series of standards covering all areas of internal auditing. The standards comprise five general standards supported by more specific standards with accompanying guidance.

3.2 Professional proficiency

Internal audits should be performed with **proficiency** and **due professional care**. There are specific standards on the following areas.

- Appropriate staffing
- Knowledge, skills and disciplines
- Supervision
- Compliance with professional standards
- Human relations and communications
- Continuing education
- Due professional care

3.3 Scope of work

The scope of internal audit's work should include **assessment** of the **adequacy** and **effectiveness** of the internal control system and quality of performance. The assessment should include consideration of whether the organisation has met the following objectives.

- Reliability and integrity of information
- Compliance with policies, plans, procedures, laws and regulations
- Safeguarding of assets
- Economical and efficient use of resources
- Accomplishment of established objectives and goals for operations and programmes

3.4 Performance of audit work

Performance should include the following stages.

- Planning the audit
- Examining and evaluating information
- Communicating results
- Follow up of work

3.5 Management of internal audit

The chief internal auditor should manage the internal audit department properly. If the department is running well, it should have the following features.

- A statement of purpose, authority and responsibility
- Thorough planning
- Written policies and procedures
- A programme for personnel management and development
- Co-ordination with external auditors
- A quality assurance system

3.6 Independence of internal audit

We discussed independence in Section 1.

The IIA attribute standards are reproduced below. Internal auditors should:

- Be **independent**, and internal auditors should be **objective** in performing their work

- Report to an **appropriate level** so that they can fulfil their responsibilities

- Be **free from interference** in determining the scope of their work, performing the audit and communicating results

- Have an **impartial**, **unbiased attitude** and avoid conflicts of interest

- **Refrain from assessing specific operations** for which they are responsible

3.7 Authority of internal audit

To perform work effectively the internal auditors need **authority**; this may be of four types (Peabody).

- **Legitimacy**: the authority to demand sight of documents, and the resources to execute this authority

- **Position**: senior auditors should be used to dealing with sensitive issues

- **Competence**: for example computer auditing skills

- **Charismatic**: good communication and inter-personal skills

4 Reporting the results of internal audit

FAST FORWARD

Reports on the results of internal audits should highlight the **risks** identified, the **weaknesses** found in controls, the **consequences** of the problems found and **recommendations** for improvements.

4.1 Objectives of reporting

4.1.1 Recommendations for change

The most important element of internal audit reporting is to **promote change** in the form of either **new or improved controls**. Descriptions of failings should promote change by emphasising the problems that need to be overcome and advising management on the steps needed to improve risk management strategies.

4.1.2 Assisting management identification of risk and control issues

We shall consider the review managers carry out of risk and control issues in Chapter 9. The auditors' report can emphasise the **importance of control issues** at times when other issues are being driven forward, for example new initiatives. Auditors can also help managers **assess the effect of unmitigated risk**. If auditors find that the internal control system is sound, then resources can be directed towards developing other areas.

4.1.3 Ensuring action takes place

Auditors should aim to have their **recommendations agreed by operational managers** and staff, as this should enhance the chances of their being actioned.

4.2 Forms of report

There are **no formal requirements** for such reports as there are for the statutory audit. The statutory audit report is a highly stylised document that is substantially the same for any audit.

4.2.1 Contents of the report

The **executive summary** of an internal audit report should give the following information.

- **Objectives** of the assignment
- **Major outcomes** of the work
- Key **action points**
- **Summary of the work** left to do

The **main body** of the report will contain the detail; for example the audit tests carried out and their findings, full lists of action points, including details of who has responsibility for carrying them out, the future time-scale and costs.

4.2.2 Format of observations and recommendations

One clear way of presenting observations and findings in individual areas is as follows:

- **Business objective** that the manager is aiming to achieve
- **Operational standard**
- The **risks** of current practice
- **Control weaknesses** or lack of application of controls
- The **causes** of the weaknesses
- The **effect** of the weaknesses
- **Recommendations** to solve the weaknesses

The results of individual areas can be summarised in the main report:

- The **existing culture of control**, drawing attention to whether there is a lack of appreciation of the need for controls or good controls but a lack of ability to ensure compliance
- Overall opinion on **managers' willingness** to address risks and improve
- Implications of **outstanding risks**
- Results of **control evaluations**
- The **causes of basic problems**, including links between the problems in various areas

When drafting recommendations internal audit needs to consider:

- The **available options**, although the auditors' preferred solution needs to be emphasised

- The **removal of obstacles to control**. It may be most important to remove general obstacles such as poor communication or lack of management willingness to enforce controls before making specific recommendations to improve controls

- **Resource issues**, how much will recommendations actually cost and also the costs of poor control

Recommendations should be linked in with the **terms of reference**, the **audit performed** and the **results**.

5 Assessing the performance of internal audit

FAST FORWARD

Formal **assessment procedures** should be used to assess the work of **internal audit**.

5.1 Assessment criteria

The performance of internal audit can be judged by various criteria. The standards set by the Institute of Internal Auditors discussed in Section 3, can be used.

The chief internal auditor will also need to be mindful of how external audit may use the work of internal audit.

5.2 Quality control and internal auditing

Whatever the criteria used to judge effectiveness, quality control procedures will be required to monitor the professional standards of internal audit. Internal audit departments should establish and monitor quality control policies and procedures designed to ensure that **all audits** are **conducted** in **accordance** with **internal standards**. They should communicate those policies and procedures to their personnel in a manner designed to provide reasonable assurance that the policies and procedures are understood and implemented.

Quality control policies will vary depending on factors such as the following.

- The size and nature of the department
- Geographic dispersion
- Organisation
- Cost-benefit considerations

Policies and procedures and related documentation will therefore vary from company to company.

The Institute of Internal Auditors has suggested that a formal system of quality assurance should be implemented in the internal audit department. This should cover the department's compliance with appropriate standards, encompassing quality, independence, scope of work, performance of audit work and management of the internal audit department.

5.3 Annual review of internal audit

The board or internal audit committee (discussed in Section 6) should conduct an annual review of the internal auditors' work. The reviews should include the following areas:

5.3.1 Scope of work

The review will be particularly concerned with the work done to test:

- The **adequacy, effectiveness** and **value for money** of internal control
- **Risk assessment** and **management processes**
- **Compliance with laws, regulations** and **policies**
- **Safeguarding** of assets
- **Reliability** of information
- **Value for money**
- **Attainment** of organisation's **objectives** and **goals**

It should be possible to see from the plans that internal audit submits to the audit committee that internal audit's work forwards the organisation's aims and that internal audit is **responsive** to organisational change.

5.3.2 Authority

The review should cover the formal **terms of reference** and assess whether they are adequate.

It should consider whether there are senior personnel in the organisation who can ensure that the scope of internal audit's work is **sufficiently broad**, that there is **adequate consideration** of **audit reports** and **appropriate action** on audit findings and recommendations.

5.3.3 Independence

The review should consider carefully whether there are **adequate safeguards** in place to ensure the independence of internal audit. These include reporting by the head of internal audit to the audit committee, **dismissal of the head of internal audit** being the responsibility of the board or audit committee, internal auditors not assuming operational responsibilities and internal auditors being excluded from systems, design, installation and operation work.

5.3.4 Resources

Again the review should consider the documentation provided by internal audit and confirm that resourcing plans indicate that there will be **sufficient resources** to review all areas. This should be assessed not just in terms of the hours set aside but also physical resources such as computers, and also of course the necessary **knowledge, skills and experience**.

Exam focus point	The annual review of internal audit is a likely subject of a part-question in the exam.

6 The internal audit committee

6.1 Role and function of internal audit committee

FAST FORWARD

An internal audit committee of **independent non-executive directors** should **liaise with external audit, supervise internal audit**, and review **the annual accounts and internal controls**.

Exam focus point

Audit committees are very significant because of their responsibilities for supervision and overall review. In particular they should have a close interest in the work of internal audit; the UK Cadbury report emphasised the importance of internal audit having unrestricted access to the audit committee.

The UK Cadbury report summed up the benefits that an audit committee can bring to an organisation.

'If they operate effectively, audit committees can bring significant benefits. In particular, they have the potential to:

(a) improve the quality of financial reporting, by reviewing the financial statements on behalf of the Board;

(b) create a climate of discipline and control which will reduce the opportunity for fraud;

(c) enable the non-executive directors to contribute an independent judgement and play a positive role;

(d) help the finance director, by providing a forum in which he can raise issues of concern, and which he can use to get things done which might otherwise be difficult;

(e) strengthen the position of the external auditor, by providing a channel of communication and forum for issues of concern;

(f) provide a framework within which the external auditor can assert his independence in the event of a dispute with management;

(g) strengthen the position of the internal audit function, by providing a greater degree of independence from management;

(h) increase public confidence in the credibility and objectivity of financial statements.'

The Cadbury report warns, however, that the effectiveness of the audit committee may be compromised if it acts as a **'barrier'** between the external auditors and the main (executive) board, or if it allows the main board to **'abdicate its responsibilities** in the audit area' as this will weaken the board's responsibility for reviewing and approving the financial statements. The audit committee must also avoid falling under the influence of a **dominant board member**.

Audit committees are now compulsory for companies trading on the New York Stock Exchange.

In order to be effective, the audit committee has to be well-staffed. The UK Smith report recommends that the **audit committee** should consist entirely of **independent non-executive directors** (excluding the chairman), and should include at least one member with **significant and recent financial experience**. The Singapore code suggests that at least two members should have accounting or related financial management expertise.

The main duties of the audit committee are likely to be as follows.

6.2 Review of financial statements and systems

The committee should review both the **quarterly/interim** (if published) and **annual accounts**. This should involve assessment of the judgements made about the overall appearance and presentation of the accounts, key accounting policies and major areas of judgement.

As well as reviewing the accounts, the committee's review should cover the financial reporting and budgetary systems. This involves considering **performance indicators** and **information systems** that allow **monitoring** of the **most significant business and financial risks**, and the progress towards financial objectives. The systems should also highlight developments that may require action (for example large variances), and communicate these to the right people.

6.3 Liaison with external auditors

The audit committee's tasks here will include:

(a) Being responsible for the **appointment or removal of the external auditors** as well as fixing their remuneration.

(b) Considering whether there are **any other threats to external auditor independence.** In particular the committee should consider **non-audit services** provided by the external auditors, paying particular attention to whether there may be a **conflict of interest.**

(c) **Discussing the scope of the external audit** prior to the start of the audit. This should include consideration of whether external audit's coverage of all areas and locations of the business is fair, and how much external audit will rely on the work of internal audit.

(d) Acting as a **forum for liaison** between the external auditors, the internal auditors and the finance director.

(e) **Helping the external auditors to obtain the information** they require and in resolving any problems they may encounter.

(f) **Making themselves available** to the external auditors for consultation, with or without the presence of the company's management.

(g) Dealing with any **serious reservations** which the external auditors may express either about the accounts, the records or the quality of the company's management.

6.4 Review of internal audit

The review should cover the following aspects of internal audit.

- **Standards** including **objectivity, technical knowledge** and **professional standards**
- **Scope** including how much emphasis is given to different types of review
- **Resources,** is the number of staff hours enough and are the technical and personal skills of the staff collectively sufficient for the work they are required to do?
- **Reporting arrangements**
- **Work plan**, especially review of controls and coverage of high risk areas
- **Liaison** with external auditors
- **Results**

The head of internal audit should have **direct access** to the audit committee.

6.5 Review of internal control

The audit committee should play a significant role in reviewing internal control.

(a) Committee members can use their own experience to **monitor** continually the **adequacy** of **internal control systems**, focusing particularly on the control environment, management's attitude towards controls and overall management controls.

(b) The audit committee's review should cover **legal compliance** and **ethics**, for example listing rules or environmental legislation. Committee members should check that there are systems in place to promote compliance. They should review reports on the operation of **codes of conduct** and review violations.

(c) The committee should also address the risk of **fraud**, ensuring employees are aware of risks and that there are mechanisms in place for staff to report fraud, and fraud to be investigated.

(d) Each year the committee should be responsible for **reviewing the company's statement on internal controls** prior to its approval by the board.

(e) The committee should consider the **recommendations of the auditors** in the management letter and management's response. Because the committee's role is ongoing, it can also ensure that recommendations are publicised and see that actions are taken as appropriate.

(f) The committee may play a **more active supervisory role**, for example reviewing major transactions for reasonableness.

6.6 Review of risk management

The audit committee can play an important part in the review of risk recommended by the Turnbull report This includes confirming that there is a **formal policy** in place for **risk management** and that the policy is backed and regularly monitored by the board. The committee should also **review** the **arrangements**, including training, for ensuring that managers and staff are aware of their responsibilities. Committee members should use their own knowledge of the business to confirm that risk management is updated to **reflect current positions and strategy**. The extent of their work may depend on whether there is a separate **risk management committee** (see Chapter 8).

6.7 Investigations

The committee will also be involved in implementing and reviewing the results of **one-off investigations**. The Cadbury report recommends that audit committees should be given specific authority to investigate matters of concern, and in doing so have access to sufficient resources, appropriate information and outside professional help.

Chapter Roundup

- The role of internal audit will **vary** according to the **organisation's objectives** but is likely to include **review of internal control systems, risk management, legal compliance** and **value for money**.

- **Internal auditors** are **employees** of the organisation whose work is designed to **add value** and who report to the **audit committee**. **External auditors** are from **accountancy firms** and their role is to **report on the financial statements** to **shareholders**.

- Both **internal and external auditors** review controls, and **external auditors** may **place reliance** on **internal auditors' work** providing they assess its worth.

- Internal audit standards cover **professional proficiency**, **scope of work**, **performance**, **management**, and most importantly **independence**.

- Reports on the results of internal audits should highlight the **risks** identified, the weaknesses found in control, the **consequences** of the problems found and the **recommendations** for improvements.

- Formal **assessment procedures** should be used to assess the work of **internal audit**.

- An intend audit committee of **independent non-executive directors** should liaise with **external audit**, **supervise internal audit**, and **review the annual accounts and internal controls**.

BPP
LEARNING MEDIA

Quick Quiz

1   What is internal audit?

2   What are the main elements of internal audit's review of the accounting and control systems?

3   Name three key differences between internal and external audit.

4   What matters would the external auditors consider when assessing the internal audit function?

5   Which of the following is not a measure designed to enhance the independence of internal audit?

   A   Internal audit should have unrestricted access to records, assets and personnel.

   B   Internal audit should report ultimately to the finance director.

   C   Internal auditors should not audit systems that they have designed.

   D   The terms of reference of the internal audit department should draw a clear distinction between regular audit services and consultancy work.

6   What are the most important aspects of the assessment of the professional proficiency of internal audit?

7   List the main responsibilities of internal audit committees.

8   Internal audit committees are generally staffed by executive directors.

   True   ☐

   False   ☐

Answers to Quick Quiz

1   Internal audit is an appraisal or monitoring activity established by management and directors, for the review of the accounting and internal control systems as a service to the entity.

2   • Reviewing the design of systems
    • Monitoring the operation of systems by risk assessment and detailed testing
    • Recommending cost effective improvements

3   • External report to members, internal to directors
    • External report on financial statements, internal on systems, controls and risks
    • External are independent of the company, internal often employed by it

4   • Organisational status
    • Scope of function
    • Technical competence
    • Due professional care

5   B   Internal audit should ultimately report to the internal audit committee.

6   • Appropriate staffing
    • Knowledge, skills and disciplines
    • Supervision
    • Compliance with professional standards
    • Human relations and communication
    • Continuing education
    • Due professional care

7   • Review of financial statements and systems
    • Liaison with external auditors
    • Review of internal audit
    • Review of internal control
    • Review of risk management
    • Investigations

8   False   Non-executive directors should staff the internal audit committee to enhance its function as an independent monitor, and a forum to which internal and external audit can address their concerns.

Now try the question below from the Exam Question Bank

Number	Level	Marks	Time
Q5	Introductory	n/a	35 mins

BPP
LEARNING MEDIA

Part C
Identifying and assessing risks

6

Business risks

Topic list	Syllabus reference
1 The nature of risks	C1
2 Strategic and operational risks	C2
3 Examples of risks faced by organisations	C2

Introduction

We have already mentioned risks when discussing internal controls. In this chapter we look at the risks organisations face. You will have encountered categorisation of risks in your auditing studies – the inherent, control, audit classification. Whilst useful in an external audit context, there are more useful ways of classifying risks faced by organisations, partly because the external auditors are most concerned with risks relating to financial statements, whereas directors have to take a wider perspective.

In the first section we look at key considerations affecting risks, particularly the relationship of risk and return. It is important to emphasise straightaway that organisations do not seek to eliminate all risks. A business that does not take any risks will not make any profits. Instead businesses are trying to make returns that are acceptable for the risks that they take.

In Section 2 we draw the important distinction between the strategic risks (integral, long-term risks that the board is likely to be most concerned with) and operational risks (largely the concern of line management). Section 3 lists many of the common business risks. However it is not comprehensive and you may have to use your imagination to identify other risks.

Study guide

		Intellectual level
C1	**Risks and the risk management process**	
(a)	Define and explain risk in the context of corporate governance	2
(b)	Define and describe management responsibilities in risk management	2
C2	**Categories of risk**	
(a)	Define and compare (distinguish between) strategic and operational risks	2
(b)	Define and explain the sources and impacts of common business risks	2
(c)	Recognise and analyse the sector or industry specific nature of many business risks	2

Exam guide

You may be able to gain some marks for understanding basic risk concepts. When trying to identify risks in the exam, consider the scenario and in particular what aspects of the scenario are currently changing – these will point you towards important risks. The most important question though when considering what risks could affect an organisation is 'What could go wrong?'

1 The nature of risks

FAST FORWARD

Risks can be **classified** by **who they affect** and whether they have **positive or negative outcomes**.

The **level of risk** that an organisation bears relates to the **level of return** it desires.

Key terms

Risk is a condition in which there exists a quantifiable dispersion in the possible results of any activity.

Hazard is the impact if the risk materialises.

In other words, risk is the probability, hazard is the consequences, of results deviating from expectations. However, risk is often used as a generic term to cover **hazard as well**.

Question

Risks

What sort of risks might an organisation face?

Answer

Make your own list, specific to the organisations that you are familiar with. Here is a list extracted from an article by Tom Jones 'Risk Management' (*Administrator*, April 1993). It is illustrative of the range of risks faced and is not exhaustive.

- Fire, flood, storm, impact, explosion, subsidence and other disasters

- Accidents and the use of faulty products

- Error: loss through damage or malfunction caused by mistaken operation of equipment or wrong operation of an industrial programme

- Theft and fraud

- Breaking social or environmental regulations

- Political risks (the appropriation of foreign assets by local governments, or of barriers to the repatriation of overseas profit)

- Computers: fraud, viruses, and espionage

- Product tamper

- Malicious damage

1.1 Types of risk

Key terms

> **Fundamental risks** are those that affect society in general, or broad groups of people, and are beyond the control of any one individual. For example there is the risk of atmospheric pollution which can affect the health of a whole community but which may be quite beyond the power of an individual within it to control.
>
> **Particular risks** are risks over which an individual may have some measure of control. For example there is a risk attaching to smoking and we can mitigate that risk by refraining from smoking.
>
> **Speculative risks** are those from which either good or harm may result. A business venture, for example, presents a speculative risk because either a profit or loss can result.
>
> **Pure risks** are those whose only possible outcome is harmful. The risk of loss of data in computer systems caused by fire is a pure risk because no gain can result from it.

There are various types of risk that exist in business and in life generally.

 Case Study

You only need to glance at the business pages of a newspaper on any day you like to find out why risk management is a key issue in today's business world. For example, look at some of the main stories in the UK on the *Telegraph's* business pages on a single day.

(a) A story about the then likely failure of **MG Rover**. This was in spite of the fact that the four owners of Phoenix Venture Holdings, who bought MG Rover for just £10 in 2000, had made more than £30m for themselves since. They had been heavily criticised for handing themselves a four-way split of a £10m 'IOU' note within months of the deal's completion in 2000. They also set up a £16.5m pension fund for company directors and separately took control of a lucrative car financing business.

(b) A story about employees of the Bermuda office of the insurer **American International Group (AIG)**, who were caught trying to destroy documents as the company faced ever-expanding enquiries into the conduct of the business.

(c) A story about how **Glaxo** faces claims in the US courts that its patents for the Aids drug AZT are invalid. The patents are worth around £1.1bn a year to Glaxo which controls 40% of the lucrative Aids drug market.

(d) A story about clothing retailer **Alexon**, which estimated that £3m would be knocked off its profits as a result of the collapse of **Allders**, the stores where it ran 118 concessions. The story also notes poor sales at the Alexon group's youth fashion chain Bay Trading. 'The company refused to blame the weather. Robin Piggot, finance director, said: "We were trimming the value of our garments, making them cheaper and cheaper but less interesting.

(e)   A story about how shoppers may face shortages of pasta and garlic bread as a result of a fire in a factory at Burton-on-Humber owned by chilled food producer **Geest**.

Here we can observe risks to the well-being of companies arising from questionable dealings by **directors**, questionable actions of **employees**, the actions of competitors, the problems of **customers/partners**, the **weather**, poor **product design**, and **fire**. And all on a single day!

1.2 Negative risks

A simple view of risk would see it in negative terms, as **downside** or **pure risk** and risk management would involve minimising the chances that adverse events will happen. However even under this viewpoint, organisations should be aware that it may **not be possible to eliminate risks** without undermining the whole basis on which the business operates or without incurring excessive costs and insurance premiums. Therefore in many situations there is likely to be a level of residual or remaining risk which it is simply not worth eliminating.

However there are some benefits to be derived from the management of risk, possibly at the expense of profits such as:

- **Predictability** of **cash flows**
- **Limitation of the impact** of potentially **bankrupting events**
- **Increased confidence** of shareholders and other investors

1.3 Risk and uncertainty

A complication in dealing with risks is the level of uncertainty involved. Ultimately risk assessment may be able to tell you the **possible impacts (hazard)**, and the **chances** that each outcome will occur **(risk probability)**. All that is unknown is the actual outcome. Uncertainty however means that you do not **know the possible** and/or the **chances of each outcome occurring**. It may arise from a lack of information about input/output relationships or the environment within which the business operates.

Exam focus point	Another good question to keep asking when analysing scenarios: 'Are we sure we know what could happen?'

1.4 Risk and return

We shall talk more about attitudes to risk when, in Chapter 8, we consider how organisations respond to risk. However there is one key point that we need to make now; **risk-averse** businesses may be willing to **tolerate a higher level of risk** provided they receive **a higher level of return**, or if risk is 'two-way' or symmetrical, that it has both positive and negative outcomes. Indeed a willingness to take certain risks in order to seize new opportunities may be **essential for business success** and expected by shareholders who themselves ultimately bear the risk of a business.

Under this view a business should be concerned with reducing risk where possible and necessary, but not eliminating all risks, whilst managers try to **maximise the returns** that are possible given the levels of risk. Most risks must be managed to some extent, and some should be eliminated as being outside the scope of the remit of the management of a business. Risk management under this view is an integral part of **strategy**, and involves analysing what the **key value drivers are** in the organisation's activities, and the risks tied up with those value drivers

For example, a business in a high-tech industry, such as computing, which evolves rapidly within ever-changing markets and technologies, has to accept high risks in its research and development activities; but should it also be speculating on interest and exchange rates within its treasury activities?

Case Study

Since risk and return are linked, one consequence of focusing on achieving or maintaining high profit levels may mean that the organisation bears a large amount of risk. The decision to bear these risk levels may not be conscious, and may go well beyond what is considered desirable by shareholders and other stakeholders.

This is illustrated by the experience of the National Bank of Australia, which announced it had lost hundreds of millions of pounds on foreign exchange trading, resulting in share price instability and the resignation of both the Chairman and Chief Executive. In the end the ultimate loss of A$360 million was 110 times its official foreign exchange trading cap of A$ 3.25 million.

The bank had become increasingly reliant on speculation and high-risk investment activity to maintain profitability. Traders had breached trading limits on 800 occasions, and at one stage had unhedged foreign exchange exposures of more than $A2 billion. These breaches were reported internally, as were unusual patterns in trading (very large daily gains) but senior managers took no action. For 3 years, the currency options team had been the most profitable team in Australia, and had been rewarded by bonuses greater than their annual salaries. Eventually however the team came unstuck, and entered false transactions to hide their losses.

The market however was unimpressed by the efforts of the bank to make members of the team scapegoats, and market pressure forced changes at the top of the organisation, a general restructuring and a more prudent attitude to risk. Observers, however, questioned whether this change in attitude would survive the economic pressures that the bank was under in the long term.

1.5 Risk and corporate governance

One obvious link between risk and corporate governance is the issue of shareholders' concerns, here about the relationship between the level of risks and the returns achieved, being addressed.

A further issue is the link (or lack of it) between **directors' remuneration** and risks taken. If remuneration does not link directly with risk levels, but does link with turnover and profits achieved, directors could decide that the company should bear risk levels that are higher than shareholders deem desirable. It has therefore been necessary to find other ways of ensuring that directors pay sufficient attention to risk management and do not take excessive risks. Corporate governance guidelines therefore require directors to:

- **Establish appropriate control mechanisms** for dealing with the risks the organisation faces
- **Monitor risks** themselves by regular review and a wider annual review
- **Disclose their risk management processes** in the accounts

2 Strategic and operational risks

FAST FORWARD

Strategic risks are risks that relate to the fundamental and key decisions that the directors take about the future of the organisation.

Operational risks relate to matters that can go wrong on a day-to-day basis while the organisation is carrying out its business.

Key term

Strategic risk is the potential volatility of profits caused by the nature and type of the business operations.

2.1 Strategic risk

The most significant risks are focused on the **strategy** the organisation adopts including concentration of resources, mergers and acquisitions and exit strategies. These will have major impacts on **costs, prices, products and sales**. Organisations also need to guard against the risks that **business processes and operations** are **not aligned** to strategic goals.

2.1.1 Relationships with stakeholders

Relations with stakeholders will have a significant impact upon strategic risks because of the **consequences of non-cooperation**, for example investors not contributing new funds, suppliers not delivering on time, employees disrupting production and ultimately of course customers not buying goods and services. Organisations must be aware of the key factors that may lead to problems in relations with stakeholders.

- **Investors** will be concerned with financial returns, accuracy and timeliness of information and quality of leadership

- Relations with **suppliers** and **employees** will be influenced by the terms and conditions of business. With employees, the organisation also needs to consider whether they have the appropriate knowledge and attitudes

- **Customers** will obviously be influenced by the **level** of **customer service,** also product safety issues and perhaps whether the organisation is 'ethical' in matters such as marketing practice; their changing attitudes and expectations will also be influential

2.1.2 Other factors

Other factors contributing to strategic risks will include:

- The types of industries/markets within which the business operates
- The state of the economy
- The actions of competitors and the possibility of mergers and acquisitions
- The stage in a product's life cycle, higher risks in the introductory and declining stages
- The dependence upon inputs with fluctuating prices, eg wheat, oil etc
- The level of operating gearing – the proportion of fixed costs in total costs
- The flexibility of production processes to adapt to different specifications or products
- The organisation's research and development capacity and ability to innovate
- The significance of new technology

There may be little management can do about some of these risks, they are inherent in business activity. However, strategies such as **diversification** can contribute substantially to the reduction of many business risks.

2.2 Operational risk

Key term

> **Operational or process risk** is the risk of loss from a failure of internal business and control processes.

Operational risk can be defined as including losses from internal control or audit inadequacies, information technology failures, human error, loss of key-person risk, fraud and business interruption events.

BPP LEARNING MEDIA

2.3 Strategic and operational risks

The main difference between strategic and operational risks is that strategic risks relate to the organisation's **longer-term** place in, and relations with, the **outside environment**. Although some of them relate to internal functions, they are internal functions or aspects of internal functions that have a **key bearing** on the organisation's situation in relation to its environment. Operational risks are what could go wrong on a **day-to-day basis**, and are not generally very relevant to the key strategic decisions that affect a business, although some (for example a major disaster) can have a major impact on the business's future.

You may also think that as strategic risks relate primarily to an outside environment that is not under the organisation's control, it is more difficult to mitigate these risks than it is to deal with the risks that relate to the internal environment that is under the organisation's control.

3 Examples of risks faced by organisations

FAST FORWARD

> Risks can be **classified** in various ways, including financial, legal, IT, operational, fraud and reputation.

There are many different types of risks faced by organisations, particularly those with commercial or international activities. The nature of these risks is discussed briefly below.

Exam focus point

Questions for this paper will undoubtedly cover a range of risks, not just financial risks.

3.1 Financial risk

The ultimate financial risk is that the organisation will not be able to continue to function as a going concern.

Financial risks include the risks relating to the **structure of finance** the organisation has, in particular the risks relating to the mix of equity and debt capital, also whether the organisation has an insufficient long-term capital base for the amount of trading it is doing (overtrading). Organisations also must consider the risks of **fraud and misuse** of financial resources. **Longer-term risks** include **currency and interest rate risks**, also market risk. **Shorter-term financial risks** include **credit risk** and **liquidity risk.**

3.1.1 Currency risk

Key term

Currency risk is the possibility of loss or gain due to future changes in exchange rates.

When a firm trades with an overseas supplier or customer, and the invoice is in the overseas currency, it will expose itself to exchange rate or currency risk. Movement in the foreign exchange rates will create risk in the settlement of the debt – ie the final amount payable/receivable in the home currency will be uncertain at the time of entering into the transaction. Investment in a foreign country or borrowing in a foreign currency will also carry this risk.

There are three types of currency risk.

  (a) **Transaction risk** – arising from exchange rate movements between the time of entering into an international trading transaction and the time of cash settlement.

  (b) **Translation risk** – the changes in balance sheet values of foreign assets and liabilities arising from retranslation at different prevailing exchange rates at the end of each year.

  (c) **Economic risk** – the effect of exchange rate movements on the international competitiveness of the organisation, eg in terms of relative prices of imports/exports, the cost of foreign labour etc.

Of these three, transaction risk has the greatest immediate impact on day to day cash flows of an organisation, and there are many ways of reducing or eliminating this risk, for example by the use of **hedging** techniques.

3.1.2 Interest rate risk

As with foreign exchange rates, future interest rates cannot be easily predicted. If a firm has a significant amount of variable (floating) rate debt, interest rate movements will give rise to uncertainty about the cost of servicing this debt. Conversely, if a company uses a lot of fixed rate debt, it will lose out if interest rates begin to fall.

There are many arrangements and financial products that a firm's treasury department can use to reduce its exposure to interest rate risk for example, involving **hedging** techniques similar to those used for the management of currency risk.

3.1.3 Market risk

Key term

> **Market risk** is a risk of loss due to an adverse move in the market value of an asset – a stock, a bond, a loan, foreign exchange or a commodity – or a derivative contract linked to these assets.

Market risk is thus connected to interest rate or exchange when derivatives are used to hedge these risks. Market risk can be analysed into various other risks that cover **movements in the reference asset**, the **risk of small price movements** that change the **value of the holder's position**, and the risks of losses relating to a change in the **maturity structure** of an asset, the **passage of time** or **market volatility**. Market risk can also apply to making a major investment, for example a recently-floated company, where the market price has not yet reached a 'true level', or if there are other uncertainties about the price, for example lack of information.

Basis risk is particularly relevant to derivative hedging because it is the risk that the derivative price may not move as expected in relation to the underlying asset being hedged.

3.1.4 Credit risk

Key term

> **Credit risk** is the risk to a company from the failure of its debtors to meet their obligations on time.

Management of **credit risk** is of particular importance to exporters and various instruments and you may remember from earlier studies that various arrangements are available to assist in this, such as **documentary credits**, **bills of exchange**, **export credit insurance**, **export factoring** and **forfaiting**.

3.1.5 Liquidity risk

Key term

> **Liquidity risk** is the risk of loss due to a mismatch between cash inflows and outflows.

To trading businesses, the risk can relate to the need to obtain short-term funding to **cover liquidity problems**, and having to pay a **high borrowing rate**. It can also be extended to cover the risk of gaining a poor liquidity reputation, and therefore having existing sources of finance withdrawn as well. There is also **asset liquidity risk,** failure to realise the expected value on the sale of an asset due to lack of demand for the asset or having to accept a lower price due to the need for quick funds.

3.1.6 Financial records and reporting risks

Financial risks can also be said to include **misstatement risks** relating to published financial information. This in turn may arise from **breakdown in the accounting systems**, **unrecorded liabilities** and **unreliable accounting records**.

3.1.7 Finance providers' risk

There are also risks to the organisation if it provides finance for others. If it lends money, there is the **risk of default** on debt payments, and ultimately the risk that the borrower will become insolvent. If it invests in shares, there is a risk that it will receive **low or no dividends**, and share price volatility will mean that it does not receive any **capital gains** on the value of the shares.

3.2 Legal and political risks

Breaches of legislation, regulations or codes of conduct can have very serious consequences for organisations. Risks include **financial or other penalties** (including ultimately closedown), having to **spend money and resources** in fighting litigation and **loss of reputation**. Key areas include health and safety, environmental legislation, trade descriptions, consumer protection, data protection and employment issues.

Governance codes are a particularly important example of best practice, and organisations must consider the risks of breaching provisions relating to integrity and objectivity, and also control over the organisation.

Political risk is the risk that political action will affect the position and value of an organisation. It is connected with **country risk**, the risk associated with undertaking transactions with, or holding assets in, a particular country.

3.3 Technological risk

3.3.1 Physical damage risks

Fire is the **most serious hazard** to computer systems. Destruction of data can be even more costly than the destruction of hardware. **Water** is also a serious hazard. In some areas flooding is a natural risk, for example in many towns and cities near rivers or coasts. Basements are therefore generally not regarded as appropriate sites for large computer installations. Wind, rain and storms can all cause substantial **damage to buildings. Lightning and electrical storms** can play havoc with power supplies, causing power failures coupled with power surges as services are restored.

Organisations may also be exposed to physical threats through the actions of humans. **Political terrorism** is the main risk, but there are also threats from individuals with **grudges.** Staff are a physical threat to computer installations, whether by spilling a cup of coffee over a desk covered with papers, or tripping and falling, doing some damage to themselves and to an item of office equipment.

3.3.2 Data and systems integrity risk

The **risks** include **human error** such as entering incorrect transactions, failing to correct errors, processing the wrong files and failing to follow prescribed security procedures. Possible **technical errors** include malfunctioning hardware or software and supporting equipment such as communication equipment, normal and emergency power supplies and air conditioning units.

Other threats include commercial espionage, malicious damage and industrial action.

These risks may be particularly significant because of the nature of computer operations. The **processing** capabilities of a computer are **extensive**, and enormous quantities of data are processed without human intervention, and so without humans necessarily knowing what is going on.

3.3.3 Fraud risk

Computer fraud usually involves the theft of funds by **dishonest use** of a computer system. **Input fraud** is where data input is falsified; good examples are putting a **non-existent employee** on the salary file or a non-existent supplier on the purchases file. With **processing fraud** a programmer or someone who has broken into this part of the system may **alter a program**. **Output fraud** involves **documents** being **stolen or tampered with** and control totals being altered. Cheques are the most likely document to be stolen, but other documents may be stolen to hide a fraud.

Over the last few years there have been rapid developments in all aspects of computer technology and these have increased the opportunities that are available to commit a fraud. The most important of the recent developments is **increased computer literacy**. The use of public communication systems has increased the ability of people outside the organisation to break into the computer system. These 'hackers' could not have operated when access was only possible on site. A consequence of increased use of computers is often a **reduction** in the number of **internal checks** carried out for any transaction.

3.3.4 Internet risk

Establishing organisational links to the Internet brings numerous security dangers.

- Corruptions such as **viruses** on a single computer can spread through the network to all of the organisation's computers.

- If the organisation is linked to an external network, **hackers** may be able to get into the organisation's internal network, either to steal data or to cause damage.

- Employees may **download inaccurate information** or imperfect or **virus-ridden software** from an external network.

- Information transmitted from one part of an organisation to another may be **intercepted**. Data can be 'encrypted' (scrambled) in an attempt to make it unintelligible to hackers.

- The **communications link itself may break down or distort data**.

3.3.5 Denial of service attack

A fairly new threat, relating to Internet websites and related systems is the 'Denial of Service (DoS)' attack. A denial of service attack is characterised by an attempt by attackers to prevent legitimate users of a service from using that service. Examples include attempts to:

- 'Flood' or bombard a site or network, thereby preventing legitimate network traffic (major sites, such as Amazon.com and Yahoo! have been targeted in this way)

- Disrupt connections between two machines, thereby preventing access to a service

- Prevent a particular individual from accessing a service

3.4 Health and safety risk

Health and safety risks include loss of employees' time because of injury and the risks of having to pay compensation or legal costs because of breaches. Health and safety risks can arise from:

- **Lack of health and safety policy** – due to increased legislation in this area this is becoming less likely

- **Lack of emergency procedures** – again less likely

- **Failure to deal with hazards** – often due to a failure to implement policies such as inspection of electrical equipment, labelling of hazards and training

- **Poor employee welfare** – not just threats to health such as poor working conditions or excessive exposure to VDUs, but also risks to quality from tired staff making mistakes

- Generally **poor health and safety culture**

Question

Can you think of some signs of a poor health and safety culture in an organisation?

Answer

Glynis Morris in the book *An Accountant's Guide to Risk Management* lists a number of signs:

- Trailing wires and overloaded electricity sockets
- Poor lighting
- Poor ventilation
- Uneven floor surfaces
- Sharp edges
- Cupboards and drawers that are regularly left open
- Poorly stacked shelves or other poor storage arrangements
- Excessive noise and dust levels
- Poor furniture design, workstation or office layout

Morris points out that all these problems can be solved with thought.

3.5 Environmental risk

Key term

> **Environmental risk** is the risk of loss to the business arising out of the environmental effects of its operations.

The risk is possibly greatest with business activities such as agriculture and farming, the chemical industry and transportation generally. These industries have the greatest direct impact on the environment and so face the most significant risks. However other factors may be significant. A business located in a **sensitive area**, such as near a river, may face increased risks of causing pollution. A key element of environmental risk is likely to be waste management, particularly if waste materials are toxic.

3.6 Fraud risk

All businesses run the risk of loss through the fraudulent activities of employees including management.

The list of possible fraud risks below is partly based on a list given in the UK Auditing Practices Board's auditing standard SAS 110 *Fraud and error*. You can see that a number of the signs listed are examples of poor corporate governance procedures, such as over-domination by one person or pressures on the accounting or internal audit departments.

Fraud and error	
Previous experience or incidents which call into question the integrity or competence of management	Management dominated by one person (or a small group) and no effective oversight board or committee
	Complex corporate structure where complexity does not seem to be warranted
	High turnover rate of key accounting and financial personnel
	Personnel (key or otherwise) not taking holidays
	Personnel lifestyles that appear to be beyond their known income
	Significant and prolonged under-staffing of the accounting department
	Poor relations between executive management and internal auditors
	Lack of attention given to, or review of, key internal accounting data such as cost estimates
	Frequent changes of legal advisors or auditors
	History of legal and regulatory violations
Particular financial reporting pressures within an entity	Industry volatility
	Inadequate working capital due to declining profits or too rapid expansion
	Deteriorating quality of earnings, for example increased risk taking with respect to credit sales, changes in business practice or selection of accounting policy alternatives that improve income
	The entity needs a rising profit trend to support the market price of its shares due to a contemplated public offering, a takeover or other reason
	Significant investment in an industry or product line noted for rapid change
	Pressure on accounting personnel to complete financial statements in an unreasonably short period of time
	Dominant owner-management
	Performance-based remuneration
Weaknesses in the design and operation of the accounting and internal controls system	A weak control environment within the entity
	Systems that, in their design, are inadequate to give reasonable assurance of preventing or detecting error or fraud
	Inadequate segregation of responsibilities in relation to functions involving the handling, recording or controlling of the entity's assets
	Poor security of assets
	Lack of access controls over IT systems
	Indications that internal financial information is unreliable
	Evidence that internal controls have been overridden by management
	Ineffective monitoring of the operation of system which allows control overrides, breakdown or weakness to continue without proper corrective action
	Continuing failure to correct major weakness in internal control where such corrections are practicable and cost effective

BPP
LEARNING MEDIA

Fraud and error	
Unusual transactions or trends	Unusual transactions, especially near the year end, that have a significant effect on earnings
	Complex transactions or accounting treatments
	Unusual transactions with related parties
	Payments for services (for example to lawyers, consultants or agents) that appear excessive in relation to the services provided
	Large cash transactions
	Transactions dealt with outside the normal systems
	Investments in products that appear too good to be true, for example low risk, high return products
	Large changes in significant revenues or expenses
Problems in obtaining sufficient appropriate audit evidence	Inadequate records, for example incomplete files, excessive adjustments to accounting records, transactions not recorded in accordance with normal procedures and out-of-balance control accounts
	Inadequate documentation of transactions, such as lack of proper authorisation, supporting documents not available and alteration to documents (any of these documentation problems assume greater significance when they relate to large or unusual transactions)
	An excessive number of differences between accounting records and third party confirmations, conflicting audit evidence and unexplainable changes in operating ratios
	Evasive, delayed or unreasonable responses by management to audit enquiries
	Inappropriate attitude of management to the conduct of the audit, eg time pressure, scope limitation and other constraints
Some factors unique to an information systems environment which relate to the conditions and events described above	Inability to extract information from computer files due to lack of, or non-current, documentation of record contents or programs
	Large numbers of program changes that are not documented, approved and tested
	Inadequate overall balancing of computer transactions and data bases to the financial accounts

Question

Procurement fraud

Give examples of indicators of fraud in the tendering process.

Answer

(a)   **Suppliers**

Examples include **disqualification of suitable suppliers**, a very **short list of alternatives** and **continual use** of the **same suppliers** or a single source. The organisation should also be alert for any signs of personal relationships between staff and suppliers.

(b)   **Contract terms**

Possible signs here include **contract specifications** that do not make commercial sense and contracts that include special, but unnecessary specifications, that only one supplier can meet.

(c) **Bid and awarding process**

Signs of doubtful practice include **unclear evaluation criteria**, **acceptance of late bids** and **changes in the contract specification** after some bids have been made. Suspicions might be aroused if reasons for awarding the contract are unclear or the contract is awarded to a supplier with a **poor performance record** or who appears to **lack the resources** to carry out the contract.

(d) **After the contract is awarded**

Changes to the contract after it has been awarded should be considered carefully, also a large number of **subsequent changes in contract specifications** or **liability limits**.

This is perhaps one of the risk areas over which the company can exert the greatest control, through a coherent corporate strategy set out in a **fraud policy statement** and the setting up of strict **internal controls**.

3.7 Knowledge management risk

Knowledge management risk concerns the effective management and control of knowledge resources. Threats might include unauthorised use or abuse of intellectual property, area or system power failures, competitor's technology or loss of key staff.

3.8 Property risk

Property risks are the risks from **damage**, **destruction** or **taking of property.** Perils to property include fire, windstorms, water leakage and vandalism.

If the organisation suffers damage, it may be liable for repairs or ultimately the building of an entirely new property. There may also be a risk of **loss of rent**. If a building is accidentally damaged or destroyed, and the tenant is not responsible for the payment of rent during the period the property cannot be occupied, the landlord will lose the rent.

If there is damage to the property, the organisation could suffer from having to **suspend or reduce** its **operations**.

3.9 Trading risk

Both domestic and international traders will face trading risks, although those faced by the latter will generally be greater due to the increased distances and times involved. The types of trading risk include the following.

3.9.1 Physical risk

Physical risk is the risk of goods being **lost** or **stolen in transit**, or **the documents** accompanying the goods **going astray**.

3.9.2 Trade risk

Trade risk is the risk of the customer refusing to accept the goods on delivery (due to sub-standard/ inappropriate goods), or the cancellation of the order in transit.

3.9.3 Liquidity risk

Liquidity risk is the inability to finance the organisation's trading activities.

3.10 Disruption risk

Obviously one of most important disruptions is a failure of information technology, but operations may be delayed or prevented for other reasons as well. These include employee error, product problems, health and safety issues, losses of employees or suppliers, or legal action.

3.11 Cost and resource wastage risk

Important operational risks for most organisations are incurring excessive costs (through poor procurement procedures, lack of control over expenditure) or waste of employees' time and resources (employees being unproductive or their efforts being misapplied).

3.12 Product risk

Product risks will include the risks of financial loss due to producing a poor quality product. These include the need to **compensate dissatisfied customers**, possible **loss of sales** if the product has to be withdrawn from the market or because of loss of reputation (see below) and the need for **expenditure on improved quality control procedures**.

Question   Managing risk

How might you attempt to manage the risk that you would lose money developing an entirely new product that turned out to be unsuccessful?

Answer

Conduct market research, even if it is only possible to describe the concept of the new product to potential customers.

Perhaps only develop product ideas that derive from customers. (Though there is a risk that they might not be good ideas, and you may miss the opportunity to develop ideas that would appeal to customers, if only they were asked.)

Do not commit to major expenditure (for example a new factory, large inventories of raw materials) without creating and market testing a prototype.

You may have had other ideas. The key is to gather as much information as possible.

3.13 Organisational risk

Organisational risks relate to the behaviour of groups or individuals within the organisation. These are particularly important to organisations that are going through **significant change**, as failure by people or teams to adapt may jeopardise change.

3.14 Reputation risk

Key term

> **Reputation risk** is a loss of reputation caused as a result of the adverse consequences of another risk.

The loss of reputation will be usually perceived by external stakeholders, and may have serious consequences, depending on the **strength of the organisation's relationship** with them.

Case Study

In an interview Bob Marshall, the chief executive of Railtrack, the body formerly responsible for running the railway infrastructure in the UK, pointed out that the management of reputation risk had to take into account the views of all the organisation's stakeholders. For Railtrack these included the travelling public, passenger pressure groups, various government departments, the Health and Safety Executive, financers, shareholders, employees and contractors. Not surprisingly many in the company felt that it was suffering from 'stakeholder overload'.

In Autumn 2000 a number of passengers died in an accident because of track problems at Hatfield, north of London. Railtrack's attempts to repair the cataclysmic loss of reputation that resulted included talking directly to stakeholders, being open and honest and admitting mistakes.

At the same time the railway network had to keep running, Railtrack meet its financial obligations and undertake negotiations with the government. They achieved this by splitting teams between business continuation work and emergency risk management procedures. Managers also talked to the workforce with the idea that they could help restore the company's reputation by conveying a positive picture to people outside the organisation.

The major lessons learnt were the importance of identifying how business identifies risk, the need for senior staff to be expert enough to identify potential problems. There were also lessons in dealing with stakeholders, in particular tightening relations with contractors and building better relations with the media. The company also needed to keep abreast of changing public attitudes towards risk, with public tolerance of failures in rail safety being, rightly, much lower than twenty to thirty years previously.

So what are likely to be the most significant risks to a business's reputation?

3.14.1 Poor customer service

This risk is likely to arise because of failure to understand **why** the customers buy from the business, how they view the business and what they expect from the business in terms of product quality, speed of delivery and value for money. Early indications of potential reputation risks include **increasing levels** of returns and customer complaints followed inevitably by loss of business.

3.14.2 Failure to innovate

We have discussed this under strategic risks.

3.14.3 Poor ethics

We shall consider ethics in detail in Part E of this text. For now, a poor ethical reputation can have the following consequences:

- Suppliers and customers unwillingness to deal with the organisation for fear of being victims of sharp practice
- Inability to recruit high-quality staff
- Fall in demand because of consumer boycotts
- Increased public relation costs because of adverse stories in the media
- Increased compliance cost because of close attentions from regulatory bodies or external auditors
- Loss of market value because of a fall in investor confidence

Exam focus point

> Reputation risk came up on the Pilot paper, and is likely to be an issue in many scenarios. Since the risks you'll be considering for organisations will often be serious, therefore the threat to organisations' reputation will also be high.

3.15 Industry-specific risks

Key term

> **Industry-specific risks** are the risks of unexpected changes to a business's cash flows from events or changing circumstances in the industry or sector in which the business operates.

Unexpected changes can arise for example due to new technology, a change in the law or a rise or fall in the price of a key commodity.

Question
Significant risks

Try listing as many significant risk areas that you think might be of relevance to major international banks. Try to list at least ten risks.

Answer

There isn't a 'correct' answer to this question, but shown below are the top 18 risks mentioned by senior bankers in a survey of risks in the banking industry, and published by the Centre for the Study of Financial Innovation in March 2005 (*Banana Skins 2005*). This list is not comprehensive, and you might have thought of others.

- Too much regulation
- Credit risk
- Corporate governance
- Complex financial instruments
- Hedge funds
- Fraud
- Currencies
- High dependence on technology
- Risk management techniques

- Macro-economic trends
- Insurance sector problems
- Interest rates
- Money laundering
- Commodities
- Emerging markets
- Grasp of new technology
- Legal risk
- Equity markets

A notable extra was environmental risk which, while positioned low in the overall ranking (28th), was seen to be gaining strongly because of fears about the impact of pollution claims and climate change on bank assets and earnings.

Exam focus point

> In the exam you may be given a scenario of a specific business and asked to identify the risks; some of the most significant risks for that business may be industry specific risks. You may therefore have to use some imagination to identify risks, but don't be too worried about this sort of question; the sector the business operates in is likely to be fairly mainstream, and the risks therefore will not be too esoteric.

Chapter Roundup

- Risks can be classified by **who they affect** and whether they have **positive or negative outcomes**.

- The **level of risk** that an organisation relates to with the **level of return** it desires.

- **Strategic risks** are risks that relate to the fundamental and key decisions that the directors take about the future of the organisation.

- **Operational risks** relate to matters that can go wrong on a day-to-day basis while the organisation is carrying out its business.

- Risks can be **classified** in various ways, including financial, legal, IT, operational, fraud and reputation.

Quick Quiz

1   What is the difference between pure risks and speculative risks?

2   Fill in the blank

    .... risks are risks from which good or harm may result.

3   Risk-averse businesses always seek to minimise the levels of risk that they face.

    True ☐

    False ☐

4   Which of the following would not normally be classified as a strategic risk?

    A   The risk that a new product will fail to find a large enough market

    B   The risk of competitors moving their production to a different country and being able to cut costs and halve sale prices as a result

    C   The risk that a senior manager with lots of experience will be recruited by a competitor

    D   The risk of resource depletion meaning that new sources of raw materials will have to be found

5   What are the major property risks that organisations face?

6   List three business risks that are associated with the Internet.

7   What are the main signs of fraud identified by SAS 110?

8   The level of reputation risk depends significantly on the level of other risks.

    True ☐

    False ☐

Answers to Quick Quiz

1   Pure risks just relate to harmful outcomes whereas speculative risks relate to positive as well as harmful outcomes.

2   Speculative risks

3   False. Risk-averse businesses may be prepared to tolerate risks provided they receive appropriate returns.

4   C The risk that a senior manager with lots of experience will be recruited by a competitor would normally be classified as an operational risk.

5   Damage, destruction or taking of property

6   Hackers accessing the internal network; staff downloading viruses; staff downloading inaccurate information; information being intercepted; the communication link breaking down or distorting data

7   • Previous experience or incidents that call into question the integrity or competence of management
    • Particular financial reporting pressures within an entity
    • Weaknesses in the design and operation of the accounting and internal control systems
    • Unusual transactions or trends
    • Problems in obtaining sufficient audit evidence
    • Information systems factors

8   True, although the threat to reputation also depends on how likely it is that the organisation will suffer bad publicity if risks in other areas materialise.

Now try the question below from the Exam Question Bank

Number	Level	Marks	Time
Q6	Introductory	n/a	45 mins

BPP
LEARNING MEDIA

Risk assessment

Topic list	Syllabus reference
1 Risk analysis	C3
2 Impact of risk on stakeholders	C3
3 Board consideration of risk	C3

Introduction

Having seen the risks that organisations might face, in this chapter we examine how they assess the significance of these risks. In Section 1 we discuss a framework for analysing risks; you may encounter other slightly different frameworks but they all involve the same activities. However, you need to understand that risk analysis has its limitations. As we saw in Chapter 6 risks are not easily categorisable and can arise from all kinds of familiar and unfamiliar sources. Both the probability of the risk materialising and the consequences (hazard) can be difficult to quantify.

To use the results of risk analysis as a basis for taking action involves judgement; we have already seen the impact of stakeholders upon organisations, so it follows that a particular concern for the board and management of organisations will be how their stakeholders judge the risks that the organisation faces.

Provided with the results of the risk analysis and having a hopefully good understanding of stakeholder views, one of the board's most important tasks should be consideration of risks. We look briefly at the key aspects the board will consider in the last section of the chapter.

Study guide

		Intellectual level
C3	**Identification, assessment and measurement of risk**	
(a)	Identify, and assess the impact upon, the stakeholders involved in business risk	3
(b)	Explain and analyse the concepts of assessing the severity and probability of risk events	2
(c)	Describe and evaluate a framework for board level consideration of risk	3

Exam guide

You may be asked to describe the risk analysis framework in the exam, or be given details about particular stakeholders whose views are important.

Most importantly when considering risks described or implied in a scenario, you need to assess the risk probabilities and the hazards (what will happen if the risk materialises). Although you may only be able to do this very roughly, it may well determine which risks you concentrate on in your answer; the more significant the risk, the more depth of discussion will most likely be required.

1 Risk analysis

FAST FORWARD

Risk analysis involves **identifying, assessing, profiling, quantifying and consolidating risks**.

1.1 Analysis framework

A commonly used framework for analysing risk is made up of five stages:

- Identification
- Assessment
- Profiling
- Quantification
- Consolidation

1.2 Risk identification

No-one can manage a risk without first being aware that it exists. Some knowledge of perils, what items they can affect and how, is helpful to improve awareness of whether **familiar risks** (potential sources and causes of loss) are present, and the extent to which they could harm a particular person or organisation. Managers should also keep an eye open for **unfamiliar risks** which may be present.

Actively identifying the risks before they materialise makes it easier to think of methods that can be used to manage them.

Risk identification is a **continuous process**, so that new risks and changes affecting existing risks may be identified quickly and dealt with appropriately, before they can cause unacceptable losses.

1.2.1 Risk conditions

Means of identifying conditions leading to risks (potential sources of loss) include:

(a)   **Physical inspection**, which will show up risks such as poor housekeeping (for example rubbish left on floors, for people to slip on and to sustain fires)

(b)   **Enquiries**, from which the frequency and extent of product quality controls and checks on new employees' references, for example, can be ascertained

(c)   **Checking** a copy of every letter and memo issued in the organisation for early indications of major changes and new projects

(d)   **Brainstorming** with representatives of different departments

(e)   **Checklists** ensuring risk areas are not missed

(f)   **Benchmarking** against other sections within the organisation or external experiences

1.2.2 Event identification

A key aspect of risk identification, emphasised by the Committee of Sponsoring Organisations of the Treadaway Commission's report *Enterprise Risk Management Framework* is identification of events that could impact upon implementation of strategy or achievement of objectives.

Events analysis includes identification of:

(a)   **External events** such as economic changes, political developments or technological advances

(b)   **Internal events** such as equipment problems, human error or difficulties with products

(c)   **Leading event indicators**. By monitoring data correlated to events, organisations identify the existence of conditions that could give rise to an event, for example customers who have balances outstanding beyond a certain length of time being very likely to default on those balances

(d)   **Trends and root causes**. Once these have been identified, management may find that assessment and treatment of causes is a more effective solution than acting on individual events once they occur

(e)   **Escalation triggers**, certain events happening or levels being reached that require immediate action

(f)   **Event interdependencies**, identifying how one event can trigger another and how events can occur concurrently. For example a decision to defer investment in an improved distribution system might mean that downtime increases and operating costs go up

Once events have been identified, they can be **classified** horizontally across the whole organisation and vertically within operating units. By doing this management can gain a better understanding of the interrelationships between events, gaining enhanced information as a basis for risk assessment.

1.3 Risk assessment

It is not always simple to forecast the financial effect of a possible disaster, as it is not until *after* a loss that all the hazards – the extra expenses, inconveniences and loss of time can be recognised. Even then it can be difficult to identify all of them.

Case Study

If your car is stolen, for example, and found converted to a heap of scrap metal, in addition to the cost of replacing it you can expect to pay for some quite **unexpected items**:

(a)   Fares home, and to and from work until you have a replacement

(b)   Telephone calls to the police, your family, your employer, and others affected

(c)   Movement and disposal of the wrecked car

(d)   Increased grocery bills from having to use corner shops instead of a distant supermarket

(e)   Notifications to the licensing authority that you are no longer the owner

(f)   Work you must turn down because you have no car

(g)   Lease charges on the new car because you have insufficient funds to buy one, when all this happens

(h)   Your time (which is difficult to value)

These are all hazards.

1.4 Risk profiling and prioritisation

This stage involves using the results of a risk assessment to group risks into risk families. One way of doing this is a likelihood/consequences matrix.

Consequences (hazard)

	Low	*High*
Low	Loss of suppliers of small scale and unimportant inputs	Loss of key customers Failure of computer systems
		Loss of senior or specialist staff
High	Loss of lower-level staff	Loss of sales to competitor Loss of sales due to macroeconomic factors

Likelihood (risk probability)

This profile can then be used to set priorities for risk mitigation.

This diagram maps two continuums on which risks are plotted. The **nearer the risk is** towards the **bottom right-hand corner** (the high-high corner), the **more important** and the **more strategic** the risk will be. The position of risks can vary over time as environmental conditions vary. The diagram is very similar to Mendelow's stakeholder map covered in Chapter 1, and in that map as well the position of stakeholders can move over time.

The main limitation of this approach is that it rests upon the assumption that both hazard and risk can be quantified or at least ranked.

Although the response to the threat of the millennium bug in the year 2000 is now often dismissed as something of an embarrassment, it does appear to have changed attitudes towards business continuity planning for low likelihood-high consequences risks. It meant that organisations now think more broadly about the possibility of threats like sabotage and consider how their business interacts with customers and suppliers. The Year 2000 threat also meant that organisations have updated technology and systems applications to more current technology and introduced uninterrupted power supply.

Exam focus point

Analysing risks using the likelihood/consequences matrix is a vital technique for your exam.

Case Study

CIMA's guide to risk management provides a list of factors that can help determine in which section of the quadrant the risk is located:

- The importance of the strategic objective to which the risk relates
- The type of risk and whether it represents an opportunity or a threat
- The direct and indirect impact of the risk
- The likelihood of the risk
- The cost of different responses to the risk
- The organisation's environment
- Constraints within the organisation
- The organisation's ability to respond to events

1.5 Risk quantification

Risks that require more analysis can be quantified, where **possible results or losses** and **probabilities** are **calculated** and **distributions** or **confidence limits** added on. From this exercise the organisation can ascertain certain key figures.

- **Average or expected result or loss**
- **Frequency of losses**
- **Chances of losses**
- **Largest predictable loss**

to which the organisation could be exposed by a **particular risk**. The risk manager must also be able to estimate the effects of each possible cause of loss, as some of the effects that he needs to consider may not be insured against.

Exam focus point

The examiner has stated that you won't be expected to carry out calculations using any of these methods in the exam.

The likely **frequency** of losses from any particular cause can be predicted with some degree of confidence, from studying available records. This confidence margin can be improved by including the likely effects of **changed circumstances** in the calculation, once they are identified and quantified. Risk managers must therefore be aware of the possibility of the **increase of an existing risk**, or the **introduction** of a **new risk**, affecting the probability and/or possible frequency of losses from another cause.

Ultimately the risk manager will need to know the **frequency** or **magnitude** of **losses** that could place the organisation in serious difficulties.

1.6 Risk consolidation, risk review and portfolio management

Risk that has been analysed and quantified at the divisional or subsidary level needs to be aggregated to the corporate level and grouped into categories (categorisation). This aggregation will be required as part of the overall review of risk that the board needs to undertake which we shall look at in more detail in later chapters. For now there should be systems in place to:

- **Identify changes in risks** as soon as they occur
- Enable management to **monitor risks regularly**
- Enable managers to carry out a **wider annual review** covering the way the organisation deals with risk

The process of risk categorisation also enables the risks categorised together to be managed by the use of **common control systems**.

2 Impact of risk on stakeholders

FAST FORWARD

Organisations' attitudes to risks will be influenced by the **priorities** of their stakeholders and how much **influence** stakeholders have. Stakeholders that have significant influence may try to prevent an organisation bearing certain risks.

2.1 Stakeholders' attitudes to risk

Businesses have to be aware of **stakeholder responses to risk** – the risk that organisations will take actions or events will occur that will generate a response from stakeholders that has an adverse effect on the business.

To assess the importance of stakeholder responses to risk, the organisation needs to determine how much leverage its stakeholders have over it. As we have seen, Mendelow provides a mechanism for classifying stakeholders that is along the same lines as the risk profiling matrix described above.

2.2 Shareholders

They can affect the **market price of shares** by selling them or they have the **power to remove management**. It would appear that the key issue for management to determine is whether shareholders:

(a) Prefer a **steady income from dividends** (in which case they will be alert to threats to the profits that generate the dividend income such as investment in projects that are unlikely to yield profits in the short-term)

(b) Are **more concerned with long-term capital gains**

2.2.1 Risk tolerances of shareholders

However the position is complicated by the different risk tolerances of shareholders themselves. Some shareholders will, for the chances of higher level of income, be prepared to **bear greater risks** that their investments will not achieve that level of income. Therefore some argue that because the shares of listed companies can be freely bought and sold on stock exchanges, if a company's risk profile changes, its existing shareholders will sell their shares, but the shares will be bought by new investors who prefer the company's new risk profile. The theory runs that it should not matter to the company who its investors are. This theory relates to the capital asset pricing model, which we shall cover in Chapter 8.

However, we have seen that the corporate governance reports have stressed the importance of maintaining links with individual shareholders. It is therefore unlikely that the directors will be indifferent to who the company's shareholders are.

2.3 Debt providers and creditors

Debt providers are most concerned about threats to the amount the organisation owes and can take various actions with potentially serious consequences such as **denial of credit**, higher interest charges or ultimately putting the company into liquidation.

When an organisation is seeking credit or loan finance, it will obviously consider what action creditors will take if it does default. However it also needs to consider the ways in which **debt finance providers** can **limit the risks of default** by for example requiring companies to meet **certain financial criteria**, provide security in the form of assets that can't be sold without the creditors' agreement or personal guarantees from directors.

These mechanisms may have a significant impact on the development of an organisation's strategy. There may be a conflict between strategies that are **suitable** from the viewpoint of the business's long-term strategic objectives, but are **unacceptable** to existing providers of finance or are **not feasible** because finance suppliers will not make finance available for them, or will do so on terms that are unduly restrictive.

2.4 Employees

Employees will be concerned about threats to their **job prospects** (money, promotion, benefits and satisfaction) and ultimately threats to the jobs themselves. They will also be concerned about threats to their personal **well-being**, particularly health and safety issues.

The variety of actions employees can take would appear to indicate the risk is significant. Possible actions include pursuit of their own goals rather than shareholder interests, industrial action, refusal to relocate or resignation.

Risks of adverse reactions from employees will have to be managed in a variety of ways:

- **Risk avoidance** – legislation requires that some risks, principally threats to person, should be avoided

- **Risk reduction** – limiting employee discontent by good pay, conditions etc

- **Risk transfer** – for example taking out insurance against key employees leaving

- **Risk acceptance** – accepting that some employees will be unhappy but believing the company will not suffer a significant loss if they leave

2.5 Customers and suppliers

We have already discussed suppliers in the context of their providing (possibly unwillingly) short-term finance. As well as that suppliers will be concerned about the risk of making unprofitable sales. Customers will be concerned with **threats to their getting the goods or services** that they have been promised, or not getting the **value** from the **goods or services** that they expect.

The impact of customer-supplier attitudes will partly depend on how much the organisation wants to **build long-term relationships** with them. A desire to build relationships implies involvement of the staff who are responsible for building those relationships in the risk management process. It also may imply a **greater degree of disclosure** about risks that may arise to the long-term partners in order to maintain the relationship of trust.

2.6 The wider community

Governments, regulatory and other bodies will be particularly concerned with risks that the organisation does not act as a good corporate citizen, implementing for example **poor employment or environmental policies**. A number of the variety of actions that can be taken could have serious consequences. Government can impose **tax increases or regulation** or take **legal action**. Pressure groups tactics can include **publicity, direct action, sabotage or pressure on government**.

Although the consequences can be serious, the risks that the wider community are concerned about can be rather less easy to predict than for other stakeholders, being governed by varying political pressures. This emphasises the need for careful monitoring as part of the risk management process, of changing attitudes and likely responses to the organisation's actions.

3 Board consideration of risk

FAST FORWARD

> The risks facing an organisation should influence the ways in which the board **develops its internal control systems**. This is a key component of good corporate governance.

3.1 Turnbull guidance

The UK *Guidance on Internal Control* (the Turnbull guidance) laid out a framework for board consideration of risk and internal control. As we have seen, Turnbull stated that when determining its policies on internal control, the board should consider:

- The **nature and extent of the risks** facing the company

- The **extent** and **categories of risk** which it regards as acceptable for the company to bear

- The **likelihood** of the **risks materialising**

- The company's ability to **reduce the incidence and impact** on the business of risks that do materialise

- The **costs** of **operating particular controls** relative to the **benefits obtained** in managing the related risks

3.2 Monitoring in practice

A number of points arise from the Turnbull recommendations:

(a)   Corporate governance best practice requires boards to draw up a **schedule of matters** that should be considered by the board itself; this should include to which risks the board give particular attention.

(b)   Boards will obviously **consider strategic risks**, but this will form part of their overall objectives anyway.

(c)   Boards will also pay most attention to **significant consequences – high likelihood risks**. However this implies confidence that the system of risk assessment will identify these risks, emphasising the need for boards to gain **assurance** on the monitoring process.

3.3 Board review of risk

The Turnbull report recommends that the board should regularly **receive and review reports on risk management and internal control**. Effective monitoring by senior management below board level is essential, but not enough.

Turnbull also recommends that directors should conduct an **annual review** of risk and internal control. This should be wider-ranging than their regular reviews of risk management.

We shall consider board reviews further in Chapter 9.

Case Study

A good example of risk monitoring in action is the briefing documentation that UK Prime Minister James Callaghan required to be sent to him weekly. Callaghan asked to be briefed on small problems that could turn out to be big problems (low likelihood, significant consequences problems) such as a worsening of relationships with Spain over Gibraltar and relationships with Argentina over sovereignty of the Falkland Isles.

The report on internal control that was sent to Prime Minister Callaghan was a map of the world the size of a desk blotter showing the disposition of the Royal Navy's ships. The map demonstrated how long it would take for a significant force of ships to arrive at any potential trouble spot.

One result of this system of risk management was that when Argentina's government started making threatening noises about regaining the sovereignty of the Falklands, Callaghan was able to send the message warning accurately what the consequences would be. As a result, on that occasion the Argentineans backed off.

Chapter Roundup

- **Risk analysis** involves **identifying, assessing, profiling, quantifying and consolidating risks**.

- Organisations' attitudes to risks will be influenced by the **priorities** of their stakeholders and how much **influence** stakeholders have. Stakeholders that have significant influence may try to prevent an organisation bearing certain risks.

- The risks facing an organisation should influence the ways in which the board **develops its internal control systems**. This is a key component of good corporate governance.

Quick Quiz

1   What are the main stages of the risk analysis framework?

2   What does event analysis aim to identify?

3   Give five examples of factors that will determine the chances of a risk materialising and the consequences of materialising.

4   Shareholders' principal concern is always threats to the level of dividend they receive.

    True   ☐
    False   ☐

5   What key indicators should risk quantification provide?

6   According to the Turnbull report, what factors should the board consider when determining their policy on internal control?

7   What risks are the board most likely to be concerned about?

8   How according to the Turnbull report should the board of directors review risks?

Answers to Quick Quiz

1   Identification; Assessment; Profiling; Quantification; Consolidation

2
- External events
- Internal events
- Escalation triggers
- Leading event indicators
- Trends and root causes
- Event interdependencies

3
- The importance of the strategic objective to which the risk relates
- The type of risk and whether it represents an opportunity or a threat
- The direct and indirect impact of the risk
- The likelihood of the risk
- The cost of different responses to the risk
- The organisation's environment
- Constraints within the organisation
- The organisation's ability to respond to events

4   False. Shareholders may prefer to make a long-term capital gain.

5
- Average or expected result
- The frequency of losses
- The chances of loss
- The largest predictable loss

6
- The nature and extent of the risks facing the company
- The extent and categories of risk that it regards as acceptable for the company to bear
- The likelihood of the risk materialising
- The company's ability to reduce the incidence and impact on the business of risks that do materialise
- The costs of operating particular controls relative to the benefits obtained in managing the related risks

7   Strategic, significant consequences-high likelihood risks

8   Regularly reviewing reports on risk management and internal control; conducting a wider-ranging annual review of risk and control.

Now try the question below from the Exam Question Bank

Number	Level	Marks	Time
Q7	Examination	25	45 mins

Part D
Controlling risk

Controlling risk

Topic list	Syllabus reference
1 Risk attitudes	D3
2 Risk management systems	D2
3 Embedding risk awareness and assessment	D2, D3
4 Risk management responsibilities	B1, C1, D1
5 Risk management strategies	D2, D3

Introduction

In this chapter we look at how directors and managers respond to risk, and try
to control risk exposure. The first section highlights that what management
does is not automatic, but is dependent on its appetite for taking risks, which in
turn is affected by various organisational and personal influences.

Sections 2 and 3 build on issues we covered in Chapter 4. Section 2 highlights
the importance of clearly-defined control systems to deal with risk, while
Section 3 deals with the control environment considerations that relate to risk.

In Section 4 we examine the responsibilities of various members of an
organisation for risk management. The larger the organisation, the more likely
it is to have a risk management committee and a specialist risk management
function.

Section 5 covers the various ways in which risk can be dealt with, and is one of
the most important sections in this Text.

Study guide

		Intellectual level
B1	**Internal control and review**	
(d)	Identify, explain and evaluate the corporate governance and executive management roles in risk management (in particular the separation between responsibility for ensuring that adequate risk management systems are in place and the application of risk management systems and practices in the organisation)	3
C1	**Risks and the risk management process**	
(b)	Define and describe management responsibilities in risk management	2
D1	**Targeting and monitoring of risk**	
(a)	Explain the assess the role of a risk manager in identifying and monitoring risk	3
(b)	Explain and evaluate the role of the risk committee in identifying and monitoring risk	3
D2	**Methods of controlling and reducing risks**	
(a)	Explain the importance of risk awareness at all levels of an organisation	2
(b)	Describe and analyse the concept of embedding risk in an organisation's systems and procedures	3
(c)	Describe and evaluate the concept of embedding risks in an organisation's culture and values	3
(d)	Explain and analyse the concepts of spreading and diversifying risk and when this would be appropriate	2
D3	**Risk avoidance, retention and modelling**	
(a)	Define the terms risk avoidance and risk retention	2
(b)	Explain and evaluate the different attitudes to risk and how these can affect strategy	3
(c)	Explain and assess the necessity of incurring risk as part of competitively managing a business organisation	3
(d)	Explain and assess attitudes towards risk and the ways in which risk varies in relation to the size, structure and development of an organisation	3

Exam guide

The chapter contents could be examined in overview (the key features of a good risk management system) or you may be asked more specific questions about various aspects such as the responsibilities of senior management or when different methods of dealing with risk might be appropriate.

1 Risk attitudes

Management responses to risk are not automatic, but will be determined by their **own attitudes to risk**, which in turn may be influenced by **shareholder attitudes** and **cultural factors**.

1.1 Factors influencing risk attitudes

Because risk management is bound up with strategy, how organisations deal with risk will not only be determined by events and the information available about events, but also **management perceptions or willingness** to take risk. These factors will also influence risk **culture**, the values and practices that influence how an organisation deals with risk in its day-to-day operations.

What therefore influences risk attitudes?

1.2 Personal views

Surveys suggest that managers acknowledge the **emotional satisfaction** from successful risk-taking, although this is unlikely to be the most important influence on appetite. Individuals vary in their attitudes to risk and this is likely to be transferred to their roles in organisations.

Case Study

Consider a company such as **Virgin**. It has many stable and successful brands, and healthy cash flows and profits: little need, you would have thought, to consider risky new ventures.

Yet in 2004 Virgin established a new company called **Virgin Galactic** to own and operate privately-built spaceships, and to offer 'affordable' sub-orbital **space tourism to everybody** – or everybody willing to pay US$200,000 for the pleasure. The risks are enormous: developing the project will involve investing very large amounts of money, there is no guarantee that the service is wanted by sufficient numbers of people to make it viable, and the risks of catastrophic accidents are self-evident.

There is little doubt that Virgin's risk appetite derives directly from the risk appetite of its chief executive, Richard Branson – a self-confessed adrenaline junkie – who also happens to own most parts of the Virgin Group privately, and so faces little pressure from shareholders.

1.3 Response to shareholder demand

Shareholders demand a **level of return** that is consistent with taking a certain level of risk. Managers will respond to these expectations by viewing risk-taking as a key part of decision-making.

Case Study

To some extent it must be true that risk appetite is allied to **need**. If Company A is cash rich in a stable industry with few competitors and satisfied shareholders it has little need to take on any more risky activities. If, a few years later, a significant number of competitors have entered the market and Company A's profits start to be eroded then it will **need** to do something to stop the rot, and it will face demands for change from investors.

A classic example is Marks and Spencer. For decades M&S was regarded as a British institution. The brand never traded on cutting-edge trends, but it did stand for quality, even a kind of 'posh-ness'. Consumers were not distracted by the likes of Topshop, New Look, Monsoon, Next, and so on because they either hadn't been thought of or they existed in a very different formula from their modern incarnations. M&S was considered a safe and highly stable investment, and there is little doubt that it became complacent. In the late 1990s M&S profits declined sharply and since then a number of management teams have attempted to restore its fortunes, so far with mixed success. That is to say the fortunes of the company have forced it to adjust its risk appetite.

1.4 Organisational influences

Organisational influences may be important, and these are not necessarily just a response to shareholder concerns. Organisational attitudes may be influenced by **significant losses** in the past, **changes in regulation and best practice**, or even **changing views** of the benefits risk management can bring.

Attitudes to risk will also depend on the **size, structure and stage of development** of the organisation.

(a)   A **larger organisation** is likely to require more **formal systems** and will have to take account of **varying risk appetites** and **incidence** amongst its operations. However a large organisation will also be able to justify employing risk specialists, either generally or in specific areas of high risk such as treasury.

(b)   The risk management systems employed will be dependent on the organisation's management control systems that will depend on the formality of **structure**, the autonomy given to local operations and the degree of centralisation deemed desirable.

(c)   Attitudes to risk will change as the **organisation develops** and its **risk profile changes**; for example attitudes to financial risk and gearing will change as different sources of finance become necessary to fund larger developments.

1.5 National influences

There is some evidence that national culture influences attitudes towards risk and uncertainty. Surveys suggest that attitudes to risk vary nationally according to how much people are shielded from the consequences of adverse events.

1.6 Cultural influences

Adams argued that there are four viewpoints that are key determinants in how risk is viewed.

(a)   **Fatalists** see themselves as having no control over their own lives and hence risk management is pointless; nothing they can do can make any difference to a situation.

(b)   **Hierarchists** can exist in most organisations, but are most likely to exist in a bureaucratic organisation, with formal structures and procedures. They are likely to emphasise risk reduction through formal risk management procedures including research to establish the facts, increased regulation, and an emphasis on risk reduction, avoidance and discouraging risk-taking behaviour.

(c)   **Individualists** seek to control their environment rather than let their environment control them. They will often be found in small single-person dominated organisations with less formal structures, and hence risk management too will be informal, if indeed it is considered at all.

(d)   **Egalitarians** are loyal to groups but have little respect for procedures. They are often found in charities and public sector, non-profit making activities. Their preference will be for sharing of risks as widely as possible, or transfer of risks to those best able to bear them.

1.7 Risk thermostat

Adams illustrated the links between perceptions of risk, influences on risk taking, and results of risk-taking by a risk thermostat.

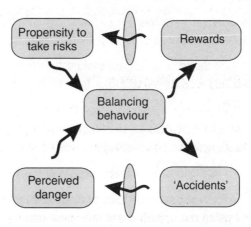

Source: **J Adams**, *Risk*

1.8 Entrepreneurial risk

Key term

> **Entrepreneurial risk** is the risk that is integral to the pursuit of business opportunities.

Whatever the other influences affecting management attitudes, boards of businesses have to bear some risks if they are to succeed in business. Risk is bound up with entrepreneurship, the factor of production that relates to competitively managing an organisation.

Surveys have found that there are different types of **entrepreneurial risk** and that entrepreneurs may have different attitudes to each type. Wu and Knott's 2005 paper *Entrepreneurial risk and market entry* suggested that entrepreneurial attitudes were affected by two types of uncertainty:

- Uncertainty regarding market demand
- Uncertainty regarding their own entrepreneurial ability

Entrepreneurs tended to be risk-averse as far as demand uncertainty was concerned. However they were overconfident with respect to ability uncertainty. Some commentators have claimed that this reflects a distinguishing feature of entrepreneurs, their level of confidence in being able to handle unforeseen events. This appears to relate to entrepreneurial belief that they **have a high level of control** over events of their lives, **including their own success or failure.** (They are individualists who have an internal locus of control, a concept that we shall discuss in connection with ethics).

Case Study

Risk-taking: is it behavioural, genetic, or learned?

Behaviour of individuals

Risky business has never been more popular. Mountain climbing is among the fastest growing sports. Extreme skiing – in which skiers descend cliff-like runs by dropping from ledge to snow-covered ledge – is drawing ever-wider interest. The adventurer-travel business, which often mixes activities like climbing or river rafting with wildlife safaris, has grown into a **multimillion-dollar** industry.

Under conventional personality theories, **normal individuals** do everything possible to **avoid tension and risk**, and in the not-too-distant past, students of human behaviour might have explained such activities as an abnormality, a kind of death-wish. But in fact researchers are discovering that the psychology of risk involves far more than a simple 'death wish'. Studies now indicate that the inclination to take high risks may be **hard-wired into the brain**, intimately linked to **arousal and pleasure mechanisms**, and may offer such a thrill that it functions like an addiction. The tendency probably affects **one in five** people, mostly young males, and declines with age.

It may **ensure our survival**, even **spur our evolution** as individuals and as a species. Risk taking probably bestowed a crucial evolutionary advantage, inciting the fighting and foraging of the hunter-gatherer.

In mapping out the mechanisms of risk, psychologists hope to do more than explain why people climb mountains. **Risk-taking**, which one researcher defines as **'engaging in any activity with an uncertain outcome'** arises in nearly all walks of life.

Asking someone on a date, accepting a **challenging work assignment**, raising a sensitive issue with a spouse or a friend, **confronting an abusive boss** – these all involve uncertain outcomes, and present some level of risk.

High risk-takers

Researchers don't yet know precisely how a risk-taking impulse arises **from within** or what role is played by **environmental factors**, from **upbringing** to the **culture** at large. And, while some level of risk taking is clearly necessary for survival (try crossing a busy street without it!), scientists are divided as to whether, in a modern society, a **'high-risk gene'** is still advantageous.

Some scientists see a willingness to take big risks as **essential for success**, but research has also revealed the **darker side** of risk taking. High-risk takers are easily bored and may suffer low job satisfaction. Their craving for stimulation can make them more likely to abuse drugs, gamble, commit crimes, and be **promiscuous**.

Indeed, this peculiar form of dissatisfaction could help explain the explosion of high-risk sports in post-industrial Western nations. In **unstable cultures**, such as those **at war** or **suffering poverty**, people rarely seek out additional thrills. But in rich and safety-obsessed countries, full of guardrails, seat belts, and with personal-injury claims companies swamping TV advertising, **everyday life may have become too safe, predictable, and boring** for those programmed for risk-taking.

Until recently, researchers were baffled. Psychoanalytic theory and learning theory relied heavily on the notion of **stimulus reduction**, which saw all human motivation geared toward eliminating tension. Behaviours that created tension, such as risk taking, were deemed **dysfunctional**, masking anxieties or feelings of inadequacy.

Yet as far back as the 1950s, research was hinting at alternative explanations. British psychologist Hans J Eysenck developed a scale to measure the personality trait of **extroversion**, now one of the most consistent predictors of risk taking. Other studies revealed that, contrary to Freud, the brain not only **craved arousal**, but somehow regulated that arousal at an optimal level. Researchers have extended these early findings into a host of **theories about risk taking**.

Some scientists concentrate on risk taking primarily as a **cognitive or behavioural** phenomenon, an element of a larger personality dimension which measures individuals' sense of **control over their environment** and their willingness to **seek out challenges**.

A second line of research focuses on risk's **biological** roots. Due to relatively low levels of certain **enzymes and neurotransmitters** the cortical system of a risk taker can handle higher levels of stimulation without overloading and switching to the fight-or-flight response. Their brains automatically dampen the level of incoming stimuli, leaving them with a kind of excitement deficit. The brains of people who don't like taking risks, by contrast, tend to augment incoming stimuli, and thus desire less excitement.

Even then, enzymes are only part of the risk-taking picture. **Upbringing, personal experience, socio-economic status, and learning** are all crucial in determining how that risk-taking impulse is ultimately expressed. For many climbers their interest in climbing was often **shaped externally**, either through contact with older climbers or by reading about great expeditions. Upon entering the sport, novices are often immersed in a tight-knit climbing **subculture, with its own lingo, rules of conduct, and standards of excellence**.

This **learned** aspect may be the most important element in the formation of the risk-taking personality.

This is much abridged and somewhat adapted from an article in Psychology Today.

Behaviour of organisations

To what extent can these ideas be **applied to organisations?** The case study indicates that the tendency to take risks or not depends on cognitive psychological factors (willingness to take on challenges), and genetic factors (the relative absence of certain chemicals in the brain that suppress the fear that most people feel when confronted with risk). None of this makes much sense when talking about an abstract non-living thing like a company, which exists only on paper and in the eyes of the law.

But the case study also indicates that upbringing, personal experience, socio-economic status, and learning play a part and that risk-takers tend to be immersed in a subculture, with its own language, rules of conduct, and standards of excellence.

Equally, organisations have a history and have unique experiences, and are wealthy or struggling. They set rules of conduct and standards of excellence. Their people possess knowledge and talk in organisational jargon. This is commonly called the organisation's **culture**.

Exam focus point

> Remember that in many instances response to risk won't be clearcut, and so you may need to suggest that the response may ultimately depend on how much risk managers are willing to tolerate.

2 Risk management systems

FAST FORWARD

Enterprise risk management provides a coherent framework for organisations to deal with risk, based on the following components:

- Internal environment
- Objective setting
- Event identification
- Risk assessment
- Risk response
- Control activities
- Information and communication
- Monitoring

2.1 Nature of enterprise risk management

Key term

> **Enterprise risk management** is a process, effected by an entity's board of directors, management and other personnel, applied in strategy setting and across the enterprise, designed to identify potential events that may affect the entity and manage risks to be within its risk appetite, to provide reasonable assurance regarding the achievement of entity objectives.
>
> **COSO**

The Committee of Sponsoring Organisations of the Treadway Commission (COSO) goes on to expand its definition. It states that enterprise risk management has the following characteristics.

(a) It is a **process**, a means to an end, that should ideally be intertwined with existing operations and exist for fundamental business reasons.

(b) It is operated by **people at every level** of the organisation and is not just paperwork. It provides a mechanism helping people to understand risk, their responsibilities and levels of authority.

(c) It is applied in **strategy setting,** with management considering the risks in alternative strategies.

(d) It is applied **across the enterprise.** This means it takes into account activities at all levels of the organisation from enterprise-level activities such as strategic planning and resource allocation, to business unit activities and business processes. It includes taking an entity level portfolio view of risk. Each unit manager assesses the risk for his unit. Senior management ultimately consider these unit risks and also **interrelated risks.** Ultimately they will assess whether the overall risk portfolio is consistent with the organisation's risk appetite.

(e) It is designed to **identify events** potentially affecting the entity and manage risk within its **risk appetite,** the amount of risk it is prepared to accept in pursuit of value. The risk appetite should be aligned with the desired return from a strategy.

(f) It provides **reasonable assurance** to an entity's management and board. Assurance can at best be reasonable since risk relates to the uncertain future.

(g) It is geared to the **achievement of objectives** in a number of categories, including **supporting** the **organisation's mission**, making **effective and efficient use** of the **organisation's resources**, ensuring **reporting is reliable**, and **complying** with **applicable laws and regulations.**

Because these characteristics are broadly defined, they can be applied across different types of organisations, industries and sectors. Whatever the organisation, the framework focuses on **achievement of objectives.**

An approach based on **objectives** contrasts with a **procedural approach** based on rules, codes or procedures. A procedural approach aims to eliminate or control risk by requiring conformity with the rules. However a procedural approach cannot eliminate the possibility of risks arising because of poor management decisions, human error, fraud or unforeseen circumstances arising.

2.2 Framework of enterprise risk management

The COSO framework consists of eight interrelated components.

Component	Explanation
Internal or control environment (Chapter 4)	This covers the tone of an organisation, and sets the basis for how risk is viewed and addressed by an organisation's people, including risk management philosophy and risk appetite, integrity and ethical values, and the environment in which they operate.
Objective setting (see below)	Objectives for the entity should be in place and the chosen objectives should support and align with the entity's mission and be consistent with its risk appetite.
Event identification (Chapter 7)	Both internal and external events which affect the achievement of an entity's objectives must be identified, distinguishing between risks and opportunities.
Risk assessment (Chapter 7)	Risks are analysed, considering likelihood and impact, as a basis for determining how they should be managed.

Component	Explanation
Risk response (see below)	Management selects risk responses such as avoidance, reduction, transfer, or acceptance which are used to develop a set of actions to align risks with the entity's risk tolerances and risk appetite.
Control activities or procedures (Chapter 4)	Policies and procedures are established and implemented to help ensure the risk responses are effectively carried out.
Information and communication (Chapter 9)	Relevant information is identified, captured and communicated in a form and timeframe that enable people to carry out their responsibilities. Effective communication should be broad – flowing up, down and across the entity. There should also be effective communication with third parties such as shareholders and regulators.
Monitoring (Chapter 7)	Risk management processes are monitored and modifications are made if necessary.

Diagrammatically all of the above may be summarised as follows.

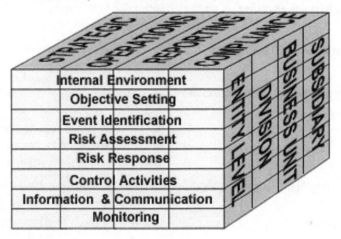

 Case Study

Different commentators have developed guidance on enterprise risk management in different ways. Arthur Andersen, as was, argued that enterprise risk management must begin with the following actions:

- Establishing an oversight structure
- Defining a common language and framework
- Targeting risks and processes
- Establishing goals, objectives and a uniform process
- Assessing risk management capability

Ernst and Young identified six components of risk management:

- Risk strategy
- Risk management processes
- Appropriate culture and capability
- Risk management functions
- Enabling technologies
- Governance

2.2.1 Objective setting

Enterprise risk management emphasises the importance of **setting strategic objectives** at entity and activity levels and **identifying critical success factors,** which feed into operations, reporting and compliance objectives.

2.3 Benefits of enterprise risk management

COSO highlights a number of advantages of adopting the process of enterprise risk management.

Alignment of risk appetite and strategy	The framework demonstrates to managers the need to consider risk toleration. They then set objectives aligned with business strategy and develop mechanisms to manage the accompanying risks and to ensure risk management becomes part of the culture of the organisation, embedded into all its processes and activities.
Link growth, risk and return	Risk is part of value creation, and organisations will seek a given level of return for the level of risk tolerated.
Choose best risk response	Enterprise risk management helps the organisation select whether to reduce, eliminate or transfer risk.
Minimise surprises and losses	By identifying potential loss-inducing events, the organisation can reduce the occurrence of unexpected problems.
Identify and manage risks across the organisation	As indicated above, the framework means that managers can understand and aggregate connected risks. It also means that risk management is seen as everyone's responsibility, experience and practice is shared across the business and a common set of tools and techniques is used.
Provide responses to multiple risks	For example risks associated with purchasing, over and under supply, prices and dubious supply sources might be reduced by an inventory control system that is integrated with suppliers.
Seize opportunities	By considering events as well as risks, managers can identify opportunities as well as losses.
Rationalise capital	Enterprise risk management allows management to allocate capital better and make a sounder assessment of capital needs.

2.4 Risk architecture

In their 1999 report *Enhancing shareholder wealth by better managing business risk* the International Federation of Accountants (IFAC) argued for the development of a **risk architecture** within which risk management processes could be developed. The architecture involves designing and implementing **organizational structures**, **systems** and **processes to manage risk**. This is a slightly different framework to that of enterprise risk management.

IFAC argued that developing a risk architecture is not just a response to risk but marks an organisational shift, changing the way the organisation:

- Organises itself
- Assigns accountability
- Builds risk management as a core competency
- Implements continuous, real-time risk management

Best practice, IFAC argued, is to develop a highly integrated approach to risk management, using a common language, shared tools and techniques and periodic assessments of the risk profile for the entire organisation. Integration is particularly important when most units have **many risks in common**, and when there is **significant interdependency** between units. It is vital when managers are trying to achieve a **shared corporate vision**.

The risk architecture developed by IFAC has eight components:

- Acceptance of a risk management framework
- Commitment from executives
- Establishment of a risk response strategy
- Assignment of responsibility for risk management process
- Resourcing
- Communication and training
- Reinforcing risk cultures through human resources mechanisms
- Monitoring of the risk management process

IFAC identified four components of risk management:

- **Structure** to facilitate the identification and communication of risk
- **Resources** – sufficient to support implementation
- **Culture** – reinforcing decision-making processes
- **Tools and techniques** developed to enable organisation-wide management of risk

2.5 Other frameworks

CIMA's suggested approach to risk management is illustrated in the diagram below. It is based on the idea of **continual feedback** that is inherent in management control systems; that feedback on issues and problems results in improvements in the risk management process.

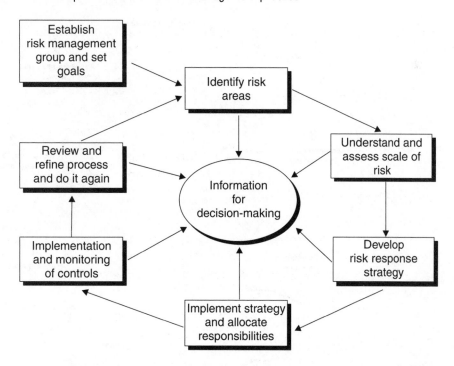

For comparative purposes, the risk management process described in the UK IRM/AIRMIC/ ALARM *Risk Management Standard* may be summarised diagrammatically as follows.

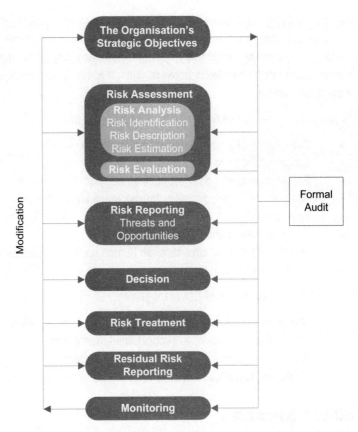

The Canadian *Integrated Risk Management Framework* summarises the process like this.

The *Australian and New Zealand Standard on Risk Management* looks like this.

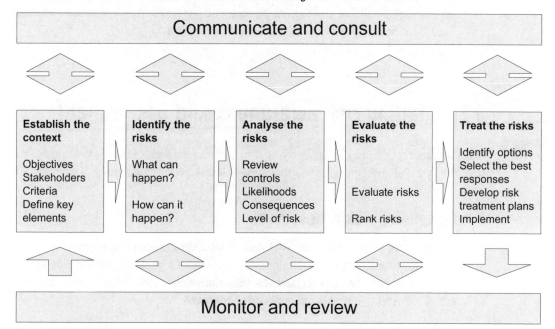

Question

Diagrams

You may find it helpful to look at each of the diagrams above and try to find the similarities and differences. This will help to fix the process in your mind.

Question

Risk management techniques

Risk management techniques can be applied in any type of organisation, although they are more commonly associated with large companies.

If you were involved in the management of a secondary school (a school for children between the ages of 11-18), what might be some of the risks that you would need to consider and adopt a policy for managing?

Answer

Of course there is no definitive solution to this question. In no particular order a list of risks to be assessed might include:

- The risk of failing to attract sufficient numbers of students
- The risk of poor examination results
- The risk of inadequate numbers of students going on to higher education
- The risk of focusing too much on academic subjects, and ignoring broader aspects of education
- Physical security: risks to students, teachers and school property
- The risk of theft of individuals' property
- Inability to recruit sufficient teachers
- Not having enough money to spend on essential or desirable items
- The risk of an adverse report from school inspectors

- The risk of an adverse report on the quality of school meals! (This is a little tongue in cheek, but a serious point could be made, given the recent adverse publicity given to school dinners in the UK and the impact on pupils' concentration and behaviour.)

3 Embedding risk awareness and assessment

Risk assessment should be embedded within an organisation's **processes, environment, culture, structure and systems**. Organisations should **issue a risk policy statement** and **maintain a risk register**.

3.1 Embedding risk assessment

The Ernst and Young report *Managing Risk Across the Enterprise* emphasises that risk assessment should evolve into a consistent, embedded activity within a company's strategic, business, budget and audit planning process rather than be executed as a significant stand-alone process. Ernst and Young identifies a number of elements of a **consistent, embedded approach**.

3.1.1 Focus on risk to stakeholder/shareholder value

The Ernst and Young report states that an embedded approach needs to focus not on risks to processes but on **risks to shareholder value**:

'Identifying these risks and ensuring that they are properly managed ... and appropriately monitored.

Share value is driven by looking at risks in two key areas; **future growth opportunities** and **core business operations**.

(a) **Future growth opportunities**

These are strategies and objectives that the organisation pursues to **increase competitive advantage** and **shareholder value** over time. Ernst and Young argues that risks to realising these opportunities are often overlooked. However the solution is simple; since future growth opportunities and supporting actions are described in external reports and internal planning documents, all that is required is to identify the most significant risks preventing achievement of these objectives.

(b) **Core business operations**

These comprise the assets and processes in the company that **generate or support the largest proportion of profit or revenues**. Organisations should identify the key risks inherent in these processes. They should also identify processes that are significantly risky and place a substantial portion of capital of risk, but may not generate significant revenues or profits (for example financial derivative trading).

3.1.2 Consistent action-oriented risk assessment criteria

Ernst and Young suggests the criteria used should **direct and drive monitoring and improvement actions**, also **focus and accountability**. For this to happen, the report emphasises that as well as considering impact and likelihood, organisations should also focus on management response to risk. This will drive the potential improvement or assurance actions.

3.1.3 Common reporting elements and style

Reporting of risks should be **consistent** across processes and functions, fully **support board needs**, be concise and be updated routinely.

3.2 Internal environment

The internal environment is an essential element of the risk management approach defined in the COSO Guide *Enterprise Risk Management – Integrated Framework*. It encompasses the tone of an organisation, and sets the basis for how risk is viewed and addressed. It includes:

- Risk management philosophy
- Risk appetite
- Integrity
- Ethical values
- The environment in which they operate

3.3 Risk culture

Key term

> **Culture** is 'the pattern of basic assumptions that a given group has invented, discovered, or developed, in learning to cope with its problems of external adaptation and internal integration, and that have worked well enough to be considered valid and, therefore, to be taught to new members as the correct way to perceive, think and feel in relation to these problems.' Schien

 Case Study

Learning a culture

Suppose you get a new job that involves operating a machine of some kind. Your induction training taught you that you are expected to spend 15 minutes at the beginning of every production session (morning and afternoon) carrying out routine maintenance on the machine you operate: checking the oil levels, looking out for wear and tear, making sure all the parts are in alignment and properly sharp, and so on. The detailed checks to do are set out in your new department's procedures manual.

Of course you will diligently do all this on your first few days, but let's suppose you quickly become aware that the other machine operators around you start productive work long before you do, and are laughing at you for being so cautious.

By Wednesday lunchtime you have received a visit from your manager who wants to know why your daily output is so much lower than that of the other members of the team. You are also concerned about this because along with your basic pay you are paid a small bonus for every job that you finish, and your colleagues seem to produce far more per day than you do.

You explain that you are just doing what you were taught to do in induction but the manager takes you aside and explains that the more experienced operators 'know' when their machines need oiling or adjusting and so on, just from the sound they make and how much they vibrate, and you will soon get to know too. The manager admits that if machines are not properly maintained there is a risk that they will be seriously damaged and production will be lost. But the manager also says that if your machine goes wrong you won't actually be seriously affected anyway: you will get the rest of the day off, on whatever is your average day's pay, while it is being fixed. So, 'between you and your manager', it is actually in your interests to produce as much as you possibly can, and ignore your supposed maintenance responsibilities.

The manager then mentions that a more senior manager has asked the department to fulfil an unusually large order that week, and your relative lack of productivity may mean that the more senior manager is let down.

By Wednesday afternoon, at the latest, you will probably have concluded that your supposed routine maintenance responsibilities are not actually necessary at all and will get on with productive work immediately. Perhaps you will be looking around to see if, when, and why your colleagues get the oil can out, if they ever do, but you will care a lot less about your machine going wrong.

Question

What organisational problems are revealed by the case study above?

Answer

The procedures laid down are probably inappropriate: the people who actually do the job understand the risks far better than the people who devised the induction training and the people who wrote the procedures manual.

The motivation and rewards system is badly designed: for experienced machine operators the risk is that they will lose a small amount of bonus, but even if they do they get a day off.

For the company the risk is lost production and extra expense on repairing machines that have not been as well maintained as they should have been.

'You' (the new employee) are a problem, though this is harsh: strictly you should have reported the fact that you were being pressured into doing something that was in breach of official procedures, but this is very hard. Most people tend to try to fit in, at least at first. In any case, who would you report to?

You may have had additional ideas.

3.4 Types of culture

Different writers have identified different types of culture, based on particular aspects of organisation and management. Knowledge of some of the most prominent ideas may be helpful in tackling exam questions both on risk management in general and on corporate governance.

3.4.1 Miles and Snow: strategic cultures

Miles and Snow identify three 'superior performing' cultures.

(a) **Defenders.** Firms with this culture like low risks, secure markets, and tried and trusted solutions. These companies have cultures whose stories and rituals reflect historical continuity and consensus. Decision taking is relatively formalised. (There is a stress on 'doing things right', that is, efficiency.)

(b) **Prospectors** are organisations where the dominant beliefs are more to do with results (doing the right things, that is, effectiveness), and therefore prospectors take risks.

(c) **Analysers** try to balance risk and profits. They use a core of stable products and markets as a source of earnings to move into innovative prospector areas. Analysers follow change, but do not initiate it.

(d) **Reactors**, unlike the three above, do not have viable strategies. Arguably, they do not have a strategy at all, unless it is simply to carry on living from hand to mouth, muddling through.

3.4.2 Deal and Kennedy: risk, feedback and reward

Deal and Kennedy (*Corporate Cultures*) consider cultures to be a function of the level of **risks** that **employees** need to take, and how quickly they get **feedback** on whether they got it right or wrong and/or rewards for doing so.

	Risk	
	Low	High
Rapid	Work hard, play hard culture	Tough guy macho culture
Slow	Process culture	Bet your company culture
	Low	High
	Risk	

(Feedback and reward — Rapid / Slow shown on both left and right sides)

(a) **Low risk cultures**

(i) **Process culture**

The process culture occurs in organisations where there is low risk and little or no feedback. People become bogged down with how things are done, not with what is to be achieved. This is often associated with **bureaucracies**. Whilst it is easy to criticise these cultures for being over-cautious or bogged down in red tape, they do produce consistent results, which is ideal in, for example, public services, banking and insurance.

(ii) **Work hard, play hard culture**

This culture is characterised by few risks being taken, all with rapid feedback. This is typical in large organisations such as retailers which strive for high quality customer service. They are often characterised by team meetings, jargon and buzzwords.

(b) **High risk cultures**

(i) **Bet your company culture**

In the bet your company culture big stakes decisions are taken, but it may be years before the results are known. Typically, these might involve development or exploration projects, which take years to come to fruition, such as could be expected with oil exploration, development of drugs or aircraft manufacturers.

(ii) **Tough-guy macho culture**

Feedback is quick and the risks and rewards are high. This often applies to fast-moving financial activities such as brokerage, but could also apply to the police, athletes competing in team sports, advertising and certain types of construction. This can be a very stressful culture in which to operate.

3.4.3 Handy: power, role, task and person cultures

Charles Handy discusses four cultures and their related structures.

(a)   A **Power culture** that concentrates power in a few pairs of hands. Control radiates from the centre like a web. Power cultures have few rules and little bureaucracy; swift decisions can be taken.

(b)   In a **Role culture**, people have clearly delegated authorities within a highly defined structure. Typically, these organisations form hierarchical bureaucracies. Power derives from a person's position and little scope exists for expert power.

(c)   By contrast, in a **Task culture**, teams form to solve particular problems. Power derives from expertise so long as a team requires expertise. These cultures often feature the multiple reporting lines of a matrix structure.

(d)   In a **Person culture** the individual and individual talent is the central focus. If however it is appropriate, the assumption is that people will contribute out of a sense of commitment to a group or organisation of which they feel they are truly members and in which they have a personal stake. Examples of this culture are universities, barristers, architects, and doctors.

 Case Study

Cultures to manage different risks

Handy acknowledges that different cultures may exist in different parts of the organisation, and in different circumstances, in order to best manage the sort of risks that may arise in different parts of the organisation.

For example an airline operates and maintains aircraft and gets passengers from one place to another. It would be reasonable in this case to assume that engineering is essentially a **Role** culture, and administration, accounting and the administrative parts of personnel should be so too. The customer-facing divisions should be essentially **Task** cultures, getting passengers and planes to their destinations on time, to quality and budget. The (non-executive) board and possibly some other parts of the organisation such as training/people development, should perhaps be **Person** cultures. But when crises hit there is likely to be an ultimate **Power** culture based on the dominant personalities, who will take the toughest decisions. Hopefully this will be the board.

(Adapted from Garratt, *The Fish Rots from the Head* (2003))

3.5 Changing a culture

3.5.1 Risk awareness and communication

In the first place people cannot be expected to avoid risks if they are not aware that they exist in the first place. Embedding a risk management frame of mind into an organisation's culture requires top-down communications on what the risk philosophy is and what is expected of the organisation's people.

Here is an example of an internal communications programme slightly adapted from an example in the COSO *Framework*.

Internal communications programme

- Management discusses risks and associated risk responses in regular briefings with employees.

- Management regularly communicates entity-wide risks in employee communications such as newsletters, an intranet.

- Enterprise risk management policies, standards, and procedures are made readily available to employees along with clear statements requiring compliance.

- Management requires employees to consult with others across the organisation as appropriate when new events are identified.

- Induction sessions for new employees include information and literature on the company's risk management philosophy and enterprise risk management programme.

- Existing employees are required to take workshops and/or refresher courses on the organisation's enterprise risk management initiatives.

- The risk management philosophy is reinforced in regular and ongoing internal communication programmes and through specific communication programmes to reinforce tenets of the company's culture.

The COSO framework also recommends certain organisational measures for spreading ownership of risk management.

(a)   Enterprise risk management should be an explicit or implicit part of **everyone's job description**.

(b)   Personnel should understand the need to **resist pressure from superiors to participate in improper activities**, and **channels outside normal reporting lines** should be available to permit reporting such circumstances.

3.5.2 Training and involvement

Training is of course essential, especially for new employees and for all when new procedures are introduced. Aside from practical matters like showing employees which buttons to press or how to find out the information they need, training should include **explanation** of why things are done in the way that they are. If employees are asked to carry out a new type of check but are **not told why** there is every chance that **they won't bother** to do it, because they don't understand its relevance: it just seems to mean more work for them and to slow up the process for everyone.

The people who are expected to own risks and risk management will be more inclined to do so if they are **involved** in the process of identifying risks in the first place and in developing responses and controls. This enhances understanding and gives them a stake in risk management.

3.5.3 Changing attitudes

The biggest problems are likely to arise when a risk culture already exists but has become inappropriate and needs to be changed. Some people embrace change and thrive on it, but many resist it. There may be a variety of reasons.

(a)   Change involves the **extra effort** of 'unlearning' old knowledge and the learning of new knowledge.

(b)   **Self-interest** may be a factor: a new procedure may entail the involvement of another person or department and be seen as an erosion of power.

(c)   People may **misunderstand** the nature of the change.

(d)   Staff may simply **mistrust** management.

(e)   Employees may **not agree** that the change is needed.

Coercion and autocratic methods may be necessary on occasions, especially when time is limited, but in the longer term **resistance must be overcome** if people are ever to accept ownership of risk management. As usual, **communication** and **dialogue** are key to this. Here are some other possible methods.

(a)   **Incentives**

Those driving the change must identify what constitutes job satisfaction for the relevant group in the organisation and provide incentives as appropriate. This may entail setting performance targets and tying results to performance pay. Rewards must be tied to actions that **promote the new practices and behaviours.**

(b)   **Learning experiences**

A change is more likely to be accepted if people have the **opportunity to experience** first hand what it means for them in a 'safe' environment that allows them to make mistakes and to experiment and ask questions to resolve personal concerns. It is often useful to involve people from other parts of the organisation who have already made the transition and can help ease the fears of those who have yet to experience it.

(c)   **Key personnel**

Some individuals are more important than others, for example, individuals with significant **power to disrupt**, individuals with important **technical expertise**, or individuals whose **influence** over other people is significant. These people need to be persuaded to buy in to the change as a first priority.

(d)   **Infrastructure**

Change – especially sudden change – is often hampered because staff do not have adequate tools. For example it may be **more difficult to obtain the information** needed, or staff may have to override old software controls while programs are being rewritten. These are problems that need to be addressed as soon as possible.

 Case Study

Writing in *Risk Management* magazine, Gayle Tollifson, chief risk officer at QBE Insurance Company, emphasises the importance of culture. She comments that in a number of corporate collapses, the tone or culture that boards set for their companies was flawed or ignored; in many instances boards were not aware of problems until too late.

Tollifson emphasises the board's responsibility to ensure the right culture exists at all levels of an organisation. At the board level selecting a chief executive who embraces the company's cultural values is vital, and board-approved policies and standards must lead the way in risk management practice. Communication is also important. This includes a risk management policy, ensuring the right mechanisms are in place for disclosing issues and that there is a culture of disclosure. This must mean sending a message to staff that the sooner bad news is identified and reported, the sooner the problem can be solved.

As well as embedding risk into the culture, Tollifson explains that companies need to ensure that risk management is an essential part of business operations, considered as part of doing business **every day**. Risk appetite needs to be considered when overall strategy and policy are set; risk analysis must form a key part of the business planning framework.

Tollifson also stresses that whilst a risk management team can make a significant contribution, the board must set the culture entrenching risk awareness, disclosure and transparency; the business managers who create risks must also take responsibility for managing them.

3.6 Risk policy statement

Organisations ought to have a statement of risk policy and strategy that is distributed to all managers and staff and covers the following areas:

- Definitions of risk and risk management
- Objectives of risk policy
- Regulatory requirements
- Benefits of risk management
- How risk management is linked into strategic decision-making and performance
- What areas of risk management (risk avoidance, risk reduction) are particularly important
- Risk classification
- Roles of board, managers, staff and audit and risk committees
- Internal control framework and important controls
- Other tools and techniques
- Assurance reporting
- Role of training
- How to obtain help

3.7 Risk register

Organisations should have formal methods of collecting together information on risk and response. A risk register **lists and prioritises the main risks** an organisation faces, and is used as the basis for decision-making on how to deal with risks. The register also details **who is responsible for dealing** with risks and the **actions taken**. The register should show the risk levels **before** and **after** control action is taken, to facilitate a cost-benefit analysis of controls.

 Case Study

The Ernst and Young report recommends a simpler key risk summary report, ideally fitting on a single page and covering

- Risk type (financial, operations, compliance and strategic)
- Risk description
- Overall ratings (impact, likelihood, control effectiveness)
- Key risk management activities
- Monitoring approach and results
- Gaps, issues and actions
- Risk owner/ Accountable party
- Processes, initiatives and objectives affected

4 Risk management responsibilities

The **board** has overall responsibility for **risk management** as an essential part of its corporate governance responsibilities. Responsibilities below board level will depend on the extent of delegation to **line managers** and whether there is a **separate risk management function**.

4.1 Responsibilities for risk management

Everyone who works for the organisation has responsibilities for risk management, not just risk specialists whose roles we shall discuss below.

4.1.1 The board

As we have seen, the board's role in managing risk is one of its most important. The board is responsible for **determining risk management strategy and monitoring risks** as part of its responsibility for the organisation's overall strategy and its responsibilities to shareholders and other stakeholders. It is also responsible for **setting appropriate policies on internal controls** and **seeking assurance** that the internal control system is **functioning effectively**. It should also communicate the organisation's strategy to employees.

4.1.2 Risk management committee

Boards also need to consider whether there should be a separate board committee, with responsibility for monitoring and supervising risk identification and management. If the board doesn't have a separate committee, under the UK Combined Code the audit committee will be responsible for risk management.

As we have seen consideration of risk certainly falls within the remit of the audit committee. However there are a number of arguments in favour of having a separate risk management committee.

(a) A risk management committee can be **staffed by executive directors**, whereas an **audit committee** under **corporate governance best practice** should be **staffed by non-executive directors**. However if there are doubts about the **competence and good faith** of executive management, it will be more appropriate for the committee to be staffed by non-executive directors.

(b) As a key role of the audit committee will be to liase with the external auditors, much of their time could be focused on **financial risks**.

(c) A risk management committee can take the lead in **driving changes in practice**, whereas an audit committee will have a purely monitoring role, checking that a satisfactory risk management policy exists.

Companies that are involved in significant financial market risk will often have a risk management committee. The potential for large losses through misuse of derivatives was demonstrated by the Barings bank scandal. A risk management committee can help provide the supervision required; clearly though to be effective, the members collectively will need a high level of financial expertise.

4.1.3 Role and function of risk management committee

Evidence of companies that have operated a risk management committee suggests that a risk management committee will be far more effective if it has clear terms of reference. Morris in *An Accountant's Guide to Risk Management* suggests that written terms of reference might include the following:

- **Approving the organisation's risk management strategy** and **risk management policy**

- **Reviewing reports on key risks** prepared by business operating units, management and the board

- **Monitoring overall exposure** to risk and ensuring it remains within limits set by the board

- **Assessing the effectiveness** of the organisation's **risk management systems**

- **Providing early warning to the board** on emerging risk issues and significant changes in the company's exposure to risks

- In conjunction with the audit committee, **reviewing the company's statement on internal control** with reference to risk management, prior to endorsement by the board.

Having a separate risk management committee can aid the board in its responsibility for ensuring that **adequate risk management systems** are in place. The application of risk management policies will then be the responsibility of operational managers, and perhaps specialist risk management personnel, as described below.

Case Study

Risk management groups

Strode's College

The key tasks of the Risk Management Group are to:

- Take overall responsibility for the administration and implementation of the risk management process;

- Identify and evaluate the significant risks faced by the College and produce a Risk Management Action Plan for consideration by the Senior Management Team and the Board of Governors;

- Provide adequate information in a timely manner to the Board of Governors and its committees on the status of risks and controls;

- Report regularly on the Risk Management Action Plan implementation to the Senior Management Team and the Board of Governors and to undertake an annual review of effectiveness of the system of internal control to be presented to the Board of Governors.

The membership of the Risk Management Group will reflect the full range of the College's activities and will include the Principal, Vice Principal, Finance Manager, Resources Manager, Estates Manager and a Director of Faculty.

The Risk Management Group will report on a regular basis to the Senior Management Team.

The Risk Management Group will prepare a report of its review of the effectiveness of the internal control system annually for consideration by the Senior Management Team, the Audit Committee and the Board of Governors.

Argyll & Clyde NHS board

The Risk Management Steering Group will be responsible for Strategic Planning. Its purpose and remit will be to:

- Identify risk.

- Review Directorate risk registers and action plans.

- Provide assurance to the Health Governance Committee that all identified risks are being managed.

- Raise awareness of risk throughout the organisation.

- Provide education on risk throughout the organisation.

- Provide regular reports to the Health Governance Committee highlighting risks which are more severe due to change in circumstances ie organisational, legal or environmental.

- Review incident reporting statistics and investigation reports.

- Effectively communicate risk issues within the organisation.

- Monitor and review the risk management process.

The Risk Management Steering Group will receive reports from an established network of groups dealing with Risk Management as part of its remit. These groups will reflect the joint clinical and non-clinical approach to Risk Management.

The Membership of the Risk Management Steering Group is:

Chief Executive (Chair)
Director of Public Health or Representative
Director of Corporate Affairs
Health and Safety Adviser
Chief Internal Auditor
Organisational Performance Manager
Emergency Planning Officer
Director of Information
Assistant Director – Planning and Performance

The Risk Management Steering Group will meet every 2 months and report to the Health Governance Committee quarterly.

4.1.4 Risk management group

A risk management group, staffed by senior managers, may be responsible for building on the overall strategy and framework prescribed by the board. This group will add more detail and will prescribe **methods of risk management** that operating units will employ. The risk management group will concentrate on **risk responses** and will also **monitor risk management** to see that the strategies and policies are operating effectively. They will also consider issues such as the staffing of a risk management function (discussed below), also how risk management impacts on the relations between central management and operating units.

The risk management group will report to the board and in turn will receive reports from line managers and employees.

4.1.5 Internal and external audit

Risk is integral to the work of internal and external audit, both in terms of influencing **how much work** they do (with more work being done on riskier areas) and also **what work** they actually do. The external auditors will be concerned with risks that impact most on the figures shown in the **financial accounts**. Internal auditors' role is **more flexible**, and their approach will depend on whether they **focus on the controls** that are being operated or the **overall risk management process**.

4.1.6 Line managers

The UK Turnbull report stresses the role of management in implementing broad policies on risk and control, including **identifying and evaluating risk** and **designing and operating an appropriate system of internal control.** Managers should have an awareness of the risks that fall into their areas of responsibility and possible links with **other areas.** The **performance indicators** they use should help them monitor key business and financial activities and highlight when intervention is required.

Line managers will be involved in communicating risk management policies to staff and will of course 'set a good example'. Line managers are also responsible for **preparing reports** that will be considered by the board and senior managers.

Depending on whether specialist risk managers are involved, part of the role of line managers may be to carry out detailed risk management functions. The office manager may deal with fire precautions and the managing director with buying insurances, for example, and each may call in experts to assist with these functions.

In much smaller organisations, all such jobs are naturally dealt with by the **executive manager**, who may well have an outside expert such as an insurer's inspector or broker's account handler to do much of the technical planning.

4.1.7 Staff

Staff will be responsible for following the **risk management procedures** the organisation has established, and should be alert for any conditions or events that may result in problems. Staff need an understanding of their **accountability** for individual risks and that **risk management** and **risk awareness** are a key part of the organisation's culture. They must be aware of how to **report** any concerns they have, particularly reports of risk, failures of existing control measures, variances in budgets and forecasts.

The UK Turnbull report emphasises the need for employees to take responsibility for risk management and internal control. This requires them to have the necessary **knowledge, skills, information and authority** to operate and monitor the control system. This requires understanding the **company,** its **objectives,** the **industries and markets** in which it operates and the **risks** it faces.

4.2 Risk management personnel

4.2.1 Risk specialists

Most individuals have little time for looking after their personal safety and security, still less for searching the market for the most suitable insurances; they frequently employ agents to help manage some of their risks.

A **specialist** advising on management of personal risks can work only as well as the client allows. A good specialist will ask for information and for co-operation with the expert surveys that enable him to provide a proper service; he will ensure that the client understands what safety measures are required and he will see that they are put into practice.

4.2.2 Risk manager

The risk manager will need technical skills in **credit, market, and operational risk**. Leadership and persuasive skills are likely to be necessary to overcome resistance from those who believe that risk management is an attempt to stifle initiative.

Lam (*Enterprise Risk Management*) includes a detailed description of this role, and the COSO framework also has a list of responsibilities. Combining these sources we can say that the risk manager is typically responsible for:

(a) Providing the **overall leadership, vision and direction** for enterprise risk management.

(b) Establishing an **integrated RM framework** for all aspects of risk across the organisation, integrating enterprise risk management with other business planning and management activities and framing authority and accountability for enterprise risk management in business units.

(c) Promoting an **enterprise risk management competence** throughout the entity, including facilitating development of technical enterprise risk management expertise, helping managers align risk responses with the entity's risk tolerances and developing appropriate controls.

(d) **Developing RM policies**, including the quantification of management's risk appetite through specific risk limits, defining roles and responsibilities and participating in setting goals for implementation.

(e) **Establishing a common risk management language** that includes common measures around likelihood and impact, and common risk categories. Developing the analytical systems and data management capabilities to support the risk management programme.

(f) **Implementing a set of risk indicators and reports** including losses and incidents, key risk exposures, and early warning indicators. Facilitating managers' development of reporting protocols, including quantitative and qualitative thresholds, and monitoring the reporting process.

(g) **Dealing with insurance companies;** an important task because of increased premium costs, restrictions in the cover available (will the risks be excluded from cover) and the need for negotiations with insurance companies if claims arise. If insurers require it demonstrating that the organisation is taking steps actively to manage its risks. Arranging financing schemes such as self-insurance or captive insurance.

(h) **Allocating economic capital to business activities** based on risk, and optimising the company's risk portfolio through business activities and risk transfer strategies.

(i) **Reporting to the chief executive on progress** and recommending action as needed. Communicating the company's risk profile to key stakeholders such as the board of directors, regulators, stock analysts, rating agencies and business partners.

The risk manager's contribution will be judged by how much he **increases the value of the organisation**. The specialist knowledge a risk manager have should allow the risk manager to assess **long-term risk** and hazard outcomes and therefore decide what resources should be allocated to combating risk.

Clearly certain strategic risks are likely to have the biggest impact on corporate value. Therefore a risk manager's role may include management of these strategic risks. These may include those having a **fundamental effect on future operations** such as mergers and acquisitions or risks that have the potential to cause **large adverse impacts** such as currency hedging and major investments

4.2.3 Risk management function

Larger companies may have a bigger risk management function whose responsibilities are wider than a single risk manager or risk specialist. The Institute of Risk Management's Risk Management standard lists the main responsibilities of the risk management function:

- **Setting policy and strategy** for risk management

- **Primary champion of risk management** at a strategic and operational level

- Building a **risk aware culture** within the organisation including appropriate education

- Establishing **internal risk policy** and structures for business units

- **Designing and reviewing processes** for risk management

- **Coordinating the various functional activities** which advise on risk management issues within an organisation

- **Developing risk response processes**, including contingency and business continuity programmes

- **Preparing reports on risks** for the board and stakeholders

Exam focus point

The study guide emphasises the roles of the risk management committee and (specialist) risk management function so you may well be asked to explain what they do.

4.3 Risk resourcing

Whatever the division of responsibilities for risk management, the organisation needs to think carefully about how risk management is resourced; sufficient resources will be required to implement and monitor risk management (including the resources required to obtain the necessary information). Management needs to consider not only the **expenditure** required, but also the **human resources** in terms of skills and experience.

5 Risk management strategies

5.1 Dealing with risk

FAST FORWARD

Methods for dealing with risk include **risk avoidance, risk reduction, risk acceptance** and **risk transference**.

In the rest of the chapter we shall consider **risk portfolio management**, the various ways in which organisations can try to mitigate risks or indeed consider whether it will be worthwhile for them to accept risks.

Risk management strategies can be linked into the likelihood/consequences matrix, discussed earlier.

Consequences (hazard)

	Low	*High*
Low	**Acceptance** Risks are not significant. Keep under view, but costs of dealing with risks unlikely to be worth the benefits.	**Transference** Insure risk or implement contingency plans. Reduction of severity of risk will minimise insurance premiums.
High	**Reduction** Take some action, eg self-insurance to deal with frequency of losses.	**Avoidance** Take immediate action to reduce severity and frequency of losses, eg charging higher prices to customers or ultimately abandoning activities.

Likelihood

Exam focus point

> This diagram is worth committing to memory. The mnemonic is TARA (Transfer, Avoid, Reduce, Accept).

5.2 Avoidance of risk

Organisations will often consider whether risk can be avoided and if so whether avoidance is desirable. That is, will the possible savings from losses avoided be greater than the advantages that can be gained by not taking any measures, and running the risk?

An extreme form of business risk avoidance is **termination of operations**, for example operations in politically volatile countries where the risks of loss (including loss of life) are considered to be too great or the costs of security are considered to be too high.

Case Study

In 1976 M&M Mars reacted to adverse publicity about the carcinogenic effects of red dye Number 2 by removing red M&Ms from the market. Although red M&Ms were not actually made with red dye Number 2, the public perceived that they **were,** and thus management felt compelled to counter the risk to the company's reputation by removing the product from sale.

The scare subsequently disappeared, and red M&Ms were re-introduced in the late 1980s.

5.3 Reduction of risk

Often risks can be avoided in part, or reduced, but not avoided altogether. This is true of many business risks, where the risks of launching a new product can be reduced by market research, advertising and so on.

Question

What measures could you take to reduce the risk that suppliers do not deliver supplies of the required quality or do not deliver on time?

Answer

Measures might include:

- Getting references from the suppliers' other customers

- Setting standards for quality and delivery time and monitoring suppliers' delivery performance against those standards (eventually eliminating those who are consistently unreliable)

- Developing good relationships with suppliers

- Ensuring that suppliers have all the information they need

- Insisting that suppliers are ISO 9001 certified

- Regularly scanning the market for new suppliers

You may have had other ideas. The point is that 'risk reduction' techniques may not be given that name: they are simply a matter of good management. If you mentioned methods such as imposing penalties for poor performance or incentives for good performance that's fine, but such approaches are really risk **sharing**, and we'll come to that in a moment.

Other risk reduction measures include contingency planning and loss control.

5.3.1 Contingency planning

Contingency planning involves identifying the **post-loss needs** of the business, **drawing up plans** in advance and **reviewing them regularly** to take account of changes in the business. The process has three basic constituents.

Information	How, for example, do you turn off the sprinklers once the fire is extinguished? All the information that will need to be available during and after the event should be gathered in advance. This will include names and addresses of staff, details of suppliers of machinery, waste disposal firms and so on. The information should be kept up to date and it should be circulated so that it will be readily available to anyone who might need it.
Responsibilities	The plan should lay down what is to be done by whom. Duties should be delegated as appropriate; deputies should be nominated to take account of holidays and sickness. Those who hold responsibilities should be aware of what they are, how they have changed, who will help them and so on.
Practice	Unless the plan has been tested there is no guarantee that it will work. A full-scale test may not always be possible; simulations, however, should be as realistic as possible and should be taken seriously by all involved. The results of any testing should be monitored so that amendments can be made to the plan as necessary.

5.3.2 Loss control

Control of losses also requires careful advance planning. There are two main aspects to good loss control, the physical and the psychological.

(a)   There are **many physical devices** that can be installed to minimise losses when harmful events actually occur. Sprinklers, fire extinguishers, escape stairways, burglar alarms and machine guards are obvious examples.

It is **not enough** however to **install such devices**. They will need to be **inspected** and **maintained** regularly, and back-up measures will be needed for times when they are inoperational. Their adequacy and appropriateness in the light of changes to the business also needs to be kept under constant review.

(b)   The key psychological factors are **awareness** and **commitment**. Every person in the business should be made aware that losses are possible and that they can be controlled. Commitment to loss control can be achieved by making individual managers accountable for the losses under their control. Staff should be encouraged to draw attention to any aspects of their job that make losses possible.

5.3.3 Risk pooling and diversification

Risk pooling and diversification involves using portfolio theory to manage risks. Portfolio theory is an important part of an organisation's financial strategy, but its principles can be applied to non-financial risks as well.

Risk pooling or diversification involves creating a **portfolio of different risks** based on a number of events, which, if some turn out well others will turn out badly, and the average outcome will be neutral. What an organisation has to do is to avoid having all its risks **positively correlated**. This means that everything will turn out **extremely well** or **extremely badly.**

Portfolio theory draws a distinction between systematic and unsystematic risk:

(a)   Risks that can be diversified away are referred to as **unsystematic risk**.

(b)   Some business opportunities are by their very nature more risky than others. This has nothing to do with chance variations up or down in actual returns compared with what an investor should expect. This inherent risk – the **systematic risk** or **market risk** – cannot be diversified away (see Figure 1).

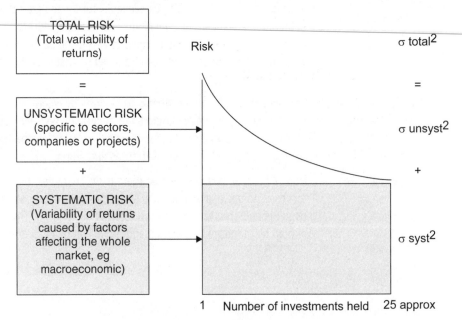

Figure 1

Systematic risk must be accepted by any investor or any company, unless their activities are entirely risk-free investments. In return for accepting systematic risk, an investor will expect to earn a **return** that is **higher** than the return on a risk-free investment. For example the systematic risk in the operating cash flows of a tourism company that will be highly sensitive to consumers' spending power might be greater than the systematic risk for a company that operates a chain of supermarkets.

5.3.4 The Capital Asset Pricing Model

The capital asset pricing model is mainly concerned with how **systematic risk is measured** and with how systematic risk affects required returns and share prices. You do not need to know the formulae involved in this paper, just the broad principles.

CAPM theory includes the following propositions.

(a) Investors in shares require a return in **excess** of the **risk-free rate**, to compensate them for systematic risk.

(b) Investors should **not require** a **premium** for **unsystematic risk**, because this can be diversified away by holding a wide portfolio of investments.

(c) Because systematic risk varies between companies, investors will require a **higher return** from shares in those companies where the **systematic risk** is **greater**.

The same propositions can be applied to **capital investments by companies**.

(a) Companies will want a return on a project to **exceed** the **risk-free rate**, to compensate them for systematic risk.

(b) **Unsystematic risk** can be **diversified away**, and so a premium for unsystematic risk should not be required.

(c) Companies should want a **bigger return** on projects where **systematic risk is greater**.

5.3.5 Risk hedging

Hedging means taking an action that will **offset** an **exposure to a risk** by incurring a **new risk** in the **opposite direction.** Hedging is perhaps most important in the area of currency or interest rate risk management, and hedging methods include forward agreements, futures and options. What these have in common generally speaking is that the organisation makes a commitment, possibly to undertake a contract in the future at a set price, to offset the risk of a transaction that will take place in the future, the value of which is currently uncertain.

5.4 Acceptance of risks

Risk retention is where the organisation bears the risk itself, and if an unfavourable outcome occurs, it will suffer the full loss. Risk retention is inevitable to some extent. However good the organisation's risk identification and assessment processes are, there will always be some unexpected risk. Other reasons for risk retention are that the risk is considered to be **insignificant** or the cost of avoiding the risk is considered to be too great set against the potential loss that could be incurred.

The decision of whether to retain or transfer risks depends first on whether there is anyone to transfer a risk to. The answer is more likely to be 'no' for an individual than for an organisation, because:

(a) Individuals have **more small risks** than do organisations and the administrative costs of transferring and carrying them can make the exercise impracticable for the insurer.

(b) The individual has **smaller resources** to find a carrier.

In the last resort organisations usually have customers to pass their risks or losses to, up to a point, and individuals do not.

5.4.1 Self-insurance

An option sometimes associated with accepting risks is **self-insurance**. In contrast to non-insurance, which is effectively gritting one's teeth and hoping for the best, self-insurance is putting aside funds of whatever size, in a lump or at intervals, in a reserve dedicated to defraying the expenses involved should a particular sort of loss happen.

A **more sophisticated method of self-insurance** is setting up a **captive**.

5.4.2 Captive insurance

> A **captive**, or **captive insurer**, is an insurance company wholly owned by a commercial organisation, and usually dedicated solely to the underwriting of its parent company's risks. Its primary purpose, therefore, is to be a vehicle for transfer of the parent company's risks.

An organisation with a risk that it cannot carry, which cannot find one or more insurers to take the bulk of that risk from it, may form a **captive insurer** to carry that risk. The captive insurer has all the parent's experience of the risk to call on, so its premiums will not be unnecessarily large, and its policy terms will be reasonable.

5.5 Transfer of risk

Alternatively, risks can be transferred – to other internal departments or externally to suppliers, customers or insurers. Risk transfer can even be to the state.

Decisions to transfer should not be made without careful checking to ensure that as many influencing factors as possible have been included in the assessment. A decision not to rectify the design of a product, because rectification could be as expensive as paying any claims from disgruntled customers, is in fact a decision to transfer the risk to the customers without their knowledge: it may not take into account the possibility of courts awarding exemplary damages to someone injured by the product, to discourage people from taking similar decisions in the future.

Internal risk transfer can also cause problems if it is away from departments with more 'clout' (eg sales) and towards departments such as finance who may be presumed to downplay risks excessively.

5.5.1 Hold harmless agreements

Indemnity or **hold harmless agreements** can be useful. They:

- **Reduce the price of goods** for a party who takes on extra responsibility
- **Preserve good trading relations** by avoiding arguments
- **Preserve good public relations** if efficiently and sympathetically operated

5.5.2 Limitation of liability

Some contracts, in which one party accepts strict liability up to a set limit, or liability which is wider than the law would normally impose, follow very ancient customs. Examples are contracts for carriage of passengers or goods by air or sea.

5.5.3 Legal and other restrictions on transferring risks

The first restriction is that a supplier or customer may **refuse** to enter a contract unless your organisation agrees to take a particular risk. This depends on the trading relationship between the firms concerned, and not a little on economics: how many suppliers could supply the item or service in question, for example, and how great is your need for the item?

5.5.4 Risk sharing

Risks can be partly held and partly transferred to someone else. An example is an insurance policy, where the insurer pays any losses incurred by the policyholder above a set amount.

Risk-sharing arrangements can be very significant in business strategy. For example in a **joint venture** arrangement each participant's risk can be limited to what it is prepared to bear.

5.6 Communication of risk

Communicating to shareholders and other stakeholders particularly those risks that cannot be avoided is an important aspect of risk management. Of course the stock market may react badly to this news. If risks are to be successfully communicated, the messages need to be consistent and the organisation has to be trusted by the recipients.

The Institute of Risk Management's Risk Management standard suggests that **formal reporting** of risk management should address:

- **Control methods** – particularly management responsibilities for risk management
- **Processes used to identify risks** and how they are addressed by the risk management systems
- **Primary control systems** in place to manage significant risks
- **Monitoring and review** systems

We consider reporting in the context of directors' review of risk and internal control in Chapter 9.

Chapter Roundup

- Management responses to risk are not automatic, but will be determined by their **own attitudes to risk**, which in turn may be influenced by **shareholder attitudes** and **cultural factors**.

- **Enterprise risk management** provides a coherent framework for organisations to deal with risk, based on the following components:

    - Internal environment
    - Objective setting
    - Event identification
    - Risk assessment
    - Risk response
    - Control activities
    - Information and communication
    - Monitoring

- **Risk assessment** should be embedded within an organisation's **processes, environment, culture, structure and systems**. Organisations should **issue a risk policy statement** and **maintain a risk register**.

- The **board** has overall responsibility for **risk management** as an essential part of its corporate governance responsibilities. Responsibilities below board level will depend on the extent of delegation to **line managers** and whether there is a **separate risk management function**.

- Methods for dealing with risk include **risk avoidance, risk reduction, risk acceptance,** and **risk transference**.

Quick Quiz

1 Match the viewpoint to the attitude to risk.

(a) Fatalist

(b) Hierarchist

(c) Individualist

(d) Egalitarian

(i) Risk reduction through formal risk management procedures
(ii) Sharing or transfer of risk
(iii) Informal risk management systems
(iv) Risk management is pointless

2 What according to COSO are the key characteristics of enterprise risk management?

3 What are the main elements that should be covered by a risk policy statement?

4 Complete the likelihood-consequences matrix in relation to methods of dealing with risk

Consequences

	Low	*High*

Low

Likelihood

High

5 Which of the following is not an argument in favour of establishing a risk management committee that is separate from the internal audit committee?

A The risk management committee can be staffed by executive directors.

B Because they are non-executive directors, members of the internal audit committee may have insufficient time to consider in sufficient detail all the major risks faced by the company.

C The risk management committee can concentrate on areas where risks are particularly high.

D The role of the internal audit committee is constrained by corporate governance codes, whereas a risk management committee can have a much wider brief.

6 Systematic risks are risks that are specific to sectors, companies or projects

True ☐

False ☐

7 What is a captive insurer?

8 Fill in the blank.

.... is taking an action that will offset an exposure to a risk by incurring a new risk in the opposite direction.

Answers to Quick Quiz

1   (a) (iv); (b) (i); (c) (iii); (d) (ii)

2
- Process
- Operated by people at every level
- Applied in strategy setting
- Applied across the organisation
- Identifies significant events
- Provides reasonable assurance
- Geared to the achievement of objectives

3
- Definitions of risk and risk management
- Objectives of risk policy
- Regulatory requirements
- Benefits of risk management
- How risk management is linked into strategic decision-making and performance
- What areas of risk management (risk avoidance, risk reduction) are particularly important
- Risk classification
- Roles of board, managers, staff and audit and risk committees
- Internal control framework and important controls
- Other tools and techniques
- Assurance reporting
- Role of training
- How to obtain help

4

	Consequences	
	Low	*High*
Low	**Acceptance** Risks are not significant. Keep under view, but costs of dealing with risks unlikely to be worth the benefits.	**Transference** Insure risk or implement contingency plans. Reduction of severity of risk will minimise insurance premiums.
Likelihood	**Reduction** Take some action, eg self-insurance to deal with frequency of losses.	**Avoidance** Take immediate action to reduce severity and frequency of losses, eg charging higher prices to customers or ultimately abandoning activities.
High		

5   D   The role of the internal audit committee can go beyond what is suggested in the corporate governance codes.

6   False. Unsystematic risks relate to specific, sectors, companies or projects

7   An insurer whose main purpose is to underwrite its owner's risks

8   Risk hedging

Now try the question below from the Exam Question Bank

Number	Level	Marks	Time
Q8	Examination	25	45 mins

Information requirements and reporting

9

Topic list	Syllabus reference
1 Information requirements of directors	B4
2 Communication with employees and internal control	D2
3 Management review and reporting	B3, C3

Introduction

This chapter brings together a number of themes we have discussed earlier. Its key theme is communication, and the first two sections emphasise the significance of **two-way** communication; what the directors are looking to receive and what should be communicated to staff. In the last section we cover in detail the board review of risk and internal control that we have mentioned in earlier chapters. One objective of this review is to produce a report communicating to shareholders how the organisation has been addressing the major risks it faces.

The board has to try to obtain strong assurance that the internal control systems are working well, since internal control failures can cause strategic failure as well as loss of capital value.

Study guide

		Intellectual level
B3	**Internal control and reporting**	
(a)	Describe and assess the need to report on internal controls to shareholders	3
(b)	Describe the content of a report on internal control and audit	2
B4	**Management information in audit and internal control systems**	
(a)	Explain and assess the need for adequate information flows to management for the purposes of the management of internal control and risk	3
(b)	Evaluate the qualities and characteristics of information required in internal control and risk management and monitoring	3
C3	**Identification, assessment and measurement of risk**	
(c)	Describe and evaluate a framework for board level consideration of risk	3
(d)	Describe the process of externally reporting on internal control and risk	2
D2	**Methods of controlling and reducing risk**	
(a)	Explain the importance of risk awareness at all levels in an organisation	2

Exam guide

In scenarios, look out for information on communication links; poor communication is often an important sign of a weak control system. Board review and reporting are key elements in the control system and you'll need to know what an effective board review involves.

1 Information requirements of directors

 FAST FORWARD

Directors need **information** from a **large variety of sources** to be able to supervise and review the operation of the internal control systems. Information sources should include normal reporting procedures, but staff should also have channels available to report problems or doubtful practices of others.

1.1 Needs of directors

We have emphasised above that board and senior manager involvement is a critical element of internal control systems and the control environment. There are various ways in which management can obtain the information they need to play the necessary active part in control systems.

1.2 Information sources

The information directors need to be able to monitor controls effectively comes from a wide variety of sources.

1.2.1 The directors' own efforts

Directors will receive reports from the internal audit committee and risk committee. Management by **walking about**, regular visits by the directors to operations, may yield valuable insights and should help the directors understand the context in which controls are currently operating.

1.2.2 Reports from subordinates

There should be systems in place for all staff with supervisory responsibilities to report on a regular basis to senior managers, and senior managers in turn to report regularly to directors. The COSO guidelines comment:

> 'Among the most critical communications channels is that between top management and the board of directors. Management must keep the board up-to-date on performance, developments, risk and the functioning of enterprise risk management and other relevant events or issues. The better the communications, the more effective the board will be in carrying out its oversight responsibilities, in acting as a sounding board on critical issues and in providing advice, counsel and direction. By the same token the board should communicate to management what information it needs and provide feedback and direction'.

1.2.3 Lines of communication

Very importantly directors must ensure that staff have lines of communication that can be used to **address concerns**. There should be normal communication channels through which most concerns are addressed, but there should also be failsafe mechanisms for reporting, or **whistleblowing**, particularly serious problems and perhaps active seeking of feedback through **staff attitude surveys.**

As well as channels existing, it is also important that staff believe that directors and managers want to know about problems and will deal with them effectively. Staff must believe that there will be **no reprisals** for **reporting relevant information.**

1.2.4 Reports from control functions

Organisational functions that have a key role to play in internal control systems must report on a regular basis to the board and senior management. One example is the need for a close relationship between **internal audit** and the **audit committee**. The **human resources function** should also report regularly to the board about personnel practices in operational units. Poor human resource management can often be an indicator of future problems with controls, since it may create dissatisfied staff or staff who believe that laxness will be tolerated.

1.2.5 Reports on activities

The board should receive regular reports on **certain activities**. A good example is major developments in computerised systems. As well as board approval before the start of key stages of the development process, the board needs to be informed of progress and any problems during the course of the project, so that any difficulties with potentially serious consequences can be rapidly addressed.

1.2.6 Reports on resolution of weaknesses

Similarly the board should obtain evidence to confirm that control weaknesses that have previously **been identified** have been **resolved**. When it has been agreed that action should be taken to deal with problems, this should include **timescale** for action and also **reporting** that the actions have been implemented.

1.2.7 Results of checks

The board should receive confirmation as a matter of course that necessary **checks** on the operation of the controls have been **carried out** satisfactorily and that the results have been clearly reported. This includes gaining assurance that the **right sort** of check has been **performed**. For example **random checks** may be required on high risk areas such as unauthorised access to computer systems. Sufficient **independent** evidence from external or internal audit should be obtained to reinforce the evidence supplied by operational units.

1.2.8 Exception reporting

Exception reports highlighting variances in **budgeting systems**, **performance measures**, **quality targets** and **planning systems** are an important part of the information that management receives. You will remember from your management accounting studies that adverse variances are often an important sign of problems, and indicate a need to tighten internal control.

Managers may consider the following issues when deciding whether to investigate further:

(a) **Materiality – Small variations in a single period** are bound to occur and **are unlikely to be significant**. Obtaining an 'explanation' is likely to be time-consuming and irritating for the manager concerned. The explanation will often be 'chance', which is not particularly helpful.

(b) **Controllability** – Controllability must also influence the decision whether to investigate further. If there is a general worldwide price increase in the price of an important raw material there is **nothing that can be done internally** to control the effect of this.

(c) **Variance trend** – If, say, an efficiency **variance** is £1,000 adverse in month 1, the obvious conclusion is that the process is **out of control** and that corrective action must be taken. This may be correct, but what if the same variance is £1,000 adverse every month? The **trend** indicates that the process is **in control** and the standard has been wrongly set.

(d) **Cost** – The likely cost of an investigation needs to be weighed against the cost to the organisation of allowing the variance to continue in future periods.

(e) **Interrelationship of variances** – Quite possibly, individual variances should not be looked at in isolation. One variance might be inter-related with another, and much of it might have occurred only because the other, inter-related, variance occurred too.

1.2.9 Feedback from customers

Customer responses, particularly complaints, are important evidence for the board to consider, particularly as regards how controls ensure the **quality of output**.

1.3 Making best use of information

1.3.1 Comparison of different sources of information

The pictures gleaned from different sources must be compared and discrepancies followed up and addressed. Not only does the board need to have a **true picture** of what is happening but discrepancies might highlight problems with existing sources of information that need to be addressed. In particular if random or special checks identify problems that should have been picked up and reported through regular channels, then the **adequacy** of these channels needs to be considered carefully.

1.3.2 Feedback to others

Directors need to ensure that as well as their obtaining the information they need to review internal control systems, **relevant information on controls** is also **passed to all those** within the organisation who need it directly. For example sales staff who obtain customer feedback on product shortcomings need to be aware of the channels for communicating with staff responsible for product quality and also staff responsible for product design.

1.3.3 Review procedures

As well as investigating and resolving problems with the information they receive, the board ought to undertake a **regular review** of the information sources that they need. They should, as we will see in Section 3, review in general the whole system of supervision and review to assess its adequacy and also to assess whether any layers of supervision or review can be reduced.

A key question to ask when analysing control systems is how strong do the feedback mechanisms appear to be and are they appropriate for the organisation.

2 Communication with employees and internal control

FAST FORWARD

Procedures improving staff abilities and attitudes should be built into the control framework. **Communication** of control and risk management issues and strong **human resource procedures** reinforce the control systems.

2.1 Importance of human element

It is very easy to design a control system that appears good on paper but is unworkable, because it is **not geared** to the **user's practicality and usefulness.** A detailed technical manual covering information technology controls may be of little use if staff lack sufficient knowledge of information technology. Controls may not work very well if staff lack motivation or the basic skills for the job in the first place. On the other hand, if good staff are taken on, they may well develop the necessary controls as part of their day-to-day work.

2.2 Important human resource issues

The UK Turnbull report stresses that all employees have some responsibility for internal control and need to have the **necessary skills**, **knowledge** and **understanding** in particular of the risks the organisation faces.

2.3 Improving staff awareness and attitudes

Turnbull stresses that it is important that all staff understand that risk management is an **integral, embedded part** of the **organisation's operations**. Elaborate risk management innovations may not be the best way to improve performance; it may be better to build **warning mechanisms** into existing information systems rather than develop separate risk reporting systems.

Turnbull suggests that it is vital to communicate policies in the following areas in particular:

- Customer relations
- Service levels for both internal and outsourced activities
- Health, safety and environmental protection
- Security of assets and business continuity
- Expenditure
- Accounting, financial and other reporting

The briefing suggests that the following steps can be taken:

- **Initial guidance** from the Chief Executive

- **Dissemination of the risk management policy** and codes of conduct, also key business objectives and internal control

- **Workshops** on risk management and internal control

- A **greater proportion of the training budget** being spent on internal control

- Involvement of staff in **identifying and responding** to change and in operating warning mechanisms

- **Clear channels of communication** for reporting breaches and other improprieties

2.4 Training staff

An interactive training event, with participants identifying for themselves the most significant risks and key controls, is likely to be most valuable.

Training days can be particularly useful in emphasising to staff the importance of different types of control (preventative, detective etc) and also the need for some controls to assist staff development, but others to enforce sanctions particularly in cases of dishonesty or negligence.

 Case Study

Here is an example of an internal communications programme slightly adapted from an example in the COSO *Framework*.

Internal communications programme

- Management discusses risks and associated risk responses in regular briefings with employees.

- Management regularly communicates entity-wide risks in employee communications such as newsletters, an intranet.

- Enterprise risk management policies, standards, and procedures are made readily available to employees along with clear statements requiring compliance.

- Management requires employees to consult with others across the organisation as appropriate when new events are identified.

- Induction sessions for new employees include information and literature on the company's risk management philosophy and enterprise risk management programme.

- Existing employees are required to take workshops and/or refresher courses on the organisation's enterprise risk management initiatives.

- The risk management philosophy is reinforced in regular and ongoing internal communication programmes and through specific communication programmes to reinforce tenets of the company's culture.

2.5 Problems of communication

Large companies, particularly those operating in several jurisdictions, may face particular problems when communicating with and training staff through cultural and ethical local filters. We shall discuss the influence of the country in which individuals work upon their ethical attitudes in the next chapter.

Exam focus point

> The examiner has stressed the influence of cultural factors upon control systems, so when assessing the strength of the control systems, it's normally worth asking whether their effectiveness may vary due to differences in culture over the whole organisation.

3 Management review and reporting

Boards should review **risks** and the **effectiveness of internal controls regularly**.
They should carry out an **annual review** that looks more widely at risks faced and control systems and also how these issues should be reported.

3.1 Audit and board review

We mentioned in Section B the importance of manager review of internal controls and the results of internal audit work obviously play a major part in this review. In the last section of this chapter we shall look in more detail at management's review of internal controls since it is effectively the last stage of the audit process.

3.2 Review of internal controls

The UK **Turnbull committee** suggests that review of internal controls should be an **integral part** of the **company's operations**; the board, or board committees, should actively consider reports on control issues from others operating internal controls.

In order to be able to carry out an effective review, boards should regularly receive and review reports and information on internal control, concentrating on:

(a)   What the **risks** are and strategies for **identifying**, **evaluating** and **managing** them

(b)   The **effectiveness** of the management and internal control systems in the management of risk, in particular how risks are **monitored** and **how** any **weaknesses** have been dealt with

(c)   Whether **actions** are being taken to **reduce** the risks found

(d)   Whether the results indicate that **internal control** should be **monitored more extensively**

Question

Internal control review

(a)   What sort of information would help the board carry out an effective review of internal control?
(b)   What sort of employee attitudes would help or hinder an effective review of internal control?

Answer

(a)   **The UK's Institute of Internal Auditors suggests that the board needs to consider the following information in order to carry out an effective review**.

- The organisation's **Code of Business Conduct** (if it has one – see Chapter 11)

- Confirmation that line managers are **clear as to their objectives**

- The overall results of a **control self assessment** process by line management or staff

- **Letters of representation** ('comfort letters') on internal control from line management (confirmations about the operation of systems or specific transactions)

- A **report** from the audit committee on the **key procedures** which are designed to provide effective internal control

- **Reports from internal audit** on audits performed

- The audit committee's **assessment** of the **effectiveness of internal audit**

- Reports on **special reviews** commissioned by the audit committee from internal audit or others

- Internal audit's **overall summary opinion on internal control**

- The **external auditors' report on weaknesses** in the accounting and internal control systems and other matters, including errors, identified during the audit

- **Intelligence** gathered by board members during the year

- A **report on avoidable losses** by the finance director

- A **report on any material developments** since the balance sheet date and up to the present

- The board's proposed wording of **the internal control report** for publication

(b) The following employee attitudes will be relevant.

Response to management behaviour

Employees may take controls with the **same degree of seriousness** that management does. They will take into account how strictly controls are applied by senior managers, whether senior managers override controls, and whether follow-up action is taken by management if control weaknesses are identified.

Realism of controls

If employees see **controls as unrealistic** because for example there is insufficient time to operate them, they may not take management review of controls seriously.

Employee collusion

If employees do collude, the evidence available to management may be **undermined**. Collusion may not necessarily be hiding fraud; it could be a shared intention to thwart what is seen as unnecessary bureaucracy. The fact for example that there are two signatures on a document does not necessarily mean that it has been checked properly.

Focus on certain controls

If a **lot of emphasis is placed on certain controls**, reports on which the annual review is based will stress the operation of those controls and provide less detail of other controls that are also significant.

Prioritisation

Many employees may feel that controls are bureaucracy and as such interfere with more important day-to-day work. This may mean for example that controls are **not operated when they should be**, but some time later, and so the evidence the annual review is relying on may not be as strong as it appears.

Reliance on memory

Some controls may be dependent on **knowledge held in the mind of employees**. The employees concerned may be happy about this because it reinforces their position, but it can lead to a lack of clarity about whether controls have operated, and also inconsistency and misunderstanding when controls depend on the attitudes of the person operating them.

In an appendix Turnbull provides more detailed guidance on what should be assessed as part of the regular review of internal controls:

Risk assessment	• Does the organisation have clear objectives and have they been communicated to provide direction to employees (examples include performance targets)?
	• Are significant risks identified and assessed on an ongoing basis?
	• Do managers and employees have a clear understanding of what risks are acceptable?
Control environment and control activities	• Does the board have a risk management policy and strategies for dealing with significant risks?
	• Do the company's culture, code of conduct, human resource policies and performance reward systems support the business objectives and risk management and control systems?
	• Does senior management demonstrate commitment to competence, integrity and fostering a climate of trust?
	• Are authority, responsibility and accountability defined clearly?
	• Are decisions and actions of different parts of the company appropriately coordinated?
	• Does the company communicate to its employees what is expected of them and the scope of their freedom to act?
	• Do company employees have the knowledge, skills and tools necessary to support the company's objectives and manage risks effectively?
	• How are processes and controls adjusted to reflect new or changing risks or operational deficiencies?
Information and communication	• Do managers receive timely, relevant and reliable reports on progress against business objectives and risks to provide the information needed for decision-making and review processes?
	• Are information needs and systems reassessed as objectives and related risks change or reporting deficiencies are identified?
	• Do reporting procedures communicate a balanced and understandable account of the company's position and prospects?
	• Are there communication channels for individuals to report suspected breaches of law or regulations or other improprieties?
Monitoring	• Are there ongoing embedded processes for monitoring the effective application of the policies, processes and activities relating to internal control and risk management?
	• Do these processes monitor the company's ability to re-evaluate risks and adjust controls effectively in response to changes in objectives, business and environment?
	• Are there effective follow-up procedures to ensure action is taken in response to changes in risk and control assessments?
	• Are there specific arrangements for management monitoring and reporting to the board matters of particular importance (including fraud or illegal acts)?

3.3 Annual review of controls

In addition, when directors are considering annually the disclosures they are required to make about internal controls, the Turnbull report states they should conduct an **annual review** of internal control. This should be wider-ranging than the regular review; in particular it should cover:

(a) The **changes** since the last **assessment** in **risks** faced, and the company's **ability** to **respond** to **changes** in its business environment

(b) The **scope** and **quality** of management's monitoring of risk and internal control, and of the work of internal audit, or consideration of the need for an internal audit function if the company does not have one

(c) The **extent** and **frequency** of reports to the board

(d) **Significant controls**, **failings** and **weaknesses** which have or might have material impacts upon the accounts

(e) The **effectiveness** of the **public reporting** processes

3.4 Reporting on risk management and internal controls

Per the Turnbull report the board should disclose as a minimum in the accounts, the existence of a **process** for **managing risks**, how the board has **reviewed** the **effectiveness** of the process and that the **process accords** with the **Turnbull guidance**. The board should also include:

(a) An **acknowledgement** that they are **responsible** for the **company's system of internal control** and **reviewing its effectiveness**

(b) An **explanation** that such a system is designed to **manage** rather than eliminate the **risk of failure** to **achieve business objectives**, and can only provide **reasonable** and not absolute **assurance** against material misstatement or **loss**

(c) A **summary** of the process that the **directors** (or a board committee) have **used to review the effectiveness** of the system of internal control and consider the need for an internal audit function if the company does not have one. There should also be disclosure of the process the board has used to deal with **material internal control aspects** of **any significant problems** disclosed in the annual accounts

(d) **Information** about those **weaknesses** in internal control that have resulted in material losses, contingencies or uncertainties which require disclosure in the financial statements or the auditor's report on the financial statements.

3.5 Significance of Turnbull recommendations

The system recommended by the Turnbull report is notable because of the following.

(a) It is **forward looking**.

(b) It is **open**, requiring appropriate disclosures to all stakeholders in the company about the risks being taken.

(c) It does **not seek** to **eliminate risk**. It is constructive in its approach to opportunity management, as well as concerned with 'disaster prevention'. To succeed companies are not required to take fewer risks than others but they do need a good understanding of what risks they can handle.

(d) It **unifies all business units** of a company into an integrated risk review, so that the same 'language' of risk (risk terminology) is applied throughout the company.

(e)   It is **strategic**, and driven by business objectives, particularly the need for the company to adapt to its changing business environment.

(f)   It should be **re-evaluated on a regular basis**.

(g)   It should be **durable**, evolving as the business and its environment changes.

(h)   In order to create shareholder value, a company needs to **manage the risks** it faces and communicate to the capital markets how it is carrying out this task. Communication of risks helps shareholders make informed decisions –remember shareholders are prepared to tolerate risk provided they receive an acceptable level of return. It will also provide more confidence in the company and hence lower the required return of shareholders and lenders. However this will be balanced against the need to avoid excessive disclosures to competitors.

Exam focus point

> Although the Turnbull report was issued in the UK, it can be regarded as setting out best practice on board review and reporting for most jurisdictions.

 Case Study

Diageo, the global premium drinks business, discloses risks under the following headings in its 2006 accounts.

- Competition reducing market share and margins

- Not deriving expected benefits from strategy of focusing on premium drinks or its change and cost-saving programmes

- Not deriving expected benefits from systems change programmes and disruption caused by systems failures

- Regulatory decisions and changes resulting in increased costs and liabilities, or limitation of business activities

- Decreased demand due to changes in consumer preferences and tastes

- Decreased demand due to decline in social acceptability of products

- Poorer results due to increased costs or shortages of raw materials or labour or disruption to production facilities

- Impact of unfavourable economic developments or political development

- Disruption to operations caused by failure to renegotiate distribution and manufacturing rights

- Inability to protect intellectual property rights

- General factors affecting US food industry

- Inability to enforce judgements in directors under UK law

Diageo's corporate governance statement includes a general statement on risks and internal controls, It stresses that the business is aiming to avoid or reduce risks that can cause loss, reputational damage or business failure; nevertheless the company aims to control business cost-effectively and exploit profitable business opportunity in a disciplined way. Each year risk is assessed as an integral part of strategic planning by:

- All significant business units
- Groups of business units
- The Diageo executive committee

and these assessments are reviewed by relevant executives and the audit and risk committees. The committees gain assurance from:

- Summary information in relation to the management of identified risks

- Detailed review of the management of selected key risks

- The work of the audit and risk function which supports and challenges risk assessments, supports and challenges management to improve the effectiveness of management of identified key risks and conducts internal audits.

Risk assessment also covers major business decisions and initiatives and significant operational risks such as health and safety, product quality and environmental risk management.

There is also specific detail on how treasury risks such as currency, interest rate, liquidity, credit and commodity price risks are being managed.

3.6 Sarbanes-Oxley requirements

The requirements relating to companies that are under the Sarbanes-Oxley regime are rather stricter than under the UK Combined Code derived from the Turnbull recommendations.

The most significant difference is that the Combined Code requires directors to say that they have assessed the effectiveness of internal controls **in general**, Sarbanes-Oxley requires the directors to say specifically in the accounts whether or not internal controls **over financial reporting** are **effective.** The directors cannot conclude that controls are effective if there are **material weaknesses** in controls, severe deficiencies that result in a more than remote likelihood that material misstatements in the financial statements won't be prevented or detected.

The disclosures should include a **statement of management responsibility**, details of the **framework** used, disclosure of **material weaknesses**, and also a **statement of attestation by the external auditors** on management's assessment of the effectiveness of internal control.

Chapter Roundup

- Directors need **information** from a **large variety of sources** to be able to supervise and review the operation of the internal control systems. Information sources should include normal reporting procedures, but staff should also have channels available to report problems or doubtful practices of others.

- Procedures improving staff abilities and attitudes should be built into the control framework. **Communication** of control and risk management issues and strong **human resource procedures** reinforce the control systems.

- Boards should review **risks** and the **effectiveness of internal controls regularly**.

- They should carry out an **annual review** that looks more widely at risks faced and control systems and also how these issues should be reported.

Quick Quiz

1   What are the key elements of an action plan for dealing with internal control weaknesses?

2   In what areas of control systems are exception reports an important feature?

3   According to the Turnbull report, in what areas do internal controls particularly need to be communicated?

4   Turnbull suggests that businesses can best enhance their risk management systems by developing additional risk reporting systems.

   True   ☐

   False   ☐

5   What according to the Turnbull report should be the main elements of the board's regular review of internal controls?

6   And what should be the main elements of the board's annual review of internal controls?

7   Fill in the blanks

   The board should report that the control system is designed to .... the risk of failure to achieve business objectives and can only provide .... assurance against material misstatement or loss.

8   Under the Sarbanes-Oxley rules, when will the directors be unable to conclude that controls are effective?

Answers to Quick Quiz

1
- The actions to be taken to resolve the weakness
- The timescale for the action to be taken
- Reporting provisions

2
- Budgets
- Performance measures
- Quality targets
- Planning systems

3
- Customer relations
- Service levels for both internal and outsourced activities
- Health, safety and environmental protection
- Security of assets and business continuity
- Expenditure
- Accounting, financial and other reporting

4   False; not necessarily. Turnbull suggests that sometimes it may be better to build warning mechanisms into existing systems.

5
- What the risks are and strategies for identifying, evaluating and managing them
- The effectiveness of the management and internal control systems
- Whether actions are being taken to reduce the risks found
- Whether the results indicate that internal control should be monitored more extensively

6
- The changes since the last assessment in risks faced and the company's ability to respond to changes in its business environment

- The scope and quality of management's monitoring of risk and internal control, and of the work of internal audit

- The extent and frequency of reports to the board

- Significant controls, failings, and weaknesses having material impacts upon the accounts

- The effectiveness of the public reporting processes

7   Manage; reasonable

8   When there are material weaknesses that result in a more than remote likelihood that material misstatements in the financial statements won't be prevented or detected.

Now try the question below from the Exam Question Bank

Number	Level	Marks	Time
Q9	Examination	25	45 mins

Part E
Professional values and ethics

Ethics and the public interest

10

Topic list	Syllabus reference
1 Ethical theories	E1
2 Influences on ethics	E2
3 Organisations' ethical and social responsibility stances	E2
4 Professionals and the public interest	E3

Introduction

This chapter begins the detailed coverage of ethics, which is a core topic not only in this paper, but generally in ACCA's professional exams. ACCA has introduced an on-line ethics module as part of its training and this section of the syllabus develops ethical themes covered in the on-line module. Remember when working through this chapter that **personal ethics** are emphasised by ACCA as well as business ethics.

We start by examining certain important ethical theories and in doing so, highlight a couple of key issues; whether there are objective, universal standards and how much ethics should be concerned with the consequences of actions. We then look at what may influence approaches to ethics; in particular Kohlberg's framework of ethical maturity is very important.

Having focused on individuals, we widen the rest of the chapter to discuss organisations' approaches to ethics and lastly the approach of the accountancy profession to serving the public interest. Defining an acceptable position for the profession has proved very difficult, because partly of the varying definition of public interest, and how much weight to give the interests of different stakeholders.

Study guide

		Intellectual level
E1	**Ethical theories**	
(a)	Explain and distinguish between the ethical theories of relativism and absolutism	2
(b)	Explain, in an accounting and governance context, Kohlberg's stages of human moral development	3
(c)	Describe and distinguish between deontological and teleological/consequentialist approaches to ethics	2
(d)	Apply commonly-used ethical decision-making models in accounting and professional contexts: American Accounting Association model; Tucker's 5 question model	3
E2	**Different approaches to ethics and social responsibility**	
(a)	Describe and evaluate Gray, Owen and Adams seven positions on social responsibility	2
(b)	Describe and evaluate other constructions of the corporate and personal ethical stance	2
(c)	Describe and analyse the variables determining the cultural context of ethics and corporate social responsibility.	2
E3	**Professions and the public interest**	
(a)	Explain and explore the nature of a profession and professionalism	2
(b)	Describe and assess what is meant by the public interest	2
(c)	Describe the role of, and assess the influence of, accounting as a profession in the organisational context	3
(d)	Analyse the role of accounting as a profession in society	2
(e)	Recognise accounting's role as a value-laden profession capable of influencing the distribution of power and wealth in society	3
(f)	Describe and critically evaluate issues surrounding accounting and acting against the public interest	3

Exam guide

The pilot paper asked for a straightforward description of certain approaches to ethics. Other questions may be more complex, requiring consideration of influences on a person or organisation's ethical position. You should also expect to see some discussion questions on the neutrality (or otherwise) of the accountancy profession and whether its activities unduly support certain interests in society. A typical question might ask you to interpret people's actions or attitudes in the light of the ethical theories or suggest how one of the theories might affect behaviour.

1 Ethical theories

A key debate in ethical theory is whether ethics can be determined by **objective**, **universal principles**. How important the **consequences of actions** should be in determining an ethical position is also a significant issue.

1.1 Role of ethical theory

Ethics is concerned with right and wrong and how conduct should be judged to be good or bad. It is about how we should live our lives and, in particular, how we should **behave towards other people**. It is therefore relevant to all forms of human activity.

Business life is a fruitful source of ethical dilemmas because its whole purpose is **material gain**, the making of profit. Success in business requires a constant, avid search for potential advantage over others and business people are under pressure to do whatever yields such advantage.

It is important to understand that if ethics is applicable to corporate behaviour at all, it must therefore be a fundamental aspect of **mission**, since everything the organisation does flows from that. Managers responsible for strategic decision making cannot avoid responsibility for their organisation's ethical standing. They should consciously apply ethical rules to all of their decisions in order to filter out potentially undesirable developments. The question is however what ethical rules should be obeyed. Those that always apply or those that hold only in certain circumstances?

Ethical assumptions underpin all business activity as well as guiding behaviour. The continued existence of capitalism makes certain assumptions about the 'good life' and the desirability of private gain, for example. As we shall see in Section 4, accountancy is allegedly not a value-neutral profession. It establishes and follows rules for the protection of shareholder wealth and the reporting of the performance of capital investment. Accordingly accounting, especially in the private sector, can be seen as a servant of capital, making the implicit assumptions about morality that capitalism does.

1.2 Non-cognitivism and ethical relativism

The approach called **non-cognitivism** denies the possibility of acquiring objective knowledge of moral principles. It suggests that all moral statements are essentially subjective and arise from the culture, belief or emotion of the speaker.

Non-cognitivism recognises the differences that exist between the rules of behaviour prevailing in different cultures. The view that right and wrong are culturally determined is called **ethical relativism** or **moral relativism**. This is clearly a matter of significance in the context of international business. Managers encountering cultural norms of behaviour that differ significantly from their own may be puzzled to know what rules to follow.

Question

Morality

What can be said about the morality of a society that allows abortion within certain time limits in certain circumstances, or which allows immigration if immigrants fulfil certain requirements (will benefit the local economy)?

Answer

The suggested treatment of these issues suggests that the society is a non-cognitivist, ethically relative society. Banning abortion would be one sign of an ethically absolute society.

1.2.1 Strengths of relativism

(a) Relativism highlights our **cognitive bias** in observing with our senses (we see only what we know and understand) and our **notational bias** (what we measure without using our senses is subject to the bias of the measurement methods used).

(b) Relativism also highlights differences in **cultural beliefs**; for example all cultures may say that it is wrong to kill innocents, but different cultures may have different beliefs about who innocents actually are.

(c) The philosopher Bernard Crick argued that differing absolutist beliefs result in **moral conflict** between people; (relativist) ethics should act to resolve such conflicts.

1.2.2 Criticisms of relativism

(a) Put simply, strong relativism is a based on a **fundamental contradiction**; the statement that 'All statements are relative' is itself an absolute, non-relative statement. However it is possible to argue that some universal truths (certain laws of physics) exist, but deny other supposedly objective truths.

(b) A common criticism of relativism, particularly by religious leaders, is that it leads to a **philosophy of 'anything goes'**, denying the existence of morality and permitting activities that are harmful to others.

(c) Alternatively some critics have argued for the existence of **natural moral laws** (discussed below). These are not necessarily religious laws; the atheist scientist Richard Dawkins has argued in favour of natural laws.

(d) Ideas such as **objectivity and final truth** do have value – consider for example the ethical principle that we shall discuss later for accountants to be objective.

(e) If it's valid to say that everyone's differing opinions are **right**, then it's equally valid to say that **everyone's differing opinions are wrong**.

1.3 Cognitivism and ethical absolutism

Cognitivist approaches to ethics are built on the principle that **objective, universally applicable moral truths** exist and can be known. There are various methods of establishing these:

(a) **Religions** are based on the concept of universally applicable principles.

(b) **Law** can be a source of reference for establishing principles. However, ethics and law are not the same thing. Law must be free from ambiguity. However, unlike law, ethics can quite reasonably be an arena for debate, about both the principles involved and their application in specific rules.

(c) **Natural law** approaches to ethics are based on the idea that a set of objective or 'natural' moral rules exists and we can come to know what they are. In terms of business ethics, the natural law approach deals mostly with **rights and duties**. Where there is a right, there is also a duty to respect that right. For those concerned with business ethics there are undeniable implications for behaviour towards individuals. Unfortunately, the implications about duties can only be as clear as the rights themselves and there are wide areas in which disagreement about rights persists.

(d) **Deontological approaches** (see below).

1.3.1 Strengths of absolutism

(a) Fundamentally the statement that **absolute truth does not exist** is **flawed**; if it does not exist, then the statement that it does not exist cannot be true.

(b) Absolutism lays down their certain unambiguous rules that people are able to follow, knowing that their **actions are right**.

1.3.2 Criticisms of absolutism

(a) Absolutist ethics takes **no account of evolving norms** within society and the development of 'advances' in morality, for example development of the belief that slavery is wrong.

(b) From **what source** should absolutist ethics be derived? Should it be religion, universal laws, human nature? Whatever source is used, it is then possibly subject to human interpretation with the result that different views may exist on the same issue and there will never be universal agreement.

(c) What happens when **two absolutist positions** appear **incompatible**. For example is it permissible to tell a lie in order to save an innocent life?

(d) A theory can be **true according to a relative framework** as well as true according to an absolute framework; what differs is the nature of the framework and not the truth of the statement.

1.4 Deontological ethics

Key term

> **Deontology** is concerned with the application of universal ethical principles in order to arrive at rules of conduct, the word deontology being derived from the Greek for 'duty'.

Whereas the consequentialist approach judges actions by their outcomes, deontology lays down **criteria** by which they may be judged in advance. The definitive treatment of deontological ethics is found in the work of the eighteenth century German philosopher, *Immanuel Kant*.

Kant's approach to ethics is based on the idea that facts themselves are neutral: they are what is; they do not give us any indication of what should be. If we make moral judgements about facts, the criteria by which we judge are separate from the facts themselves. Kant suggested that the criteria come from within ourselves and are based on a **sense of what is right**; an intuitive awareness of the nature of good.

Kant spoke of motivation to act in terms of 'imperatives'. A **hypothetical imperative** lays down a course of action to achieve a certain result. For instance, if I wish to pass an examination I must study the syllabus. A **categorical imperative**, however, defines a course of action in terms of acting in accordance with **moral duty** without reference to outcomes, desire or motive. For Kant, moral conduct is defined by categorical imperatives. We must act in certain ways because it is right to do so – right conduct is an **end in itself**.

Kant arrived at three formulations of the categorical imperative.

(a) 'So act that the maxim of your will could hold as a principle establishing universal law.'

This is close to the common sense maxim called the golden rule found in many religious teachings, for example the bible:

In everything do to others what you would have them do to you, for this sums up the Law and the Prophets (Matthew 7:12)

The difference between Kant's views and the golden rule is that under the golden rule, one could inflict harm on others if one was happy for the same harm to be inflicted on oneself.

Kant however would argue that certain actions were universally right or wrong, irrespective of the personal, societal or cultural conditions.

Kant went on to suggest that this imperative meant that we have a duty not to act by maxims that result in logical contradictions. Theft of property for examples implies that it is permissible to steal, but also implies the existence of property; however if theft is allowed there can be no property, a logical contradiction. Kant also argued that we should act only by maxims that we believe should be universal maxims. Thus if we only helped others when there was advantage for ourselves, no-one would ever give help to others.

(b)   'Do not treat people simply as means to an end but as an end in themselves.'

The point of this rule is that it distinguishes between **people** and **objects**. We use objects as means to achieve an end: a chair is for sitting on, for instance. People are different.

We regard people differently from the way we regard objects, since they have unique intellects, feelings, motivations and so on of their own: treating them as objects denies their rationality and hence rational action.

Note, however, that this does not preclude us from using people as means to an end as long as we, at the same time, recognise their right to be treated as autonomous beings. Clearly, organisations and even society itself could not function if we could not make use of other people's services.

(c)   'So act as though you were through your maxims a law-making member of the kingdom of ends.'

Autonomous human beings are not subject to any particular interest and are therefore only subject to the universal laws which they make for themselves. However they must regard those laws as binding on others, or they would not be universal and would not be laws at all.

1.4.1 Criticisms of Kant

(a)   Critics have pointed out a dualism in Kant's views; he sees humans as part of nature whose actions can be explained in terms of natural causes. Yet Kant also argues that human beings are **capable of self-determination** with full freedom of action and in particular an ability to act in accordance with the principles of duty. Man is therefore capable in effect of rising above nature, which appears to conflict with the view that man is a natural animal.

(b)   It is argued that you cannot take actions in a vacuum and must have regard for their **consequences**. The Swiss philosopher Benjamin Constant put forward the 'enquiring murderer' argument; if you agree with Kant and hold that Truth telling must be universal, then one must, if asked, tell a known murderer the location of his prey. Kant's response was that lying to a murderer denied the murderer's rationality, and hence denied the possibility of there being free rational action at all. In addition Kant pointed out that we cannot always know what the consequences of our actions would be.

(c)   Kierkegaard argued that, whatever their expectations of others, **people failed to apply Kant's duties** to themselves, either by not exercising morally laws or not punishing themselves if they morally transgressed.

1.5 Teleological or consequentialist ethics: utilitarianism

There are two versions of consequentialist ethics:

- Utilitarianism – what is best for the greatest number
- Egoism – what is best for me

The teleological approach to ethics is to make moral judgements about courses of action by reference to their **outcomes or consequences**. The prefix *telios* is derived from the Greek and refers to issues of ends or outcomes.

Right or wrong becomes a question of **benefit or harm** rather than observance of universal principles.

Utilitarianism is the best-known formulation of this approach and can be summed up in the '**greatest good'** principle – 'greatest happiness of the greatest number'. This says that when deciding on a course of action we should choose the one that is likely to result in the greatest good for the greatest number of people. It therefore contrasts sharply with any absolute or universal notion of morality. The 'right' or 'wring' can **vary between situations and over time** according to the greatest happiness of the greatest number.

1.5.1 Problems with utilitarianism

There is an immediate problem here, which is how we are to define what is good for people. Bentham, a philosopher who wrote on utilitarianism, considered that **happiness** was the measure of good and that actions should therefore be judged in terms of their potential for promoting happiness or relieving unhappiness. Others have suggested that longer lists of harmful and beneficial things should be applied.

Case Study

A connected problem lies in outcomes that may in fact be beneficial but are not recognised as such. The **structural adjustment programmes** provided by the International Monetary Fund are a case in point. They are designed to align a country's economic incentives so that, by improving trade and public finances, to meet an objective, such as debt repayment. The IMF might argue, therefore, that the pain and dislocation suffered are short-term difficulties for long-term well-being. Critics of IMF structural adjustment programmes might suggest the opposite: that they are designed to remove money from the very poorest. The rights of the poor are more important than those of bondholders and to insist on repayment is unethical.

The utilitarian approach may also be questioned for its potential effect upon minorities. A situation in which a large majority achieved great happiness at the expense of creating misery among a small minority would satisfy the 'greatest good' principle. It could not, however, be regarded as ethically desirable.

However, utilitarianism can be a useful guide to conduct. It has been used to derive wide ranging rules and can be applied to help us make judgements about individual, unique problems.

Exam focus point

> The Pilot paper asked for the consequentialist and deontological approaches to ethics to be contrasted.

1.6 Teleological or consequentialist ethics: egoism

Key term

> **Egoism** states that an act is ethically justified if decision-makers freely decide to pursue their own short-term desires or their long-term interests. The subject to all ethical decisions is the self.

Adam Smith argued that an egoistic pursuit of individual self-interest produced a desired outcome for society through **free competition and perfect information** operating in the marketplace. Producers of goods for example have to offer value-for-money, since competition means that customers will buy from competitors if they don't. Egoism can also link in with enlightened self-interest; a business investing in good facilities for its workforce to keep them content and hence maintain their loyalty.

1.6.1 Criticisms of egoism

One criticism of pure egoism is that it makes short-term selfish desires equivalent to longer-term, more beneficial, interests. A modified view would give most validity to exercising those short-term desires that were in long-term interests. A more serious criticism has been that the markets do not function perfectly, and that some participants can benefit themselves at the expense of others and also the wider environment – hence the debate on sustainability which we shall consider in Chapter 12. Most fundamentally egoism is argued to be the **ethics of the thief** as well as the short-termist.

1.7 Pluralism

Pluralism accepts that different views may exist on morality, but suggests a consensus may be able to be reached in certain situations. A pluralist viewpoint is helpful in business situations where a range of perspectives have to be understood in order to establish a **course of action**. It emphasises the importance of morality as a **social phenomenon**; that some rules and arrangements need to be established for us to live together and we therefore need a good understanding of the different moralities that we will encounter.

2 Influences on ethics

FAST FORWARD

Ethical decision making is influenced by **individual and situational factors**.

Individual factors include **age and gender**, **beliefs, education and employment**, how much **control** individuals believe they have over their own situation and their **personal integrity**.

Kohlberg's framework relates to individuals' degree of **ethical maturity**, the extent to which they can take their own ethical decisions.

Situational factors include **the systems of reward**, **authority** and **bureaucracy**, **work roles**, **organisational factors**, and the **national and cultural contexts**.

2.1 The cultural context of ethics and corporate social responsibility

Models of ethical decision-making divide the cultural factors that influence decision-making into two categories:

- **Individual** – the characteristics of the individual making the decision
- **Situational** – the features of the context which determine whether the individual will make an ethical or unethical decision

The problem with identifying these factors is that it is difficult to break them down individually since many of them are interdependent. Also evidence on the importance of **individual factors** seems to be mainly from the **USA**, whereas information on **situational factors** seems mainly to be from **Europe**. This arguably reflects an American focus on individual economic participants, whereas European attention is more focused on the design of economic institutions and how they function morally and promote moral behaviour in others.

2.2 Individual influences

2.2.1 Age and gender

Although some evidence suggests that the ways in which men and women respond to ethical dilemmas may differ, empirical studies do not clearly show whether men or women can be considered as more ethical. Similarly, although different age groups have been influenced by different experiences, again empirical evidence does not suggest that certain age groups are more moral than others.

2.2.2 National and cultural beliefs

By contrast national and cultural beliefs seem to have a significant effect on ethical beliefs, shaping what individuals regard as acceptable business issues. Hofstede has indicated that significant differences lie in the following four areas:

(a) **Individualism/collectivism** – the extent to which the culture emphasises the autonomous individual as opposed to group and community goals

(b) **Power distance** – how much acceptance there is in the society of the unequal distribution of power, and the perceived gap between juniors and seniors in a society or social structure (eg children/parents, students/teachers, citizens/legislators)

Hickson and Pugh describe power distance as 'how removed subordinates feel from superiors in a social meaning of the word distance. In a high power distance culture, inequality is accepted… in a low power distance culture inequalities and overt status symbols are minimised and subordinates expect to be consulted and to share decisions with approachable managers'.

(c) **Uncertainty avoidance** – individuals' preferences for certainties, rules and absolute truths

(d) **Masculinity/femininity** – or the extent to which money and possessions are valued as against people and relationships

These factors may influence how an individual tackles an ethical problem; alone (in an individualist culture) or in consultation (in a collectivist situation). Other influences might be on how individuals respond to ethically questionable directives from their superiors; in power distance cultures, where hierarchy is respected, commands are less likely to be questioned (I was only obeying orders). Globalisation may weaken the influence of national factors, although there is often a close connection between the local culture and a particular geographical region.

2.2.3 Education and employment

By contrast globalisation might be expected to strengthen the influence of education and employment. There do appear to be some differences in ethical decision-making between those with different educational and professional experiences.

2.2.4 Psychological factors

Psychological factors are concerned with the ways in which people think, and hence
decide what is the morally right or wrong course of action. Discussion has centred on **cognitive moral development** and **locus of control.**

2.2.5 Cognitive moral development

Kohlberg explains the ethical development of individuals in terms of progression through three levels of moral development with two planes within each level. Although these levels are meant to relate to an individual's experience, in fact all three levels can be related to ethical behaviour. They show the **reasoning process** of individuals; it is possible that individuals at different levels will make the same moral decisions, but they will do so as a result of different reasoning processes. Kohlberg emphasises **how** the decision is reached, not **what** is decided.

Level 1 External rewards/punishment and self-interest

Individuals will define right or wrong in terms of the magnitude of expected rewards or punishment, or on a higher plane in terms of the deals they make to achieve their interests being **fair**. These are concepts that seem to be associated with children, but employees' actions may be governed by whether they think they will be rewarded or penalised.

- On the lower plane individuals see morality in terms of the questions: 'Will I be punished? Will I be rewarded?'.

- On the higher plant it means acquiescing in others' behaviour in return for others supporting them.

Level 2 Conventional

In terms of individual development, this level can be defined as individuals learning to live up to what is **expected** of them. On the lower plant this relates the expectations of their immediate circle. This can work both ways in a business context; an individual might feel pressurised into staying out for a long lunch because everybody else in his team does; on the other hand individuals may feel they have to be at work by a certain time because everybody else is, even if it is earlier than their prescribed hours.

Individuals are seen as operating on a higher plane within this level if they operate in line with social or cultural accord rather than just the opinion of those around them. This certainly means **complying with the law** as it codifies social accord but it doesn't just mean that. Directors may for example decide to offer better terms to overseas workers because of the activities of pressure groups campaigning against 'sweatshop labour'. Many business managers appear to think with Level 2 reasoning.

Level 3 Post-conventional

The most advanced level relates to individual development towards making their **own ethical decisions** in terms of what they believe to be right, not just acquiescing in what others believe to be right. Individuals are **separate entities** from **societies**:

- On the lower plane what individuals believe to be right is in terms of the **basic values** of their society.

- On the higher plane, individuals base their decisions on **wider universal ethical principles** such as justice, equity or rights, or Kant's framework. Business decisions made on these grounds could be disclosure on grounds of right-to-know that isn't compelled by law, or stopping purchasing from suppliers who test products on animals, on the grounds that animal rights to be free from suffering should be respected.

2.2.6 Criticisms of Kohlberg

Kohlberg argued that the higher the stage, the more ethical a decision was. However Kohlberg's work has been criticised for:

(a) Being **narrowly founded** on the typical abstract principles of American males such as fairness, impartiality, rights, maintenance of rules. Carol Gilligan, one of Kohlberg's former students(!), argued that women tend to use an ethic of care with a focus on empathy, harmony and interdependent relationships.

(b) Basing the **framework on his own value judgements**. Critics argue that the framework values rights and justice above other bases of morality such as basing actions upon social consequences or the need to achieve a peaceful settlement of conflict or problems.

(c) Arguing that the **acceptability of a solution** depends on the method of reasoning; the stage of moral development reached here would also appear to be significant.

(d) Assuming that moral action is **primarily decided by formal reasoning**. Social intuitionists argue that people make moral judgements in real-life without necessarily considering concerns such as fairness, law, human rights and abstract values; the judgements they make to solve a problem in real-life may be different to those if given the same problem as a theoretical problem.

(e) **Assuming individual development.** This is perhaps the most serious criticism of Kohlberg, that individuals do not necessarily progress during their lives, and even if they do progress, it may only be in certain situations; they may use different methods of moral reasoning inside and outside the workplace.

Exam focus point

Kohlberg's framework is emphasised significantly in the syllabus, and you therefore will need to consider it when dealing with various ethical situations. For example does the organisation's ethical framework allow people to make up their own minds on ethics, or does it assume (or promote) a lower level of ethical awareness.

You may also need to identify the Kohlberg level that someone is at given that he is behaving in a certain way, and produce arguments for and against operating at certain levels.

2.2.7 Locus of control

The locus of control is **how much influence individuals believe** they have over the course of their own lives. Individuals with a high internal locus believe that they can shape their own lives significantly, whereas those with external locus believe that their lives will be shaped by circumstances or luck. This distinction suggests that those with an internal locus will take more responsibility for their actions and are more likely to consider the moral consequences of what they do. Research however does not clearly indicate whether this is true in practice. As we saw in Chapter 8, this may also link into attitudes towards risk and what can be done to deal with risk.

2.2.8 Personal integrity

Integrity can be defined as adhering to moral principles or values. Its ethical consequences are potentially very significant, for example in deciding whether to **whistleblow** on questionable practice at work, despite pressure from colleagues or superiors or negative consequences of doing so. However evidence of its importance is limited because strangely it has not been included in many ethical decision models.

2.2.9 Moral imagination

Moral imagination is the level of awareness individuals have about the variety and moral consequences of what they do, how creatively they reflect on ethical dilemmas. The consequences of having a wide moral imagination could be an ability to see beyond the conventional organisational responses to moral difficulties, and formulate different solutions. Again there is little research on this subject, but differing levels of moral imagination would seem to be a plausible reason why individuals with the same work background view moral problems in different ways.

2.3 Situational influences

The reason for considering situational influences on moral decision-making is that individuals appear to have 'multiple ethical selves' – they make different decisions in different circumstances. These circumstances might include **issue-related factors** (the nature of the issue and how it is viewed in the organisation) and **context-related factors** (the expectations and demands that will be placed on people working in an organisation).

2.4 Issue-related factors

2.4.1 Moral intensity

Thomas Jones proposed a list of six criteria that decision-makers will use to decide how ethically significant an issue was, and hence what they should do:

- **Magnitude of consequences** – the harms or the benefits that will result

- **Social consequences** – the degree of general agreement about the problem

- **Probability of effect** – the probability of the harms or benefits actually happening

- **Temporal immediacy** – the speed with which the consequences are likely to occur; if they are likely to take years, the moral intensity may be lower

- **Proximity** – the feelings of nearness that the decision-maker has for those who will suffer the impacts of the ethical decision

- **Concentration of effect** – whether some persons will suffer greatly or many people will suffer lightly

Research suggests that moral intensity is significant but has to be seen in the context of how an issue is perceived in an organisation.

2.4.2 Moral framing

Moral framing sets the context for how issues are **perceived** in organisations. Language is very important. Using words such as fairness and honesty is likely to trigger moral thinking. However evidence suggests that many managers are reluctant to frame issues in moral terms seeing it as promoting disharmony, distorting decision-making and suggesting that they are not practical. Instead issues are more likely to be discussed in terms of **rational corporate self-interest**.

2.5 Context-related factors

2.5.1 Systems of reward

Reward mechanisms have obvious potential consequences for ethical behaviour. This works both ways. Basing awards on sales values achieved may encourage questionable selling practices; failing to reward ethical behaviour (or worst still penalising whistleblowers or other staff who act ethically) will not encourage an ethical culture.

Sadly a majority of studies on this area seem to indicate that there is a significant link between the rewarding of unethical behaviour and its continuation.

2.5.2 Authority

There are various ways in which managers may encourage ethical behaviour; by **direct instructions** to subordinates, by setting subordinates **targets** that are so challenging that they can only be achieved through taking unethical shortcuts. Failing to act can be as bad as acting, for example failing to prevent bullying. Studies suggest that many employees perceive their managers as lacking ethical integrity.

2.5.3 Bureaucracy

Key term

> **Bureaucracy** is a system characterised by detailed rules and procedures, impersonal hierarchical relations and a fixed division of tasks.

Bureaucracy underpins the authority and reward system, and may have a number of impacts on individual's reactions to ethical decision-making:

- **Suppression of moral autonomy** – individual ethical beliefs tend to be overridden by the rules and roles of the bureaucracy

- **Instrumental morality** – seeing morality in terms of following procedures rather than focusing on the moral substance of the goals themselves

- **Distancing** individuals from the consequences of what they do

- **Denial of moral status** – that ultimately individuals are resources for carrying out the organisation's will rather than autonomous moral beings

2.5.4 Work roles

Education and experience build up expectations of how people in particular roles will act. Strong evidence suggests that the expectations staff have about the roles that they adopt in work will override the individual ethics that may influence their decisions in other contexts.

2.5.5 Organisational field

Key term

> An **organisational field** is a community of organisations with a common 'meaning system' and whose participants interact more frequently with one another than those outside the field.

Organisations within an organisation field tend to share a common business environment, such as a common system of training or regulation. This means that they tend to cohere round common norms and values.

Within an organisational field a **recipe** is a common set of assumptions about organisational purposes and how to manage organisations. If the recipe is followed, it means that organisations within the organisational field can provide consistent standards for consumers for example. However it can also mean that managers within the field cannot appreciate the lessons that could be learnt from organisations outside the field, and therefore transition outside the field may be difficult.

 Case Study

An example would be a private sector manager joining a public service organisation and having to get used to different traditions and mechanisms, for example having to build consensus into the decision-making process.

The result of being in an organisational field can be a desire to achieve **legitimacy** – meeting the **expectations** that those in the same organisational field have in terms of the assumptions, behaviours and strategies that will be pursued.

2.5.6 Organisational culture

Key term

> **Organisational culture** is the 'basic assumptions and beliefs that are shared by members of an organisation, that operate unconsciously and define in a basic taken-for-granted fashion an organisation's view of itself and its environment.'
>
> (Handy)

Organisational culture relates to ways of acting, talking, thinking and evaluating. It can include shared:

- **Values** that often have 'official' status being connected to the organisation's mission statement but which can be vague (acting in the interests of the community)

- **Beliefs** that are more specific than assumptions but represent aspects of an organisation that are talked about, for example using 'ethical suppliers'

- **Behaviours**, the ways in which people within the organisation and the organisation itself operates, including work routines and symbolic gestures

- **Taken** for **granted assumptions**, which are at the core of the organisation's culture which people find difficult to explain but are central to the organisation. The **paradigm** represents the common assumptions and collective experience that an organisation must have to function meaningfully

Organisational culture may be different to (may conflict with) the official rules of the bureaucracy. Unsurprisingly it has been identified as a key element in decisions of what is morally right or wrong, as employees become conditioned by it into particular attitudes to ethical decision making.

 Case Study

In his memoirs the journalist Hunter Davies related that when he started working on a newspaper in London, he discovered that he was financially rather better off than he thought he would be because of being able to claim expenses. 'This was something that was explained to me on my very first day, not by the management, but by other reporters.' Staff would spend the first working morning of their week filling out their expenses 'for some the hardest part of their week'.

Davies was told what the normal expense claim for his role as a junior reporter was. All he had to do in order to claim that amount was submit bills for lunch or dinner with anyone; it didn't matter who they were so long as he had a piece of paper and could name them as a potential contact. Davies was informed that management knew, that it was an accepted part of national newspaper life and he would undermine the system if he didn't do what everyone else did.

In addition to the main organisational culture, there may also be **distinct subcultures** often dependent upon the way the organisation is structured, for example function or division subcultures.

2.5.7 National and cultural context

In an organisational context, this is the **nation** in which the ethical decision is made rather than the nationality of the decision-maker. If someone spends a certain length of time working in another country, their views of ethical issues may be shaped by the norms of that other country, for example on sexual harassment. Globalisation may complicate the position on this.

3 Organisations' ethical and social responsibility stances

An organisation's ethical stance relates to how it **views its responsibilities** to shareholders, stakeholders, society and the environment.

3.1 The ethical stance

Key term

An organisation's **ethical stance** is defined by *Johnson and Scholes* as the extent to which it will exceed its minimum obligation to stakeholders.

Crane and Matten and Johnson and Scholes have identified a number of key assumptions (in the form of questions) upon which ethical and social responsibility stances are based:

Who is responsible for ethical conduct in business?	Is it the individual, or is control exercised socially, by governments
Who is the key actor in business ethics?	Is it the corporation, or is it the government or other collective bodies such as trade unions
What are the key guidelines for ethical behaviour?	Again does it rest with the corporation in the form of corporate codes of ethics, or is the key guidance a legal framework negotiated with, or imposed on, business
What are the key issues in business ethics?	Are they single decision issues involving misconduct and immorality, or are they social issues surrounding the framework of business
To whom are businesses responsible?	Whether to focus on enhancing shareholder value or multiple stakeholders
How should performance be measured?	Should it be measured by bottom line financial results or by pluralistic measures
How should an ethical stance be incorporated into business activity?	Should an ethical stance be seen primarily in terms of compliance with law/corporate governance codes, or should it be actively incorporated into an organisation's mission and strategy
How important is reputation?	Does it make any difference to financial results? Should organisations strive to have a good reputation even if doing so makes no demonstrable difference to their bottom line profits

Johnson and Scholes illustrate the range of possible ethical stances by giving four illustrations.

- **Short-term shareholder interest**
- **Long-term shareholder interest**
- **Multiple stakeholder obligations**
- **Shaper of society**

3.1.1 Short-term shareholder interest

An organisation might limit its ethical stance to taking responsibility for **short-term shareholder interest** on the grounds that it is for **government** alone to impose wider constraints on corporate governance. This minimalist approach would accept a duty of obedience to the demands of the law, but would not undertake to comply with any less substantial rules of conduct. This stance can be justified on the grounds that going beyond it can **challenge government authority**; this is an important consideration for organisations operating in developing countries.

3.1.2 Long-term shareholder interest

There are two reasons why an organisation might take a wider view of ethical responsibilities when considering the **longer-term interest of shareholders**.

(a)   The organisation's **corporate image** may be enhanced by an assumption of wider responsibilities. The cost of undertaking such responsibilities may be justified as essentially promotional expenditure.

 Case Study

The *Cooperative Bank* has estimated that it made £40m profit in 2003 as a result of its ethical policies.

Research showed that the Bank's ethical stance attracted business far in excess of that lost by turning away customers with poor human rights records or weak environmental performance.

(b)   The responsible exercise of corporate power may prevent a build-up of social and political **pressure for legal regulation**. Freedom of action may be preserved and the burden of regulation lightened by acceptance of ethical responsibilities.

3.1.3 Multiple stakeholder obligations

An organisation might accept the **legitimacy of the expectations and/or claims of stakeholders other than shareholders** and build those expectations into its stated purposes. This would be because without appropriate relationships with groups such as suppliers, employers and customers, the organisation would not be able to function.

Clearly, organisations have a duty to respect the **legal rights** of stakeholders other than shareholders. These are extensive in the UK, including wide-ranging **employment law** and **consumer protection law**, as well as the more basic legislation relating to such matters as contract and property. Where **moral entitlements** are concerned, organisations need to be practical: they should take care to establish just what expectations they are prepared to treat as **obligations,** bearing in mind their general ethical stance and degree of concern about bad publicity.

Acceptance of obligations to stakeholders implies that **measurement of the organisation's performance** must give due weight to these extra imperatives. For instance the British entrepreneur Anita Roddick has not cared to have the performance of Body Shop assessed in purely financial terms.

3.1.4 Shaper of society

It is difficult enough for a commercial organisation to accept wide responsibility to stakeholders. The role of **shaper of society** is even more demanding and largely the concern of public sector organisations and charities, though some well-funded private organisations might act in this way. The legitimacy of this approach depends on the framework of **corporate governance** and **accountability.** Where organisations are clearly set up for such a role, either by government or by private sponsors, they may pursue it. However, they must also satisfy whatever requirements for financial viability are established for them.

Traidcraft aims to fight poverty through a wide-range of trade related activities. The company's structure is that of a trading company and a development charity working together, pioneering the development of fair trade by:

- Building lasting relationships with small-scale producers in developing countries
- Supporting people to trade out of poverty
- Working to bring about trade justice and fair business practices
- Striving to be transparent and accountable

In poorer countries Traidcraft supports traders by providing business training, information and help in winning sales. In the UK Traidcraft works to encourage business to apply corporate social responsibility and provide social accounts. It aims to persuade UK businesses to change their practices so that they have a positive impact on their suppliers.

Traidcraft's policy unit exists to campaign for changes in the rules of trade and work with business and institutions to deliver poverty-alleviating policies. The organisation has recently campaigned against European partnership agreements – agreements between European countries and their former colonies – on the grounds that these are forcing the colonies' economies to liberalise too fast. This will result in farmers and industries having to compete openly with EU corporations before they are ready, and resulting in their losing markets and going out of business.

3.2 Social responsibility stances

Gray, Owen and Adams in their book *Accounting and accountability* identify seven viewpoints of social responsibility.

Pristine capitalists	Support liberal economic democracy, **private property system** is the best system, companies exist to **make profits** and **seek economic efficiency**. Businesses therefore have **no moral responsibilities** beyond their obligations to shareholders and creditors.
Expedients	Modified liberal economic democracy, economic systems do generate some **excesses**, therefore businesses have to accept some (limited) **social legislation and moral requirements**. Some social responsibility may be appropriate if such behaviour is in **the business's economic interests**.
Proponents of the social contract	An organisation's survival and prosperity is based on **delivery of benefits to society** in general and distribution of economic, social or political benefits to groups from which it derives its power. Organisations therefore believe they should behave in a way broadly in conformance with the ethical norms in society because there is effectively a contract or agreement between the organisations in power and those who are **affected by the exercise of this power.** This may necessitate some modifications to behaviour, reporting, etc but these are necessary to underpin **mutual confidence**.
Social ecologists	Problems exist with the human environment that large organisations have created and need to eradicate. Economic processes that result in **resource exhaustion, waste and pollution** must be **modified**. Organisations must adopt socially responsible positions accordingly.

Socialists	Socialists see the business relationship reflected in business reporting as one class (capitalists) manipulating and oppressing another class (workers and the socially oppressed). Ownership and structure of society should no longer be determined by the requirements of capitalism and materialism but should **promote equality**. Attempts to enhance corporate social responsibility will fail if they continue to take place in the existing framework.
Radical feminists	Economic and social systems emphasise masculine qualities such as aggression, conflict and competition rather than **feminine values such as cooperation and reflection**; developing corporate social responsibility in the existing masculine framework won't work. A fundamental re-adjustment is required in the ownership and structure of society with potentially far-reaching implications for accountability relationships.
Deep ecologists	Human beings have **no greater rights to resources or life** than other species. Economic systems that trade off threats to the existence of species with economic imperatives are flawed. Arguably businesses cannot be trusted to maintain something as important as the environment. This viewpoint is connected with ideas on sustainability which are covered in Chapter 12 of this text.

Question

Briefly explain the main ethical issues that are involved in the following situations.

(a)   Dealing with a repressive authoritarian government abroad
(b)   An aggressive advertising campaign
(c)   Employee redundancies
(d)   Payments or gifts to officials who have the power to help or hinder the payees' operations

Answer

(a)   Dealing with unpleasantly authoritarian governments can be supported on the grounds that it **contributes to economic growth and prosperity** and all the benefits they bring to society in both countries concerned. This is a consequentialist argument. It can also be opposed on consequentialist grounds as **contributing to the continuation of the regime,** and on deontological grounds as **fundamentally repugnant**.

(b)   Honesty in advertising is an important problem. Many products are promoted exclusively on image. Deliberately creating the impression that purchasing a particular product will enhance the happiness, success and sex-appeal of the buyer can be attacked as **dishonest.** It can be defended on the grounds that the supplier is actually **selling a fantasy or dream** rather than a physical article.

(c)   Dealings with employees are coloured by the **opposing views of corporate responsibility and individual rights**. The idea of a job as property to be defended has now disappeared from labour relations in many countries, but corporate decisions that lead to redundancies are still deplored. This is because of the obvious **impact of sudden unemployment on aspirations and living standards**, even when the employment market is buoyant. Nevertheless businesses have to consider the cost of employing labour as well as its productive capacity.

(d)   The main problems with payments or gifts to officials are making distinction between those that should never be made, and those that can be made in certain cultural circumstances.

   (i)   **Extortion**. Foreign officials have been known to threaten companies with the complete closure of their local operations unless suitable payments are made.

(ii) **Bribery**. This is payments for services to which a company is not legally entitled. There are some fine distinctions to be drawn; for example, some managers regard political contributions as bribery.

(iii) **Grease money**. Multinational companies are sometimes unable to obtain services to which they are legally entitled because of deliberate stalling by local officials. Cash payments to the right people may then be enough to oil the machinery of bureaucracy.

(iv) **Gifts**. In some cultures (such as Japan) gifts are regarded as an essential part of civilised negotiation, even in circumstances where to Western eyes they might appear ethically dubious. Managers operating in such a culture may feel at liberty to adopt the local customs.

4 Professions and the public interest

FAST FORWARD

Professionalism means **avoiding actions** that bring **discredit on the accountancy profession**.

Acting in the public interest means acting for the welfare of society at large.

Various commentators have argued that the **figures** accountants produce are **not neutral**, but incorporate value judgements and are in accordance with the wishes of certain viewpoints in society.

4.1 Professions and professionalism

IFAC's code of ethics defines professionalism in terms of professional behaviour. Professional behaviour imposes an obligation on professional accountants to **comply with relevant laws and regulations** and **avoid any action** that may **bring discredit to the profession**. In marketing themselves and their work, professional accountants should not bring the profession into disrepute. They should avoid making exaggerated claims for their own services, qualifications and experience and should not refer to others disparagingly.

An ACCA survey in 2005 produced a wider definition of professionalism. The survey suggested that the most important competencies for modern professionals were:

- Maintaining confidentiality and upholding ethical standards
- Preparing financial information
- Complying with legal and regulatory requirements
- Interpreting financial statements
- Communicating effectively
- Preparing financial statements
- Problem-solving and managerial skills

4.2 The public interest

Key term

The **public interest** is considered to be the collective well-being of the community of people and institutions the professional accountant serves, including clients, lenders, governments, employers, employees, investors, the business and financial community and others who rely on the work of professional accountants. (IFAC)

IFAC comments that an accountant's responsibility is not exclusively to satisfy the needs of an **individual client or employer**.

One fundamental problem with the debate about accountants acting in the public interest is the lack in most jurisdictions of a robust definition of what the public interest is that is backed by enforcement mechanisms. Within UK law for example there is no statutory definition of the public interest. As one critic, Lovell, comments 'Its malleability possibly explains both its longevity and its unreliability in a court of law.'

Critics of the view that accountants act in the public interest have focused on the alleged closeness between accountants' definition of the public interest and the profession's own self-interest. Critics have claimed that accountants' insistence on self-regulation indicates where their priorities lie. Some believe that the accountancy profession has always been vulnerable to this charge. Lee's history of the accountancy profession in the nineteenth century comments: 'The most obvious feature of early UK professionalisation is the pursuit by accountants and their institutions of economic self-interest in the name of a public interest'.

 Case Study

A more recent example of confusion about what the accountancy profession's interests should be is the Institute of Chartered Accountants in England and Wales's attempts to introduce a mission statement in the early 1990s. Its first draft was a simple statement that it was working in the public interest. Many members however objected on the grounds that they saw the Institute as a trade association, with its purpose being to represent their sectional interests.

As a result the ICAEW revised its mission statement to read: 'The Institute's mission is to promote high standards of objectivity, integrity and technical competence, thereby serving the interests of both the public and its members and enhancing the value of the qualification chartered accountant'. The ICAEW's leadership tried to put a positive spin on this: 'Over the longer term there is a natural convergence between the public interest and members' interest'. Critics however were not convinced.

4.3 Influence of the accountancy profession on organisations

That the influence of the accountancy profession is potentially huge can be established simply by considering all the different involvements that accountants have:

- Financial accounting
- Audit
- Management accounting
- Consulting
- Tax
- Public sector accounting

 Case Study

Accountants dominate senior business positions in many countries. In the UK for example in April 2006, 101 chief executive officers, finance directors and company secretaries in the FTSE 100 held accountancy qualifications.

The variety of involvements accountants have within each area of their expertise is also very large. The Institute of Chartered Accountants in England and Wales' recruitment literature highlights for example the role of tax accountants:

'Some professionals will advise on policy for our tax system, others will write the tax law. Someone else will administer the collection of taxes for the government. Others will act for businesses of all types who have to pay these taxes. Marketing, IT, media and publishing all need tax specialists.'

Accountants therefore have a significant impact, a significant footprint, on the organisations for which they work. Is this always for the best?

Case Study

In the book *Ethical Issues in Accounting* a chapter by Alan Lovell points out accountants will be responsible for managing public sector organisations in as cost effective a way as possible, which may not necessarily be compatible with the service objectives of those organisations nor the codes of other professional staff who work within those organisations.

Lovell utilises Kohlberg's view of ethical hierarchy to explain how accountants effectively view other professionals. The accounting system in effect assumes that as the other professionals do not trust the system or those who operate it, this illustrates that they have a low level of moral reasoning and therefore justifies a strict performance management system, together with anti-whistleblowing codes designed to deter employees from revealing shortcomings in patient care.

However the ethical codes to which doctors and nurses adhere are founded on the idea that they are their patients' advocates and this implies that they need to use a much higher level of moral reasoning.

4.4 The accountancy profession in society

At one level the numbers included within accounts can have a number of impacts:

(a)   **Mechanistic issues** are where the accounts are used to judge the performance of a company or its directors in line with a regulation or contract. Examples are company borrowing limits which are frequently defined as a multiple of share capital and reserves and directors' bonus schemes that are based on some proportion of reported profits.

(b)   **Judgemental issues** are where the figures in the accounts influence the judgement of their users. The accounts may influence not just the view of investors, but governments seeking to assess what a reasonable tax burden would be and employees determining their wage claims.

4.5 Accountancy as a value-laden profession

Many accountants would suggest that the numbers in accounts support no cause and it is for others to draw conclusions on the figures produced. If pressed they might argue that they are following the requirements of laws or of their clients. However the laws may be ethically suspect and following the requirements of clients' argument does not support ideas of accountants' independence, or, worse, leads to the suspicion that accountants are pursuing ethically dubious courses.

Even if the ends are not explicitly ethically suspect, much accounting literature assumes that accountants are producing information for individuals or corporations seeking to **maximise their personal wealth**. If this has a moral justification, it is based on the ideas of **liberal economic democracy** (the pristine capitalist position identified above). These ideas are that individuals should be free to **exercise their economic choices** and are equally able to do so. No group in society dominates either economically or politically. The result of the individual pursuit of economic benefit is economic efficiency, maximum profits and economic growth, and everyone within society being better off.

4.5.1 Criticisms of liberal economic democracy

Critics have claimed that the model of liberal economic democracy is far from reality and has various flaws. By providing the information that supports the present systems, accountants are complicit in perpetuating its flaws.

(a) **Lack of equality**

One significant criticism is that individuals are not equal economically and are evidently **not able to make economic choices** that will benefit themselves. The argument that people make a rational economic choice to be homeless is clearly wrong. Accountants are therefore accused of supporting those who can make economic choices and by doing so perpetuate social inequality, ensure wealth continues to be distributed amongst the already wealthy, and suppress minorities and the disenfranchised and powerless.

(b) **Role of institutions**

A related criticism is that individuals do not exercise the real power but institutions – principally the **government and corporations**. Indeed critics point to many instances of governments acting to protect the interests of shareholders and the information rights of the financial community against less well-off groups in society.

Marxist arguments take this viewpoint to its furthest conclusion, arguing that power is held by **capital**, that capital and labour are inevitably in conflict and that the state acts to protect capital and suppress labour; accountants too are complicit in this.

(c) **Failure to increase social welfare**

The argument that the pursuit of individual self-interest leads to maximum social welfare appears tenuous. Even if wealth is maximised, there is **no guarantee** that all aspects of **social welfare** will be **maximised**; indeed some aspects of social welfare such as quality of life or health would not seem to have an obvious link with maximising income. In addition maximisation of wealth does not imply that wealth will be fairly distributed. Critics have claimed that economic growth has been at the expense of a widening gap between rich and poor, both within developed countries and between developed countries and the third world.

(d) **Environmental problems**

As we have seen above, critics such as the 'deep ecologists' have claimed that the pursuit of growth has been at the expense of **environmental degradation** and that society needs to change its priorities. By aiding the promotion of economic growth, accountants are complicit in supporting activity that harms the environment.

(e) **Ethical viewpoint**

Some critics have gone back to ethical theories outlined earlier and have claimed accountants are complicit in a version of **utilitarianism** with the economic ends justifying the means rather than another (preferable) ethical position.

Exam focus point	The examiner has stressed that students must be able to discuss whether accountants' role is that of the servant of capital.

4.6 Criticisms of the accountancy profession

Inevitably perhaps it has been the critics of the accountancy profession who have been most vocal in highlighting the influence of accounting in resource allocation, seeking to demonstrate its complicity in wealth distribution and its role as the agent of capital.

4.6.1 Accountants in management accounting

In his book *The Social and Organisational Context of Management Accounting* Puxty argued that the 'received wisdom' of management accounting cannot legitimately be taken for granted.

Case Study

Puxty highlighted behavioural studies of budgeting that use the phrase 'dysfunctional behaviour', meaning behaviour that is harmful to the **organisation**. But why should this be so? Is it not 'dysfunctional' from the point of view of the **manager** that he is expected to suffer the misery of having his actions constrained by budget targets? There are many other examples: what, for instance, is 'favourable' about a favourable labour rate variance, from the point of view of the workforce?

Puxty went on to show that traditional management accounting is rooted in modes of thought that are only considered to be 'common sense' for the time being. 'Common sense' he asserted, is determined by the **beliefs** and **values** of the society in which it supposedly applies; it is not common to all eras (it is relativist).

In particular the ideas that considerations of society (of which businesses are a part and a microcosm) should take the individual as their starting point, and that individuals have rights to liberty and property are fundamental to accounting, yet they only originated with philosophers like Hobbes and Locke in the seventeenth century.

Case Study

One very controversial instance of the involvement of a leading accountant in a key business decision was the involvement of Professor Edward Stamp with the National Coal Board in early 1980s. Stamp had previously campaigned to launch a UK accounting standards programme and had had input into the mid 1970s document *The Audit Report* which explored the case for wider accountability for accountants. Stamp went on to become the member of a group that the National Coal Board asked to review the accounting practices that it used as a basis for deciding on pit closures. The group Stamp belonged to largely endorsed these practices.

Stamp's critics claimed that the Coal Board's accounts did not provide a basis for informed management decisions and that his group failed to take into account that a range of **political** choices could be justified from the data. What primarily drove the criticism however was that the decision management made had considerable social consequences:

'Professor Stamp's approval of the National Coal Board's accounting practices played a part in the coalmine closure programme which eventually decimated many people's lives and destroyed whole communities. Many would question whether the professional judgments which take no account of the consequences could ever be described as ethical'. *Prem Sikka*

Critics of the views of Sikka and others have claimed that their agenda is overtly political and what Stamp has been criticised for is endorsing a political decision with which they disagree.

Puxty also argues that Foucault's ideas about the way in which **regimes of power** have grown and been sustained through **disciplinary mechanisms** and the **institution of norms** for human behaviour.' are very relevant to the role of the accountancy profession.

Case Study

Other studies along similar lines to Puxty have attempted to show how the origins of accounting reside in the exercise of social power and how accounting is 'implicated in the creation of structures of surveillance and power that permit modern management to function at a distance from the work process itself.'

One study considers the development of standard costing and budgeting in the 1920s as simply one part of a general widening of the apparatus of power at this time.

'The practices that developed were intended to make the person ... more amenable to being managed and controlled',

and this should be seen in the context of other drives current at the time, such as the wide advocacy of eugenics (the sterilisation of the 'unfit', to improve the country's breeding stock) and an interest in 'mental hygiene', to be promoted by means of such methods as IQ testing.

Macintosh, *Management Accounting and Control Systems* (1994) looks at Foucault's ideas about the general principles of discipline and control that became widespread in the Western world from about 1700 onwards.

(a)   The **enclosure principle**, in essence keeping people in confined spaces (at the desk, at their workstation).

(b)   The **efficient body principle**, which disciplines individuals' time when they are in their confined spaces.

(c)   The **correct comportment principle,** disciplining behaviour through surveillance, through the imposition of norms of behaviour, and through examination.

Macintosh has little difficulty in drawing parallels with management accounting – responsibility accounting, standard costing practices and performance measurement systems being amongst the examples chosen.

4.6.2 Accountants and financial accounting

Unsurprisingly accountants have been criticised in similar terms for the picture published financial accounts give and the support they provide to capital markets. Prem Sikka argues that many accountants

'believe that mobilising accounting and auditing practices in support of markets and financial capital (held by shareholders) is ethically acceptable but mobilising accounting to give visibility to poverty and institutionalised exploitation is somehow unethical...Accounting and auditing practices remain preoccupied with prioritising capital over labour (in the profit and loss account) and the property rights (in the balance sheet). Most accounting books have little to say about social justice or the rights of employees.'

Thus for example Professor Sikka and others proposed expanding the level of disclosures in accounts in the early 1990s to include disclosures of low pay. This proposal was made at a time when the Labour party was pressing for the introduction of the minimum wage.

Sikka and others have thus emphasised the idea that accountancy decisions inevitably have **political consequences** and that it is difficult to see how accountants could hold positions that are not influenced by wider values. However one criticism of their view is that accountants are not free to determine their own stance, and that instead they are constrained by politicians' attitudes expressed in legislation.

 Case Study

A good example of this is the response to the 1970s UK document *The Corporate Report* which put the case for accountability by companies to a wider range of groups. However the UK Law Society's standing committee on company law made the following representations:

'If (the Corporate Report's) wider philosophy was to be adopted it would, in our judgment, diminish the legal rights of shareholders and creditors. While these rights are not immutable, any changes should be made by deliberate alteration of the law.'

Many of the ideas of the Corporate Report were taken up by a government green paper in 1977; however, after a change of government in the UK in 1979, reform was abandoned.

4.7 Acting against the public interest

Criticism of the accountancy profession has extended to the rules that it follows. Critics have argued that the rules:

(a)   Are **too passive,** allowing too great a variety of accounting treatments, and failing to impose meaningful responsibilities on auditors such as an explicit responsibility to detect and report fraud

(b)   **Emphasise the wrong principles**, giving priority to client confidentiality over disclosure in the wider public interest

Arguably these views depend to some extent on hindsight; the implication being that as auditors and governance structures have failed to identify corporate malpractice, there must be something wrong with the rulebook that is being followed.

However we've seen how the fallout from the Enron case influenced the development of the stricter Sarbanes-Oxley rules in the United States. Partly this was due to a belief that in a number of ways Enron did 'tick the right boxes'; it had a good number of non-executive directors on its board with a strong range of experience for example.

Chapter Roundup

- A key debate in ethical theory is whether ethics can be determined by **objective**, **universal principles**. How important the **consequences of actions** should be in determining an ethical position is also a significant issue.

- Ethical decision-making is influenced by **individual and situational factors**.

- **Individual factors** include **age and gender**, **beliefs, education and employment**, how much **control** individuals believe they have over their own situation and their **personal integrity**.

- **Kohlberg's** framework relates to individuals' degree of **ethical maturity**, the extent to which they can take their own ethical decisions.

- **Situational factors** include **the systems of reward**, **authority** and **bureaucracy**, **work roles**, **organisational factors**, and the **national and cultural contexts**.

- An organisation's ethical stance relates to how it **views its responsibilities** to shareholders, stakeholders, society and the environment.

- Professionalism means **avoiding actions** that bring **discredit on the accountancy profession**.

- **Acting in the public interest** means acting for the welfare of society at large.

- Various commentators have argued that the **figures** accountants produce are **not neutral**, but incorporate value judgements and are in accordance with the wishes of certain viewpoints in society.

Quick Quiz

1   Which view of ethics states that right and wrong are culturally determined?

    A   Ethical relativism
    B   Cognitivism
    C   Teleological
    D   Deontological

2   Fill in the blank

    The .... approach to ethics is to make moral judgements about courses of action by reference to their outcomes or consequences.

3   Match the position on social responsibility with the viewpoint held.

    (a)   Pristine capitalist

    (b)   Expedient

    (c)   Social contract proponent

    (d)   Social ecologist

    (e)   Socialist

    (f)   Radical feminist

    (g)   Deep ecologist

        (i)   Economic systems that trade off threats to the existence of species with economic imperatives are flawed

        (ii)   Businesses have to accept some social legislation and moral requirements if they are to be able to generate profits

        (iii)   Companies exist to make profits and seek economic efficiency

        (iv)   The economic framework should change from being one that promotes materialism to one that promotes equality

        (v)   Economic processes that result in resource exhaustion, waste and pollution must be modified

        (vi)   Economic systems emphasise aggression, conflict and competition rather than cooperation and reflection

        (vii)   An organisation's survival and prosperity is based on delivery of benefits to society in general

4   In what areas of national and cultural beliefs has Hofstede identified significant differences?

5   What is the significance of the post-conventional stage of an individual's moral development according to Kohlberg?

6   What is the locus of control?

7   What are the six criteria that Jones suggests will be used to determine how significant an ethical issue is?

8   What is the public interest in the context of accountancy?

Answers to Quick Quiz

1   A   Ethical relativism

2   Teleological or consequentialist

3   (a) (iii); (b) (ii); (c) (vii); (d) (v); (e) (iv); (f) (vi); (g) (i)

4   • Individualism vs collectivism
     • Acceptance of unequal distribution of power and status
     • How much individuals wish to avoid uncertainties
     • Masculinity vs femininity, money and possessions vs people and relationships

5   The post-conventional stage is when individuals make their own ethical decisions in terms of what they believe to be right, not just acquiescing in what others believe to be right.

6   The amount of influence individuals believe they have over the course of their own lives.

7   • Magnitude of consequences
     • Social consequences
     • Probability of effect
     • Temporal immediacy
     • Proximity
     • Concentration of effect

8   The collective well-being of the community of people and interests that the accountant serves

Now try the question below from the Exam Question Bank

Number	Level	Marks	Time
Q10	Introductory	n/a	45 mins

BPP
LEARNING MEDIA

Ethics and professional practice

Introduction

In this chapter we examine the guidance that organisations and professional bodies issue to encourage ethical behaviour. In Section 1 we look at corporate codes, covering their typical contents and how much impact they actually have.

In Section 2 we discuss the main features of professional codes. You will see that as with corporate governance codes, a key issue with professional ethical codes is whether the guidance should be based largely on principles or on detailed rules. In Section 3 we examine conflicts of interest and independence in detail. You will have covered these before, but we spend time recapping them because they are emphasised in the Study guide.

In the last two sections of the chapter we concentrate on how ethical problems should be approached in practice and also the way to tackle exam questions that are focused on ethical scenarios.

Study guide

		Intellectual level
E4	**Professional practice and codes of ethics**	
(a)	Describe and explore and areas covered by corporate codes of ethics	3
(b)	Describe, and assess the content of, and principles behind, professional codes of ethics	3
(c)	Describe and assess the codes of ethics relevant to accounting professionals such as IFAC or professional body codes eg ACCA	3
E5	**Conflicts of interest and the consequences of unethical behaviour**	
(a)	Describe and evaluate issues associated with conflicts of interest and ethical conflict resolution	3
(b)	Explain and evaluate the nature of impacts of ethical threats and safeguards	3
(c)	Explain and explore how threats to independence can affect ethical behaviour	3
E6	**Ethical characteristics of professionalism**	
(a)	Explain and analyse the content and nature of ethical decision-making using content from Kohlberg's framework as appropriate	2
(b)	Explain and analyse issues related to the application of ethical behaviour in a professional context	2
(c)	Describe and discuss rules based and principles based approaches to resolving ethical dilemmas encountered in professional accounting	2

Exam guide

You may gain a few marks for describing basic ethical threats, but the main focus in questions on ethics will be on practical situations. In these the ethical issues, or at any rate the solutions, will not be clearcut. Although resignation or withdrawing from an audit or assurance engagement may be the last resort that has to be adopted in certain circumstances, it will **not** always be the solution.

Although we have quoted from IFAC and ACCA guidance as obvious examples of best practice, the examiner has emphasised that these are not the only sources of ethical guidance. Using examples from other, relevant codes will also gain you credit.

1 Corporate codes of ethics

Organisations have responded to pressures to be seen to act ethically by publishing **ethical codes**, setting out their **values and responsibilities** towards stakeholders.

1.1 Corporate codes and corporate culture

Case Study

British Airways got caught in 1993 waging a 'dirty tricks' campaign against its competitor Virgin Atlantic. British Airways maintained that the offending actions (essentially, the poaching of Virgin's customers) were those of a small group of employees who overstepped the bounds of 'proper' behaviour in their eagerness to foster the interests of their employer.

An alternative view digs a little deeper. Some observers believed that the real villain of the piece was British Airways' abrasive corporate culture, inspired by the then chairman of BA, Lord King.

One of BA's responses to its defeat in the courts against Virgin and the bad publicity arising from the case was to introduce a code of ethics.

Exam focus point

An examination question may include an extract from a set of corporate guidelines on which you will be expected to comment. Even if you are not given specific information about a company's policy, though, remember that all organisations have ethical standards. There will almost certainly be something in the information that you are given that will enable you to infer at least some of the values held by the people or departments involved.

You may also be asked to criticise or evaluate a code of ethics, to interpret actions in a case scenario in the light of a code or to argue the pros and cons of adopting corporate codes of ethics.

Question

Code of ethics

Here are some extracts from an article that appeared in the UK *Financial Times*:

'Each company needs its own type of code: to reflect the national culture, the sector culture, and the exact nature of its own structure.

The nature of the codes is changing. NatWest's code, for example, tries to do much more than simply set out a list of virtues. Its programme involves not only the production of a code, but a dedicated effort to teach ethics, and a system by which the code can be audited and monitored.

For example, it has installed a 'hot-line' and its operation is monitored by internal auditors. The board of NatWest wanted it to be confidential – within the confines of legal and regulatory requirements – and the anonymity of 'whistle-blowers' has been strictly maintained.

The code contains relevant and straightforward advice. For example: 'In recognising that we are a competitive business, we believe in fair and open competition and, therefore, obtaining information about competitors by deception is unacceptable. Similarly, making disparaging comments about competitors invariably invites disrespect from customers and should be avoided.' Or: 'Employment with NatWest must never be used in an attempt to influence public officials or customers for personal gain or benefit.'

Jonathan Bye, manager of public policy at NatWest, said the bank is continually looking at ways of refreshing the code and measuring its effectiveness.

How would you suggest that the effectiveness of a company's policy on ethics could be measured?

Answer

Some ideas that you might think through are: **training effectiveness measures; breaches of the code dealt with; activity in the ethics office; public perceptions of the company.** Try to flesh them out and think of some other ideas. The extract above should suggest some.

1.2 Company code of conduct

An **ethical code** typically contains a **series of statements setting out the organisation's values and explaining how it sees its responsibilities towards stakeholders.**

Codes of corporate ethics normally have the following features.

- They **focus on regulating individual employee behaviour.**

- They are **formal documents.**

- They **cover specific areas** such as gifts, anti-competitive behaviour and so on.

- Employees may be **asked to sign** that they will comply.

- They may be **developed from third party codes** (eg regulators) or use third parties for monitoring.

- They tend to **mix moral with technical imperatives.**

- Sometimes they do **little more than describe current practices.**

- They can be used to **shift responsibility** (from senior managers to operational staff).

1.2.1 Example of code of conduct

<table>
<tr><td align="center">**Typical statements in a corporate code**</td></tr>
<tr><td>

- The company conducts all of its business on **ethical principles** and expects staff to do likewise.

- **Employees** are seen as the most important component of the company and are expected to work on a basis of trust, respect, honesty, fairness, decency and equality. The company will only employ people who follow its ethical ideals.

- **Customers** should be treated courteously and politely at all times, and the company should always respond promptly to customer needs by listening, understanding and then performing to the customer requirements.

- The company is dedicated to complying **with legal or regulatory standards** of the industry, and employees are expected to do likewise.

- The company's relationship with **suppliers and subcontractors** must be based on mutual respect. The company therefore has responsibilities including ensuring fairness and truthfulness in all of its dealings with suppliers, including pricing and licensing, fostering long-term stability in the supplier relationship, paying suppliers on time and in accordance with agreed terms of trade and preferring suppliers and subcontractors whose employment practices respect human dignity.

- The company has a responsibility to: foster open markets for trade and investment; promote **competitive behaviour** that is socially and environmentally beneficial and demonstrates mutual respect among competitors; and refrain from either seeking or participating in questionable payments or favours to secure competitive advantages.

</td></tr>
</table>

- A business should protect and, where possible, improve **the environment**, promote sustainable development, and prevent the wasteful use of natural resources.
- The company has a responsibility in **the community** to: respect human rights and democratic institutions, and promote them wherever practicable; recognise government's legitimate obligation to the society at large and support public policies and practices that promote human development through harmonious relations between business and other segments of society; collaborate with those forces in the community dedicated to raising standards of health, education, workplace safety and economic well-being; respect the integrity of local cultures; and be a good corporate citizen through charitable donations, educational and cultural contributions and employee participation in community and civic affairs.

Question	Employee behaviour

How can an organisation influence employee behaviour towards ethical issues?

Answer

Here are some suggestions.

- Recruitment and selection policies and procedures
- Induction and training
- Objectives and reward schemes
- Ethical codes
- Threat of ethical audit

1.3 The impact of codes of conduct

A code of conduct can set out the company's expectations, and in principle a code such as that outlined above addresses many of the problems that the organisations may experience. However, **merely issuing a code is not enough**.

(a) The **commitment of senior management** to the code needs to be real, and it needs to be very clearly communicated to all staff. Staff need to be persuaded that expectations really have changed.

(b) Measures need to be taken to **discourage previous behaviours** that conflict with the code.

(c) **Staff need to understand** that it is in the **organisation's best interests** to change behaviour, and become committed to the same ideals.

(d) Some employees – including very able ones – may find it very difficult to buy into a code that they **perceive may limit their own earnings** and/or restrict their freedom to do their job.

(e) In addition to a general statement of ethical conduct, **more detailed statements** (codes of practice) will be needed to set out formal procedures that must be followed.

1.4 Problems with codes of conduct

1.4.1 Inflexibility

Inflexible rules may not be practical. One example would be a **prohibition on accepting gifts from customers**. A simple prohibition that would be quite acceptable in a Western context would not work in other cultures, where non-acceptance might be seen as insulting.

1.4.2 Clarity

It is difficult to achieve **completely unambiguous wording**.

1.4.3 Irrelevancy

Surveys suggest that ethical codes are often perceived as irrelevant, for the following reasons:

(a)   They failed to say anything about the sort of **ethical problems that employees encounter.**

(b)   Other people in the organisation **pay no attention** to them.

(c)   They are **inconsistent with the prevailing organisational culture**.

(d)   Senior managers' behaviour is **not seen as promoting ethical codes**. Senior managers rarely blatantly fail to comply, rather they appear out-of-touch on ethics because they are too busy or unwilling to take responsibility.

Exam focus point

> One area explored by a question issued by the examiner was the justification for issuing a code of ethics. The viewpoints were roughly a normative code is justified because being ethical is desirable in itself vs an instrumental code is justified if it gives strategic advantage and doesn't cost too much.

1.5 Identity and values guidance

Corporate ethical codes are often **rather legalistic documents**, consisting largely of prohibitions on specific undesirable actions such as the acceptance of gifts from suppliers. More general guidance with an emphasis on principles may be more appropriate.

Identity and values programmes describe corporate values without specifying in detail what they mean. Rather than highlighting compliance with negatives they **promote positive values** about the company and form part of its culture. (Compliance programmes are about limiting legal and public relations disasters.) Even so, they need to be integrated with a company's values and leadership.

1.6 Other measures

To be effective, ethical guidance needs to be accompanied by **positive attempts to foster guiding values, aspirations and patterns of thinking that support ethically sound behaviour** – in short a **change of culture**.

Increasingly organisations are responding to this challenge by devising **ethics training programmes** for the entire workforce, instituting comprehensive **procedures for reporting and investigating ethical concerns** within the company, or even setting up an **ethics office** or department to supervise the new measures.

 Case Study

'The view from the trenches'

Badaracco and Webb (1995) carried out in-depth interviews with 30 recent Harvard MBA graduates. They found that unethical behaviour appeared to be widespread in the middle layers of business organisations.

'...in many cases, young managers received explicit instructions from their middle-manager bosses or felt strong organisational pressures to do things that they believed were sleazy, unethical, or sometimes illegal.'

However, these young managers categorised only a few of their superiors as fundamentally unethical; most were basically decent, but themselves pushed into requiring unethical behaviour by four strong organisational pressures.

(a) Performance outcomes are what really count.
(b) Loyalty is very important.
(c) Don't break the law.
(d) '…don't over-invest in ethical behaviour'.

The outcome of these pressures was a firm impression that ethical conduct was a handicap and a willingness to evade ethical imperatives an advantage in career progression.

Exam focus point

You may need to discuss corporate ethical behaviour as part of a wider discussion on the control environment. There is a good example of this sort of question in the Pilot paper.

2 Professional codes of ethics

FAST FORWARD

Professional codes of ethics apply to the **individual behaviour** of professionals and are often based on principles, supplemented by guidance on **threats and safeguards**.

2.1 Contents of professional codes

The IFAC Code of Ethics in 2005 is a good illustration of how codes not just for accountants but for other professionals are constructed:

(a) The Code begins by stating that it reflects the acceptance by the accountancy profession of the responsibility to act in the **public interest**.

(b) The detailed guidance begins with establishment of **fundamental principles of ethics**.

(c) The guide then supplies a **conceptual framework** that requires accountants to identify, evaluate and address **threats to compliance**, applying **safeguards** to eliminate the threats to reduce them to an acceptable level.

2.1.1 Advantages of principles-based guidance

IFAC suggests that the sheer variety of threats to compliance with the fundamental principles mean that no guidance can cover every situation where there is a potential threat. Therefore requiring use of a principles-based framework rather than a set of specific rules is in the public interest for the following reasons:

(a) A framework of guidance places the onus on the professional to **consider actively** relevant issues in a given situation, rather than just agreeing action with a checklist of forbidden items. It also requires him to **demonstrate** that a responsible conclusion has been reached about ethical issues.

(b) The framework **prevents professionals interpreting legalistic requirements narrowly** to get around the ethical requirements. There is an extent to which rules engender deception, whereas principles encourage compliance.

(c) A framework **allows for variations** that are found in every **individual situation**. Each situation is likely to be different.

(d) A framework can accommodate a **rapidly changing environment**, such as the one in which auditors are.

(e)   However, a **framework can contain prohibitions** where these are necessary when principles are not enough.

(f)   A code prescribes **minimum standards of behaviour** that are expected.

(g)   Codes can include **examples** to illustrate how the principles are applied.

2.1.2 Disadvantages of principles-based guidance

(a)   As ethical codes cannot include all circumstances and dilemmas, accountants need a very good understanding of the **underlying principles**.

(b)   **International codes** such as the IFAC code cannot fully capture **regional variations in beliefs and practice.**

(c)   The **illustrative examples** can be interpreted mistakenly as rules to follow in all similar circumstances.

(d)   Principles– based codes can be difficult to enforce legally, unless the breach of the code is blatant. Most are therefore **voluntary** and perhaps therefore less effective.

> **Exam focus point**
>
> A question in the Pilot paper asked whether the benefits of codes of ethics outweighed the costs of producing them.

2.2 Accountancy ethical codes

ACCA publishes guidance for its members, the *Code of Ethics and Conduct*. IFAC publishes a *Code of Ethics for Professional Accountants*. Both are based on very similar fundamental principles

2.2.1 Fundamental principles

Fundamental principles	
Integrity	Members should be **straightforward** and **honest** in all business and professional relationships.
Objectivity	Members should not allow **bias**, **conflicts of interest** or **undue influence** of others to override professional or business judgements.
Professional competence and due care	Members have a continuing duty to maintain **professional knowledge and skill** at a level required to ensure that a client or employer receives competent professional service based on current developments in practice, legislation and techniques. Members should act diligently and in accordance with applicable technical and professional standards when providing professional services.
Confidentiality	Members should respect the **confidentiality of information** acquired as a result of professional and business relationships and should not disclose any such information to third parties without proper or specific authority or unless there is a legal or professional right or duty to disclose. Confidential information acquired as a result of professional and business relationships should not be used for the personal advantage of members or third parties.
Professional behaviour	Members should comply with relevant laws and regulations and should avoid any action that discredits the profession.

2.3 Threats to compliance with the Fundamental principles

Both IFAC and ACCA identify certain threats to compliance with the Fundamental principles.

- **Self-interest** threat (example, having a financial interest in a client)
- **Self-review** threat (example, auditing financial statements prepared by the firm)
- **Advocacy** threat (example, advocating for the client in a lawsuit)
- **Familiarity** threat (example, an audit team member having family at the client)
- **Intimidation** threat (example, threats of replacement due to disagreement)

As we shall see in the next section, these threats are particularly relevant in the context of threats to independence.

2.4 Safeguards

There are three general categories of safeguard identified in the IFAC and ACCA guidance:

- Safeguards created by the profession, legislation or regulation
- Safeguards within the assurance client/ the firm's own systems and procedures

2.4.1 Examples of safeguards created by the profession, legislation or regulation

- Educational training and experience requirements for entry into the profession

- Continuing professional development requirements

- Corporate governance regulations

- Professional standards

- Professional or regulatory monitoring and disciplinary procedures

- External review by a legally empowered third party of the reports, returns, communication or information produced by a professional accountant

IFAC issues ethical standards, quality control standards and auditing standards that work together to ensure independence is safeguarded and quality audits are carried out.

2.4.2 Examples of safeguards in the assurance client/firm's own systems and procedures

- Involving an additional professional accountant to review the work done or otherwise advise as necessary

- Consulting an independent third party, such as a committee of independent directors, a professional regulatory body or another professional accountant

- Rotating senior personnel

- Discussing ethical issues with those in charge of client governance

- Disclosing to those charged with governance the nature of services provided and extent of fees charged

- Involving another firm to perform or reperform part of the engagement

2.5 Ethical conflict resolution

The IFAC Code states that firms should have established policies to resolve conflict and should follow those established policies.

Professional accountants should consider:

- The facts
- The ethical issues involved
- Related fundamental principles
- Established internal (firm) procedures
- Alternative courses of action, considering the consequences of each

2.5.1 American Accounting Association Model

This frames the ethical decision as a series of answers to questions.

- What are the facts of the case?

- What are the ethical issues in the case?

- What are the norms, principles and values related to the case?

- What are the alternative courses of action?

- What is the best course of action that is consistent with the norms, principles and values identified?

- What are the consequences of each course of action?

- What is the decision?

2.5.2 Tucker's 5 question model

One benchmark against which to test ethical decisions is Tucker's 5 question model.

Is the decision:

- Profitable
- Legal
- Fair
- Right
- Sustainable or environmentally sound

Debates on this model concentrate on definitions of what is **fair** and **right**.

2.6 Ethical codes and Kohlberg's guidance

One key aim of a principles-based ethical code is in effect to move subjects to **post-conventional levels of reasoning** as defined in Kohlberg's framework. The principles are meant to provide ideals towards which ethical decisions should aspire. The emphasis in the code that the examples given are not a comprehensive list of every situation that could be affected by the code indicates the expectation that the code is aiming beyond giving examples of common situations in which individuals follow set behaviour. It is aiming to encourage individuals to make their own ethical judgements.

2.7 Responsibilities to employer and responsibilities as a professional

Clearly there is a lot of overlap between an accountant's employment and professional responsibilities. The professional body and (hopefully) the employer would expect the accountant to act with **integrity** and **probity**. Both would require the accountant to act with **diligence and due care**.

There may however be conflict in the following areas:

(a)   **Confidentiality** may be a major issue. An employer will wish for the employee to respect confidentiality about all sensitive matters both during and after the period of employment. Confidentiality is a professional duty too; however the accountants may, in the **public interest**, have to report an errant employer to the relevant authorities.

(b)   The employer may wish the accountant to put shareholder interests above all others. The accountant however may believe that a duty is owed to a **wider stakeholder group**.

Exam focus point

Situations where professional and employer responsibilities conflict are likely to occur frequently in this exam. Question 4 in the pilot paper is an example.

3 Independence and conflicts of interest

FAST FORWARD

Threats to independence include **self-interest**, **self-review**, **advocacy**, **familiarity** and **intimidation**.

Accountants may face **conflicts of interest** between their own and clients' interests, or between the interests of different clients.

3.1 Independence

We have looked at independence guidelines relating to internal auditors in Chapter 5. You will have encountered the guidance relating to external auditors in your earlier studies, but we cover the main threats here. Both IFAC and ACCA list examples of threats to independence and applicable safeguards. Most of the guidance also applies to accountants providing assurance services as well as audit.

Key term

An **assurance engagement** is one in which a practitioner expresses a conclusion designed to enhance the degree of confidence of the intended users other than the responsible party about the outcome of the evaluation or measurement of a subject matter against criteria.

There are **two general types** of assurance engagement:

(a)   An **assertion based** engagement where the accountant declares that a given premise (assertion) is either correct or not

(b)   A **direct reporting** engagement, where the accountant reports on issues that have come to his attention during his evaluation

Exam focus point

Remember in this exam, it is important that you can apply the spirit of the guidance to a given situation rather than just learning and regurgitating the guidance.

3.2 Self-interest threat

The ACCA Code of Ethics and Conduct highlights a great number of areas in which a self-interest threat to independence might arise.

3.2.1 Financial interests

Key term

Financial interests exist where an audit firm has a financial interest in a client's affairs, for example, the audit firm owns shares in the client, or is a trustee of a trust that holds shares in the client.

A financial interest in a client constitutes a substantial self-interest threat. According to both ACCA and IFAC, **the parties listed below are not allowed to own a direct financial interest or an indirect material financial interest in a client:**

- The **assurance firm**
- **Partners in the same office** as the engagement partner (and their immediate families)
- A **member of the assurance team**
- An **immediate family member of a member of the assurance team**

The following safeguards will therefore be relevant:

- Disposing of the interest
- Removing the individual from the team if required
- Keeping the client's audit committee informed of the situation
- Using an independent partner to review work carried out if necessary

3.2.2 Close business relationships

Examples of when a firm and client have an inappropriately close business relationship include:

- Having a **material financial interest** in a joint venture with the assurance client

- **Arrangements to combine one or more services or products** of the firm with one or more services or products of the assurance client and to market the package with reference to both parties

- **Distribution or marketing arrangements** under which the firm acts as distributor or marketer of the assurance client's products or services or vice versa

Again, it will be necessary to judge the materiality of the interest and therefore its significance. However, unless the interest is clearly insignificant, an **assurance provider should not participate** in such a venture with a client. Appropriate safeguards are therefore to end the assurance provision or to terminate the (other) business relationship.

3.2.3 Employment with client

It is possible that staff might transfer between a firm and a client, or that negotiations or interviews to facilitate such movement might take place. Both situations are a threat to independence:

- An audit staff member might be **motivated by a desire to impress a future possible employer** (objectivity is therefore affected)

- A former partner turned Finance Director has **too much knowledge of the audit firm's systems** and procedures

The extent of the threat to independence depends on various factors, such as the **role** the individual has taken up at the client, the **extent of his influence** on the audit previously, the length of time that has passed between the individual's connection with the audit and the new role at the client.

Various safeguards might be considered:

- Considering **modifying the assurance plan**

- Ensuring the audit is assigned to someone of **sufficient experience** as compared with the individual who has left

- Involving an **additional professional accountant** not involved with the engagement to review the work done

- Carrying out a **quality control review** of the engagement

In respect of audit clients, ethical guidance states that a partner should not **accept a key management position** at an audit client until **at least two years** have elapsed since the conclusion of the audit he was involved with. An individual who has moved from the firm to a client should **not be entitled to any benefits or payments** from the firm unless these are made in accordance with pre-determined arrangements. A firm should have procedures setting out that an individual involved in serious employment negotiations with an audit client should **notify the firm** and that this person would then be removed from the engagement.

3.2.4 Partner on client board

A partner or employee of an audit/assurance firm should **not serve on the board** of an assurance client. It may be acceptable for a partner or an employee of an assurance firm to perform the role of company secretary for an assurance client, if the role is essentially administrative (however don't forget the increased emphasis on the role of the company secretary in governance reports, aiming to enhance the secretary's role to go beyond routine administrative tasks).

3.2.5 Family and personal relationships

Family or close personal relationships between assurance firm and client staff could seriously threaten independence. Each situation has to be evaluated individually. Factors to consider are:

- The individual's responsibilities on the assurance engagement
- The closeness of the relationship
- The role of the other party at the assurance client

When an immediate family member of a member of the assurance team is a **director, an officer or an employee of the assurance client** in a position to exert direct and significant influence over the assurance engagement, the individual should be removed from the assurance team.

The audit firm should also consider whether there is any threat to independence if an employee who is not a member of the assurance team has a **close family or personal relationship** with a director, an officer or an employee of an assurance client.

A firm should have **quality control policies and procedures** under which staff should disclose if a close family member employed by the client is promoted within the client.

3.2.6 Gifts and hospitality

Unless the value of the gift/hospitality is clearly insignificant, a firm or a member of an assurance team should not accept it.

3.2.7 Loans and guarantees

The advice on loans and guarantees falls into two categories:

- The client is a bank or other similar institution
- Other situations

If a **lending institution client** lends an **immaterial amount to** an audit firm or member of assurance team on normal commercial terms, there is no threat to independence. If the loan were material it would be necessary to apply safeguards to bring the risk to an acceptable level. A suitable safeguard is likely to be an **independent review** (by a partner from another office in the firm).

Loans to members of the assurance team from a bank or other lending institution client are likely to be **material to the individual,** but provided that they are on normal commercial terms, these do not constitute a threat to independence.

However an audit firm or individual on the assurance engagement should not enter into any loan or guarantee arrangement with a client that is not a bank or similar institution.

3.2.8 Overdue fees

In a situation where there are overdue fees, the auditor runs the risk of, in effect, making a loan to a client, whereupon the guidance above becomes relevant.

Audit firms should guard against fees building up and being significant by **discussing the issues with the audit committee or others involved in governance,** and, if necessary, the possibility of resigning if overdue fees are not paid.

3.2.9 Percentage or contingent fees

Key term

> **Contingent fees** are fees calculated on a predetermined basis relating to the outcome or result of a transaction or the result of the work performed.

Ethical guidelines state that a firm should not enter into any fee arrangement for an assurance engagement under which the amount of the fee is contingent on the result of the assurance work or on items that are the subject matter of the assurance engagement. It would also usually be inappropriate to accept a contingent fee for non assurance work from an assurance client.

3.2.10 High percentage of fees

A firm should be alert to the situation arising where when the **total fees generated by an assurance client** represent a **large proportion of a firm's total fees**. Factors such as the **structure of the firm** and the length of time it has been trading will be relevant in determining whether there is a threat to independence. It is also necessary to beware of situations where the fees generated by an assurance client are a large proportion of the revenue of an individual partner.

BPP LEARNING MEDIA

Safeguards in these situations might include:

- Discussing the issues with the audit committee
- Taking steps to reduce the dependency on the client
- Obtaining external/internal quality control reviews
- Consulting a third party such as ACCA

Ethical guidance states that the public may perceive that a member's objectivity is likely to be in jeopardy where the fees for audit and recurring work paid by one client or group of connected clients **exceed 15%** of the firm's total fees. Where the entity is listed or public interest, this figure should be 10%.

It will be difficult for new firms establishing themselves to keep within these limits and firms in this situation should make use of the safeguards outlined.

3.2.11 Lowballing

When a firm quotes a significantly lower fee level for an assurance service than would have been charged by the predecessor firm, there is a significant self-interest threat. If the firm's tender is successful, the firm must apply safeguards such as:

- **Maintaining records** such that the firm is able to demonstrate that appropriate staff and time are spent on the engagement

- **Complying with all applicable assurance standards**, guidelines and quality control procedures

3.2.12 Recruitment

Recruiting senior management for an assurance client, particularly those able to affect the subject matter of an assurance engagement creates a self-interest threat for the assurance firm.

Assurance providers must not make management decisions for the client. Their involvement could be limited to reviewing a shortlist of candidates, providing that the client has drawn up the criteria by which they are to be selected.

3.3 Self-review threat

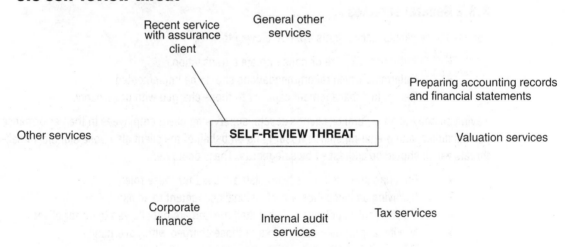

The key area in which there is likely to be a self-review threat is where an assurance firm provides services other than assurance services to an assurance client (providing multiple services). There is a great deal of guidance in the ACCA and IFAC rules about various other services accountancy firms might provide to their clients, and these are dealt with below.

The distinction between listed companies, or public limited companies, and private companies is perceived to be an important issue in the question of providing other services to clients.

Key term

Public interest companies are those that for some reason (size, nature, product) are in the 'public eye'. Auditors should treat these as if they are listed companies.

Exam focus point

In exam questions, bear in mind the nature of the entity being audited. Is it a small owner-managed business where the auditor is in effect an all-round business adviser and accountant, or is it a listed company where the above rule is relevant?

In the United States the Sarbanes-Oxley rules concerning auditor independence for **listed** companies state that an accountant is not independent if they provide certain non-audit services to an audit client. The relevant services are:

- Bookkeeping
- Financial information systems design and implementation
- Appraisal or valuation services or fairness opinions
- Actuarial services
- Internal audit services
- Management functions
- Human resources
- Broker-dealer services
- Legal services

3.3.1 Recent service with an assurance client

Ethical guidance focuses on individuals who have been a **director or officer of the client**, or an employee in a position to exert **direct and significant influence** over the subject matter information of the assurance engagement in the period under review or the previous two years to the assurance team.

If an individual had been closely involved with the client prior to the time limits set out above, the assurance firm should consider the threat to independence arising and apply appropriate safeguards, such as:

- Obtaining a quality control review of the individual's work on the assignment
- Discussing the issue with the audit committee

3.3.2 General services

For assurance clients, accountants are not allowed to:

- Authorise, execute or consummate a transaction
- Determine which recommendations should be implemented
- Report in a management capacity to those charged with governance

Having custody of an assurance client's assets, supervising client employees in the performance of their normal duties, and preparing source documents on behalf of the client also pose significant self-review threats which should be addressed by safeguards. These could be:

- Ensuring non assurance team staff are used for these roles
- Involving an independent professional accountant to advise
- Quality control policies on what staff are and are not allowed to do for clients
- Making appropriate disclosures to those charged with governance
- Resigning from the assurance engagement

3.3.3 Preparing accounting records and financial statements

There is clearly a significant risk of a self-review threat if a firm prepares **accounting records and financial statements** and then audits them. On the other hand auditors routinely assist management with the preparation of financial statements and give advice about accounting treatments and journal entries.

Therefore, assurance firms must analyse the risks arising and put safeguards in place to ensure that the risk is at an acceptable level. Safeguards include:

- **Using staff members other than assurance team members** to carry out work
- **Obtaining client approval for work** undertaken

The rules are more stringent when the client is listed or public interest. Firms should not prepare accounts or financial statements for listed or public interest clients, unless an emergency arises.

For any client, assurance firms are also not allowed to:

- Determine or change journal entries without client approval
- Authorise or approve transactions
- Prepare source documents

3.3.4 Valuation services

Key term

> A **valuation** comprises the making of assumptions with regard to future developments, the application of certain methodologies and techniques, and the combination of both in order to compute a certain value, or range of values, for an asset, a liability or for a business as a whole.

If an audit firm performs a valuation for which will be included in financial statements audited by the firm, a self-review threat arises.

Audit firms should not carry out valuations on matters that will be material to the financial statements.

If the valuation is for an immaterial matter, the audit firm should **apply safeguards** to ensure that the risk is reduced to an acceptable level. Matters to consider when applying safeguards are the extent of the audit client's knowledge of the relevant matters in making the valuation and the degree of judgement involved, how much use is made of established methodologies and the degree of uncertainty in the valuation. Safeguards include:

- Second partner review
- Confirming that the client understands the valuation and the assumptions used
- Ensuring the client acknowledges responsibility for the valuation
- Using separate personnel for the valuation and the audit

3.3.5 Taxation services

The **provision of taxation services** is generally not seen to impair independence.

3.3.6 Internal audit services

A firm may provide internal audit services to an audit client in most jurisdictions, but not in America under Sarbanes-Oxley. However, it should ensure that the client **acknowledges its responsibility** for **establishing, maintaining and monitoring the system** of internal controls. It may be appropriate to use safeguards such as ensuring that an employee of the client is designated as responsible for internal audit activities and that the board or internal audit committee approve all the work that internal audit does.

3.3.7 Corporate finance

Certain aspects of corporate finance will create self-review threats that cannot be reduced to an acceptable level by safeguards. Therefore, assurance firms are **not allowed to promote, deal in or underwrite** an assurance client's shares. They are also not allowed to commit an assurance client to the terms of a transaction or consummate a transaction on the client's behalf.

Other corporate finance services, such as assisting a client in defining corporate strategies, assisting in identifying possible sources of capital and providing structuring advice may be acceptable in jurisdictions other than the USA, providing that safeguards are in place, such as using different teams of staff, and ensuring no management decisions are taken on behalf of the client.

3.3.8 Other services

The audit firm might sell a variety of other services to audit clients, such as:

- IT services
- Temporary staff cover
- Litigation support
- Legal services

The assurance firm should consider whether there are any barriers to independence. Examples include the firm being asked to design internal control IT systems, which it would then review as part of its audit, or the firm being asked to provide an accountant to cover the chief accountant's maternity leave. The firm should consider whether the threat to independence could be reduced by appropriate safeguards. Again the rules in America are stricter than elsewhere.

3.4 Advocacy threat

An advocacy threat arises in certain situations where the assurance firm is in a position of **taking the client's part** in a dispute or somehow **acting as their advocate.** The most obvious instances of this would be when a firm offered legal services to a client and, say, defended them in a legal case or provided evidence on their behalf as an expert witness. An advocacy threat might also arise if the firm carried out corporate finance work for the client, for example, if the audit firm was involved in advice on debt reconstruction and negotiated with the bank on the client's behalf.

As with the other threats above, the firm has to appraise the risk and apply safeguards as necessary. Relevant safeguards might be using **different departments** in the firm to carry out the work and making disclosures to the audit committee. Remember, the ultimate option is always to withdraw from an engagement if the risk to independence is too high.

3.5 Familiarity threat

A familiarity threat is where independence is jeopardised by the audit firm and its staff becoming over familiar with the client and its staff. There is a substantial risk of loss of professional scepticism in such circumstances.

We have already discussed some examples of when this risk arises, because very often a familiarity threat arises in conjunction with a self-interest threat.

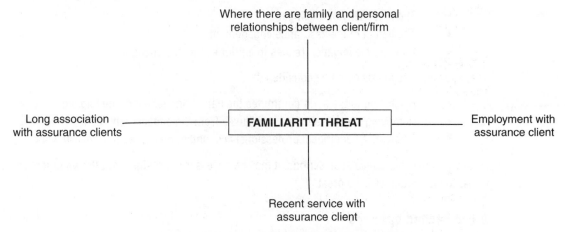

3.5.1 Long association of senior personnel with assurance clients

Senior members of staff at an audit firm having a long association with a client is a significant threat to independence. All firms should therefore monitor the relationship between staff and established clients and use safeguards to independence such as **rotating senior staff off the assurance team**, involving **second partners** to carry out reviews and obtaining independent (but internal) quality control reviews.

3.6 Intimidation threat

An intimidation threat arises when members of the assurance team have reason to be intimidated by client staff.

These are also examples of self-interest threats, largely because intimidation may only arise significantly when the assurance firm has something to lose.

3.6.1 Actual and threatened litigation

The most obvious example of an intimidation threat is when the client threatens to sue, or indeed sues, the assurance firm for work that has been done previously. The firm is then faced with the **risk of losing the client, bad publicity** and the **possibility that they will be found to have been negligent,** which will lead to further problems. This could lead to the firm being under pressure to produce an unqualified audit report when they have been qualified in the past, for example.

Generally, assurance firms should seek to avoid such situations arising. If they do arise, factors to consider are:

- The materiality of the litigation
- The nature of the assurance engagement
- Whether the litigation relates to a prior assurance engagement

The following safeguards could be considered:

- Disclosing to the audit committee the nature and extent of the litigation
- Removing specific affected individuals from the engagement team
- Involving an additional professional accountant on the team to review work

However, if the litigation is at all serious, it may be necessary to **resign from the engagement**, as the threat to independence is so great.

3.6.2 Second opinions

Another way that auditors can suffer an intimidation threat is when the audit client is unhappy with a proposed audit opinion, and seeks a **second opinion** from a different firm of auditors.

In such a circumstance, the second audit firm will not be able to give a formal audit opinion on the financial statements – only an appointed auditor can do that. However, the problem is that if a different firm of auditors indicates to someone else's audit client that a different audit opinion might be acceptable, the appointed auditor may feel under pressure to change the audit opinion. In effect, a self-interest threat arises, as the existing auditor may feel that he will lose next year's audit if he does not change this year's opinion.

There is nothing to stop a company director talking to a second firm of auditors about treatments of matters in the financial statements. However, the firm being asked for a second opinion should be very careful, because it is very possible that the opinion they form could be incorrect anyway if the director has not given them all the relevant information. For that reason, firms giving a second opinion should ensure that they **seek permission** to communicate with the existing auditor and they are appraised of all the facts. If permission is not given, the second auditors should decline to comment on the audit opinion.

Given that second opinions can cause independence issues for the existing auditors, audit firms should generally take great care if asked to provide one anyway.

3.7 Conflicts of interest

Audit firms should take reasonable steps to identify circumstances that could pose a conflict of interest. This is because a conflict of interest could result in the ethical code being breached (for example, if it results in a self-interest threat arising).

3.7.1 Conflicts between members' and clients' interests

A conflict between members' and clients' interests might arise if members compete directly with a client, or have a joint venture or similar with a company that is in competition with the client.

The rules state that members and firms should not accept or continue engagements in which there are, or are likely to be, significant conflicts of interest between members, firms and clients.

3.7.2 Conflicts between the interests of different clients

Assurance firms can have clients who are in competition with each other. However, the firm should ensure that it is **not the subject of a dispute** between the clients. It must also manage its work so that the interests of one client do not adversely affect the other client. Where acceptance or continuance of an engagement would, even with safeguards, **materially prejudice** the interests of any client, the appointment should not be accepted or continued.

Auditors often give their clients business advice unrelated to audit. In such a position, they may well become involved when clients are involved in issues such as:

- Share issues
- Takeovers

Neither situation is inherently wrong for an auditor to be in. With regard to **share issues**, audit firms should not underwrite an issue of shares to the public of a client they audit. In a **takeover situation**, if the auditors are involved in the audits of both predator and target company, they must take care in a takeover situation. They should not:

- Be the principal advisers to either party
- Issue reports assessing the accounts of either party other than their audit report

If they find they possess material confidential information, they should contact the appropriate body or regulator.

3.7.3 Managing conflicts between clients' interests

When considering whether to accept a client or when there is a change in a client's circumstances, assurance firms should take reasonable steps to ascertain whether there is a **conflict of interest** or if there is likely to be one in the future. Relationships that ended two or more years earlier are unlikely to create a conflict.

Disclosure is the most important safeguard in connection of conflicts between clients' interests. Safeguards would usually include:

- **Notifying the client** of the interest/activities that may **cause a conflict of interest** and obtaining their consent to act in the circumstances, or

- **Notifying all known relevant parties** that the member is **acting for two or more parties** in respect of a matter where their respective interests are in conflict, and obtaining their consent so to act, or

- Notifying the client that the member **does not act exclusively for any one client** in the provision of proposed services, and obtaining their consent so to act

Other safeguards

- Using separate engagement teams
- Procedures to prevent access of information (such as special passwords)
- Clear guidelines for the respective teams on issues of security and confidentiality
- The use of confidentiality agreements signed by the partners and staff
- Regular review of the safeguards by an independent partner
- Advising one or both of the clients to obtain additional independent advice

4 Practical situations

FAST FORWARD

Exam questions will often be founded on what should be done if breaches of laws, regulations or ethical guidelines occur. **Close relationships** between the parties or other **conflicts of interest** will often be a complication.

4.1 Examination questions

Examination questions will expect you to be able to apply your understanding of ethical issues to practical problems arising in organisations. Later in this chapter we are going to suggest an approach that you may find helpful in dealing with such questions, but first we are going to take the bare bones of a situation and see how it might be built up into the kind of scenario you will have to face.

4.2 The problem

The exam may present you with a scenario, typically containing an array of detail much of which is potentially relevant. The problem, however, will be one or other of two basic types.

    (a)   **A wishes B to do C which is in breach of D**

            where A = a situation, person, group of people, institution or the like
                       B = you/an accountant, the person with the ethical dilemma
                       C = acting, or refraining from acting, in a certain way
                       D = an ethical principle, quite possibly one of ACCA's fundamental principles

    (b)   Alternatively, the problem may be that A has done C, B has become aware of it and D requires some kind of response from B.

4.3 Example: the problem

An accountant joined a manufacturing company as its Finance Director. The company had acquired land on which it built industrial units. The Finance Director discovered that, before he had started at the company, one of the units had been sold and the selling price was significantly larger than the amount which appeared in the company's records. The difference had been siphoned off to another company – one in which his boss, the Managing Director, was a major shareholder. Furthermore, the Managing Director had kept his relationship with the second company a secret from the rest of the board.

The Finance Director confronted the Managing Director and asked him to reveal his position to the board. However, the Managing Director refused to disclose his position to anyone else. The secret profits on the sale of the unit had been used, he said, to reward the people who had secured the sale. Without their help, he added, the company would be in a worse position financially.

The Finance Director then told the Managing Director that unless he reported to the board he would have to inform the board members himself. The Managing Director still refused. The Finance Director disclosed the full position to the board.

The problem is of the **second basic type. B** is of course the easiest party to identify. Here it is the **Finance Director. A** is clear, as well: it is the **Managing Director. C** is the **MD's breach of his directorial duties** regarding related party transactions not to obtain any personal advantage from his position of director without the consent of the company for whatever gain or profit he has obtained. **D** is the **principle that requires B not to be a party to an illegal act**. (Note that we distinguish between ethical and legal obligations. B has legal obligations as a director of the company. He has ethical obligations not to ignore his legal obligations. In **this** case the two amount to the same thing.)

4.4 Relationships

You may have a feeling that the resolution of the problem described above is just too easy, and you would be right. This is because A, B, C and D are either people, or else situations involving people, who stand in certain relationships to each other.

- A may be B's boss, B's subordinate, B's equal in the organisational hierarchy, B's husband, B's friend.

- B may be new to the organisation, or well-established and waiting for promotion, or ignorant of some knowledge relevant to the situation that A possesses or that the people affected by C possess.

- C or D, as already indicated, may involve some person(s) with whom B or A have a relationship – for example the action may be to misrepresent something to a senior manager who controls the fate of B or A (or both) in the organisation.

Question

Relationships

Identify the relationships in the scenario above. What are the possible problems arising from these relationships?

Answer

The MD is the Finance Director's boss. He is also a member of the board and is longer established as such than B the Finance Director.

In outline the problems arising are that **by acting ethically the Finance Director will alienate the MD**. Even if the problem were to be resolved the episode would sour all future dealings between these two parties. Also, **the board may not be sympathetic to the accusations of a newcomer**. The Finance Director may find that he is ignored or even dismissed.

Relationships should never be permitted to affect ethical judgement. If you knew that your best friend at work had committed a major fraud, for example, **integrity** would demand that **in the last resort** you would have to bring it to the attention of somebody in authority. But note that this is only in the last resort. Try to imagine what you would do in practice in this situation.

Surely your **first course** would be to try to **persuade your friend** that what they had done was wrong, and that they themselves had an ethical responsibility to own up. Your **second option**, if this failed, might be to try to get **somebody** (perhaps somebody outside the organisation) that you knew could **exert pressure** on your friend to persuade him or her to own up.

There is obviously a limit to how far you can take this. The important point is that just because you are dealing with a situation that involves ethical issues, this **does not mean that all the normal principles of good human relations and good management have to be suspended**. In fact this is the time when such business principles are most important.

4.5 Consequences

Actions have consequences and the consequences themselves are quite likely to have their own ethical implications (remember the teleological approach we covered in Chapter 10).

In the example given above, we can identify the following further issues.

(a) The MD's secret transaction appears to have been made in order to secure the sale of an asset the proceeds of which are helping to prop up the company financially. Disclosure of the truth behind the sale may mean that the company is pursued for compensation by the buyer of the site. The **survival of the company** as a whole may be jeopardised.

(b) If the truth behind the transaction becomes public knowledge this could be highly damaging for the company's **reputation**, even if it can show that only one person was involved.

305

(c)   The board may simply rubber stamp the MD's actions and so the Finance Director may still find that he is expected to be party to dishonesty. (This assumes that the **company as a whole is amoral** in its approach to ethical issues. In fact the MD's refusal to disclose the matter to the board suggests otherwise.)

In the last case we are back to square one. In the first two cases, the Finance Director has to consider the ethicality or otherwise of taking action that could lead to the collapse of the company, extensive redundancies, unpaid creditors and shareholders and so on.

4.6 Actions

In spite of the difficulties, your aim will usually be to reach a satisfactory resolution to the problem. **The actions that you recommend** will often include the following.

(a)   **Informal discussions** with the parties involved.

(b)   **Further investigation** to establish the full facts of the matter. What extra information is needed?

(c)   The **tightening up of controls or the introduction of new ones**, if the situation arose due to laxity in this area. This will often be the case and the principles of professional competence and due care and of technical standards will usually be relevant.

(d)   **Attention to organisational matters** such as changes in the management structure, improving communication channels, attempting to change attitudes.

Question

Cunning plan

Your finance director has asked you to join a team planning a takeover of one of your company's suppliers. An old school friend works as an accountant for the company concerned, the finance director knows this, and has asked you to try and find out 'anything that might help the takeover succeed, but it must remain secret'.

Answer

There are three issues here. Firstly you have a **conflict of interest** as the finance director wants you to keep the takeover a secret, but you probably feel that you should tell your friend what is happening as it may affect their job.

Second, the finance director is asking you to deceive your friend. Deception is unprofessional behaviour and will break your ethical guidelines. Therefore the situation is presenting you with **two conflicting demands**. It is worth remembering that no employer should ask you to break your ethical rules.

Finally, the request to break your own ethical guidelines constitutes **unprofessional behaviour** by the finance director. You should consider reporting him to the relevant body.

Exam focus point

> In an internal company role, ethical problems could be in the following forms.
> *   Conflict of duties to different staff superiors
> *   Discovering an illegal act or fraud perpetrated by the company (ie its directors)
> *   Discovering a fraud or illegal act perpetrated by another employee
> *   Pressure from superiors to take certain viewpoints, for example towards budgets (pessimistic/ optimistic etc) or not to report unfavourable findings

5 Examination questions: an approach

5.1 Dealing with questions

FAST FORWARD

In a situation involving ethical issues, there are **practical steps** that should be taken.

- Establish the facts of the situation by further investigation and work.
- Identify the ethical issues at stake.
- Consider the alternative options available for action.
- State the best course of action based on the steps above.
- Justify your recommendation.

An article in a student magazine contained the following advice for candidates who wish to achieve good marks in ethics questions. (The emphasis is BPP's.)

'The precise question requirements will vary, but in general marks will be awarded for:

- **Analysis of the situation**

- **A recognition of ethical issues**

- **Explanation if appropriate of relevant part of ethical guidelines,** and **interpretation** of its relevance to the question

- Making clear, logical, and appropriate **recommendations** for action. Making inconsistent recommendations does not impress examiners

- **Justifying recommendations** in practical business terms and in ethical terms

As with all scenario based questions there is likely to be **more than one acceptable answer**, and marks will depend on how well the case is argued, rather than for getting the 'right' answer.

However, questions based on ethical issues tend to produce a range of possible solutions which are, on the one hand, consistent with the ethical guidelines and acceptable, and on the other hand, a range of clearly inadmissible answers which are clearly in breach of the ethical guidelines and possibly the law.'

5.2 Step-by-step approach

We suggest that:

(a) **You use the question format to structure your answer**.

(b) **You bear in mind what marks are being awarded for** (see above).

(c) **You adhere to the following list of do's and don'ts** based on the **American Accounting Association** model. Be sure to read the notes following.

DO	Note	DON'T
Identify the key facts as briefly as possible (one sentence?)	1	Merely paraphrase the question
Identify the ethical issues at stake, and the related norms, principles and values	2	Regurgitate the entire contents of the Ethical Guidelines
Consider alternative reasonable actions and their consequences	3	List every single possible action and then explain how all the unsuitable ones can be eliminated
Make a decision and recommend the best course of action as appropriate, based on consistency with the norms, principles and values	4	Fail to make a decision or recommend action. Propose actions in breach of the *Ethical Guidelines* or the law
Justify your decision	5	Be feeble. 'This should be done because it is ethical' is not terribly convincing

Notes

1   **One sentence** is an ideal to aim for.

2   (a)   **Use the terminology of the ethical guidelines, but not *ad nauseam*.** Don't forget the words 'fairness', 'bias', and 'influence' when discussing 'objectivity'.

     (b)   **Don't torture the case study to make it fit a fundamental principle**: if, say, 'justice' is the most persuasive word for a situation don't be afraid of using it.

     (c)   If the law is involved, don't get carried away – this is **not a law exam**. 'The director has a statutory duty to ...' is sufficient: there is no need to go into legal detail.

3   Useful ways of generating alternatives are:

     (a)   To **consider the problem from the other side of the fence**: imagine you are the guilty party

     (b)   To **consider the problem from the point of view of the organisation** and its culture and environment

4   Making a decision is often very hard, but if you cannot do this you are simply not ready to take on the responsibilities of a qualified accountant. There are usually a number of decisions that could be justified, so **don't be afraid of choosing the 'wrong' answer.**

5   This is not actually as hard as you might think.

5.3 Regurgitating the question

Possibly the most **common fault** in students' answers to questions on ethics is that they include large **amounts of unanalysed detail copied out from the question** scenarios in their answers. This earns no marks.

5.4 Justifying your decision

The article quoted above says that **marks will be awarded for 'justifying recommendations in practical business terms and in ethical terms'.** We shall conclude by examining a passage from a model solution to a question on ethics to see how this can be done.

> 'Perhaps the first thing to do is to **report** the whole matter, **in confidence** and **informally**, to the chief internal auditor with suggestions that a **tactful investigation** is undertaken to **verify as many of the facts** as possible. The fact that the sales manager has already been tackled (informally) about the matter may be a positive advantage as **he/she may be recruited** to assist in the investigation. It could however be a problem as the information needed for further **investigation** may have already been removed. **Tact** is crucial as handling the matter the wrong way could adversely influence the whole situation. An understanding of who participants are and how they are implicated can be used positively to bring about change with the **minimum of disruption**.'

The key to this approach is **using the right language**, and to a large extent you cannot help doing so if you have sensible suggestions to make. The real problem that many students experience with questions of this type is lack of confidence in their own judgement. If you have sound business and managerial sense and you know the ethical guidelines there is every reason to suppose that an answer that you propose will be acceptable, so don't be shy of expressing an opinion.

Chapter Roundup

- Organisations have responded to pressures to been seen to act ethically by publishing **ethical codes**, setting out their **values and responsibilities** towards stakeholders.

- Professional codes of ethics apply to the **individual behaviour** of professionals and are often based on principles, supplemented by guidance on **threats and safeguards**.

- Threats to independence include **self-interest**, **self-review**, **advocacy**, **familiarity** and **intimidation**.

- Accountants may face **conflicts of interest** between their own and clients' interests, or between the interests of different clients.

- Exam questions will often be founded on what should be done if breaches of laws, regulations or ethical guidelines occur. **Close relationships** between the parties or other **conflicts of interest** will often be a complication.

- In a situation involving ethical issues, there are **practical steps** that should be taken.

  - Establish the facts of the situation by further investigation and work.
  - Identify the ethical issues at stake.
  - Consider the alternative options available for action.
  - State the best course of action based on the steps above.
  - Justify your recommendations.

Quick Quiz

1   What does an organisation's ethical code usually contain?

2   What are the key elements of IFAC's Code of Ethics?

3   Which of the following is not an advantage of a principles-based ethical code?

    A   It prevents narrow, legalistic interpretations
    B   It can accommodate a rapidly-changing environment
    C   The illustrative examples provided can be followed in all similar situations
    D   It prescribes minimum expected standards of behaviour

4   Fill in the blank

    .... means that members should be straightforward and honest in all business and professional relationships.

5   According to the IFAC code of ethics, what should professional accountants consider when attempting to resolve ethical issues?

6   What actions should a firm take if it believes that an assurance client is generating too high a proportion of its fees?

7   Give four examples of a familiarity threat.

8   A firm that is sued by a client must resign from engagement with that client.

    True ☐
    False ☐

Answers to Quick Quiz

1   A statement of the organisation's values and an explanation of its responsibilities towards its stakeholders

2   • An acceptance by the accountancy profession of the responsibility to act in the public interest

    • Fundamental principles of ethics

    • Conceptual framework, requiring accountants to address threats to compliance and apply safeguards

3   C   Although the examples may be good guides for conduct in many instances, circumstances will vary, so they should not be seen as totally prescriptive.

4   Integrity

5   • The facts
    • The ethical issues involved
    • Related fundamental principles
    • Established internal procedures
    • Alternative courses of action, considering the consequences of each

6   • Discuss the issue with the audit committee
    • Take steps to reduce the dependence
    • Obtain quality control reviews
    • Consult a third party

7   • Family and personal relationships between the client and the firm
    • Long association with assurance client
    • Employment with assurance client
    • Recent service with assurance client

8   False. Not necessarily. Other safeguards can be used (disclosure to the audit committee, removing certain individuals from the team, involving an additional professional accountant on the team to review work.) Resignation may however be required in the end.

Now try the question below from the Exam Question Bank

Number	Level	Marks	Time
Q11	Examination	25	45 mins

Social and
environmental issues

Topic list	Syllabus reference
1 Social and environmental effects of economic activity	E7
2 Sustainability	E7
3 Environmental management systems	E7
4 Social and environmental audits	E7

Introduction

In this last chapter we focus on the ethical and corporate social responsibilities
organisations have towards the natural environment. We examine the impact
organisations have upon the environment; the concept of sustainability,
discussed in Section 2, is particularly important, as it relates to whether the
impact the organisation makes on the environment can be limited to what the
environment can bear. We also consider aspects of reporting, managing and
auditing the environmental effects of organisations' activities.

Study guide

		Intellectual level
E7	**Social and environmental issues in the conduct of business and ethical behaviour**	
(a)	Describe and assess the social and environmental effects that economic activity can have (in terms of social and environmental footprints)	3
(b)	Explain and assess the concept of sustainability and evaluate the issues concerning accounting for sustainability (including the contribution of full cost accounting)	3
(c)	Describe the main features of internal management systems for underpinning environmental accounting such as EMAS and ISO 14000	1
(d)	Explain the nature of social and environmental audit and evaluate the contribution it can make to the development of environmental accounting	3

Exam guide

You may see a whole optional question on the issues covered in this chapter as it covers various aspects of organisations' activities and control systems. Alternatively, as in Pilot Paper Question 1, some of the themes may be brought in as part of a wider question.

1 Social and environmental effects of economic activity

FAST FORWARD

> There is increasing concern about businesses' relationship with the natural environment. Businesses may suffer **significant costs** and a **loss of reputation** if problems arise.

1.1 Significance of environmental effects

Is there a problem and how serious is it?

  Case Study

The World Wildlife Fund warned in a report published in October 2006 that current global consumption levels could result in a large scale ecosystem collapse by the middle of the twenty-first century. It warned that if demand continued at the current rate, two planets worth of resources would be needed to meet the consumption demand by 2050. The loss in biodiversity is the result of resources being consumed faster than the planet can replace them.

The report based its findings on two measures:

Living Planet Index – assessing the health of the planet's ecosystems by tracking the population of over 1,000 vertebrate species. It found that species had declined by about 30% since 1970.

The Ecological Footprint – measuring the amount of biologically productive land and water to meet the demand for food, timber and shelter and absorb the pollution from economic activity. The report found that the global footprint exceeded the world's biocapacity by 25% in 2003, which meant that the earth could no longer meet what was being demanded of it.

Case Study

Most seriously of all, there is the issue of whether business activities have contributed to climate change.

Intergovernmental Panel

The Intergovernmental Panel on Climate Change reported in February 2007. The report emphasised that global atmospheric concentrations of carbon dioxide, methane and nitrous oxide have increased markedly as a result of human activities since 1750 and now exceed pre-industrial values. The main causes are fossil-fuel usage (the most significant cause), land-use change and agriculture.

The report stated that evidence of warming of the climate system is unequivocal, as is seen from observations of increases in global average air and ocean temperatures, widespread melting of snow and ice, and rising global average sea level. Numerous changes in climate are long-term. These are most likely due to increases in greenhouse gas concentrations.

For the next two decades a warming of about 0.2ºC is projected based on projected levels of greenhouse gas emissions. Continued greenhouse gas emissions at or above current rates would cause further warming and induce many climate changes in the 21st century that will be larger than those observed in the 20th century. These include increases in heatwaves, spells of heavy rain and intensity of tropical cyclones.

Stern report

A few months before the Intergovernmental panel report was published, a UK report was published on the costs of climate change. The report's author was Sir Nicholas Stern, former chief economist at the World Bank, and adviser to the UK Chancellor of the Exchequer Gordon Brown who commissioned the report. The report warned of a global recession that could cut between 5% and 20% from the world's wealth later this century, unless the world invests now in the technologies needed to create a global low-carbon economy.

The effects would be on a scale similar to those associated with the two World Wars and the 1930s depression. They include huge disruption to African economies as drought hits food production, up to a billion people losing water supplies, hundreds of millions losing their homes to sea level rises and potentially big increases in damage from hurricanes.

Stern calls for a global investment of about 1% per year of global GDP over the next 50 years to combat these threats. His findings contradict past claims from economists that the world would do better adapting to climate change rather than trying to halt it. In response to the report Gordon Brown has called for industrialised countries to cut their carbon dioxide emissions by at least 30% by 2020 and by at least 60% by 2050.

World Wildlife Fund

The World Wildlife Fund's Climate Savers programme encourages companies to reduce carbon dioxide emissions by:

* Increasing the energy efficiency of buildings and factories

* Taking advantage of recent advances in combined heat and power to increase energy efficiency and lower energy costs

* Purchasing power generated from renewable energy sources

* Integrating next-generation efficiency measures into the design of new buildings, factories and products

* Integrating energy and environmental efficiency into building, product and process design

* Optimising existing manufacturing processes

* Educating employees, customer base and supply chain to help take advantage of best practices for greenhouse gas mitigation

Examples of companies who have joined the programme include:

- Johnson & Johnson, 30% of whose total US energy use is from green power sources such as wind power, on-site solar, low-impact hydro, renewable energy sources

- IBM, whose energy savings methods include installing motion detectors for lighting in bathrooms and copier rooms, rebalancing heating and lighting systems and resizing high purity water pumping systems in semi-conductor manufacturing lines

- Polaroid, which is upgrading and replacing compressors, chillers, boilers, hot water systems, lighting systems and motors; purchasing green power and switching to cleaner forms of fuel for on-site operations. Polaroid's Facilities organisation now requires each employee to identify energy-saving projects as part of their performance evaluation

- Nike, which offsets the majority of its business travel carbon dioxide emissions through partnerships with air carriers, rental car companies, government energy departments and the retail market

- Lafarge, the cement manufacturer which uses industrial by-products such as fly-ash from coal-fired power plants and slag from the steel industry as substitutes for raw materials that consume significant energy to produce. Lafarge has also shifted some of its fuel use to waste fossil fuels (industrial waste, tyres, oils, plastic and solvents) and waste biomass (rice husks, coffee shells, animal meal)

The WWF points out the following benefits of joining Climate Savers:

- **Knowledge increase**, providing an opportunity to develop relationships with other stakeholders, business colleagues and technology experts

- **Visibility** through publicity in the WWF's literature and press reports

- **Cost advantages**, greater efficiency leading to reduction in energy costs

Climate change will be one of the most topical areas of your syllabus, so we would advise you to read and keep copies of stories on how businesses are responding to climate change.

Clearly there are concerns which need to be closely examined.

1.2 Impact on environment of economic activities

Key term

> **Environmental footprint** is the impact that a business's activities have upon the environment including its resource environment and pollution emissions.

At a individual firm or business level environmental impact can be measured in terms of environmental costs in various areas. Much business activity takes place at some cost to the environment. A 1998 IFAC report identified several examples of impacts on the environment

- Depletion of natural resources
- Noise and aesthetic impacts
- Residual air and water emissions
- Long-term waste disposal (exacerbated by excessive product packaging)
- Uncompensated health effects
- Change in the local quality of life (through for example the impact of tourism)

1.3 Impact on organisation of environmental costs

In addition the IFAC report listed a large number of costs that the business might suffer internally:

Direct or indirect environmental costs

- Waste management
- Remediation costs or expenses
- Compliance costs
- Permit fees
- Environmental training
- Environmentally driven research and development
- Environmentally related maintenance
- Legal costs and fines
- Environmental assurance bonds
- Environmental certification and labelling
- Natural resource inputs
- Record keeping and reporting

Contingent or intangible environmental costs

- Uncertain future remediation or compensation costs
- Risk posed by future regulatory changes
- Product quality
- Employee health and safety
- Environmental knowledge assets
- Sustainability of raw material inputs
- Risk of impaired assets
- Public/customer perception

Exam focus point

A Pilot paper question asked for a definition of environmental footprint.

Clearly failing to take sufficient account of environmental impact can have a significant impact on the business's accounts as well as the outside world.

Exam focus point

You may be asked about the main impacts on the environment that a particular organisation's activities are likely to have. You will need to use a little imagination, but hopefully the ideas we suggest in this chapter will help you come up with suggestions.

1.4 Social impacts of activities

Partly because of the publicity generated by reports like the recent WWF report, there is now significant focus on the environmental impact of business's activities. However corporate social responsibility does not start and end with the environment; organisations need to consider other aspects of corporate social responsibilities.

Case Study

It is unethical for US researchers to test expensive treatments on people in Third World countries who would be unable to afford those drugs, a bioethics commission warned in a published report. In an article in the New England Journal of Medicine, the National Bioethics Advisory Commission also said it was unethical to give volunteers placebos instead of treatments that are known to work.

These warnings by Harold Shapiro and Eric Meslin, the chairman and executive director respectively of the presidential commission, mark the latest round in a debate over the rules for conducting studies in countries where ethical standards may be less stringent than in the United States.

The issue surfaced in the Journal in 1997 when Drs. Peter Lurie and Sidney M Wolfe of Public Citizen's Health Research Group cited 15 government-financed studies that, they said, were using unethical methods to test whether various treatments could block the spread of the AIDS virus from a woman to her newborn child. All were being done in developing countries.

Some of the women in those studies were given placebos, even though the GlaxoSmithKline drug AZT had been shown to prevent babies from contracting AIDS from their infected mothers. At the time, it was regarded as unethical in the United States and other countries to test alternative AIDS treatments by giving pregnant volunteers a placebo.

Supporters of the studies had argued that giving placebos was valid because the radically different economic conditions in developing countries, where AZT was not widely available, made it virtually impossible to do the type of research that had become the standard in developed countries.

Shapiro and Meslin, who lead the 17 member advisory council established by former President Bill Clinton in 1995, wrote in the Journal that the experimental treatment should be tested against the best established treatment, 'whether or not that treatment is available in the host country.'

Giving placebos when an effective treatment exists 'is not ethically acceptable,' they said.

Shapiro and Meslin also said it was important to 'avoid the exploitation of potentially vulnerable populations in developing countries.'

If an experiment is testing a drug or device that ' is not likely to be affordable in the host country or if the health care infrastructure cannot support its proper distribution and use, it is unethical to ask persons in that country to participate in the research, since they will not enjoy any of its potential benefits,' they said.

There have been suggestions that researchers or drug companies may be testing products in poor countries because the cost is less and the rules are less stringent.

'Conducting a trial in a developing country because it is more convenient or efficient or less troublesome to do is never a sufficient justification,' said Shapiro and Meslin.

The two also said that if tests show that the experimental treatment turns out to be more effective, it should be made available to all the people who participated in the study.

Researchers should not abandon their volunteers after the study is completed, they said.

Reuters

1.4.1 Stakeholder expectations

Pressures on organisations to widen the scope of their corporate public accountability come from **increasing expectations of stakeholders** and knowledge about the **consequences of ignoring such pressures**.

Stakeholders in this respect include communities (particularly where operations are based), customers (product safety issues), suppliers and supply chain participants and competitors. Issues such as plant closures, pollution, job creation, sourcing, etc can have powerful **social effects** for good or ill on these stakeholders.

Case Study

These are a few examples in which consumers have been successful in applying pressure to seek changes in business practices.

(a)   Consumers began boycotting Shell filling stations in large numbers, leading the company to reverse its policy on a controversial environmental subject concerning the disposal of an oil drilling platform.

(b)   Pressure was applied to change the Nestlé company's practice of exploiting the market for processed milk in developing countries.

Similar campaigns have targeted Nike (alleged exploitation of overseas garment-trade workers) and McDonalds (alleged contribution to obesity and related illnesses).

1.4.2 Reputation risk

We have discussed the importance of **loss of corporate reputation** in earlier chapters. Increasingly a business must have the reputation of being a **responsible business** that enhances long-term shareholder value by addressing the needs of its **stakeholders** – employees, customers, suppliers, the community and the environment.

 Case Study

Reputation can be affected adversely even if the company has good intentions. An example was Monsanto believing that investment in genetically modified (GM) products would be seen as helping Third World farmers by increasing yields. However, they failed to take on board the fact that these farmers usually save seed from one crop to sow the following season. This would not be possible with GM crops.

Bad publicity portrayed Monsanto as exploiting, rather than helping, the Third World. In addition, inadequately addressed environmental concerns about the effect of GM crops on nature, led to:

•   A consumer boycott of GM products
•   Trial crops being destroyed
•   A tumbling share price

The final straw was the news that Monsanto's UK staff canteen was GM free!

 Case Study

Charity Oxfam recently (2005) suffered a public relations crisis when it was revealed that the overseas manufacturer of its 'Make Poverty History' wristband was, in fact, exploiting its labour force in appalling conditions. With the increase in outsourcing to developing nations, a number of key brands have either positively positioned themselves as ethical sources (eg The Body Shop) or taken steps to counter allegations of unethical employment practices (eg Nike).

2 Sustainability

Sustainability means limiting use of resources to what can be replenished.

The **Global Reporting Initiative** provides a framework for a **sustainability report**.

Full cost accounting is a method of accounting for all relevant costs including externalities.

2.1 Defining sustainability

Key terms

In relation to the development of the world's resources, **sustainability** has been defined as ensuring that development meets the needs of the present without compromising the ability of the future to meet its own needs.

For organisations, sustainability involves developing strategies so that the organisation only uses resources at a rate that allows them to be replenished (in order to ensure that they will continue to be available). At the same time emissions of waste are confined to levels that do not exceed the capacity of the environment to absorb them.

Sustainable development is development that is … 'not a fixed state of harmony, but rather a process of change in which the exploitation of resources, the direction of investments, the orientation of technological development and institutional change are made consistent with future as well as present needs'.(Brutland report)

Although it's possible to come up with a general definition of sustainability that's uncontroversial but vague, problems arise when you try to extend that definition. Key issues include whether sustainability just implies **natural sustainability**, or whether **social and economic sustainability** are important as well. Particularly if social and economic sustainability are acknowledged, there is also the issue that sustainability may vary over time and between groups.

2.2 Aspects of sustainability

2.2.1 Sustainable for whom

Issues here include the **species to be sustained other than mankind** and the **level of world population** that should be sustained, natural resources, pollution absorption and the needs of developing countries.

We saw that in Chapter 10 the deep ecologist viewpoint, that man has 'had its chance' and that socio-economic considerations are irrelevant to sustainability; they are intrusions on the natural world. Other views are that population pressures and social and economic disparities inevitably have to be addressed as well if sustainability for other species is to be maintained. However what then happens if there is conflict between social and ecological sustainability?

2.2.2 Sustainable in what way

The ecological focus would be on preserving the ability of the environment to **function as naturally as possible,** to continue to support all life forms on the planet and maintain its evolutionary potential.

Extending the definition to **social sustainability** poses various problems. Social sustainability has been defined as including personal growth and development, maintaining physical and mental health, equity and involvement in decision-making. However to what extent are these human **needs** and to what extent are they human **wants** (which may not be necessary). There is also the issue of the extent to which social sustainability means preserving the existing institutions and customary behaviours of society, or whether these need to change (see the discussion on strong sustainability below).

Economic sustainability is even more controversial. Critics claim that it defines wellbeing in terms of production of goods and services. Social and ecological sustainability are only seen as important in providing a framework for a system to operate that supports production.

Another significant issue here is whether the developing world should be encouraged to reach and sustain the **same level of economic development** as the Western economies. One argument is that without economic growth the investment necessary for ecological sustainability will not be available. However encouraging all world economies to reach the levels of economic growth that may have caused environmental degradation may lead to more, not less, rapid resource depletion.

 Case Study

Various studies have shown that we would need two or more worlds that each had the same level of natural resources that this world has to sustain this world, if all countries enjoyed the same rate of consumption per head as the developed countries.

2.2.3 Sustainable for how long

A key issue here is **generational equity,** ensuring that future generations are able to enjoy the same environmental conditions, and in social terms per capita welfare is maintained or increased.

However with raw materials having finite levels, any use of these resources ultimately cannot be sustained. In other areas the question of **how long** things can be sustained is bound up with the **level** at which they will be sustained. Perspectives on how to maintain a sustainable society indefinitely may also have to change in the light of changing climatic and ecological conditions, some of which are independent of whatever mankind does.

2.2.4 Sustainable at what cost

Again the deep ecologist view is that threats to the existence of other species are unacceptable, and that a system that rewards ecologically unsustainable behaviour is flawed and needs to be changed.

Those who hold other views must address the **issue of non-renewable resources** and whether some **ecological capital is irreplaceable**. Should therefore the emphasis be on preservation, or is substitution of other resources or capital possible? Alternatively would it be possible to compensate future generations for the resources and capital this generation exhausts?

2.2.5 Sustainable by whom

Ideally by the whole world, but meaningful global international agreements look unlikely at present. Therefore sustainability must be on an individual basis by nations, individuals – and businesses.

2.3 Strong and weak sustainability

One distinction that is often drawn in the sustainability debate is the distinction between strong and weak sustainability. These two approaches to the idea of sustainability relate to their supporters' views of the extent, causes and solutions.

2.3.1 Weak sustainability

Supporters of this view are concerned to **prevent the kind of catastrophe** that would threaten society. They believe that the focus should be on **sustaining the human species** and the natural environment can be regarded as a resource. However the human race needs to have **better mastery of the natural environment**. This can be achieved by incremental change driven by market forces and legal regulation and requiring economic development to drive the technological changes necessary. Sustainability can be achieved within the next 30-50 years.

The weak sustainability viewpoint tends to dominate discussion within the Western economic viewpoint; critics suggest however that it is based on hope rather evidence, and is ultimately underpinned by a desire to maintain existing economic and social systems.

2.3.2 Strong sustainability

Supporters of strong sustainability argue that far more fundamental changes are needed in society. The viewpoint is linked with other critiques of our society that we have seen in earlier chapters such as the feminist or anti-capitalist agenda. Supporters stress the **need for harmony** with the natural world; it is important to sustain all species, not just the human race. They see a requirement for **fundamental change**, including a change in how man perceives economic growth (and whether it is pursued at all). They suggest that we have little or no idea at present of what sustainability would be, and the **timespan** for achieving it is likely to be very long, perhaps over a century.

Supporters of strong sustainability stress the need for participation and democracy in achieving sustainable growth. However this course faces opposition from political and business leaders who are benefiting from the current system.

2.4 Businesses and sustainability

Key term

> **Externality** is the difference between the market and social costs, or benefits, of an activity. An externality is a cost or benefit that the market fails to take into account.

How can individual businesses help to promote sustainability, bearing in mind that competitors have other priorities? One important way is to provide information about the external environmental effects – the **externalities** – of their activities. This data can then be used in decision-making processes, both of government, and of other organisations, by **internalising** the costs of environmental effects. In addition better costing of externalities will **influence the price mechanism** and hence the economic decisions that are taken.

 Case Study

The British Airports Authority (BAA) has developed a sustainable development programme with a number of aspects:

- **Bio-diversity** – BAA's programme has been developed in consultation with stakeholders including Defra, English Nature and Earthwatch. All BAA airports have a local biodiversity strategy and biodiversity action plans in place.

- **Car sharing** – BAA has introduced car share schemes for its employees and employees of companies based at its airports.

- **Environmental awareness** – BAA has promoted environmental awareness by training days focused on the workplace and the home. Recycling targets have been set for the new Terminal 5 at London's Heathrow Airport.

Two developments designed to provide more information are the **Global Reporting Initiative** and the development of **full cost accounting.**

2.5 The Global Reporting initiative (GRI)

The Global Reporting Initiative is a large multi-stakeholder network of thousands of experts, in dozens of countries worldwide, who participate in working groups and governance bodies and use the GRI Guidelines to report or to contribute to develop the reporting framework. The Initiative's governance emphasises the importance of stakeholder contribution by having a stakeholder council to debate and deliberate on key policy and strategic issues as well as a board of directors and a technical advisory committee.

The Global Reporting Initiative, as its name suggests, is a reporting framework and arose from the need to **address the failure of the current governance structures to respond to changes in the global economy**.

The GRI aims to develop **transparency**, **accountability**, **reporting** and **sustainable development**. Its vision is that reporting on economic, environmental and social importance should become as routine and comparable as financial reporting.

 Case Study

In their 2006 survey *Tomorrow's Value* the forum SustainAbility identified the following trends in company reporting:

(a) Leading companies were shifting the focus of their sustainability strategy away from risk management towards a more progressive and entrepreneurial approach that seeks to identify the sustainability opportunities for strategic innovation and market building

(b) Financial markets were becoming more interested in the level of disclosure

(c) A significantly larger number of companies had reported the integration of sustainable development factors into core decision-making

(d) There was a lack of disclosure of the lobbying undertaken by many companies

(e) International frameworks had begun to provide context for sustainability reporting such as the Millennium Development Goals

 Case Study

British Telecommunications plc came out top in the *Tomorrow's Value* corporate sustainability reporting survey. BT sees sustainability reporting as part of wider corporate social reporting. The report emphasises how Information Communications Technology can support increases in productivity, and can also support economic and social development by transforming communication and access to information.

BT stresses that using their own products and services enables them to reduce consumption of finite materials and improves the work-life balance of their staff; their technology is used particularly effectively in conferencing, flexible workstyles and e-business.

One example of how BT supports sustainable development is the development of broadband technology in the UK. Broadband has extended market reach and impact, made organisational working practices more efficient, enabled staff to work flexibly and substituted electronic communication for travel and meetings (therefore reducing traffic congestion and fuel use).

BT believes that advanced telecommunications services are one of the few achievements of the consumer society that could be accessible to, and used by, every person on earth, without exceeding sustainable limits on resource-use and environmental impact. To achieve this there needs to be:

- A commercially successful sector

- An inclusive society where services are accessible to all and people have the necessary skills to exploit them

- The right checks and balances to ensure security, privacy and freedom of expression

- Networks and equipment powered by energy derived from renewable sources

- Equipment and cables made from non-oil derived plastics and polymeric conductors used in place of metals

- Optical switches and computers – reducing the need for metals and conventional semi-conductor materials

2.5.1 GRI Guidelines

The GRI published revised guidelines in 2002.

The main section of the Guidelines (Report contents) sets out the framework of a sustainability report. It consists of five sections.

(a)   **Vision and strategy.** Description of the reporting organisation's strategy with regard to sustainability, including a statement from the CEO.

(b)   **Profile.** Overview of the reporting organisation's structure and operations and of the scope of the report.

(c)   **Governance structure and management systems.** Description of organisational structure, policies and management systems, including stakeholder engagement efforts.

(d)   **GRI content index.** A table supplied by the reporting organisation identifying where the information listed in the *Guidelines* is located within the organisation's report.

(e)   **Performance indicators.** Measures of the impact or effect of the reporting organisation divided into integrated, economic, environmental, and social performance indicators.

2.5.2 Indicators in the GRI framework

GRI structures performance indicators according to a hierarchy of category, aspect and indicator. Indicators are grouped in terms of the three dimensions of the conventional definition of sustainability – economic, environmental, and social.

	Category	Aspect
ECONOMIC	Direct economic impacts	Customers Suppliers Employees Providers of capital Public sector
ENVIRONMENTAL	Environmental	Materials Energy Water Biodiversity Emissions, effluents, and waste Suppliers Products and services Compliance Transport Overall
SOCIAL	Labour practices and decent work	Employment Labour/management relations Health and safety Training and education Diversity and opportunity
	Human rights	Strategy and management Non-discrimination Freedom of association and collective bargaining Child labour Forced and compulsory labour Disciplinary practices Security practices Indigenous rights
	Society	Community Bribery and corruption Political contributions Competition and pricing
	Product responsibility	Customer health and safety Products and services Advertising Respect for privacy

2.5.3 Influence of GRI

There is a trend to report on broader sustainability issues and to include **social and economic information** alongside environmental disclosures.

An increasing number of companies, including BT, Vauxhall Motors Ltd, British Airways and Shell are following the GRI guidelines to some extent in their reporting.

2.5.4 Advantages of GRI

Adoption of the GRI framework has advantages to companies in the form of **improved reputation** and to investors who have better information. The fact that investors feel better informed can in turn impact back upon the company, as investors will see the company as lower risk as more risks are known about and reported. Hence the company's cost of capital will fall.

 Case Study

BT's Social and Environmental Report for the year ended 31 March 2006 complies with the 2002 Global Reporting Initiative Guidelines. To give an overview of the company's social and environmental performance, the report selects 12 non-financial key performance indicators.

(a)   Customer satisfaction – 3% increase in satisfaction

(b)   Employee engagement index (measure of success of BT's relationship with employees) – 65%

(c)   Diversity – 22.1% women, 9.2% ethnic minority, 2.0% disabled

(d)   Health and safety lost time injury rate – down from 0.468 cases per 100,000 working hours to 0.281 cases per 100,000 working hours

(e)   Health and safety sickness and absence rate – down from 2.53% calendar days lost due to sickness/absence to 2.35% calendar days lost

(f)   Supplier relationship success – 89% satisfaction

(g)   Ethical trading (a measure of the application of BT's supply chain human rights standard) – 230 risk assessments with 100% follow-up

(h)   Community contribution – £21.3 million in funding and support in kind (BT aims to maintain a minimum investment of 1% of pre-tax profits and to trial a new measure of community programme effectiveness)

(i)   Global warming CO_2 emissions (a measure of climate change impact) – 60% below 1996 level

(j)   Waste to landfill and recycling (a measure of use of resources) – 58% to landfill, 42% to recycling; BT aims to reduce the amount sent to landfill by 5% each year

(k)   UK addressable broadband market – a measure of the geographical reach of broadband – 99.7% of UK households. This measure ties in with the discussion about the development of broadband technology above

(l)   Ethical performance index – 72%

 Question   Indicators

Compare this brief summary with the table in 2.5.2 above, ticking off performance indicators. If you have time, look for further details and developments on www.globalreporting.org.

2.6 Full cost accounting

2.6.1 Definition

Key term

> **Full cost accounting (FCA)** is at its simplest a system that allows current accounting and economic numbers to incorporate all potential/actual costs and benefits into the equation including environmental (and perhaps social) externalities to get the prices right. *Bebbington, Gray, Hibbitt and Kirk – FCA: An Agenda for Action* (published by ACCA).

As with sustainability, this is a fairly simple definition. Attempts to provide a more helpful definition have proved problematic, with the result that different commentators use the term in different ways. A key problem is that we are not yet sure what a full cost price looks like; hence the emphasis is achieving increasingly fuller costs.

2.6.2 Elements of FCA

The Bebbington et al report for ACCA quotes and amends the USEPA/Tellus approach to FCA. The approach is of achieving increasingly full costs by a number of tiers.

Tier 0	Usual costs	Basic capital and revenue costs
Tier 1	Hidden costs	Costs usually included as overheads eg costs of management systems and safety
Tier 2	Liability costs	Contingent liability costs eg fines
Tier 3	Less tangible costs	Costs of poor environmental management eg loss of goodwill of customers and suppliers, reputation risk
Tier 4	Environment focused costs	Costs that ensure that project has zero environmental effect

Question
Full cost accounting

Compare this tiered approach with the list of costs quoted in the IFAC report in Section 1.

2.6.3 Advantages of FCA

(a) **Knowledge of full extent of environmental footprint**

As with sustainability reporting, this aids investors who are better able to assess the risks involved in the companies' activities.

(b) **Reducing environmental footprint**

A key aim of introducing FCA is to assess the significance of the organisation's environmental footprint and thus encourage reductions in per unit **and** absolute resource usage.

(c) **Assisting decision-making**

As well as making specific environmental decisions, FCA can inform decision-making by allowing comparisons between the externalities created by **different investment options**. The environmental costs identified under FCA will be indicators of future business costs in other areas.

(d) **Favourable publicity**

FCA can allow organisations to demonstrate that products or processes do **not** have significant environmental impacts.

Case Study

The Bebbington et al report quotes the example of Ontario Hydro who listed the following benefits of introducing FCA and reasons for supporting the development of FCA.

Expected benefits

- Incentive to search for ways to reduce environmental damage
- Decision-making includes consideration of present and future environmental impacts

- Promotes efficient and effective resource usage
- Helps 'level the playing field' when assessing demand and supply options

Reasons for supporting development

- Improved environmental cost management

- Cost avoidance by helping businesses anticipate future costs

- Revenue enhancements through environmental technology innovations or strategic alliances with companies using waste products as inputs

- Improved decision-making

- Environmental quality improvement, establishing an optimal level for reducing emissions/effluents/ waste

- Contribution to the development of environmental regulations/standards

- Assisting in sustainable development

Sadly after experimenting with FCA, Ontario Hydro failed to continue with the project and did not disclose why they did not pursue FCA.

2.6.4 Disadvantages of FCA

(a) **Data required**

FCA requires organisations to gather an increased amount of data, with potentially significant **information-gathering costs**. Some commentators have suggested that organisations need to adopt a **life cycle accounting** approach to identify externalities.

(b) **Which cost figures to use?**

One example is the choice between using the **costs of correction** (clean-up costs) or **using costs of prevention** (costs of changing the way business is conducted).

(c) **Translating activities into impacts**

The translation process depends on the (possibly limited) **state of scientific knowledge**.

(d) **Limitations of business level analysis**

The argument is that the individual business is too small a unit to conduct meaningful FCA and **industry** or **geographical area** data may be more useful.

(e) **Inclusion of social externalities**

If full cost accounting accounts for **environmental effects**, then it would appear logical to try to account for **social effects**. However widening the concept to include social costs would introduce additional problems of **definition and measurement** and also mean that political considerations had more significance.

(f) **Impression given**

Many organisations have reservations about introducing FCA because of the impression given; the idea that the picture would be **an alarming** one, suggesting strong sustainability rather than weak sustainability solutions and that many companies would be perceived to have **additional responsibilities** and **ultimately be shown to be unviable.** However there may be some lack of consistency in this argument; that many companies that were unwilling to introduce full cost accounting would nevertheless agree with the principle of 'polluter pays.'

(g)   **Compulsory FCA**

Insistence by governments or standard-setting bodies that businesses go further towards FCA may encourage businesses to relocate away from countries with FCA regimes and thus **export the externalities** to developing nations.

2.6.5 Impact of full cost accounting

Supporters of full cost accounting argue that its disadvantages are in a sense beside the point. The main aim of full cost accounting is not to produce an achievable measure but to **stimulate debate** about the measurement and internalisation of other costs. Full cost accounting, it is argued, demonstrates the limitations of traditional accounting and also highlights the importance of the debate we have discussed about the limits of accountability that accountants have. Full cost accounting shows that the measurement of business performance by measuring recognisable costs falls far short of the limits of business activity.

Exam focus point

A question in the Pilot paper asked for an explanation of the importance of environmental reporting.

3 Environmental management systems

 FAST FORWARD

ISO statements provide a framework for an **environmental management system** including a policy statement, assessment, functions and reporting.

Question   Environmental control systems

How do the main elements of control systems for environmental management systems differ from control systems in other areas?

Answer

As we shall see in this section, they don't. Environmental management systems are a good illustration of how control systems work in practice.

3.1 EMAS

The European Union's Eco-Management and Audit Scheme (EMAS) was adopted in 1993 as a voluntary scheme. Its emphasis is on **targets and improvements**, **on-site inspections** and requirements for **disclosure and verification**. The insistence on targets means that organisations that subscribe to it cannot just rely on monitoring; they have to **improve their environmental performance**.

The **disclosure and verification requirements** are seen as essential, as companies need to know that their performance will be subject to public scrutiny based on data that has been reliably audited, to become 'good little goldfish' (Elkington). Disclosure means that companies have to address the very real difficulties and conflicts of interest that arise in weighing the need to maximise profits against the need to comply with disclosure requirements. However many businesses were opposed to the requirement of EMAS and lobbying meant that compliance was introduced as voluntary rather than compulsory as was originally intended.

EMAS's adoption has been rather more extensive in Germany than elsewhere in the European Union. However many companies that felt that the requirements of EMAS were excessive had eventually to respond to pressures regarding their environmental performance and adopt a recognised standard (ISO 14000).

3.1.1 Requirements for EMAS registration

- An environmental policy containing commitments to comply with legislation and achieve continuous environmental performance improvement

- An on-site environmental review

- An environmental management system that is based on the environmental review and the company's environmental policy

- Environmental audits at sites at least every three years

- Audit results to form the basis of setting environmental objectives and the revision of the environmental policy to achieve those objectives

- A public environmental statement validated by accredited environmental verifiers containing detailed disclosures about policy, management systems and performance in areas such as pollution, waste, raw material usage, energy, water and noise

3.2 ISO 14000

ISO 14000 was first published in 1996 and based on earlier quality management standards. It provides a general framework on which a number of specific standards have been based (the ISO family of standards). ISO 14001 prescribes that an environmental management system must comprise:

- An environmental policy statement
- An assessment of environmental aspects and legal and voluntary obligations
- A management system
- Internal audits and reports to senior management
- A public declaration that ISO 14001 is being complied with

Critics of ISO 14000 claim that its emphasis on management systems rather than performance is misplaced, and that it is much less effective because it does not include EMAS's rigorous verification and disclosure requirements.

3.3 Environmental policy statement

The policy statement should be the basis for future action. It needs therefore to be based on **reliable data,** and allow for the development of **specific targets.**

Organisations may wish to develop their own in-house policy statement or adopt one of the public charters such as the **CERES principles** (see below) or the **ICC's Charter for Sustained Development.** An in-house charter can be tailored to the organisation's needs and be compatible with the mission statement in other areas. However it may be viewed by outsiders as too general and bland, and also may not be internationally comparable. Adopting internationally recognised standards means adherence to standards that have been **determined objectively**, and assisting stakeholders by enabling comparison with other organisations that have adopted the same standards.

 Case Study

The Coalition for Environmentally Responsible Economics, CERES, created the CERES principles in 1989. The principles are a code of environmental conduct to be publicly endorsed by companies as an environmental mission statement or ethic.

- **Protection of the biosphere** – aiming to eliminate the release of any substance that may cause environmental damage, safeguarding habitats and protecting biodiversity

- **Sustainable use of natural resources** – making sustainable use of renewable natural resources and conserving non-renewable natural resources through efficient use and careful planning

- **Reduction and disposal of waste** – elimination of waste where possible through source reduction and recycling, and disposal where necessary of waste through safe and responsible methods

- **Energy conservation** – conserving energy, improving energy of efficiency of internal operations, goods and services and making every effort to use environmentally safe and sustainable energy sources

- **Reduction in environmental and health and safety risks** through safe technologies, facilities and operating procedures, and being prepared for emergencies

- **Safe products and services** – elimination where possible of products and services that cause environmental damage or health and safety hazards, together with informing customers of environmental impacts

- **Environmental restoration** – correcting conditions caused by the organisation that have resulted in damage to the environment and aiming to redress injuries

- **Informing the public** of conditions that might endanger health and safety and the environment, regular dialogue with nearby communities and not taking any action against whistleblowing employees who report dangerous incidents or conditions

- **Management commitment** – environmental commitment being a factor in the selection of directors, board kept informed about environmental issues and acknowledgement of board responsibility for environmental issues

- **Audits and reports** – annual self-evaluation of progress in implementing principles, support for the timely creation of generally accepted environmental audit principles – and annual endorsement of the CERES principles

3.4 Management roles

Whatever the standards adopted, they must be promoted by a member of the senior management team for the standards to be **effective**, and the **audit committee** is likely to be involved in monitoring and reporting on environmental compliance. Depending on the size of the organisation and its impact on the external environment, an **environmental manager** or an **environmental management department** may be employed.

3.5 Assessment of environmental aspects and obligations

Many companies have been forced to act on environmental issues because of shocks such as environmental disasters or attention from pressure groups. To reduce the chances of these happening, organisations must not only monitor their internal performance, but also include within their monitoring of the external situation assessment of the impact of environmental issues. It will be particularly important to monitor:

- Emerging environmental issues
- Likely changes in legislation
- Changes in industry best practice
- Attitudes of suppliers, customers, media and the general public
- Activities of environmental enforcement agencies
- Activities of environmental pressure groups

3.6 Management systems

In *Accounting for the Environment* Gray and Bebbington listed the functions that environmental management systems should cover.

Environmental review and policy development	A first review of environmental impacts of materials, issues and products and of business issues arising, also the development of a tailored in-house policy or measures to ensure adherence to external standards
Objectives and target development	As with all business objectives and targets, it is preferable that those set be unambiguous and achievable. Initiatives such as the WWF initiative described above encourage quantified targets within a specified time period eg reducing carbon dioxide emissions by X% within a specified time period
Life-cycle assessment	This aims to identify all interactions between a product and its environment during its lifetime, including energy and material usage and environmental releases. • Raw materials used have to be traced back to the biosphere and the company recognise impact on habitat, gas balance, the energy used in the extraction and transportation and the energy used to produce the means of extraction • For intermediate stages, emissions, discharges and co-products • At the consumer purchase stage, the impact of manufacture and disposal of packaging, transport to shops and ultimately impacts of consumers using and disposing of the product
Establishment and maintenance of environmental management systems	Key features of environmental management systems (as with other management systems) including information systems, budgeting, forecasting and management accounting systems, structure of responsibilities, establishment of an environmentally-friendly culture, considering impact on human resource issues such as education and performance appraisal
Regulatory compliance	Making sure that current legal requirements are being fulfilled and keeping up-to-date with practical implications of likely changes in legislation
Environmental impact assessment	A regular review of interactions with the environment, the degree of impact and an environmental SWOT analysis, also the impact of forthcoming major investments
Eco-label applications	Eco-labelling allows organisations to identify publicly products and services that meet the highest environmental standards. To be awarded an eco-label requires the product to be the result of a reliable quality management system
Waste minimisation	Whether waste can be minimised (or better still eliminated), possibility of recycling or selling waste
Pollution prevention programmes	Deciding what to target
Research, development and investment in cleaner technologies	How to bring desirable features into product development, bearing in mind product development may take several years, and opinion and legal requirements may change during that period. Desirable features may include minimum resource usage, waste, emissions, packaging and transport, recycling, disassembly and longer product life
Environmental performance and issues reporting	Consideration of the benefits and costs of reporting, how to report and what to include (policies, plans, financial data, activities undertaken, sustainability)

3.7 Environmental reporting

Predictably the main arguments in favour of environmental reporting are similar to those for reporting on other aspects of internal control, including following the principles of **transparency** and **openness, disclosing matters of concern** to investors and other stakeholders and generally presenting a **balanced and understandable assessment** of the **company's position and prospects**.

4 Social and environmental audits

> **FAST FORWARD**
>
> **Social and environmental audits** are designed to ascertain whether the organisation is complying with codes of best practice or internal guidelines, and is fulfilling the wider requirements of being a good corporate citizen.

4.1 Social audits

The process of checking whether an organisation has achieved set targets may fall within a social audit that a company carries out. Social audits may cover sustainable use of resources, health and safety compliance, labour conditions (no exploitation of labour) and equal opportunities.

General social audits will involve:

- Establishing whether the organisation has a **rationale** for engaging in socially responsible activity
- Identifying that all current environment programmes are **congruent** with the mission of the company
- **Assessing objectives and priorities** related to these programmes
- **Evaluating company involvement** in such programmes past, present and future

Whether or not a social audit is used depends on the degree to which social responsibility is part of the **corporate philosophy**. A cultural awareness must be achieved within an organisation in order to implement social policy, which requires Board and staff support.

4.1.1 Specific social audits

Specific social audits may cover the consequences of a major decision, for example the costs such as unemployment costs and indirect redundancies of shutting a major manufacturing plant.

 Case Study

In the 1980s the then Sheffield City Council attempted to assess the **volume and quality** of **direct and indirect employment** resulting from council activity. The main areas that the audit examined were:

- The council's spending and its financing
- The trends of employment in Sheffield and the council's contribution
- Total jobs supported by council spending and generated by employees
- The employment effects of capital and housing revenue expenditure
- How pay and conditions compared with other employers
- Impact of rates and charges on local employment levels
- The impact of privatisation of council services
- Benchmarking Sheffield's policies against the effects of Dudley Council's different policies

 BPP LEARNING MEDIA

4.1.2 External social audits

Another type of social audit is an audit carried out by an external body with or without the organisation's co-operation. These types of audit might for example cover **involvement in controversial areas** such as animal testing, aggressive marketing, low-wage employment overseas and investment in countries governed by oppressive regimes. More positive areas that could be covered include industrial democracy, equal opportunities, community involvement and disclosure of information.

4.2 Environmental audits

Key term

> An **environmental audit** is a systematic, documented, periodic and objective evaluation of how well an entity, its management and equipment are performing, with the aim of helping to safeguard the environment by facilitating management control of environmental practices and assessing compliance with entity policies and external regulations.
>
> Environmental auditing is also used for auditing the **truth and fairness** of an environmental report rather than the organisation itself; the same is true of social auditing.

An environmental audit might be undertaken as part of obtaining or maintaining the BSI's ISO 14001 standard.

In practice environmental audits may cover a number of different areas, and some of the examples below may go beyond what you have encountered in your earlier auditing studies. The scope of the audit must be determined and this will depend on each individual organisation. Often the audit will be a general review of the organisation's environmental policy. On other occasions the audit will focus on specific aspects of environmental performance (energy or waste disposal) or particular locations, activities or processes.

There are, however, some aspects of the approach to environmental auditing which are worth mentioning.

(a) **Environmental Impact Assessments (EIAs)**

These are required, under EC directive, for all major projects which require planning permission and have a material effect on the environment. The EIA process can be incorporated into any environmental auditing strategy.

(b) **Environmental surveys**

These are a good way of starting the audit process, by looking at the organisation as a whole in environmental terms. This helps to identify areas for further development, problems, potential hazards and so forth.

(c) **Environmental SWOT analysis**

A 'strengths, weaknesses, opportunities, threats' analysis is useful as the environmental audit strategy is being developed. This can only be done later in the process, when the organisation has been examined in much more detail.

(d) **Environmental Quality Management (EQM)**

This is seen as part of TQM (Total Quality Management) and it should be built into an environmental management system. Such a strategy has been adopted by companies such as IBM, Dow Chemicals and by the Rhone-Poulenc Environmental Index which has indices for levels of water, air and other waste products.

(e) **Eco-audit**

The European Commission has adopted a proposal for a regulation for a voluntary community environmental auditing scheme, known as the eco-audit scheme. The scheme aims to promote improvements in company environmental performance and to provide the public with information about these improvements. Once registered, a company will have to comply with certain on-going obligations involving disclosure and audit.

(f)   **Eco-labelling**

Developed in Germany, this voluntary scheme will indicate those EC products which meet the highest environmental standards, probably as the result of an EQM system. It is suggested that eco-audit **must** come before an eco-label can be given.

(g)   **BS 7750 Environmental Management Systems**

BS 7750 also ties in with eco-audits and eco-labelling and with the quality BSI standard BS 5750. Achieving BS 7750 is likely to be a first step in the eco-audit process.

(h)   **Supplier audits**

They ensure that goods and services bought in by an organisation meet the standards applied by that organisation.

4.2.1 Auditor concerns

(a)   Board and management having **good understanding** of the environmental impact and related legislation of the organisation's activities in areas such as buildings, transport, products, packaging and waste

(b)   Adoption and communication of adequate policies and procedures to ensure **compliance with relevant standards and laws**

(c)   Adoption of **appropriate environmental information systems**

(d)   Adoption and **review of progress** against quantifiable targets

(e)   Assessment of whether **progress** is being made **economically and efficiently**

(f)   Implementation of **previous recommendations** of improvements to processes or systems

(g)   **True, fair and complete reporting** of environmental activities

4.2.2 Auditing environmental policy

Auditing the appropriateness of, and compliance with, the organisation's environmental policy will be at the heart of internal environmental audits.

(a)   Review evidence of the organisation's environmental interactions

(b)   Obtain a copy of the organisation's environmental policy

(c)   Assess whether the policy is likely to achieve objectives:

   (i)   Meet legal requirements
   (ii)   Meet environmental standards
   (iii) Satisfy key customers/suppliers' criteria

(d)   Test implementation and adherence to the policy by:

   (i)   Discussion
   (ii)   Observation
   (iii) 'Walk-though tests' where possible

Chapter Roundup

- There is increasing concern about businesses' relationship with the natural environment. Businesses may suffer **significant costs** and a **loss of reputation** if problems arise.

- **Sustainability** means limiting use of resources to what can be replenished.

- The **Global Reporting Initiative** provides a framework for a **sustainability report**.

- **Full cost accounting** is a method of accounting for all relevant costs including externalities.

- **ISO statements** provide a framework for an **environmental management system** including a policy statement, assessment, functions and reporting.

- **Social and environmental audits** are designed to ascertain whether the organisation is complying with codes of best practice or internal guidelines, and is fulfilling the wider requirements of being a good corporate citizen.

Quick Quiz

1   Fill in the blank.

    .... is the impact that a business's activities have upon the environment including its resource environment and pollution emissions.

2   What is sustainability in relation to a company's activities?

3   Give three examples of the environmental indicators mentioned in the Global Reporting Initiative.

4   What is full cost accounting?

5   What are the main elements of an environmental management system per ISO 14001?

6   What is eco-labelling?

    A   An indication of a product that meets the highest environmental standards

    B   Looking at the organisation as a whole in environmental terms

    C   A requirement for all major projects that need planning permission and have a material effect on the environment

    D   A voluntary community environmental auditing scheme

7   By what criteria is an auditor likely to test an organisation's environmental policy?

8   When an organisation is developing an environmental audit strategy, the first thing it should do is carry out an environmental SWOT analysis.

    True   ☐

    False   ☐

Answers to Quick Quiz

1   Environmental footprint

2   Sustainability involves developing strategies so that the company only uses resources at a rate that allows them to be replenished (in order to ensure that they will continue to be available). At the same time the company's emissions of waste are confined to levels that do not exceed the capacity of the environment to absorb them.

3   Three from:

- Materials
- Energy
- Water
- Biodiversity
- Emissions, effluent and waste
- Suppliers
- Products and services
- Compliance
- Transport
- Overall

4   Full cost accounting is a system that allows current accounting and economic numbers to incorporate all potential/actual costs and benefits into the equation including environmental and social externalities.

5   • An environmental policy
     • An assessment of environmental aspects and legal and voluntary obligations
     • A management system
     • Internal audits and reports to senior management
     • A public declaration that ISO 14001 is being complied with

6   A   An indication of a product that meets the highest environmental standards
     B   is an environmental survey.
     C   is an environmental impact assessment.
     D   is an eco-audit.

7   • Meet legal requirements
     • Meet environmental standards
     • Satisfy key customers'/suppliers' criteria

8   False. The SWOT analysis should be carried out later in the process when evidence is available of the organisation's environmental footprint.

Now try the question below from the Exam Question Bank

Number	Level	Marks	Time
Q12	Examination	25	45 mins

BPP
LEARNING MEDIA

Appendix
London Stock Exchange Combined Code

Appendix

London Stock Exchange Combined Code

1 Directors

1.1 The board

All listed companies should be led by an **effective board**. The board should meet regularly and have **certain matters** reserved for its decision. Directors should be able to obtain independent professional advice and have access to the services of the company secretary. The company secretary is **responsible for ensuring** that **board procedures** and **relevant regulations** are followed. The whole board should be responsible for removing the company secretary. Every director should use **independent judgement** when making decisions. Every director should receive appropriate **training**.

1.2 Chairman and Chief Executive

There are two leading management roles; running the board and running the company. A **clear division of responsibilities** should exist so that there is a balance of power, and no one person has unfettered powers of decision. Combination of the roles of **chairman** and **chief executive** should be **justified publicly**. There should also be a **strong and independent** body of **non-executive directors** with a recognised senior member other than the chairman.

1.3 Board balance

The board should have a **balance** of **executive and non-executive directors** so that no individual or small group is dominant. The non-executive directors should be of sufficient calibre and number to have a significant influence and should comprise at least one third of the board. The majority of non-executive directors should be independent.

1.4 Supply of information

The board should be **promptly supplied** with **enough information** to enable it to carry out its duties. Information volunteered by management will sometimes need to be supplemented by information from other sources. All directors should be properly briefed.

1.5 Appointment of directors

There should be a **clear, formal procedure** for appointing new directors. A nomination committee should make recommendations about all new board appointments.

1.6 Re-election

All directors should submit themselves for **re-election regularly**, and at least once every three years.

2 Directors' remuneration

2.1 Remuneration policy

Remuneration levels should be sufficient to attract directors of **sufficient calibre** to run the company effectively, but companies should not pay more than is necessary. A proportion of remuneration should be based on **corporate and individual performance.** Comparisons with other companies should be used with caution. When designing performance-related elements of remuneration, the remuneration committee should consider annual bonuses and different kinds of long-term incentive schemes.

2.2 Service contracts and compensation

Boards' ultimate objectives should be to set **notice periods at one year or less**. Directors should consider whether to include compensation commitments in the contracts of service.

2.3 Procedure

Companies should establish a formal and clear procedure for **developing policy** on **executive remuneration** and for fixing the remuneration package of individual directors. **Directors should not be involved** in **setting their own remuneration**. A **remuneration committee**, staffed by independent non-executive directors, should make **recommendations** about the framework of executive remuneration, and should determine specific remuneration packages. The board should determine the remuneration of non-executive directors.

2.4 Disclosure

The annual report should contain a **statement about remuneration policy** and **details of the remuneration of each director**. The report should give details about **all elements of the remuneration package,** share options, pension entitlements and service contracts or compensation in excess of one year. Shareholders should approve all new long-term remuneration schemes. The remuneration report need not be a standard AGM item, but the board should consider whether the report needs to be approved.

3 Relations with shareholders

3.1 Institutional shareholders

Companies should be prepared to **communicate** with **institutional shareholders**.

3.2 Use of the AGM

The AGM should be a **means of communication** with **private investors.** Companies should count all proxies and announce proxy votes for and against on all votes on a show of hands. Companies should propose a **separate resolution** on each substantially separate issue, and there should be a resolution covering the **board and accounts**. The chairmen of the audit, nomination and remuneration committees should be available to answer questions at the AGM. Papers should be sent to members at least 20 working days before the AGM.

4 Accountability and audit

4.1 Financial reporting

The board should present a **balanced and understandable assessment** of the **company's position and prospects** in the annual accounts and other reports such as interim reports and reports to regulators. The directors should explain their responsibility for the accounts, and the auditors should state their reporting responsibilities. The directors should also report on the going concern status of the business.

4.2 Internal control

A good system of control should be maintained. The directors should **review effectiveness** annually and report to shareholders that they have done so. The review should cover all controls including financial, operational and compliance controls and risk management. Companies who **lack** an **internal audit function** should regularly consider whether they need one.

4.3 Audit committees and auditors

There should be **formal and clear arrangements** with the **company's auditors**, and for applying the financial reporting and internal control principles. Companies should have an **audit committee** consisting of non-executive directors, the majority of whom should be independent. The audit committee should review the audit, and the independence and objectivity of the auditors. In particular the committee should keep matters under review if the auditors supply significant non-audit services.

5 Shareholder voting

Institutional shareholders should use their votes carefully and **disclose** how they have **voted** to their clients. They should also enter into a dialogue with companies, and should give appropriate weight to all relevant criteria when considering corporate governance arrangements.

6 Compliance with the Code

The Combined Code requires listed companies to include in their accounts:

(a) A narrative statement of how they **applied** the **principles** set out in the Combined Code. This should provide explanations which enable their shareholders to assess how the principles have been applied.

(b) A statement as to whether or not they **complied throughout** the **accounting period** with the provisions set out in the Combined Code. Listed companies that did not comply throughout the accounting period with all the provisions must specify the provisions with which they did not comply, and give **reasons** for **non-compliance**.

Exam question bank

1 Bonus schemes
45 mins

It has been suggested that optimal bonus schemes for profit centre managers promise significant rewards for the achievement of challenging targets in areas they can influence. These schemes balance short-term pressure with incentives to maintain a long-term focus and protect managers from the distorting effects of uncontrollable factors.

It has also been suggested that many bonus schemes have additional features with different motivational effects.

The following are possible features of bonus schemes.

- Limiting the range of performance within which rewards are linked to results, in particular ignoring losses and limiting maximum payments

- Linking incentive payments wholly or partly to the profit of the organisation as a whole

Required

(a) (i)   Explain why bonus schemes might include these features.

 (ii)   Discuss the advantages and disadvantages of incorporating these features into bonus schemes. **(16 marks)**

Bonus schemes are normally designed to motivate full-time employees who have no other employment and are wholly dependent upon the organisation for their income. Part-time employees and short-term employees might not be included.

(b)   Describe and advise on the possible features of bonus schemes which are designed to motivate non-executive directors who are part-time, remunerated by fees under contracts for a fixed number of years and required by corporate governance codes to maintain independence. **(9 marks)**

(Total = 25 marks)

2 Corporate governance requirements
45 mins

Contrast the requirements of the Sarbanes-Oxley Act 2002 with the Organisation for Economic Co-operation and Development principles of corporate governance and the International Corporate Governance Network report on corporate governance.

3 Board appraisal
45 mins

The Combined Code on Corporate Governance recommends that 'the board should undertake a formal and rigorous annual evaluation of its own performance and that of its committees and individual directors'.

Required

Write a report to the Board of Directors of a public limited company which wishes to update its board appraisal system. Your report should recommend the main areas of board and individual director's performance that should be assessed and measures that might be used to make that assessment.

4 Controls in new company

45 mins

A large local government authority in the United Kingdom has decided to seek competitive tenders for all its internal computer requirements. The present managers of the authority's Computer Services Department have decided that they wish to tender for the work, and if successful, form a company to acquire the existing assets and carry out work for the local government authority and other customers.

They think that the work that they currently do for their own local government authority is technically far in advance of that done by neighbouring local government authorities. They consider that additional volume would allow them to reward more highly the good staff who are currently employed at low public sector rates of pay.

A group of local businessmen and potential investors has discussed this proposal with the Director of Computing, who would lead the proposed management buy-out (MBO). They are quite impressed with the technical competence of the staff, and the prospects for gaining additional work.

However, they have a number of reservations, as the staff have no experience outside information technology, and no commercial experience. Their experience of budgeting is also limited. The local government authority does not subdivide its budget for the Computer Services Department. It manages this department as a cost centre, and receives reports of expenditure against budget at quarterly intervals.

The investors have asked consultants to advise on certain aspects of the proposals.

Required

Write a report to the investors. This report should:

(a)   Recommend the form and level of detail of budgetary control required in the new company.

(10 marks)

(b)   Recommend the structure and formal controls required at Board level in the new company.

(15 marks)

(Total = 25 marks)

5 Internal audit role

35 mins

You have been appointed manager of internal audit in a large organisation and asked to set up an appropriate department.

Required

Write a report for the board clarifying the role of internal audit with regard to external audit and accounting systems. In your report, you should:

(a)   Compare briefly the role of the external audit to that of the internal audit.

(b)   Describe the steps the external auditors need to take to be able to rely on specific internal audit work.

(c)   Discuss whether the existence of an internal audit function simplifies the job of the external auditors.

6 Risks

45 mins

When an organisation undertakes a major investment project, it takes on project risk. The risk in a project comes from various sources, and includes:

(i)   Project-specific risk
(ii)   Competitive risk
(iii)   Industry-specific risk
(iv)   Market risk

Required

(a)   Describe what is meant by each of these types of risk.

The most important risks that many businesses face are as follows:

(i)   Trading risk
(ii)   Cultural, country and political risks
(iii)   Currency risk
(iv)   Interest rate risk
(v)   Technological risk

Required

(b)   Describe what is meant by each of these types of risk.

(c)   Explain how following the principles laid down in the codes of corporate governance can assist in managing risks on a day-to-day basis.

7 Pacific Group

45 mins

Pacific Group Ltd (PG) is a publisher of a monthly magazine 'Sea Discovery'. Approximately 70% of the magazine's revenue is derived from advertising, the remainder being subscription income.

Individual advertisements, which may be quarter, half or whole page, are priced at £750, £1,250 and £2,000, respectively. Discounts of 10% to 25% are given for repeat advertisements and to major advertising customers.

PG's management has identified the following risks relating to its advertising revenues:

(i)   Loss of revenue through failure to invest in developments which keep the presentation of advertisements up to date with competitor publications (such as 'The Deep');

(ii)   Due to unsuitable credit limits being set, business is accepted from a small proportion of advertising customers who are uncreditworthy;

(iii)   Published advertisements may not be invoiced due to incomplete data transfer between the editorial and invoicing departments;

(iv)   Individual advertisements are not charged for at approved rates – either in error or due to arrangements with the advertisers. In particular, the editorial department does not notify the invoicing department of reciprocal advertisement arrangements, whereby advertising customers provide PG with other forms of advertising (such as website banners).

(v)   Individual advertisers refuse to pay for the inaccurate production of their advertisement;

(vi)   Cash received at a front desk, which is significant, may not be passed to cashiers, or be misappropriated;

(vii)   The risk of error arising from unauthorised access to the editorial and invoicing systems;

(viii)   The risk that the editorial and invoicing systems are not available;

(ix)   The computerised transfer of accounting information from the invoicing system to the nominal ledger may be incomplete or inaccurate;

(x)   The risk that PG may be sued for advertisements which do not meet the British Standards Authority's 'Code of Advertising'.

Risks are to be screened out, as 'non-applicable', if they meet **any** of the following criteria:

(1)   The effect of the risk can be quantified and is less than £5,000;
(2)   The risk is mitigated by an effective risk strategy e.g. insurance;
(3)   The risk is likely to be low or its effect insignificant.

Those risks not screened out, called 'applicable risks', will require further consideration and are to be actively managed.

Required

(a)   For each of the above risks identified by management, evaluate, with a reason, whether it should be considered an 'applicable risk'.   **(17 marks)**

(b)   Describe suitable internal controls to manage any FOUR of the applicable risks identified in (a).

(8 marks)

(Total = 25 marks)

8 Azure Airline   45 mins

Azure, a limited liability company, was incorporated in Sepiana on 1 April 20X6. In May, the company exercised an exclusive right granted by the government of Pewta to provide twice weekly direct flights between Lyme, the capital of Pewta, and Darke, the capital of Sepiana.

The introduction of this service has been well advertised as 'efficient and timely' in national newspapers. The journey time between Sepiana and Pewta is expected to be significantly reduced, so encouraging tourism and business development opportunities in Sepiana.

Azure operates a refurbished 35 year old aircraft which is leased from an international airline and registered with the Pewtan Aviation Administration (the PAA). The PAA requires that engines be overhauled every two years. Engine overhauls are expected to put the aircraft out of commission for several weeks.

The aircraft is configured to carry 15 First Class, 50 Business Class and 76 Economy Class passengers. The aircraft has a generous hold capacity for Sepiana's numerous horticultural products (eg of cocoa, tea and fruit) and general cargo.

The six hour journey offers an in-flight movie, a meal, hot and cold drinks and tax-free shopping. All meals are prepared in Lyme under a contract with an airport catering company. Passengers are invited to complete a 'satisfaction' questionnaire which is included with the in-flight entertainment and shopping guide. Responses received show that passengers are generally least satisfied with the quality of the food – especially on the Darke to Lyme flight.

Azure employs 10 full-time cabin crew attendants who are trained in air-stewardship including passenger safety in the event of accident and illness. Flight personnel (the captain and co-pilots) are provided under a contract with the international airline from which the aircraft is leased. At the end of each flight the captain completes a timesheet detailing the crew and actual flight time.

Ticket sales are made by Azure and travel agents in Sepiana and Pewta. On a number of occasions Economy seating has been over-booked. Customers who have been affected by this have been accommodated in Business Class as there is much less demand for this, and even less for First Class.

Ticket prices for each class depend on many factors, for example, whether the tickets are refundable/non-refundable, exchangeable/non-exchangeable, single or return, mid-week or weekend, and the time of booking.

Azure's insurance cover includes passenger liability, freight/baggage and compensation insurance. Premiums for passenger liability insurance are determined on the basis of passenger miles flown.

Required

(a)   Identify and explain the business risks facing Azure.   **(12 marks)**

(b)   Recommend how the risks identified in (a) could be managed and maintained at an acceptable level by Azure.   **(13 marks)**

Note: You should assume it is 5 December 20X6.   **(Total = 25 marks)**

9 Governance and controls   45 mins

Corporate governance issues first came to prominence in the late 1980s and early 1990s, and triggered the requirement for companies with shares traded on the main stock market to have a system of corporate governance in place.

Required

(a)   Discuss the main issues that triggered the requirement for systematised corporate governance in large public companies.   **(10 marks)**

A UK public company has an official listing for its shares, which are traded on the London Stock Exchange. The company has a small head office, including a non-executive chairman, a chief executive and a finance director. There are three major business divisions, each headed by a main board member, and each business division consists of a number of operating units (subsidiaries). The management structure is largely decentralised, and many operating and spending decisions are taken at operating unit level. Operations are carried on throughout Europe. The board consists of five executive directors, a non-executive chairman, and five non-executive directors. There is no internal audit department.

The board is required to make an annual statement in its report and accounts about the effectiveness of its internal controls.

Required

(b)   Explain what the board should do before it is in a position to make a statement about the effectiveness of its internal controls. Give particular attention to the need for a control environment, the evaluation of risks, the existence of information and communication systems, control procedures and monitoring and corrective action.   **(15 marks)**

(Total = 25 marks)

10 Ethical standards   45 mins

(a)   Identify some common barriers to the successful adoption of ethical standards in business practice.

(b)   Explain the practical steps that organisations can take towards creating an ethical framework for corporate governance.

11 Independence

45 mins

'The internal auditor should have the independence in terms of organisational status and personal objectivity which permits the proper performance of his duties.'
(*Guidance for Internal Auditors*, Auditing Practices Committee)

Required

(a) Discuss what is meant by independence in this context, listing and briefly explaining the freedoms and privileges needed for employees of an organisation to be able to act effectively as internal auditors. **(7 marks)**

(b) Discuss the alternative organisational structures that can help to achieve this independence of internal audit, and the ways in which an Audit Committee can contribute to this. **(7 marks)**

(c) Discuss the threats to the objectivity of internal audit caused by the existence of family or other close relationships between the internal auditor and the staff being audited. **(5 marks)**

(d) In many organisations, bonus payments related to annual profits form a significant part of the total remuneration of all senior managers, not just the top few managers.

Discuss whether it is appropriate for the Chief Internal Auditor to receive a bonus based on the organisation's profit, or whether it could be seen to compromise his independence. **(6 marks)**

(Total = 25 marks)

12 Environmental audit and accounting

45 mins

You have been asked to conduct an environmental audit for your organisation to assess how 'green' it is in terms of energy consumption, use of renewable resources, and employee awareness of these issues.

(a) Describe the information you would seek when planning the audit. **(9 marks)**

(b) Explain how would you test for employee awareness, and how would you involve all employees in the initiative. **(6 marks)**

(c) Discuss the reasons why companies wish to disclose environmental information in their financial statements. Discuss whether the content of such disclosure should be at the company's discretion.

(10 marks)

(Total = 25 marks)

Exam answer bank

1 Bonus schemes

Top tips. The biggest dangers in (a) are failing to read the question carefully and the temptation to overrun on the time allowed for the solution, given the marks available. Bonus schemes are a recurring feature of this exam and most candidates should be able to write about them both from theoretical and personal knowledge without too much difficulty.

(b) requires much more thought – think about the key issue of independence for NEDs. As long as the features you suggest do not compromise independence or suggest awarding too generous bonuses you will be earning marks.

(a) **Limiting the range of performance within which rewards are linked to results**

Many schemes do indeed limit the range of performance within which rewards are linked to results, in particular ignoring losses and limiting maximum payments.

Ignoring losses

Unless the organisation in question was operating in an extremely stable and predictable environment, it would be unacceptable to the vast majority of managers to be asked to participate in a remuneration system that might require them to reimburse their employer in the event of losses being incurred. In general, managers want to receive their standard salary, they do not want the threat of some of it being taken away if their organisation reports losses. If the organisation were to **impose penalties for poor performance**, managers may well **manipulate their targets to ensure that they did not suffer financially**.

Benefits and drawbacks of ignoring losses

If **losses are excluded** from the range of performance, **full participation** in the scheme is likely as no financial penalty (or negative bonus) can be imposed on a manager if levels of performance are particularly poor. Salaries will be viewed as fair payment for duties performed, with any bonus being regarded as a genuine reward for effort.

Managers may **take unnecessary risks**, however, as they are under no financial risk themselves, and **poor levels of performance may be deliberately further depressed** to ensure easier future targets.

Capping maximum payments

Reasons for capping maximum payments include a desire by risk averse managers to **limit the organisation's maximum liability** and the **prevention of payments which shareholders might regard as excessive**.

Benefits and drawbacks of capping maximum payments

Capping maximum payments should ensure that managers **concentrate on improvements which will be sustainable year-on-year**. The financial incentive provided should be large enough to motivate without being excessive.

Managers might feel **no incentive to improve performance beyond the cut-off level**, however, and they could be forced into **holding back for future periods profit-generating or cost-cutting strategies and ideas** once the maximum limit has been reached. A limit on maximum payments could also cause managers to feel **disempowered**, the message being sent out by the bonus system indicating that no matter how good their performance, the most they would receive is £X.

Linking incentive payments to the profits of the organisation as a whole

This is a **popular feature** in many bonus schemes for a number of **reasons**.

(i)   Profit is a **widely-understood measure**, and the maximisation of organisational profit is generally accepted to be congruent with the goals of shareholders.

(ii)   As **profit reporting forms** part of most organisation's **standard reporting procedures**, little additional work is required for profit to be used as the standard measure of performance (compared with more elaborate performance reward mechanisms which can generate substantial data collection costs).

(iii)   It also provides a **basis for participation** in bonus schemes by service centre staff such as those of internal audit and IT departments, for whom the use of other measures can be much more problematic.

(iv)   The profit reported by many profit centres will be **significantly affected** by **head office policies** on, for example, salary levels or stock valuation, and so overall organisational profit may be more objective.

(v)   Rather than arguing over scarce resources, the use of organisational profit may persuade **profit centre managers** to **work together** to further the aims of the organisation as a whole.

(vi)   As agents of the organisation's shareholders, **managers' rewards should be closely linked to the rewards of shareholders.**

Benefits of linking payments to organisational profits

(i)   Inter-profit centre/-divisional **conflicts should be minimised**, with all parts of the organisation concentrating on group results.

(ii)   Management attention should be focused on the need to **cut unnecessary expenditure.**

(iii)   Management will **not be diverted from performing their regular duties** to agree on more elaborate performance-reward systems.

Drawbacks of linking payments to organisational profits

(i)   If the proportion of the bonus that is linked to overall organisational performance is significant and other profit centres do not perform well, managers will get a **reduced bonus** payment or even no payment at all. Managers who consistently perform well and achieve their individual targets are likely to become demotivated if they receive no bonus because of poor levels of performance in other parts of the organisation.

(ii)   Managers could feel that their **area of responsibility** is **too small** to have a substantial impact on group profits and may become demotivated.

(iii)   Managers may **cut short-term, discretionary costs** in order to achieve current profit targets at the **expense of future profits**.

(b)   **Bonus schemes for non-executive directors (NEDs)**

The design of bonus schemes for NEDs is **problematic**. If the bonus is **too small** the NEDs may **not be motivated** to do anything more than the minimum required to collect their fees. If the bonus is **too generous** they may **stop acting in the best interests of shareholders for fear of incurring the displeasure of the executive directors** and thereby jeopardizing their bonus payments.

A bonus scheme for NEDs will therefore need to include the following **features**.

(i)   It should ensure that **high quality and motivated NEDs** are recruited, thereby ensuring that shareholders will benefit from the appointment of the NEDs.

(ii)   The bonus should be paid either **in cash or in the companies' shares**. Such methods will motivate the NED without contravening the recommendation in the Hampel report that NEDs are not granted share options.

(iii)   The bonus scheme could be **linked to the long-term performance of the company**, rather than simply to the financial performance of the current period. A **balanced range of performance measures** such as increase in market share or stock market valuation in relation to competitors over a certain period of time (depending on the NEDs' length of contract) and so on should **encourage NEDs to take a broader view of corporate governance.**

(iv)   It is important that **good corporate governance is seen to be maintained**. Shareholders' prior approval of any bonus scheme should be obtained to avoid any impression that NEDs' bonuses are being offered as a *quid pro quo* for the executive directors' remuneration.

(v)   Any bonus scheme should be designed to provide an incentive for the NED to achieve specific objectives or complete specific tasks outside his normal duties as a NED.

         Bonuses are justified for tasks such as carrying out competitor reviews or designing staff remuneration schemes, which will enhance the NED's understanding of the business without compromising his independence.

(vi)   Any **goal-oriented bonuses** should **be paid immediately following the work to which they relate**. Rolling up of bonus payments may silence any criticism from the NED as the payment date approaches.

2 Corporate governance requirements

Top tips. The answer illustrates how you should approach a comparison question; a point-by-point comparison rather than the first half of the answer dealing with the Sarbanes-Oxley Act, the second half with the OECD/ICGN principles. Although the answer does include some detail on the requirements, it also brings out the comparison by exploring what the legislation and guidelines aimed to achieve.

Purpose

The main purpose of the Sarbanes-Oxley Act was to **tackle various problems** that had been brought to light by Enron and other corporate scandals. These included poor internal controls, misleading financial statements and ineffectiveness of non-executive directors and auditor monitoring of companies. They relate to the situation in **America**, although foreign companies with a listing on the US stock market have to comply as well.

The OECD principles have been designed to establish an credible international framework that **promotes global investment**; investors who are investing in different countries can have confidence in the corporate governance of companies that adopt the OECD principles or regimes that base their own governance codes on the OECD. The ICGN report is designed to enhance the OECD principles by providing practical guidance for boards wishing to **enhance their reputation** for **good corporate governance** and to establish better dialogue with their investors.

Board roles

Sarbanes-Oxley aims to reinforce the **monitoring role of the board and the responsibility of the board** for producing true and fair financial statements. It thus lays stress on the role of the audit committee, which is compulsory for all listed companies. The audit committee should oversee the role of external auditors and establish mechanisms for dealing with complaints. Board responsibility is enforced by the chief executive officer and the chief financial officer being required to certify the financial statements, and having to forfeit their bonuses if the financial statements subsequently have to be restated.

The OECD/ICGN guidelines provide rather more general guidance on the role and responsibilities of the board. They aim to promote **board effectiveness.** The OECD principles do this by stressing the board's **overall role in strategic development**, that board members should exercise **care and good faith** and **exercise independent judgement,** and assigning non-executive directors to appropriate roles. The ICGN code gives some specific guidelines on how to achieve the OECD guidelines. These include listing **strategic matters** that would normally be considered by the board, recommending certain **board committees** (nomination, remuneration and audit) be established, suggesting that the **chairman and chief executive** should be **different people** and stating **scrutiny of director performance** would be enhanced by yearly appraisal and regular reelection.

Accounts

A major aim of the Sarbanes-Oxley legislation is to tighten up accounting rules that it was perceived were too lax, allowing Enron to produce accounts that may have complied with existing standards but were misleading. Hence the Act targets the kinds of **off-balance sheet arrangements** that Enron employed. Sarbanes-Oxley also seeks to **promote effective internal controls** by requiring disclosure of management responsibility for control system maintenance, and an audited **assessment of the effectiveness of the internal control structure and the procedures for financial reporting.**

The OECD/ICGN guidelines contain **various recommendations for disclosure** based on good practice in major jurisdictions. The disclosures reflect the important areas highlighted in the guidelines including governance structures and policies, and relationships with shareholders and stakeholders. They aim to **promote disclosure** that aids investors by recommending the provision of analysis or advice that is relevant to investors. The guidelines also stress the importance of the company **excelling in the returns it achieves** in comparison with its equity sector peer group.

Audit

Sarbanes-Oxley responded to concerns about external auditing practice by stiffening the requirements relating to auditor independence. The **enhanced role of the audit committee** was part of this, but the Act also includes **provisions limiting the non-audit services** auditors can provide and **requiring the regular rotation of lead audit partners.** The Act also includes a number of provisions relating to the **conduct of audits** and **audit firm procedures,** including retention of working papers and quality control requirements, and the requirement for auditors to review internal control systems.

The OECD/ICGN guidelines place less stress than Sarbanes-Oxley on the role of the auditor, although they do stress the importance of the auditor providing **external and objective assurance** and audit committee-auditor links. The issue of non-audit services affecting **independence is raised**, the guidance noting the various methods different regimes have used to deal with this potential problem.

Shareholders

Sarbanes-Oxley does not contain significant provisions enhancing the role of shareholders. The OECD and ICGN guidelines do contain provisions promoting shareholder interests, in line with their key objective of enhancing investor confidence. The OECD principles stress the importance of **treating all shareholders equitably** and **eliminating cross-border impediments to shareholding**. The ICGN report seeks to reinforce these general aims with some specific guidance on how **shareholder voting rights** can be **protected** and also **promoting the role of institutional shareholders,** with the idea that their active involvement can encourage better corporate governance.

Stakeholders and ethics

The provisions relating to ethics in Sarbanes-Oxley were mainly inspired by the examples of unacceptable behaviour at Enron. They are designed to reduce the chances of **poor ethical behaviour occurring** and **remaining undetected.** Hence companies are required to state whether they have **adopted a code of conduct for senior financial officers** and the **contents** of that code. The Act also contains strong provisions protecting the position of auditors, employees and lawyers who **whistleblow** on unethical behaviour.

The OECD/ICGN guidance also stresses the importance of companies establishing an ethical code and protecting whistleblowers. However these requirements are set in the rather wider context of encouraging companies to act in an **economically, socially and environmentally friendly manner** and the board promoting a **culture of integrity**. The guidance also emphasises the **importance of successful and productive relationships** with stakeholders, particularly employees, and suggests various methods of enhancing employee participation.

Enforcement

Sarbanes-Oxley has passed into US law and thus companies listed on the US Stock Exchange **have to comply** with its provisions. The OECD/ICGN principles have no legislative power; however countries are using the OECD principles as a basis for developing or judging their own regimes.

3 Board appraisal

> **Top tips.** An easy mistake to make with the question like this is to go into detail about the mechanism of the appraisal process rather than what it should cover. The question's basic themes are the practice and elements of a good board. Our answer is based on the Combined Code; it would be equally valid to base your answer on the requirements of a different Code. The measures you recommend should have been quite specific; not all of them will be numerical measures (though a lot of them should have been), but in every case you needed to recommend a tangible method to judge success.

REPORT

To: Board of directors
From: Consultant
Date: December X4
Subject: Board and directors appraisal

Introduction

The Combined Code on Corporate Governance recommends that 'the board should undertake a formal and rigorous annual evaluation of its own performance and that of its committees and individual directors.'

The recommendations in this report regarding the main areas of board and individual directors' performance to be assessed are therefore based largely upon the recommendations of the Combined Code, which is best practice in this area. This report will also discuss methods of assessing performance in both financial and non-financial terms.

Board composition and meetings

For a company to be effective and to provide value for its stakeholders it must be headed by an **effective board of directors** which is collectively responsible for the success of the company. The board must meet on a **regular basis**, with regular attendance from all directors, and there should also be the opportunity for unscheduled meetings to be called when circumstances require. All members of the board should be aware of their **roles and responsibilities** as should all members of other board committees such as the remuneration, audit and nomination committees.

This area could be assessed using the following possible measures.

- Number of scheduled board meetings held each year
- Number of unscheduled board meetings held each year
- Attendance record of individual directors
- How regularly the schedule of formal roles and responsibilities is updated

Board balance and independence

For effective and unbiased running of the company the board should include a **balance of executive** and **non-executive directors** such that no individual or small group can dominate the board's decision taking. There are two main tasks at the top of every public company – the running of the board and the executive responsibility of running the company's business. There should therefore be a clear division of responsibilities between the Chairman of the board and the Chief Executive Officer.

This area could be assessed using the following possible measures.

- The number and percentage of executive and non-executive directors
- Written evidence of a division of responsibilities between the chairman and the chief executive
- Age profile of the directors
- Up-to-date CVs of the directors to indicate the range of skills and experiences

Mission and strategy

One of the key roles of the board is to **determine the mission statement and strategy** of the company and therefore its success in achieving these aims must be assessed.

This area could be assessed using **balanced scorecard** style measures. A balanced scorecard establishes non-financial as well as financial targets, and measures actual performance in relation to all these targets. Areas covered include profitability, customer satisfaction, internal efficiency and innovation.

Board appointment and re-election

For a board to have the confidence of its shareholders and the market there should be a formal, rigorous and transparent procedure for the **appointment of new directors** to the board. In order to maintain standards, all directors should be submitted for re-election at regular intervals.

This area could be assessed using the following possible measures.

- The existence and make-up of the nomination committee
- The number of meetings of the nomination committee
- The length of tenure of each of the directors
- Whether each director is nominated for re-election at a maximum interval of three years
- Evidence of a succession policy

Directors' remuneration

Levels of remuneration for directors should be sufficient to **attract, retain and motivate directors** of the quality required to run the company successfully but should not be more than is necessary for this purpose. It is preferable for a significant proportion of directors' remuneration to be linked to **corporate** and **personal performance**. Thus there should be a remuneration committee made up of independent non-executive directors, the remuneration policy should be reported in the annual report, and any performance-related pay should ideally align the interests of the directors with those of the shareholders.

This area could be assessed using the following possible measures.

- The existence of a remuneration committee

- The proportion of the remuneration committee who are independent non-executive directors

- Whether targets such as profit margins, share price growth etc have been met for performance-related elements of pay

Information and professional development

As far as information is concerned the board should be supplied in a timely manner with information in a form and of a quality appropriate to enable it to **discharge its duties**. All directors should receive induction training on joining the board and should regularly update and refresh their skills and knowledge.

This area could be assessed using the following possible measures.

- How frequently are the directors provided with management accounting information
- How frequently have directors attended training courses during the year
- How many new directors are there and have they attended an induction course

Accountability

The board are expected to present a **balanced and understandable assessment of the company's position** and prospects in the annual report and other public statements. In order to safeguard the shareholders' investment and the company's assets the board should maintain a **sound system of internal controls**. There must also be formal and transparent arrangements for considering how the financial reporting and internal control principles should be applied and an **audit committee** to ensure that an appropriate relationship is maintained with the company's auditors.

This area could be assessed using the following possible measures.

- How frequently internal controls have been assessed during the year
- How regularly any internal audit department examines internal controls
- How regularly the audit committee meets
- The proportion of non-executive directors on the audit committee
- The number of internal control recommendations made by the external auditors

Communication

In order to maintain investor confidence companies should be ready to enter into **dialogue with institutional shareholders** and should use the AGM to communicate with private investors and encourage their participation.

This area could be assessed using the following possible measures.

- How frequently the board or the chairman meet with major shareholders
- Any other communications with shareholders during the year
- The percentage of shareholders attending the AGM

Conclusion

The role and responsibilities of the board of directors of a public listed company is many and varied but in order to maintain the confidence of the shareholders and investors at large it is important that procedures are put in place to ensure that areas such as those suggested in this report are reviewed on a regular basis and the performance of the board as a whole and individual directors is assessed on this basis.

4 Controls in new company

Top tips. The report in (a) starts by stating the main transactions that the system will have to process. It then discusses the key areas of information required and assignment of responsibility and reporting mechanisms. However your answer to (a) should only briefly mention reporting mechanisms as these are dealt with in more detail in part (b).

Part (b) covers a very important theme for this part of the syllabus, how the board acts as an overall supervisory control on the rest of the business. This involves taking the decisions that follow from the board's responsibility for strategy (such as fixed asset purchases), and also reviewing the operations of the business using internal and external data.

REPORT

To: Potential investors
From: Management Consultant
Date: XX.XX.XX
Subject: Controls in the new computer services company

(a) **Form and level of detail of budgetary control**

A useful starting point is to consider the likely revenues and costs that will have to be considered when designing the budgetary control system.

Revenues

Income will be derived from two main sources: existing local government work and new work from neighbouring authorities or commercial customers.

The local government work could be subdivided further, either according to the nature of the work (one-off data processing tasks, long-term systems development etc) and/or according to the particular local government department (education, housing, etc).

The other work may also be subdivided according to its nature and/or type of customer. This will aid analysis of profitability.

Costs

Operational costs are likely fall into the broad categories listed below. More detailed sub-categories will be desirable in practice. Most costs will be fixed costs, although there will be sundry equipment, administrative and marketing expenses that are variable.

Main areas of concern

(i) **Forecasting** the **level of income** to be derived from **new work** (the level of existing local government should be easy to predict). Assessment of likely new work will include the likely duration of contracts to be carried out, and how new contracts will be priced and billed.

(ii) **Allocating** and **monitoring expenditure** for the **areas** that are **new** to the company, particularly financial administration, working capital management and marketing. Particularly close attention should be paid to the 'set-up' costs of new systems in these areas.

Recommended system for budgetary control

(i) A recording system capable of **analysing costs** and **revenues** in the various ways suggested above. (This may seem self-evident but it has not been the norm in public sector bodies in the past.)

(ii) Clear **assignment** of **responsibility** for **controllable costs** and **revenues** to **individual managers**, using a **cost** or **profit centre system**. Again this may seem self-evident, but detailed apportionment of what have previously been regarded as lump-sum allocations has been a serious problem for public sector and former public sector bodies.

(iii) **Operational reports** at least **weekly** in the initial stages to catch bugs in the system and spot areas for improvement. Reports may be less regular once the system is up and running, especially for work that the company is already used to doing. Some of the information collected can be of a non-financial nature, for example staff and computer time for frequently performed tasks.

(iv) **Monthly reports** for **submission** to **senior management**, summarising the operational data. This area is addressed in more detail in the second part of this report.

(b) **Structure and formal controls at Board level**

Personnel

The Board is likely to consist of a Managing Director (the current Director of Computing), a Technical Director, a Finance Director and a Marketing Director. **Non-executive directors** should also be appointed. One should represent the interests of investors and may be appointed by the venture capital company involved; a second could bring in commercial sector experience and a third might have local government knowledge.

Scrutiny of budget reports

One of the key controls operated at board level will be the **monthly budget report**. Particular attention will need to be paid to the areas that are new to the proposed company's experience, most especially **control of finance** and **cash flow**. Given the Board's lack of commercial experience an **internal auditor** should be appointed to report directly to the board and provide reassurance that unfamiliar areas are being properly managed from day to day. Our firm would be pleased to undertake this role.

External monitoring

Presumably in the medium term the company will wish to reduce its reliance on existing local government work, although it will wish to retain its original main customer. **External monitoring** of **potential markets**, **competitors' activities** and of the **political environment** will therefore be crucial. This can be in the form of SWOT analysis or similar.

Analytical measures

Likewise **measurement** of **current performance** in terms of **market share**, new **business won** and so on will help to guide the overall strategy. In any case, local authorities are likely to set their own performance criteria. Board level checks therefore need to be in place to ensure that the required standards are being maintained.

Focus of Board

The Board's responsibility is the **strategy** of the company rather than its day-to-day management and this will include the long-term investment strategy. The Board should focus on **recognising future needs** and ensuring that they can be met at the appropriate time.

The Board's focus on strategy should also mean that certain matters are **reserved** for **decision** by the **full Board**. Although the company is not a listed company, they could usefully follow the Cadbury recommendations, and reserve the following decisions for full approval.

(i)   Acquisition and disposal of major assets.

(ii)   Investments, capital projects, authority levels, treasury policies and risk management policies.

Future developments

If the company is likely to be taking on new work such as systems development, there should be **formal controls** in this area, since this type of work tends to be long-term. It is also difficult to judge, and so control, what progress has been made and how much progress should have been made. **Separate reports** in addition to the main monthly package may be called for, here.

Signed: Management Accountant

5 Internal audit role

Top tips. This question brings out the need to understand the difference between the different types of audit. Most of the areas considered by external auditors when they review the work of internal audit should also be considered when the audit committee carries out its annual review of internal audit.

REPORT

To: Board of directors
From: Internal audit manager
Date: 18 November 20X6
Subject: The role of internal audit

Introduction

As requested I have produced in this report a description of the role of internal audit in comparison with that of external audit, and in the context of developing a new accounting system.

(a)   **Internal audit and external audit compared**

The main functions of internal audit and external audit are very different, although some of the means of fulfilling each function are the same.

Role of external auditors

The external auditors are appointed by the shareholders to report on the stewardship of the managers of the company on a **regular basis** (usually annually). The role of the external auditors is defined by statute and the report produced by the external auditors states whether the published financial statements show a true and fair view and adhere to accounting standards.

Role of internal auditors

In contrast, internal auditors are employed directly by the managers of the company. This means that they are **not independent** of the company and its managers, unlike the external auditors. The internal auditors normally work **full time** for the company and their role is much more varied and wide-ranging than that of the external auditors. As well as statutory matters the internal auditors will be concerned with **monitoring the effectiveness of all controls** within the business, whether financial or non-financial, and whether operational departments are **implementing new systems and company policies**. The internal auditors will normally report directly to management, but may occasionally report directly to an audit committee. The objectives of internal audit are controlled by management.

In their work, both the internal and external auditors will evaluate and test the internal control system of the business. In this overlap area, the internal auditors may aid the external auditors to avoid duplication of work and to cut costs.

(b)   **Reliance on internal audit by the external auditors**

The external auditors will assess the internal controls of a company in order to determine whether they may rely on the controls and thereby reduce the number of substantive procedures to be carried out. The internal audit function will be part of the system of controls and therefore the internal audit function must be assessed by the external auditors. There are several factors which must be examined.

(i)   How **independently** do the internal auditors **operate** within the company and to what level of management do they report?

(ii)   What are the **scope and objectives** of the internal audit department? Is it sufficiently wide-ranging and unrestricted?

(iii) What **qualifications** do the internal auditors have? Do they receive sufficient training to carry out their jobs? Are they all screened carefully and do they follow a code of conduct of some kind?

(iv) Do the internal auditors **exercise due professional care** in their work?

(v) Are the **reports** produced by internal audit of a **good standard**, sent to the appropriate senior managers, and are they acted on promptly and effectively?

(vi) What **level of resources** is the internal audit department given?

When the external auditors have considered all these points, they may feel that internal audit work can be used as part of the external audit. Any co-operation of this sort needs to be carefully negotiated to make sure that all important matters are agreed.

(c) **The impact of internal audit on external audit**

The responsibility for the external audit cannot be **reduced** or **diluted** by the presence, and reliance on, an internal audit department. The external auditors may not have to perform a great deal of testing if they rely on internal audit work, but the review of internal audit mentioned in (b) above must be carried out, and all the internal audit working papers must be reviewed by the external auditors. Thus, the amount of work might be reduced in volume, but the external auditors must exercise greater judgement.

Internal auditors will have an **in-depth knowledge** of most aspects of the company and this knowledge may be used by the external auditors and thus their work will be simplified.

There may be certain procedures which the internal auditors are much better placed to perform than the external auditors, due to the **timing of the tests** (when the external auditors did not plan to be present) and in such cases the external auditors will find it more cost effective and often simpler to use internal audit to perform the tests in question.

6 Risks

Top tips. This question is simpler than you would expect to see in your exam, but it does provide a good introduction to risk. It emphasises the need for wide-ranging knowledge of the risks an organisation could face and emphasises that adherence to the corporate governance codes will be a central part of risk management.

The risks discussed in (b) may come to mind easier than those in (a). However, don't forget the business and strategic risks in (a) as they are likely to be included somewhere in the paper.

(a) **Project risk**

The **project-specific risk** for an individual investment project occurs because the **cash flows from the project** might be **higher or lower than expected**, for reasons that are specific to the project. The cash flows might have been **estimated incorrectly**, such as an under-estimate of operating costs or an over-estimate of market demand. (However, if a company invests in a wide range of similar projects, it can be argued that much of this project risk will be diversified away in the normal course of business.) Other risk factors specific to a project could be the **location of the project**, the **quality of personnel**, or the **reliability of the equipment** to be used.

Competitive risk

This is the possibility of **unexpected effects** on the project cash flows (positive or negative), due to the **actions of competitors**. The actual actions of competitors might differ from the assumptions made by the company when it takes its project investment decision. Companies cannot diversify away competitive risk, but shareholders can, by investing in the shares of the competitor companies.

Industry-specific risk

This is the risk of unexpected changes to a project's cash flows (positive or negative) from **events or changing circumstances in the industry** in which the investment is made. Unexpected changes can arise, for example, due to new technology, or a change in the law, or a rise or fall in the price of a key commodity.

Market risk

This refers to changes that could occur in **market conditions**, that will affect the cash flows from the project. These could be unexpected changes in **interest rates**, or in the **rate of inflation**, or in the **state of the economy**.

Each of these risks is a two-way risk, in the sense that the actual cash flows could be either better or worse than expected. For example sales demand could be higher than forecast, a competitor might over-price a rival product, a new law might be introduced that has the effect of boosting demand for the output produced by the project, and exchange rates or interest rates might move favourably.

(b) **Trading risks**

Both domestic and international traders will face trading risks, although those faced by the latter will generally be greater due to the increased distances and times involved. The types of trading risk include:

(i)   **Physical risk** – the risk of goods being lost or stolen in transit, or the documents accompanying the goods going astray

(ii)   **Credit risk** – the possibility of payment default by the customer. This is discussed further below

(iii) **Trade risk** – the risk of the customer refusing to accept the goods on delivery (due to sub-standard/ inappropriate goods or other reasons), or the cancellation of the order in transit

(iv)   **Liquidity risk** – the inability to finance the credit

Cultural, country and political risks

(i)   Where a business trades with, or invests in, a foreign country **cultural risk** is introduced by the existence of different customs, laws and language. Communication between parties can be hindered, and potential deals put into jeopardy by ignorance of the expected manner in which such transactions should be conducted.

(ii)   **Country risk** is the risk associated with undertaking transactions with, or holding assets in, a particular country. Sources of risk might be political, economic or regulatory instability affecting overseas taxation, repatriation of profits, nationalisation, currency instability etc.

(iii) **Political risk** is the risk that political action (exchange controls, tax changes, pricing regulations etc) will affect the position and value of a company.

Currency risk

Currency risk is the possibility of loss or gain due to future changes in exchange rates.

When a firm trades with an overseas supplier or customer, and the invoice is in the overseas currency, it will expose itself to exchange rate or currency risk. Movements in the foreign exchange rates will create risk in the settlement of the debt – i.e. the final amount payable/receivable in the home currency will be uncertain at the time of entering into the transaction.

Investment in a foreign country or borrowing in a foreign currency will also carry this risk.

Interest rate risk

As with foreign exchange rates, future interest rates cannot be easily predicted. If a firm has a significant amount of variable (floating)-rate debt, interest rate movements will give rise to uncertainty about the cost of servicing this debt.

Conversely, if a company uses a lot of fixed-rate debt, it will lose out if interest rates begin to fall.

Technological risk

All businesses depend to some extent on technology, either in the support of its business activities (eg the computers used by the accounts, stores and treasury departments), or more directly in its production or marketing activities.

As technology evolves and develops, firms can find themselves using out of date equipment and marketing methods, which may leave them at a competitive disadvantage. Products in a high-tech industry have very short life-cycles, and a firm must recognise and plan for continual replacement and upgrading of products if it is not to lose market share.

(c) **How the codes of corporate governance can assist in managing the risks**

Corporate governance is concerned with the control and influence exerted over a company's operations and its employees by the decisions of top management, usually the Board of Directors.

Turnbull report recommendations

(i) Management should **identify** and **evaluate** the risks to which they will be exposed in the achievement of their corporate objectives. These will include both the traditional areas of risk discussed above, but also those increasingly arising from intangible assets, such as reputation and branding.

(ii) Risk control should be **embedded in the culture and processes of the business**, rather than being the subject of a completely separate management system. Each person in the organisation should be aware of, and manage, the significant risks related to the tasks they perform.

(iii) Directors should continually review and monitor risk control issues. They should regularly review **reports on internal control** from line managers and, where appropriate, from internal auditors and other specialists. **Regular discussion** of risk and control issues at board meetings should be encouraged.

(iv) **Risk analysis and assessment** should form part of the evaluation of every major capital investment or proposed acquisition.

(v) **Financial risk analysis** will very much depend upon commercial judgement, but should include assessment of effect on cash flow, profitability, liquidity and gearing.

(vi) The **relative likelihood** of the events giving rise to the risks also need to be assessed.

(vii) Once risks have been prioritised, management needs to decide what to do about them, and how they can be managed and monitored in the future. Strategies for management of a given risk include **acceptance**, **transfer**, **elimination and control**.

7 Pacific Group

> **Top tips**. This question might seem overwhelming, but bear in mind that the examiner has done the hard part already. The risks have been identified, you simply have to assess how serious they are. Make sure that you read the question properly and understand the criteria that the examiner gives you to judge whether risks are applicable or not, then apply those criteria to each risk in the question. If you are not sure, decide whether you can say more in support of classifying it as applicable or non-applicable. You gain marks for your explanations.
>
> (b) requires a bit of imagination using your knowledge of controls from Chapter 4 and your previous auditing studies.

(a) **Applicable risks**

(i) **Failure to invest in new developments**

Applicable risk

The majority of PG's income comes from advertising revenue and therefore it is crucial that they keep up to the cutting edge of advertising developments, particularly when their competitors do. This could have a substantial adverse financial impact if advertisers decide to cut advertising in PG in favour of more up to date advertising techniques in competitor publications such as The Deep.

(ii) **Unsuitable credit limits**

Non-applicable risk

As credit limits (albeit unsuitable) are set, and the majority of customers are likely to be credit worthy, the effect of a small number of advertisers being uncreditworthy is not likely to be substantial.

(iii) **Incomplete data transfer (editorial - invoicing departments)**

Applicable risk

It is crucial to cash flow and business operations that published adverts are invoiced. Only two full page adverts and a half page advert would have to be omitted from invoicing before the effect of this risk would be greater than £5,000. If the system is failing to transfer data, there is no reason to assume that the problem should be limited to so few adverts.

(iv) **Rates charged**

Applicable risk

As seen above, given the prices of adverts, a problem with a small number of adverts can have a significant (> £5,000) impact. So, for example, if two full page and three half page adverts were given a 50% discount and the same number were given 'free' for reciprocal advertising, this could have a significant financial impact.

(v) **Individual errors**

Non-applicable risk

PG is likely to have reasonable controls over production to ensure that errors in production such as typos, colour problems and such like are likely to be isolated and no individual advertisement has a significant financial effect on PG.

(vi)   **Cash misappropriation**

Applicable risk

Cash received at front desk is significant and there appear to be no controls to ensure that the cash is secure and passed on to cashiers. This is a big risk to PG as they may simply lose a large amount of income in this way. Again, it only requires payment for three full page adverts to be misappropriated to have a significant impact.

(vii)   **Errors due to unauthorised access**

Non-applicable risk

It is likely that PG has basic computer system controls making this risk a low risk.

(viii) **Availability of systems**

Applicable risk

This risk is applicable because if PG does not have contingency plans against systems failure, and many companies with computerised systems do not, then the financial and operational risk of delay in invoicing and processing advertising orders could be significant in terms of customer dissatisfaction and delayed payments.

(ix)   **Incomplete transfer of information to nominal ledgers**

Non-applicable risk

This is potentially significant to the reported results of the company but should not affect their operational or financial strength.

(x)   **Risk of litigation for inappropriate advertising**

Applicable risk

As PG carries a large amount of advertising in its publication this risk is significant. Although PG is likely to have insurance for the financial impact of such litigation, the cost in terms of loss of reputation or/and therefore customers could be significant.

(b)   **Controls**

(*Note*. the question requirement only requires you to give controls for four of the applicable risks. All six are covered in this answer for illustration purposes only).

(i)   **Failure to invest in new developments**

–   Regular review of developments in competitor products (for example, each edition, or each quarter)

–   Regular review of developments available so as to be ready to action them if necessary

–   Regular review of actual investment costs against budget, to see if any budgetary slack could be utilised

(iii)   **Incomplete data transfer (editorial – invoicing departments)**

–   Reconciliations of advertisements invoiced to advertisements appearing in publications

–   Serial numbering of advertisements and sequence checking by invoicers

(iv)   **Rates charged**

–   Authorised price list
–   Authorised discounts list
–   Comparison of PG's own advertising budget to actual (to identify uncharged adverts)
–   Monitoring of percentage yield for advertisements per issue
–   Minimum percentage yield for advertisements per issue set

(vi)   **Misappropriation of cash**

- Cashiers to supervise post opening
- Front desk staff to issue pre-numbered duplicate receipts for cash to couriers
- Two people should attend post opening
- Cash receipts should be listed

(viii) **Non availability of systems**

- Contingency plan to be established to receive/process adverts/invoices if system fails

- Tests to be run to ensure disaster plans are successful/well known

(x)   **Risk of litigation for inappropriate advertising**

- Staff training in British Standards Code of Advertising to reduce inappropriate adverts being run

- Editorial policy on adverts should be published to all staff

- Reporting system including a named responsible official for all advert queries

8 Azure Airline

Top tips. When asked to identify, you should aim to be brief and not copy out chunks of the scenario; instead concentrate on explaining the risks well. In (a) you would probably need to identify and explain half a dozen risks to gain full marks. The answer below contains more than this for illustration. Most of the risks identified below are signalled in the question. However, it is acceptable to use your general knowledge to identify a risk not signposted in the question, such as the fact that the price of fuel can escalate, and Azure needs fuel to operate. You can easily however spend too much time on competition risk and on (a) in general; it's easy to overrun on this part and hence lose the chance of gaining marks elsewhere.

In (b) you are asked for controls for the risks, and you must think widely about how the risks could be managed. For example, think about the lease contract. It must have contingencies and protections for Azure's operation in it. It's also important to make realistic suggestions. For example saying that the company should buy a new plane or employ its own captain and co-pilot would be irrelevant as it is only operating two days a week.

(a)   **Business risks**

(i)   **Leasing of equipment and specialist staff**

As Azure leases its equipment and the most specialised of its staff from another airline, there is a risk that its **equipment and/or pilots** could be **withdrawn** leaving it unable to operate.

(ii)   **Conditions of exclusive right**

The PAA requires Azure's aircraft engines be overhauled biannually. There is a risk that Azure will be **unable to meet this condition**, if the **lessor company does not agree** to regular overhaul, or that it will be **too expensive** for Azure to meet this requirement. It could then lose the right to operate, or its exclusivity, opening it up to competition. There may be other conditions which Azure has to meet, such as the two weekly flights being a minimum.

(iii)   **Necessary service suspension**

As Azure is required to overhaul its engines every two years, there will be a significant period every two years where Azure will either have to **incur the cost of leasing** other planes (assuming this is possible) or will have to **suspend services**. The cost of leasing other planes might be prohibitively expensive or the disruption to service might mean that conditions relating to the right to operate might not be met. As Azure only has one plane, service would also be interrupted if there was an emergency relating to the plane, such as fire or a crash.

(iv)   **Age of aircraft**

The aircraft being leased is old. This raises **operational risks** (it may not always be able to fly due to necessary maintenance), **finance risks** (it may require regular repair) and **compliance risks** (it may not meet environmental or safety standards, now or in the future).

(v)   **High proportion of expensive seats**

The plane leased by Azure has a **high proportion of empty expensive seats** and therefore **insufficient (overbooked) cheaper seats**. Although Azure can appease customers by upgrading them, this means the airline is operating well below capacity.

(vi)   **Cargo**

The flight route results in the airline carrying a large amount of horticultural produce. This raises various risks – that Azure might be liable to passengers if their **cargo deteriorates in transit**, that the airline might be **liable for any breaches of law** by its passengers (for example, if prohibited items are transferred into Pewta or Sepiana (many countries prohibit the importation of animals or meat products or plants).

(vii)   **On-board services**

Customers are currently **dissatisfied with the food provision** on the flight and there is a risk that food prepared in Lyme may become **less appealing** and even dangerous when served on a Darke to Lyme flight (when it has been prepared a substantial time earlier, given a six hour flight, at least an hour's turn around time, and time for getting to the airline in the first place). If the food makes customers ill, Azure might be faced with compensation claims.

(viii)   **Pricing**

There is a **complex system of pricing** and a large number of sales agents, and Azure is at risk of **operating at a sales value less than required** to cover costs (for example, if too many of the cheapest tickets are sold).

(ix)   **Safety**

The airline industry has **stringent safety conditions** and Azure may face **customer boycotts** or difficulty in recruiting staff if safety requirements are not met, as well as the threat of not being allowed to fly.

(x)   **Fuel**

The aircraft **cannot fly without fuel**, which can be a scarce or high-cost resource. If fuel prices escalate due to world conditions, the company might not be able to meet the costs of operating.

(b) **Managing risks**

(i) **Leasing of equipment and specialist staff**

Azure must ensure that the **terms of the contract** with the international airline ensure that aircraft and staff **cannot be withdrawn** without reasonable notice, and, that in the event of withdrawal, substitutes will be provided.

(ii) **Conditions of exclusive rights**

Azure must ensure that all staff are **aware of any conditions** and the **importance of meeting them**. However, this risk must simply be accepted as there is little Azure can do about conditions imposed on them by the governing body of their industry.

(iii) **Necessary service suspension**

Azure must have **contingency plans for service suspension**, such as ensuring its contract with the international airline ensures alternative aircraft will be made available in the event of maintenance or damage to the aircraft, or by making arrangements to lease from a different airline in the event of emergency. As a minimum, Azure must ensure that the airline it leases from would give it **financial compensation** in the event of aircraft or staff not being available, so that Azure's customers could be compensated.

(iv) **Age of aircraft**

Azure should have plans in place to be able to **lease/afford newer planes** if required to by law. Again, this could be written into its contract with the airline. Azure should **manage cash flow and borrowing facilities** so as to be able to afford ongoing maintenance when required.

(v) **High proportion of expensive seats**

Azure should negotiate a **reconfiguration of the plane** with the **lessor** so that business and first class seating could be reduced and more economy seats made available. If this is not possible with the current lessor, Azure should **investigate leasing differently configured planes** from a different company. If it is not feasible to adjust the plane seating, Azure should consider **its pricing and on-board facilities policies** to make business and first class seats more attractive to customers. As the seats are not being sold anyway, it is probable that a reduction in prices would increase overall revenue.

(vi) **Cargo**

Azure should **publish a cargo policy** to ensure that customers are aware of their legal obligations. They should ensure that staff are **sufficiently trained** to discuss the contents of baggage with customers and are aware what items Azure should not carry. They should insure against lost and damaged cargo.

(vii) **On-board services**

Azure should consider **entering into a contract with a company in Darke** to **provide food** for the Darke to Lyme journey. Obviously they must not breach any existing contract with the Lyme company and so in the meantime should review the type of food provided. For example, it might be safer to only offer cold food, for example sandwiches and cakes until a Darke contract can be set up. Even if a new contract is set up, it might still be best to offer cold food as there is less chance of health problems arising as a result of serving cold food rather than hot food.

(viii) **Pricing**

As discussed above, Azure should **review the pricing policy**. It should also **establish limits on how many of certain types of tickets** (non-refundable/single etc) can be issued for one flight and it should institute a **centralised system** to ensure that each agent is aware when limits have been reached. As the agents must be linked to a similar system already (to be aware of whether tickets are available for sale) this should not be too difficult to achieve.

(ix) **Safety**

The company should appoint a member of staff to be **specifically responsible for safety operations** (such as training, updating for legal requirements, educating passengers) and should ensure that staff are regularly appraised about safety issues.

(x) **Fuel**

The company could take out **hedging contracts** against the cost of fuel. Other than this, there is little it can do about this matter, and it is another risk that has to be accepted.

9 Governance and controls

> **Top tips**. (a) emphasises that pressures to improve financial reporting and auditing practices have not been the only influences on corporate governance development. There has been emphasis as well on various aspects of directors' conduct that would be considered unacceptable even if there were no problems with the financial statements and audit. Don't forget the role of globalisation as this has led to the development of international codes.
>
> In (b) you need to say something about the basics of information gathering and board and audit committee meetings before discussing the topics highlighted in the requirements. Note that the stress in (b) is on higher-level monitoring controls, rather than the detailed transaction controls you will have seen in your auditing studies. The importance of the control environment would have needed to be stressed even if the question had not asked for it.

(a) Several different issues triggered moves towards systematised corporate governance.

Global investment

The trend towards global investment has meant that large investment institutions in the US in particular, but also in other countries such as the UK, have been seeking to invest large amounts of capital in companies in other countries. US investors, expecting **similar treatment** from foreign companies that they received from US companies, expressed concern about the inadequacy of corporate governance in many countries. Many of their concerns focused on the **lack of shareholder rights**, or the disregard for minority shareholder rights shown by major shareholders or the boards of foreign companies.

The move towards systematised corporate governance still has a long way to go in many countries; however, in issuing its principles of corporate governance, the OECD recognised that the demands and expectations of global investors would have to be met if the trend towards global investment (and efficient capital allocation) is to continue.

Financial reporting and auditing

There were serious concerns about the standards of financial reporting. In the late 1980s, there were a number of well-publicised corporate failures, which were unexpected because the financial statements of those companies had not given any indication of their financial problems. This also raised questions about the **quality of external auditing** and the **effectiveness of professional auditing standards**.

Executive directors

There were also concerns that many large companies were being run for the benefit of their executive directors and senior managers, and not in the interests of shareholders. For example, there were concerns that acquisitions were sometimes made to **increase the size of a company** and the power of its chief executive, rather than as a means of adding shareholder value. These concerns raised the question of the conflict of interest between the board of directors and the shareholders.

A particular concern was the **powerful position of individuals** holding the positions of both chairman and chief executive officer in their company, and the lack of 'balance' in boards of directors.

Directors' remuneration

Directors' remuneration also became an issue. There is a widely-held view that executive directors are paid **excessive amounts**, in terms of basic salary, 'perks' and incentives. Some directors appeared to receive high rewards even when the company **performed badly** or no differently from the 'average' of other companies. Although investment institutions did not object to high pay for talented executives, they believed that incentive schemes were often badly conceived, and that executives were being rewarded for performance that was not necessarily linked to the benefits provided to shareholders, for example in terms of a higher share price.

Insider dealings

Although convictions for insider dealing have been rare, there was a suspicion that some directors might be **using their inside knowledge** about their company to make a personal gain by dealing in shares in the company. For example, directors might sell a large number of shares just ahead of a profits warning by their company, or buy shares just ahead of a public announcement that might be expected to boost the share price.

(b) **Board action**

Obtain evidence of control

In order to issue its statement about the effectiveness of controls, the board of directors must obtain evidence of the existence and effective operation of controls and procedures throughout the group.

Due to the decentralised nature of this company and the absence of an internal audit department, the confirmation of this evidence will probably have to come from the **senior managers of each operating unit**. The senior managers or directors of each operating unit would need to summarise the key internal control procedures, and provide written confirmation on a regular basis that these controls are in place and working well. The main board director responsible for each operating unit, the senior managers or directors of the operating unit and the group finance director will probably need to meet to discuss any confirmations that are given.

Site reviews

As there is no internal audit department, head office staff (probably accounts staff) should visit operating units regularly, to carry out a **financial and operational review**. The results of these reviews should be reported back to the finance director and the audit committee.

Board meetings

The board of the parent company should **meet regularly**, and **adopt a schedule of matters** to be considered for decision, so ensuring that it maintains control over strategic, financial, operational and compliance issues. The investigation of these matters will probably be delegated to the audit committee, but the main board retains responsibility.

Audit committee

The audit committee should **meet regularly**, and its remit should include a **review of the group's system of internal controls**, based on information obtained from both external sources (the external auditors) and internal sources.

Specific features

The board will also exercise control through its approval of the annual budget and performance targets, and a system of regular performance monitoring and reporting.

The need for a control environment

A suitable control environment should be provided by a combination of culture and management style, together with management control mechanisms. The necessary culture should be stimulated by the **directors' commitment to quality and competence**, and the adoption of ethical and behavioural standards throughout the group.

Lines of responsibility

Despite the decentralisation of authority within the group, management control mechanisms should ensure that there are clear **lines of responsibility and accountability** running throughout the group, that **budgeting systems** are in place, and that **management information systems** exist for the **provision of performance reports in a timely manner**. It is likely that some tasks will be performed centrally at head office, perhaps as the responsibility of the finance director. These would include statutory reporting, tax matters and arranging insurance. Budgetary control processes should be in place and operating properly.

Targets

Operating units should be given **clear and achievable targets** aligned with the group's overall objectives, and these targets should be known to the senior management in each operating unit. There will be some **delegation of authority** to spend, but within clearly stated limits. Spending decisions above a certain level should be the responsibility of the main board. The board is also required to consider each year the need for an internal audit department or unit.

Evaluation of risks

The board should have a focus on the **control and containment of risks**, based on a cost/benefit approach. Controls are likely to include a board policy not to invest in any operation outside a specific area of 'competence', so that acquisitions are not made that alter the risk profile of the company's businesses. All divisions should have **at least one main board director** actively involved, so that there is direct knowledge of operating units at main board level. The main board should discuss all major proposed new ventures, and when a new venture is given the go-ahead, it should operate with **clear financial constraints**. Spending above a certain amount should require full board approval.

Monitoring of problem operations

There should be an **information system** that reports on performance in a way that non-performing or under-performing units can be identified as soon as possible. New operations and under-performing units should be monitored closely by the board.

Other risks

The board should also consider **other risks on a regular basis**, such as the risk from new technology. The risk of non-compliance with legal and regulatory requirements might be controlled at head office level by the finance director. Insurance arrangements might also be controlled centrally.

Risks and controls

In considering the **soundness of the system of internal controls**, the board should consider the **nature and extent of the risks** facing the company, the extent and types of risk that it is reasonable for the company to bear, the likelihood of the risks materialising, the ability of the company to minimise the incidence and impact of risks when they do materialise and the costs and benefits of operating particular controls.

Information and communication systems

The group **should prepare budgets** and budget packs for **each operating unit**, and budget information should be communicated to senior managers in each unit. The budget should be approved by the main board. There should be **regular budget reports** comparing actual results against the budget. Managers in each operating unit should be able to extract up-to-date information about the current state of affairs in their unit, from the management information system.

Control procedures

The group should have a range of control procedures in place. The internal auditors should check that the **financial controls** are operating effectively. Controls include specific limits on the **authorisation of spending** at different levels of management, a suitable **segregation of duties** in the accounts department, the use of **accounting controls** (such as bank reconciliations), and suitable **controls for computer systems** (password controls, physical security for cheque books and computer equipment, etc.)

Monitoring and corrective action

There should be regular reports to the main board on internal controls, and the audit committee should be given **responsibility for monitoring the control system**. The board should also discuss the **risk and control implications** of major changes, such as new acquisitions. Whenever a weakness or failure in the control system is discovered, **corrective action** should be taken. The finance director should have specific responsibility for explaining to the board any weaknesses or deficiencies uncovered in the system of financial controls.

10 Ethical standards

Top tips. (a) requires thought; the important elements of the answer are the problems of coming up with a clear definition, how much cultural factors should be allowed to influence ethical thinking and the need for the ethical framework to be more than a superficial gloss. The compatibility of ethical and commercial concerns is also an important issue to raise.

Some of the issues covered in (b) are discussed in detail in Chapter 11, but you can apply what you've learnt about principles vs rules–based frameworks in corporate governance.

(a) **Problems with ethical framework**

Over the past few years the topic of business ethics has been examined and debated by many writers and academics. Although many organisation world-wide have adopted or redefined their business with ethics in mind, there are many people both in business and who study the area who see **many barriers to businesses** implementing an ethical framework.

What constitutes ethics

Defining **'what we mean by ethics'** is for the most part easy to understand (inappropriate gifts, accepting money, environmental protection are all ethical issues). More contentious issues are topics such as workplace safety, product safety standards, advertising content and whistle-blowing which are areas where some businesses have been considered less ethical.

Necessity for action

Actions speak **louder than words**. Ethics are **guidelines or rules of conduct** by which we **aim to live by**. It is the actual conduct of the people in the organisation that, collectively, determines the organisation's standards. In other words it is not what the organisations 'says', but rather what it 'does' which is the real issue. It is no good having a code of ethics that is communicated to the outside world, but is ignored and treated with disdain by those inside the organisation.

Varying cultures

Globalisation and the resultant need to operate within different ethical frameworks have **undermined the idea** that **ethical guidance** can be **defined in simple absolute terms**. It may be culturally acceptable to promote by merit in one country, or by seniority in another. Paying custom officials may be acceptable in some cultures, but taboo in others.

Ethical versus commercial interests

Ethical and commercial interests have, it is argued, always diverged to some extent. Some organisations have seen for example the issues of **'being seen to be ethical'** as a good business move. However this viewpoint is pragmatic rather than idealistic; being ethical is seen as a means towards the end of gaining a better reputation and hence increasing sales.

Policies of others

Modern commercialism places great demands on everyone in organisations to succeed and provide the necessary revenues for the future growth and survival of the business. Acting with social responsibility can be hard, as not everyone plays by the same rules.

(b) ### Need for practical steps

If organisations are to **achieve a more ethical stance** they **need to put into place a range of practical steps** that will achieve this. Developing an ethical culture within the business will require the organisation to communicate to its workforce the 'rules' on what is considered to be ethical and is not. Two approaches have been identified to the management of ethics in organisations.

Rules-based approach

This is primarily designed to ensure that the organisation acts within the letter of the law, and that violations are **prevented, detected and punished.** This is very much the case in the US, where legal compliance is very much part of the business environment. The problem here is that legislation alone will not have the desired effect, particularly for those businesses who operate internationally and therefore may not be subject to equivalent legislation in other jurisdictions.

Integrity-based programmes

Here the concern is not for any legal control, but with developing an **organisational culture.** The task of ethics management is to define and give life to an organisation's **defining values** and to create an environment that supports ethical behaviour and to instil a sense of **shared accountability** among all employees. Integrity-based programmes require not just words or statements, but on seeing and doing and action. The purpose with this approach is not to exact revenge through legal compliance but to develop within the workforce a **culture of ethics** that has **value and meaning** for those in it.

The integrity-based approach encompasses all aspects of the business - **behavioural assumptions** of what is right or is wrong; staffing, education and training, audits and activities that promote a social responsibility across the workforce.

Organisations can also take further steps to reinforce their values by adopting **ethical committees** who are appointed to rule on misconduct and to develop ethical standards for the business.

Kohlberg's framework

Kohlberg's ethical framework demonstrates how individuals advance through different levels of moral development, their advance relating to how their **moral reasoning develops** and it can be used to assist in developing an organisational framework. Kohlberg's framework goes from individuals who see ethical decisions solely in terms of the good or bad consequences for themselves through to individuals who choose to follow universal ethical principles, even if these conflict with the values of the organisation for which they are working.

The importance of different components of an organisation's ethical framework can indicate the level of moral reasoning that staff are in effect expected to employ.

Pre-conventional reasoning

A rules-based framework that sets out **expected behaviour** in detail and has strong provisions for punishing breaches implies that staff are at the lowest stage of development – they define right or wrong solely in terms of expected rewards or punishments. An emphasis on bureaucratic controls, including the reporting of all problems that occur with staff, would be designed to prevent 'You scratch my back, I scratch yours' behaviour that is also part of moral reasoning at this level.

Conventional reasoning

An emphasis on a **strong ethical culture** would indicate staff are expected to adopt the intermediate stage of Kohlberg's framework. **Peer pressure**, also the concepts that managers should set an **example**, are features of this sort of ethical approach; if also the organisation appears to be responding to **pressures from outside** to behave ethically, this suggests higher level reasoning within this stage.

Post-conventional reasoning

An ethical approach based on staff using post-conventional reasoning would be likely to emphasise adherence to an ethical code. A detailed code based on rights and values of society would imply ethical reasoning based on the idea of the organisation **enforcing a social contract.** Higher-level reasoning would be expected if the code was framed in terms of more abstract principles such as justice or equality.

11 Independence

Top tips. The practical aspects of **independence** are discussed here, and you should be able to describe the meaning of the term in that context. A good way to approach (a) is to think of the ways in which operational departments can have contact with or influence internal audit. (b) brings out the important links between internal audit and the audit committee.

(a)   **Extent of internal audit independence**

An internal auditor cannot have the same amount of independence as an external auditor. However, internal audit can be given various **powers and access** to senior managers that allow independent comment, in a free and professional manner, about the internal control of the business (or any matter under investigation).

Measures to ensure independence

In particular, the following points will ensure a satisfactory level of independence within the organisation.

(i)   Internal auditors should **not act** in any **operational capacity**, particularly at managerial level. They should be concerned **only** with the functioning and management of the internal audit department.

(ii)   The internal audit department should **not** be **controlled** by any **operational managers.** It should be **controlled directly** by the **board** of directors or **audit committee**.

(iii)   **No area** of records, personnel or assets should be **closed** to the internal auditor. Any such restrictions would invalidate internal audit's full power of investigation.

(iv)   **Recruitment, training** and other personnel matters within the internal audit department should be **dealt** with only by the **Chief Internal Auditor,** not by outside managers or the board.

(b)   There are two structures in which the internal audit department may operate.

Reporting to the board

Even though not a voting board member, the internal auditor will report directly to the full board. This is far superior to reporting directly to line management or to the finance director or managing director, as it does not allow an individual manager or director to suppress or neglect an internal audit report.

Reporting to the audit committee

This is the method recommended by the **Cadbury report** on corporate governance. The audit committee will consist mainly or entirely of non-executive directors, and thus internal audit will maintain the independence of its report.

This method is advantageous as it brings together people with great expertise in such control matters who have the **time to discuss** them without bias and outside any operating considerations. The committee will also be able to **advise internal audit** on procedures and further action and, because of its seniority, be able to persuade the board to take action on any matters raised by internal audit.

A further advantage of an audit committee is that it can act as a **forum for communication** between the various parties involved in financial control. The Cadbury report recommended that audit committees should be attended by the finance director, the head of internal audit and a representative of the external auditors.

(c)   **Family or other close personal or business relationships**

Where there are **family or other close relationships** between the internal auditor and other staff and the auditor, objectivity is impaired as the auditor's decisions may be affected by his wish to support the family member or friend or to enhance his own business interests.

Obviously the extent of the problem depends on the **nature of the relationship** and the **seniority** of those involved. The chief internal auditor being married to the finance director would be more of a risk than the audit junior being related to one of the sales staff.

Impact on report

Again the key issue is the **effect this may have on what the auditor reports**. The auditor may feel pressured to present the results of the audit in a better light than the facts would suggest. An auditor may also be reluctant to issue a critical audit report if this will damage a personal relationship or another business interest; this may expose the organisation to possible higher level risks, particularly perhaps the risk of fraud.

(d)   **Compromising of independence**

In external auditing it is considered to be a **compromise** of **independence** to accept presents, discounts, bonuses or commissions from audit clients. In many ways this will also apply to the chief internal auditor, as an 'officer' of the board.

Rewarding internal audit

Conversely, the chief internal auditor is an employee of the company, which pays a salary to him or her already. As part of the internal control function, helping to **keep down costs** and **increase profitability**, the chief internal auditor should arguably have a reward for adding to the profit of the business.

Residual problem

The problem remains that, if the chief internal auditor receives a bonus based on results, he or she may be tempted to allow certain actions, practices or transactions which should be stopped, but which are increasing the profit of the business, and therefore the bonus.

12 Environmental audit and accounting

Top tips. You need to use your auditing knowledge and a bit of imagination in (a). Try to use your own experience to think of what you can find out about resource usage, also what you would like to know and how you can obtain evidence of what you would like to know.

In (b) observation is likely to be the most useful audit technique, although if staff are being observed, they may behave differently. You may have come up with other means for informing staff.

(c) is good revision of issues that we have discussed throughout this text, the impact of stakeholder views and voluntary principles-based disclosure versus compulsory rules-based disclosure.

(a) **The planning process**

The planning process for any investigative activity revolves around a consideration of **what information is needed,** where it **may be found** and **how to obtain it.**

Available information

In the case of an environmental audit, much information is probably already available in the form of accounting records; **heating and lighting costs**, for instance can be related to factors such as numbers employed, floor space and building volumes.

There are some fairly **standard aspects of good practice** in terms of energy conservation such as provision of wall and roof insulation and thermostatic and time clock control of space and water heating systems. The existence and maintenance of such factors can be established from the appropriate records. In the UK, the energy utilities offer free advice on energy conservation and this should be considered. **Use of renewable resources** should be a matter of policy and the purchasing department should be able to comment on the extent to which it is achieved.

Expert advice

Other aspects of energy consumption require expert advice. For instance, the **compressed air circuits** used in many factories to power hand and machine tools can be extremely wasteful of energy if they are leaky, since this causes the compressor to be run for excessive periods to maintain pressure. However, it is a specialised engineering task to measure the actual efficiency of a pneumatic system.

If the organisation is a manufacturer, it would be appropriate to consider the extent to which the **products themselves** were **energy efficient** in use and made use of renewable resources both in use and in their construction. These are largely matters of design and it would be necessary to take technical advice.

Audit framework

The ISO family of statements, ISO 14000 and others, provides a general framework that the auditor will wish to consider and also includes a specific statement on internal audit.

(b) **Testing for employee awareness**

Employee awareness could be measured by **observation, questionnaire and interview.** In a large organisation a sampling approach could be taken. Observation could be largely unobtrusive and might provide a useful control on the results of interview, since some staff might make exaggerated claims about their environmental awareness.

Involvement of employees

The techniques of **internal marketing** could be used to involve employees. Internal marketing is the use of marketing techniques that are normally associated with communications flowing out from the organisation, for internal purposes. It is a concept associated with change management and therefore may be appropriate here.

A concerted campaign could be created. This could include messages in salary advices, posters, presentations, the **formation of discussion groups**, and the creation of a **suggestion scheme** specifically aimed at environmental issues. If there are any existing empowerment schemes such as quality circles, it may be possible to introduce an environmental dimension into them.

(c) **Stakeholder interest**

Public interest in corporate social responsibility is steadily increasing. Although financial statements are primarily intended for investors and their advisers, there is growing recognition that companies actually have **a number of different stakeholders**. These include **customers, employees and the general public,** all of whom are **potentially interested** in the way in which a company's operations affect the natural environment and the wider community. These stakeholders can have a **considerable effect on a company's performance**. As a result many companies now deliberately attempt to build a **reputation for social and environmental responsibility**. Therefore the disclosure of environmental and social information is essential.

Regulatory and professional interest

Another factor is **growing interest by governments and professional bodies**. Although there are **no IFRSs** that specifically require environmental and social reporting, it may be required by **company legislation**. There are now a number of **awards for environmental and social reports** and high quality disclosure in financial statements. These provide further encouragement to disclose information.

Performance impact

There is also growing recognition that **corporate social responsibility is actually an important part of an entity's overall performance.** Responsible practice in areas such as reduction of damage to the environment and recruitment **increases shareholder value**. Companies that act responsibly and make social and environmental disclosures are **perceived as better investments** than those that do not.

Compulsory or voluntary disclosure

At present companies are normally able to disclose **as much or as little information as they wish in whatever manner that they wish**. This causes a number of **problems**. Companies tend to disclose information **selectively** and it is difficult for users of the financial statements to **compare the performance of different companies**. However, there are **good arguments** for continuing to allow companies a certain amount of freedom to determine the information that they disclose. If detailed rules are imposed, **companies are likely to adopt a 'checklist' approach** and will **present information in a very general and standardised way**, so that it is of very little use to stakeholders.

Pilot paper questions and answers

Pilot paper

Paper P1

Professional Accountant

Time allowed

Reading and planning:	15 minutes
Writing:	3 hours

This paper is divided into two sections:

Section A – This ONE question is compulsory and MUST be attempted

Section B – TWO questions ONLY to be attempted

Do NOT open this paper until instructed by the supervisor.

During reading and planning time only the question paper may be annotated. You must NOT write in your answer booklet until instructed by the supervisor.

This question paper must not be removed from the examination hall.

Warning

The pilot paper cannot cover all of the syllabus nor can it include examples of every type of question that will be included in the actual exam. You may see questions in the exam that you think are more difficult than any you see in the pilot paper.

SECTION A: This question is compulsory and MUST be attempted

Question 1

Chemco is a well-established listed European chemical company involved in research into, and the production of, a range of chemicals used in industries such as agrochemicals, oil and gas, paint, plastics and building materials. A strategic priority recognised by the Chemco board some time ago was to increase its international presence as a means of gaining international market share and servicing its increasingly geographically dispersed customer base. The Chemco board, which operated as a unitary structure, identified JPX as a possible acquisition target because of its good product 'fit' with Chemco and the fact that its geographical coverage would significantly strengthen Chemco's internationalisation strategy. Based outside Europe in a region of growth in the chemical industry, JPX was seen by analysts as a good opportunity for Chemco, especially as JPX's recent flotation had provided potential access to a controlling shareholding through the regional stock market where JPX operated.

When the board of Chemco met to discuss the proposed acquisition of JPX, a number of issues were tabled for discussion. Bill White, Chemco's chief executive, had overseen the research process that had identified JPX as a potential acquisition target. He was driving the process and wanted the Chemco board of directors to approve the next move, which was to begin the valuation process with a view to making an offer to JPX's shareholders. Bill said that the strategic benefits of this acquisition was in increasing overseas market share and gaining economies of scale.

While Chemco was a public company, JPX had been family owned and operated for most of its thirty-five year history. Seventy-five percent of the share capital was floated on its own country's stock exchange two years ago, but Leena Sharif, Chemco's company secretary, suggested that the corporate governance requirements in JPX's country were not as rigorous as in many parts of the world. She also suggested that the family business culture was still present in JPX and pointed out that it operated a two-tier board with members of the family on the upper tier. At the last annual general meeting, observers noticed that the JPX board, mainly consisting of family members, had 'dominated discussions' and had discouraged the expression of views from the company's external shareholders. JPX had no non-executive directors and none of the board committee structure that many listed companies like Chemco had in place. Bill reported that although JPX's department heads were all directors, they were not invited to attend board meetings when strategy and management monitoring issues were being discussed. They were, he said, treated more like middle management by the upper tier of the JPX board and that important views may not be being heard when devising strategy. Leena suggested that these features made the JPX board's upper tier less externally accountable and less likely to take advice when making decisions. She said that board accountability was fundamental to public trust and that JPX's board might do well to recognise this, especially if the acquisition were to go ahead.

Chemco's finance director, Susan Brown advised caution over the whole acquisition proposal. She saw the proposal as being very risky. In addition to the uncertainties over exposure to foreign markets, she believed that Chemco would also have difficulties with integrating JPX into the Chemco culture and structure. While Chemco was fully compliant with corporate governance best practice, the country in which JPX was based had few corporate governance requirements. Manprit Randhawa, Chemco's operations director, asked Bill if he knew anything about JPX's risk exposure. Manprit suggested that the acquisition of JPX might expose Chemco to a number of risks that could not only affect the success of the proposed acquisition but also, potentially, Chemco itself. Bill replied that he would look at the risks in more detail if the Chemco board agreed to take the proposal forward to its next stage.

Finance director Susan Brown, had obtained the most recent annual report for JPX and highlighted what she considered to be an interesting, but unexplained, comment about 'negative local environmental impact' in its accounts. She asked chief executive Bill White if he could find out what the comment meant and whether JPX had any plans to make provision for any environmental impact. Bill White was able to report, based on his previous dealings with JPX, that it did not produce any voluntary environmental reporting. The Chemco board broadly supported the idea of environmental reporting although company secretary Leena Sharif recently told Bill White that she was unaware of the meaning of the terms 'environmental footprint' and 'environmental reporting' and so couldn't say whether she was supportive or not. It was agreed, however, that relevant information on JPX's environmental performance and risk would be necessary if the acquisition went ahead.

Required

(a)   Evaluate JPX's current corporate governance arrangements and explain why they are likely to be considered inadequate by the Chemco board.   **(10 marks)**

(b)   Manprit suggested that the acquisition of JPX might expose Chemco to a number of risks. Illustrating from the case as required, identify the risks that Chemco might incur in acquiring JPX and explain how risk can be assessed.   **(15 marks)**

(c)   Construct the case for JPX adopting a unitary board structure after the proposed acquisition. Your answer should include an explanation of the advantages of unitary boards and a convincing case FOR the JPX board changing to a unitary structure.   **(10 marks)**

(d)   Explain FOUR roles of non-executive directors (NEDs) and assess the specific contributions that NEDs could make to improve the governance of the JPX board.   **(7 marks)**

(e)   Write a memo to Leena Sharif defining 'environmental footprint' and briefly explaining the importance of environmental reporting for JPX.   **(8 marks)**

(Total = 50 marks)

Section B: TWO questions ONLY to be attempted

Question 2

In a recent case, it emerged that Frank Finn, a sales director at ABC Co, had been awarded a substantial over-inflation annual basic pay award with no apparent link to performance. When a major institutional shareholder, Swanland Investments, looked into the issue, it emerged that Mr Finn had a cross directorship with Joe Ng, an executive director of DEF Co. Mr Ng was a non-executive director of ABC and chairman of its remunerations committee. Swanland Investments argued at the annual general meeting that there was "a problem with the independence" of Mr Ng and further, that Mr Finn's remuneration package as a sales director was considered to be poorly aligned to Swanland's interests because it was too much weighted by basic pay and contained inadequate levels of incentive.

Swanland Investments proposed that the composition of Mr Finn's remuneration package be reconsidered by the remunerations committee and that Mr Ng should not be present during the discussion. Another of the larger institutional shareholders, Hanoi House, objected to this, proposing instead that Mr Ng and Mr Finn both resign from their respective non-executive directorships as there was "clear evidence of malpractice". Swanland considered this too radical a step, as Mr Ng's input was, in its opinion, valuable on ABC's board.

Required

(a)   Explain FOUR roles of a remuneration committee and how the cross directorship undermines these roles at ABC Co.   **(12 marks)**

(b)   Swanland Investments believed Mr Finn's remuneration package to be 'poorly aligned' to its interests. With reference to the different components of a director's remuneration package, explain how Mr Finn's remuneration might be more aligned to shareholders' interests at ABC Co.

                                                                                                                  (8 marks)

(c)   Evaluate the proposal from Hanoi House that both Mr Ng and Mr Finn be required to resign from their respective non-executive positions.   **(5 marks)**

                                                                                                  (Total = 25 marks)

Question 3

At a recent conference on corporate social responsibility, one speaker (Professor Cheung) argued that professional codes of ethics for accountants were not as useful as some have claimed because:

"they assume professional accountants to be rules-driven, when in fact most professionals are more driven by principles that guide and underpin all aspects of professional behaviour, including professional ethics."

When quizzed from the audience about his views on the usefulness of professional codes of ethics, Professor Cheung suggested that the costs of writing, implementing, disseminating and monitoring ethical codes outweighed their usefulness. He said that as long as professional accountants personally observe the highest values of probity and integrity then there is no need for detailed codes of ethics.

Required

(a) Critically evaluate Professor Cheung's views on codes of professional ethics. Use examples of ethical codes, where appropriate, to illustrate your answer. **(12 marks)**

(b) With reference to Professor Cheung's comments, explain what is meant by 'integrity' and assess its importance as an underlying principle in corporate governance. **(7 marks)**

(c) Explain and contrast a deontological with a consequentialist based approach to business ethics. **(6 marks)**

(Total = 25 marks)

Question 4

As part of a review of its internal control systems, the board of FF co, a large textiles company, has sought your advice as a senior accountant in the company.

FF's stated objective has always been to adopt the highest standards of internal control because it believes that by doing so it will not only provide shareholders with confidence in its governance but also enhance its overall reputation with all stakeholders. In recent years, however, FF's reputation for internal control has been damaged somewhat by a qualified audit statement last year (over issues of compliance with financial standards) and an unfortunate internal incident the year prior to that. This incident concerned an employee, Miss Osula, expressing concern about the compliance of one of the company's products with an international standard on fire safety. She raised the issue with her immediate manager but he said, according to Miss Osula, that it wasn't his job to report her concerns to senior management. When she failed to obtain a response herself from senior management, she decided to report the lack of compliance to the press. This significantly embarrassed the company and led to a substantial deterioration in FF's reputation.

The specifics of the above case concerned a fabric produced by FF Co, which, in order to comply with an international fire safety standard, was required to resist fire for ten minutes when in contact with a direct flame. According to Miss Osula, who was a member of the quality control staff, FF was allowing material rated at only five minutes fire resistance to be sold labelled as ten minute rated. In her statement to the press, Miss Osula said that there was a culture of carelessness in FF and that this was only one example of the way the company approached issues such as international fire safety standards.

Required

(a) Describe how the internal control systems at FF Co differ from a 'sound' system of internal control, such as that set out in the Turnbull guidance, for example. **(10 marks)**

(b) Define 'reputation risk' and evaluate the potential effects of FF's poor reputation on its financial situation. **(8 marks)**

(c) Explain, with reference to FF as appropriate, the ethical responsibilities of a professional accountant both as an employee and as a professional. **(7 marks)**

(Total = 25 marks)

1

Top tips. (a) may well be an example of the sort of governance question that will occur frequently on this paper. The answer combines some obvious points (lack of non-executive directors) with some less obvious points (the family-dominated structure, the oblique reporting). The best way to approach (a) would have been to go through the scenario carefully during the reading time, noting each point that is relevant to corporate governance, and comparing the details you're given with corporate governance best practice.

(b) covers a combination of risks; the extra risks that JPX will bring to Chemco (the environmental risk and the exchange risk), the risks of the acquisition itself (the market risk of the stock) and the risks arising from the processes of change that will be implemented once the merger takes place. Remember when trying to identify risks in the scenario that often a lot of risks will relate to what's about to change; the results of the change and the processes required for change to occur will all have risks attached.

You may see slightly different versions of the risk assessment process described in the second part of (b), but you would get full marks if you described a logical process that was similar to what's described in the answer.

The key advantages in (c) are equal legal responsibility and larger boards meaning that more viewpoints are represented and that the board is less likely to be dominated by a single director or group of directors. In relation to JPX, consistency is also an issue, but you need to show why it's important; the answer contains a good explanation. The answer also stresses the importance of culture change, an aspect of the control environment that the examiner has highlighted as very important.

(d) represents a summary of the role of non-executive directors, usefully grouped under four key headers. In the second part of (d) you need to discuss elements of what does and doesn't make a good board; that the interests of external shareholders should be represented, that all relevant viewpoints should be included and the board shouldn't be dominated by a small group. These points certainly link in with the discussion in (c).

(e) represents the ethical element that the examiner has promised will be part of all compulsory questions. It emphasises the key elements of interaction with the environment. Note that the second part of (e) includes discussion of general corporate governance principles of openness and sufficient explanation; the answer also brings out how reporting can bring home to the company its environmental impact.

In addition we have to suggest that the way the answer is presented, particularly the long paragraphs in (a) and (b), would not have made it easy to mark. The mark scheme suggests that the marker will be looking for a series of 1-2 mark points; the best way to present these would be one paragraph per point with a header at the start of each paragraph.

Easy marks. There are various general sections that don't need to be related to JPX or Chemco such as the risk assessment process or the role of non-executive directors. These represent core knowledge and should therefore be easy marks.

2

Top tips. Directors' remuneration is the type of subject that you are very likely to see in this exam as it is (always) topical and there's lots of corporate governance guidance covering it. In (a) 8 marks is quite a generous allocation for the role of the remuneration committee; the answer brings out what it does, the issues and complexities with which it has to engage, and the key corporate governance responsibilities of accountability (here the reporting requirements) and compliance. Your answer on cross-directorships needs to bring out the key principle (independence) and show how independence in breached.

In (b) the description of remuneration brings out the most important issue of links with performance, but also another important issue, that of directors getting benefits on better terms than employees. Note the stress on trying to balance short and long-term priorities; the weighting of each is not easy to determine, particularly for a sales director whose short-term performance will be significant.

In (c) the arguments for the proposal take an absolutist view of the rules, reinforced by arguments stressing the beneficial consequences (simple solution, better for reputation).

The arguments against the proposal stress that there is doubt about malpractice and also other consequences (loss of experience unbalancing the board). Remember under most governance codes not all non-executive directors have to meet the independence criteria, but there need to be sufficient non-executive directors on the board to constitute a strong presence and to staff the key corporate governance committees.

Overall (c) is a good example of weighing up a strong ethical solution against a maybe weaker, but more practical, one.

Easy marks. The descriptive sections on remuneration committee and directors' remuneration certainly offer most of the marks you need to pass this question. Remember however that in your exam, the marks may be more tilted towards application.

3

Top tips In (a) you should get a certain amount of mileage from using Professor Cheung's arguments in the question. Partly the disadvantages of codes is that accountants pay too much attention to the examples and not enough to understanding the basic principles (this point is also picked up in the answer to Question 4 (c)). The impact of regional differences is interesting; you will remember that they impact upon individuals' ethical outlook, so how can codes respond. The arguments against the opinion bring out what codes can achieve, particularly minimum standards of behaviour.

Again we would suggest in (a) that each argument for or against the viewpoint is given in a separate headed paragraph.

(b) emphasises the key concept of integrity. The definition and the importance of integrity represent knowledge you must have; the examiner has laid a lot of stress on it.

(c) just asks for a definition of these two viewpoints. You may be asked in other questions to apply them to a situation where a deontological (absolute) perspective suggests one course of action, a consequentialist (teleological) perspective another.

Easy marks. Make sure that a similar question to (b) does represent easy marks.

4

Top tips. (a) appears to be in two parts, first description of good control systems and then application to FF. The description paragraphs appear to be quite generously rewarded; don't assume that this will necessarily be the case in your exam where the majority of marks are likely to be given for application of knowledge to the scenario.

You should note a couple of things which the answer to (a) stresses. Firstly the importance of embedding internal control which has been stressed by the examiner; secondly the need for control systems to respond quickly to changing risks. You may well see scenarios in the exam where the company's business situation is changing, hence its risks are altering, and you will need to explain that the control systems have to respond.

(b) stresses the importance of reputation risk. The level of reputation risk is partly determined by the level of other risks, but, as this answer stresses, it also depends on stakeholder responses. Lost sales is the obvious consequence, but note also the non-financial consequences such as recruitment problems or increased regulator attention.

The key question (c) brings out is when the duty of confidentiality might be overridden. The discussions of professional responsibilities brings out how accountants should have recourse to the basic principles of integrity, probity and public interest in situation where the detail in codes isn't helpful.

Easy marks. The first parts of (a) and (b) are descriptive rather than application based, requiring knowledge of Turnbull and the definition of reputation risk.

1 (a) JPX's current corporate governance arrangements

Inadequacy of JPX's current corporate governance arrangements

The case highlights a number of ways in which the corporate governance at JPX is inadequate. JPX's history as a privately run family business may partly explain its apparent slowness to develop the corporate governance structures and systems expected in many parts of the world. There are five ways, from the case, that JPX can be said to be inadequate in its corporate governance although these are linked. There is overlap between the points made.

In the first instance, the case mentions that there were no non-executive directors (NEDs) on the JPX board. It follows that JPX would be without the necessary balance and external expertise that NEDs can provide. Second, there is evidence of a corporate culture at JPX dominated by the members of the family. The case study notes that they dominate the upper tier of the board. This may have been acceptable when JPX was a family owned company, but as a public company floated on a stock exchange and hence accountable to external shareholders, a wider participation in board membership is necessary. Third, the two-tier board, whilst not necessarily being a problem in itself (two-tier boards work well in many circumstances), raises concern because the department heads, who are on the lower tier of the board, are excluded from strategic discussions at board level. It is likely that as line managers in the business, the departmental heads would have vital inputs to make into such discussions, especially on such issues as the implementation of strategies. It is also likely that their opinions on the viabilities of different strategic options would be of value. Fourth, it could be argued that JPX's reporting is less than ideal with, for example, its oblique reference to a 'negative local environmental impact'. However, it might be noted that ambiguity in reporting is also evident in European and American reporting. Finally, having been subject to its own country's less rigorous corporate governance requirements for all of its previous history, it is likely that adjusting to the requirements of complying with the European-centred demands of Chemco will present a challenge.

(b) Risks of the proposed acquisition

Risks that Chemco might incur in acquiring JPX.

The case describes a number of risks that Chemco could become exposed to if the acquisition was successful. Explicitly, the case highlights a possible environmental risk (the 'negative local environmental impact') that may or may not be eventually valued as a provision (depending on whether or not it is likely to result in a liability). Other risks are likely to emerge as the proposed acquisition develops. Exchange rate risks apply to any business dealing with revenue or capital flows between two or more currency zones. The case explicitly describes Chemco and JPX existing in different regions of the world. Whilst exchange rate volatility can undermine confidence in cash flow projections, it should be borne in mind that medium term increases or decreases in exchange values can materially affect the returns on an investment (in this case, Chemco's investment in JPX). There is some market risk in Chemco's valuation of JPX stock. This could be a substantial risk because of JPX's relatively recent flotation where the market price of JPX may not have yet found its intrinsic level. In addition, it is not certain that Chemco has full knowledge of the fair price to pay for each JPX share given the issues of dealing across national borders and in valuing stock in JPX's country. All mergers and acquisitions ('integrations') are exposed to synergy risks. Whilst it is expected and hoped that every merger or acquisition will result in synergies (perhaps from scale economies as the case mentions), in practice, many integrations fail to realise any. In extreme cases, the costs arising from integration can threaten the very survival of the companies involved. Finally, there are risks associated with the bringing-together of the two board structures. Specifically, structural and cultural changes will be required at JPX to bring it in line with Chemco's. The creation of a unitary board and the increased involvement of NEDs and departmental heads may be problematic, for example, Chemco's board is likely to insist on such changes post-acquisition.

Assessment of risk

The assessment of the risk exposure of any organisation has five components. Firstly, the identity (nature and extent) of the risks facing the company should be identified (such as considering the risks involved in acquiring JPX). This may involve consulting with relevant senior managers, consultants and other stakeholders. Second, the company should decide on the categories of risk that are regarded as acceptable for the company to bear. Of course any decision to discontinue exposure to a given risk will have implications for the activities of the company and this cost will need to be considered against the benefit of the reduced risk. Third, the assessment of risk should quantify, as far as possible, the likelihood (probability) of the identified risks materialising. Risks with a high probability of occurring will attract higher levels of management attention than those with lower probabilities. Fourth, an assessment of risk will entail an examination of the company's ability to reduce the impact on the business of risks that do materialise. Consultation with affected parties (e.g. departmental heads, stakeholders, etc.) is likely to be beneficial, as information on minimising negative impact may sometimes be a matter of technical detail. Fifth and finally, risk assessment involves an understanding of the costs of operating particular controls to review and manage the related risks. These costs will include information gathering costs, management overhead, external consultancy where appropriate, etc.

(c) Unitary and two-tier board structures

Advantages of unitary board structure in general

There are arguments for and against unitary and two-tier boards. Both have their 'place' depending on business cultures, size of business and a range of other factors. In general, however, the following arguments can be put for unitary boards.

One of the main features of a unitary board is that all directors, including managing directors, departmental (or divisional) directors and NEDs all have equal legal and executive status in law. This does not mean that all are equal in terms of the organisational hierarchy, but that all are responsible and can be held accountable for board decisions. This has a number of benefits. Firstly, NEDs are empowered, being accorded equal status to executive directors. NEDs can bring not only independent scrutiny to the board, but also experience and expertise that may be of invaluable help in devising strategy and the assessment of risk. Second, board accountability is enhanced by providing a greater protection against fraud and malpractice and by holding all directors equally accountable under a 'cabinet government' arrangement. These first two benefits provide a major underpinning to the confidence that markets have in listed companies. Third, unitary board arrangements reduce the likelihood of abuse of (self-serving) power by a small number of senior directors. Small 'exclusivist' boards such as have been evident in some corporate 'scandals' are discouraged by unitary board arrangements. Fourth, the fact that the board is likely to be larger than a given tier of a two-tier board means that more viewpoints are likely to be expressed in board deliberations and discussions. In addition to enriching the intellectual strength of the board, the inclusivity of the board should mean that strategies are more robustly scrutinised before being implemented.

Relevance to JPX in particular

If the JPX acquisition was to proceed, there would be a unitary board at Chemco overseeing a two-tier board at JPX. The first specific argument for JPX adopting a unitary board would be to bring it into line with Chemco's. Chemco clearly believes in unitary board arrangements and would presumably prefer to have the benefits of unitary boards in place so as to have as much confidence as possible in JPX's governance. This may be especially important if JPX is to remain an 'arms length' or decentralised part of Chemco's international operation. Second, there is an argument for making changes at JPX in order to signal a departure from the 'old' systems when JPX was independent of the 'new' systems under Chemco's ownership. A strong way of helping to 'unfreeze' previous ways of working is to make important symbolic changes and a rearrangement of the board structure would be a good example of this. Third, it is clear that the family members who currently run JPX have a disproportionate influence on the company and its strategy (the 'family business culture'). Widening the board would, over time, change the culture of the board and reduce that influence. Fourth, a unitary board structure would empower the departmental heads at JPX whose opinions and support are likely to be important in the transition period following the acquisition.

(d) **Non executive directors**

Four roles of non-executive directors.

The Higgs Report (2003) in the United Kingdom helpfully described the function of non-executive directors (NEDs) in terms of four distinct roles. These were the strategy role, the scrutinising role, the risk advising role and the 'people' role. These roles may be undertaken as part of the general discussion occurring at Board meetings or more formally, through the corporate governance committee structure.

The strategy role recognises that NEDs are full members of a unitary board and thus have the right and responsibility to contribute to the strategic success of the organisation for the benefit of shareholders. In this role they may challenge any aspect of strategy they see fit, and offer advice or input to help to develop successful strategy.

In the scrutinising role, NEDs are required to hold executive colleagues to account for decisions taken and results obtained. In this respect they are required to represent the shareholders' interests against the possibility that agency issues arise to reduce shareholder value.

The risk role involves NEDs ensuring the company has an adequate system of internal controls and systems of risk management in place. This is often informed by prescribed codes (such as Turnbull) but some industries, such as chemicals, have other systems in place, some of which fall under International Organisation for Standardisation (ISO) standards.

Finally, the 'people' role involves NEDs overseeing a range of responsibilities with regard to the management of the executive members of the board. This typically involves issues on appointments and remuneration, but might also involve contractual or disciplinary issues.

Specific benefits for JPX of having NEDs

The specific benefits that NEDs could bring to JPX concern the need for a balance against excessive family influence and the prior domination of the 'family business culture'. Chemco, as JPX's new majority shareholder, is unlikely to want to retain a 'cabal' of an upper tier at JPX and the recruitment of a number of NEDs will clearly help in that regard. Second, NEDs will perform an important role in representing external shareholders' interests (as well as internal shareholders). Specifically, shareholders will include Chemco. Third, Chemco's own board discussion included Bill White's view that the exclusion of departmental heads was resulting in important views not being heard when devising strategy. This is a major potential danger to JPX and NEDs could be appointed to the board in order to ensure that future board discussions include all affected parties including the previously disenfranchised department heads.

(e) Environmental reporting.

Memorandum

From: Professional Accountant
To: Leena Sharif

Date: DD/MM/YYYY

Re: environmental issues at Chemco and JPX

1. **Introduction**

   I have been asked to write to you on two matters of potential importance to Chemco in respect of environmental issues. The first of these is to consider the meaning of the term, 'environmental footprint' and the second is to briefly review the arguments for inviting JPX (should the acquisition proceed) to introduce environmental reporting.

2. **'Environmental footprint'**

   Explanation of 'environmental footprint'
   The use of the term 'footprint' with regard to the environment is intended to convey a meaning similar to its use in everyday language. In the same way that humans and animals leave physical footprints that show where they have been, so organisations such as Chemco leave evidence of their operations in the environment. They operate at a net cost to the environment. The environmental footprint is an attempt to evaluate the size of Chemco's impact on the environment in three respects. Firstly, concerning the company's resource consumption where resources are defined in terms of inputs such as energy, feedstock, water, land use, etc. Second, concerning any harm to the environment brought about by pollution emissions. These include emissions of carbon and other chemicals, local emissions, spillages, etc. It is likely that as a chemical manufacturer, both of these impacts will be larger for Chemco than for some other types of business. Thirdly, the environmental footprint includes a measurement of the resource consumption and pollution emissions in terms of harm to the environment in either qualitative, quantitative or replacement terms.

3. **Environmental reporting at JPX.**

   Arguments for environmental reporting at JPX
   There are number of arguments for environmental reporting in general and others that may be specifically relevant to JPX. In general terms and firstly, I'm sure as company secretary you will recognise the importance of observing the corporate governance and reporting principles of transparency, openness, responsibility and fairness wherever possible. We should invite JPX to adopt these values should the acquisition proceed. Any deliberate concealment would clearly be counter to these principles and so 'more' rather than 'less' reporting is always beneficial. Second, it is important to present a balanced and understandable assessment of the company's position and prospects to external stakeholders. Third, it is important that JPX recognises the existence and size of its environment footprint, and reporting is a useful means if doing this. Fourth, and specifically with regard to JPX and other companies with a substantial potential environmental footprint, there is a need to explain environmental strategy to investors and other interested stakeholders (eg Chemco). Finally, there is a need to explain in more detail the 'negative local environmental impact' and an environmental report would be an ideal place for such an explanation.

Summary:

As JPX's 'environmental footprint' is potentially quite large, it is important that Chemco ensures as far as possible, that any such footprint left by JPX is known and measured. Additionally, in the interests of transparency, openness, responsibility and fairness, it is important that it is also fully reported upon for the information of both investors and other interested stakeholders.

2 **(a)** **Remunerations committees and cross directorships**

Remunerations committees
Remunerations committees comprise an important part of the standard board committee structure of good corporate governance.

The major roles of a remuneration committee are as follows. Firstly, the committee is charged with determining remunerations policy on behalf of the board and the shareholders. In this regard, they are acting on behalf of shareholders but for the benefit of both shareholders and the other members of the board. Policies will typically concern the pay scales applied to directors' packages, the proportions of different types of reward within the overall package and the periods in which performance related elements become payable.

Secondly the committee ensures that each director is fairly but responsibly rewarded for their individual contribution in terms of levels or pay and the components of each director's package. It is likely that discussions of this type will take place for each individual director and will take into account issues including market conditions, retention needs, long-term strategy and market rates for a given job.

Third, the remunerations committee reports to the shareholders on the outcomes of their decisions, usually in the corporate governance section of the annual report (usually called Report of the Remunerations Committee). This report, which is auditor reviewed, contains a breakdown of each director's remuneration and a commentary on policies applied to executive and non-executive remuneration.

Finally, where appropriate and required by statute or voluntary code, the committee is required to be seen to be compliant with relevant laws or codes of best practice. This will mean that the remunerations committee will usually be made up of non-executive members of the board and will meet at regular intervals.

Cross directorships

Cross directorships represent a threat to the efficient working of remunerations committees. A cross directorship is said to exist when two (or more) directors sit on the boards of the other. In practice, such arrangements also involve some element of cross-shareholdings which further compromises the independence of the directors involved. In most cases, each director's 'second' board appointment is likely to be non-executive. Cross directorships undermine the roles of remunerations committees in that a director deciding the salary of a colleague who, in turn, may play a part in deciding his own salary, is a clear conflict of interests. Neither director involved in the arrangement is impartial and so a temptation would exist to act in a manner other than for the benefit of the shareholders of the company on whose remunerations committee they sit. It is for this reason the cross directorships and cross shareholding arrangements are explicitly forbidden by many corporate governance codes of best practice.

(b) Mr Finn's remunerations package

Different components of directors' rewards

The components of a director's total rewards package may include any or all of the following in combination. The basic salary is not linked to performance in the short run but year-to-year changes in it may be linked to some performance measures. It is intended to recognise the basic market value of a director. A number of benefits in kind may be used which will vary by position and type of organisation, but typically include company cars, health insurance, use of health or leisure facilities, subsidised or free use of company products (if appropriate), etc. Pension contributions are paid by most responsible employers, but separate directors' schemes may be made available at higher contribution rates than other employees. Finally, various types of incentives and performance related components may be used. Short to medium term incentives such as performance-related annual bonuses will encourage a relatively short term approach to meeting agreed targets whilst long term incentives including share options can be used for longer term performance measures.

Mr Finn's remuneration package

The case mentions that, "Mr Finn's remuneration package as a sales director was considered to be poorly aligned to Swanland's interests because it was too much weighted by basic pay and contained inadequate levels of incentive."

The alignment of director and shareholder interests occurs through a careful design of the performance related components of a director's overall rewards. The strategic emphases of the business can be built into these targets and Mr Finn's position as a sales director makes this possible through incentives based on revenue or profit targets. If current priorities are for the maximisation of relatively short-run returns, annual, semi-annual or even monthly performance-related bonuses could be used. More likely at board level, however, will be a need for longer-term alignments for medium to long-term value maximisation. While Mr Finn may be given annual or even quarterly or monthly bonus payments against budget, longer-term performance can be underpinned through share options with a relevant maturity date or end-of-service payouts with agreed targets. The balance of short and longer-term performance bonuses should be carefully designed for each director with metrics within the control of the director in question.

(c) Evaluation of the proposal from Hanoi House.

The dilemma over what action to take in the light of Mr Ng and Mr Finn's cross directorship is a typical problem when deciding how to address issues of conflicts of interest. Should the situation be 'put right' at minimum cost, or should the parties in the arrangement be punished in some way as Hanoi House suggested? Swanland's more equivocal suggestion (that the remunerations committee reconsider Mr Finn's remuneration package without Mr Ng being present) may be more acceptable to some shareholders. This debate touches on the ethical issues of a pragmatic approach to some issues compared to a dogmatic approach.

For the proposal

Hanoi House's more radical proposal would have a number of potential advantages. Specifically, it could be argued that the resignation of both men from their respective NED positions would restore ABC shareholders' confidence in the remunerations committee. The appearance of probity is sometimes as important as the substance and resignations can sometimes serve to purge a problem to everybody's (except for the director in question's) benefit. The double resignation would signal a clean break in the apparently compromising relationship between Mr Finn and Mr Ng and, certainly as far as ABC was concerned, would resolve the problem decisively. It would signal the importance that ABC placed on compliance with corporate governance best practice and this, in turn, would be of comfort to shareholders and analysts concerned with the threat to the independence of ABC's remunerations committee.

Against the proposal

Hanoi House's proposal was seen as too radical for Swanland. Among its concerns was the belief that only Mr Ng's resignation from ABC's remunerations committee would be strictly necessary to diffuse the situation. Clearly Swanland saw no problem with Mr Finn's position on the ABC board in his executive capacity. Furthermore, it took a pragmatic view of Mr Ng's position as NED on ABC's board. It considered Mr Ng's input to be valuable on the ABC board and pointed out that this input would be lost if Hanoi House's proposal was put into practice. Hanoi House may therefore have been mindful of the assumed deficit of talent at senior strategic level in corporate management and accordingly, wished to retain both Mr Finn's and Mr Ng's expertise if at all possible.

3 (a) Professor Cheung's views on codes of professional ethics

Professor Cheung adopts a sceptical stance with regard to codes of ethics. There are arguments both supporting and challenging his views.

Supporting Professor Cheung's opinion

Professional codes of ethics have a number of limitations, some of which Professor Cheung referred to. Because they contain descriptions of situations that accountants might encounter, they can convey the (false) impression that professional ethics can be reduced to a set of rules contained in a code (as pointed out by Professor Cheung). This would be a mistaken impression, of course, as the need for personal integrity is also emphasised. Ethical codes do not and cannot capture all ethical circumstances and dilemmas that a professional accountant will encounter in his or her career and this reinforces the need for accountants to understand the underlying ethical principles of probity, integrity, openness, transparency and fairness. Although codes such as IFAC's are intended to apply to an international 'audience', some may argue that regional variations in cultural, social and ethical norms mean that such codes cannot capture important differences in emphasis in some parts of the world. The moral 'right' can be prescribed in every situation. Finally, professional codes of ethics are not technically enforceable in any legal manner although sanctions exist for gross breach of the code in some jurisdictions. Individual observance of ethical codes is effectively voluntary in most circumstances.

Against Professor Cheung's opinion

There are a number of arguments for codes of professional ethics that challenge Professor Cheung's views. Firstly, professional codes of ethics signal the importance, to accountants, of ethics and acting in the public interest in the professional accounting environment. They are reminded, unambiguously and in 'black and white' for example, that as with other professions, accounting exists to serve the public good and public support for the profession is likely to exist only as long as the public interest is supported over and above competing interests. The major international codes (such as IFAC) underpin national and regional cultures with internationally expected standards that, the codes insist, supersede any national ethical nuances. The IFAC (2003) code states (in clause 4), "the accountancy profession throughout the world operates in an environment with different cultures and regulatory requirements. The basic intent of the Code, however, should always be respected." The codes prescribe minimum standards of behaviour expected in given situations and give specific examples of potentially problematic areas in accounting practice. In such situations, the codes make the preferred course of action unambiguous.

A number of codes of ethics exist for professional accountants. Prominent among these is the IFAC code. This places the public interest at the heart of the ethical conduct of accountants. The ACCA code discusses ethics from within a principles-based perspective. Other countries' own professional accounting bodies have issued their own codes of ethics in the belief that they may better describe the ethical situations in those countries.

(b) Integrity

Meaning of 'integrity'

Integrity is generally understood to describe a person of high moral virtue. A person of integrity is one who observes a steadfast adherence to a strict moral or ethical code notwithstanding any other pressures on him or her to act otherwise. In professional life, integrity describes the personal ethical position of the highest standards of professionalism and probity. It is an underlying and underpinning principle of corporate governance and it is required that all those representing shareholder interests in agency relationships both possess and exercise absolute integrity at all times. To fail to do so is a breach of the agency trust relationship.

Importance of integrity in corporate governance

Integrity is important in corporate governance for several reasons. Codes of ethics do not capture all ethical situations and the importance of the virtue of the actor rather than the ethics of the action is therefore emphasised. Any profession (such as accounting) relies upon a public perception of competence and integrity and in this regard, accounting can perhaps be compared with medicine. As an underlying principle, integrity provides a basic ethical framework to guide an accountant's professional and personal life. Finally, integrity underpins the relationships that an accountant has with his or her clients, auditors and other colleagues. Trust is vital in the normal conduct of these relationships and integrity underpins this.

(c) Deontology and consequentialism

Deontological ethics

The deontological perspective can be broadly understood in terms of 'means' being more important than 'ends'. It is broadly based on Kantian (categorical imperative) ethics. The rightness of an action is judged by its intrinsic virtue and thus morality is seen as absolute and not situational. An action is right if it would, by its general adoption, be of net benefit to society. Lying, for example, is deemed to be ethically wrong because lying, if adopted in all situations, would lead to the deterioration of society.

Consequentialist ethics

The consequentialist or teleological perspective is based on utilitarian or egoist ethics meaning that the rightness of an action is judged by the quality of the outcome. From the egoist perspective, the quality of the outcome refers to the individual ("what is best for me?"). Utilitarianism measures the quality of outcome in terms of the greatest happiness of the greatest number ("what is best for the majority?"). Consequentialist ethics are therefore situational and contingent, and not absolute.

4   **(a)**   **FF plc and a 'sound' system of internal control**

Features of sound control systems

The Turnbull code employs the term 'sound' to indicate that it is insufficient to simply 'have' an internal control system. They can be effective and serve the aim of corporate governance or they can be ineffective and fail to support them. In order to reinforce 'soundness' or effectiveness, systems need to possess a number of features. The Turnbull guidance described three features of a 'sound' internal control system.

Firstly, the principles of internal control should be embedded within the organisation's structures, procedures and culture. Internal control should not be seen as a stand-alone set of activities and by embedding it into the fabric of the organisation's infrastructure, awareness of internal control issues becomes everybody's business and this contributes to effectiveness.

Secondly, internal control systems should be capable of responding quickly to evolving risks to the business arising from factors within the company and to changes in the business environment. The speed of reaction is an important feature of almost all control systems (for example a servo system for vehicle brakes or the thermostat on a heating system). Any change in the risk profile or environment of the organisation will necessitate a change in the system and a failure or slowness to respond may increase the vulnerability to internal or external trauma.

Thirdly, sound internal control systems include procedures for reporting immediately to appropriate levels of management any significant control failings or weaknesses that are identified, together with details of corrective action being undertaken. Information flows to relevant levels of management capable and empowered to act on the information are essential in internal control systems. Any failure, frustration, distortion or obfuscation of information flows can compromise the system. For this reason, formal and relatively rigorous information channels are often instituted in organisations seeking to maximise the effectiveness of their internal control systems.

Shortcomings at FF plc.

The case highlights a number of ways in which the internal control at FF fell short of that expected of a 'sound' internal control system. First, and most importantly, the case suggests that the culture of FF did not support good internal control. Miss Osula made reference to, "culture of carelessness in FF" and said that the issue over the fire safety standards, "was only one example of the way the company approached issues such as international fire safety standards." While having systems in place to support sound internal control, it is also important to have a culture that also places a high priority on it. Second, there is evidence of a lack of internal control and reporting procedures at FF. Not only was the incorrect fire-rating labelling not corrected by senior management, the attempt to bring the matter to the attention of management was also not well-received.

Third, there is evidence of structural/premeditated contravention of standards (and financial standards) at FF. In addition to the fire safety issue, the case makes reference to a qualified audit statement over issues of compliance with financial standards. There is ample evidence for shareholders to question the competence of management's ability to manage the internal control systems at FF.

(b)   **Reputation risk**

Defining reputation risk

Reputation risk is one of the categories of risk used in organisations. It was identified as a risk category by Turnbull and a number of events in various parts of the world have highlighted the importance of this risk. Reputation risk concerns any kind of deterioration in the way in which the organisation is perceived, usually, but not exclusively, from the point of view of external stakeholders. The cause of such deterioration may be due to irregular behaviour, compliance failure or similar, but in any event, the effect is an aspect of corporate behaviour below that expected by one or more stakeholder. When the 'disappointed' stakeholder has contractual power over the organisation, the cost of the reputation risk may be material.

Effects of poor reputation on financial situation

There are several potential effects of reputation risk on an affected organisation. When more than one stakeholder group has reason to question the otherwise good reputation of an organisation, the effect can be a downward spiral leading to a general lack of confidence which, in turn, can have unfortunate financial effects. In particular, however, reputation risk is likely to affect one or more of the organisation's interactions with resource providers, product buyers, investors or auditors/regulators. Resource provision (linked to resource dependency theory) may affect recruitment, financing or the ability to obtain other inputs such as (in extremis) real estate, stock or intellectual capital. Within product markets, damage to reputation can reduce confidence among customers leading to reduced sales values and volumes and, in extreme cases, boycotts. Investor confidence is important in public companies where any reputation risk is likely to be reflected in market value. Finally, auditors, representing the interests of shareholders, would have reason to exercise increased scrutiny if, say, there are problems with issues of trust in a company. It would be a similar situation if the affected organisation were in an industry subject to high levels of regulation.

FF and reputation

At FF, the sources of the potential threat to its reputation arise from a failure to meet an external standard, an issue over product confidence and a qualified audit statement. The failure to meet an external standard concerned compliance with international fire safety standards. The issue over product confidence involved selling one product falsely rated higher than the reality. These would be likely to affect customer confidence and the attitude of any fire safety accrediting body. The qualified audit statement would be likely to intensify the attention to detail paid by auditors in subsequent years.

(c) Ethical responsibilities of a professional accountant

A professional accountant has two 'directions' of responsibility: one to his or her employer and another to the highest standards of professionalism.

Responsibilities to employer

An accountant's responsibilities to his or her employer extend to acting with diligence, probity and with the highest standards of care in all situations. In addition, however, an employer might reasonably expect the accountant to observe employee confidentiality as far as possible. In most situations, this will extend to absolute discretion of all sensitive matters both during and after the period of employment. The responsibilities also include the expectation that the accountant will act in shareholders' interests as far as possible and that he or she will show loyalty within the bounds of legal and ethical good practice.

Responsibilities as a professional

In addition to an accountant's responsibilities to his or her employer, there is a further set of expectations arising from his or her membership of the accounting profession. In the first instance, professional accountants are expected to observe the letter and spirit of the law in detail and of professional ethical codes where applicable (depending on country of residence, qualifying body, etc.). In any professional or ethical situation where codes do not clearly apply, a professional accountant should apply 'principles-based' ethical standards (such as integrity and probity) such that they would be happy to account for their behaviour if so required. Finally, and in common with members of other professions, accountants are required to act in the public interest that may, in extremis, involve reporting an errant employer to the relevant authorities. This may be the situation that an accountant may find him or herself in at FF. It would clearly be unacceptable to be involved in any form of deceit and it would be the accountant's duty to help to correct such malpractice if at all possible.

P1 Pilot Paper
Professional Accountant

Marking Scheme

1 **(a)** Up to two marks per valid point made on the inadequacy of JPX's governance
(Up to a maximum of ten in total)

(b) One mark for identifying and describing each risk to Chemco in the JPX acquisition up to a maximum of six.
Up to one mark per relevant point on assessing each risk and a further one mark for development of relevant points up to a maximum of ten.
(Up a maximum of fifteen in total)

(c) Award one mark for each relevant point made.
(i) Up to four marks for an explanation of the advantages of unitary boards
(ii) Up to five marks for the case concerning the advantages of a unitary board at JPX.
(iii) Up to two marks for the clarity and persuasiveness of the argument for change in the JPX board.
(Up to a maximum of ten in total)

d) Award one mark for each explanation of the four roles of non-executive directors up to a maximum of four marks.

Award one mark for each specific benefit of NEDs to JPX up to a maximum of four marks.
(Up to a maximum of seven marks in total)

(e) Memo to Leena Sharif.
Explaining environmental footprint – one mark for each relevant point made up to a maximum of three marks.
Explaining importance of environmental reporting – one mark for each relevant point made up to a maximum of five marks.

Up to two marks for the form of the answer (memo in which content is laid out in an orderly and informative manner).
(Up to a maximum of eight in total)

(50 marks)

2 **(a)** (i) One mark for each valid point made up to a maximum of two for demonstrating an understanding of cross directorships.
(ii) Award up to two marks for each valid point made on roles of remunerations committees up to a maximum of eight.
(iii) Award up to two marks for each valid point on undermining the roles up to a maximum of four.
(Up to a maximum of twelve marks in total)

b) One mark for each components of a director's remuneration correctly identified up to a maximum of four.
One mark for each relevant point describing how Finn's remuneration might be more aligned to shareholders' interests up to a maximum of five.
(Up to a maximum of eight marks in total)

(c) Award one mark for each point evaluating the proposal from Hanoi House:
Arguments in favour – up to three marks,
Arguments against – up to three marks.
(Up to a maximum of five marks in total).

(25 marks)

3 **(a)** Award one mark for each valid point made supporting codes of professional ethics up to a maximum of six.
Award one mark for each valid point made on limitations of codes of professional ethics up to a maximum of six.
Up to two marks for using an actual code of ethics by way of example.
(Up to a maximum of eleven marks in total)

(b) Definition of integrity – one mark for each relevant point up to a maximum of four.
Importance of integrity – one mark for each relevant point up to a maximum of four.
(Up to a maximum of seven marks in total)

(c) Explanation of deontology – one mark for each valid point up to a maximum of four marks
Explanation of consequentialism – one mark for each valid point up to a maximum of four marks
(Up to a maximum of seven marks in total)

(25 marks)

4 **(a)** Description of 'sound' control systems – up to two marks for each valid point made up to a maximum of six.
Explanation of shortcomings at FF plc – one mark for each valid point made up to a maximum of six.
(Up to a maximum of ten marks in total)

(b) Definition of 'reputation risk' – one mark for each valid point made up to a maximum of three.
Explanation of the financial effects of poor reputation – one mark for each valid point made up to a maximum of four.
Recognition of the causes of FF's reputation problems – one mark for each valid point made up to a maximum of two.
(Up to a maximum of eight marks in total)

(c) Responsibilities to employer – one mark for each valid point made up to a maximum of four.
Responsibilities to professionalism – one mark for each valid point made up to a maximum of four.
(Up to a maximum of seven marks in total)

(25 marks)

Index

Note. **Key Terms** and their page references are given in **bold**.

Review Form & Free Prize Draw – P1 Professional Accountant (4/07)

All original review forms from the entire BPP range, completed with genuine comments, will be entered into one of two draws on 31 January 2008 and 31 July 2008. The names on the first four forms picked out on each occasion will be sent a cheque for £50.

Name: _____   Address: _____

_____

_____

How have you used this Text?
(Tick one box only)

☐ Home study (book only)

☐ On a course: college _____

☐ With 'correspondence' package

☐ Other _____

Why did you decide to purchase this Text? *(Tick one box only)*

☐ Have used BPP Texts in the past

☐ Recommendation by friend/colleague

☐ Recommendation by a lecturer at college

☐ Saw advertising

☐ Saw information on BPP website

☐ Other _____

During the past six months do you recall seeing/receiving any of the following?
(Tick as many boxes as are relevant)

☐ Our advertisement in *ACCA Student Accountant*

☐ Our advertisement in *Pass*

☐ Our advertisement in *PQ*

☐ Our brochure with a letter through the post

☐ Our website www.bpp.com

Which (if any) aspects of our advertising do you find useful?
(Tick as many boxes as are relevant)

☐ Prices and publication dates of new editions

☐ Information on Text content

☐ Facility to order books off-the-page

☐ None of the above

Which BPP products have you used?

Text	☑	Success CD	☐	Learn Online	☐
Kit	☐	i-Learn	☐	Home Study Package	☐
Passcard	☐	i-Pass	☐	Home Study PLUS	☐

Your ratings, comments and suggestions would be appreciated on the following areas.

	Very useful	Useful	Not useful
Introductory section (Key study steps, personal study)	☐	☐	☐
Chapter introductions	☐	☐	☐
Key terms	☐	☐	☐
Quality of explanations	☐	☐	☐
Case studies and other examples	☐	☐	☐
Exam focus points	☐	☐	☐
Questions and answers in each chapter	☐	☐	☐
Fast forwards and chapter roundups	☐	☐	☐
Quick quizzes	☐	☐	☐
Question Bank	☐	☐	☐
Answer Bank	☐	☐	☐
Index	☐	☐	☐

Overall opinion of this Study Text	Excellent ☐	Good ☐	Adequate ☐	Poor ☐

Do you intend to continue using BPP products?   Yes ☐   No ☐

On the reverse of this page are noted particular areas of the text about which we would welcome your feedback. The BPP author of this edition can be e-mailed at: nickweller@bpp.com

Please return this form to: Nick Weller, ACCA Publishing Manager, BPP Learning Media Ltd, FREEPOST, London, W12 8BR

Review Form & Free Prize Draw (continued)

TELL US WHAT YOU THINK

Please note any further comments and suggestions/errors below

Free Prize Draw Rules

1　Closing date for 31 January 2008 draw is 31 December 2007. Closing date for 31 July 2008 draw is 30 June 2008.

2　Restricted to entries with UK and Eire addresses only. BPP employees, their families and business associates are excluded.

3　No purchase necessary. Entry forms are available upon request from BPP Learning Media Ltd. No more than one entry per title, per person. Draw restricted to persons aged 16 and over.

4　Winners will be notified by post and receive their cheques not later than 6 weeks after the relevant draw date.

5　The decision of the promoter in all matters is final and binding. No correspondence will be entered into.